Palgrave Studies in Economic History

Series Editor
Kent Deng, London School of Economics, London, UK

Palgrave Studies in Economic History is designed to illuminate and enrich our understanding of economies and economic phenomena of the past. The series covers a vast range of topics including financial history, labour history, development economics, commercialisation, urbanisation, industrialisation, modernisation, globalisation, and changes in world economic orders.

More information about this series at
https://link.springer.com/bookseries/14632

Jianbo Zhou

Westernization Movement and Early Thought of Modernization in China

Pragmatism and Changes in Society, 1860s–1900s

palgrave
macmillan

Jianbo Zhou
School of Economics
Peking University
Beijing, China

Translated by
Jianhua Zhao
College of Economics
and Management
China Three Gorges University
Yichang, China

ISSN 2662-6497 ISSN 2662-6500 (electronic)
Palgrave Studies in Economic History
ISBN 978-3-030-86987-8 ISBN 978-3-030-86985-4 (eBook)
https://doi.org/10.1007/978-3-030-86985-4

Cover illustration: Antiqua Print Gallery/Alamy Stock Photo

This Palgrave Macmillan imprint is published by the registered company Springer Nature Switzerland AG
The registered company address is: Gewerbestrasse 11, 6330 Cham, Switzerland

Foreword

Dr. Zhou Jianbo's new book "The Westernization Movement and Early Thought of Modernization in China" is worth reading for its rich and innovative contents.

Research on the Westernization Movement and Westernization group has been conducted for a century. Abstracting a great number of researchers, this study is extensive and impressive, and based on abundant materials and achievements. The voluminous extant research renders it difficult to make further progress and new breakthroughs, and to achieve this goal, we must not only make painstaking efforts, but also innovate in our research methods.

Dr. Zhou Jianbo originally studied the Modern History of China and engaged in teaching for several years after obtaining a master's degree. During his teaching period, he laid a solid foundation for research in important fields and issues in Modern Chinese History. Later, he turned to study the history of Chinese economic thought, gaining a unique advantage in studying history by using an historical materialism and economics methodology, which enabled him to forge a new path in the study of the Westernization Movement. This is well manifested in this book, which focuses on the thoughts and practices of the major characters of the Westernization Movement, and considers these an important aspect by which to examine modernization in China.

After the failure of the first Opium War, the issue of development became a fundamental issue in Chinese history. The essence of development is now fully replacing individual farming and the backward productive forces of handicraft with socialized modern productivity, transforming the economic base and superstructure, and establishing productivity and a superstructure that conforms to the notion of socialized productivity. The aim of development is to enable China to achieve its conversion from an ancient feudal society to a modern one. Thus, the entire process of development has manifested as the drive to modernization.

Among all the major issues, events, and challenges in modern Chinese history linked with this fundamental issue, only when that of positioning the object studied is adequately solved can the nature, characteristics, historical significance, and role of the object be correctly understood and evaluated in the study of historical issues.

Dr. Zhou Jianbo defines the Westernization Movement as an early modernization movement in China, which is correct. In the Westernization Movement, Chinese modernization is not only the trend of thought that increasingly influences society, but also a growing practice. Although very few people (e.g., Hong Rengan) mentioned the issues of development and modernization in the field of thought before the Westernization Movement, they have not produced a way of thinking that influences society to enable relevant practices, as these issues are isolated and rare. Therefore, suffice to say that the Westernization Movement is the early modernization movement in China, and no modernization movement had existed before it.

In terms of the content studied, this book focuses on researching the modernization program of the Westernization group; specifically, its micro vision on running an enterprise and macro vision on developing all sectors of the modern economy. Most previous studies on the Westernization Movement have not emphasized these aspects. As this book studies the Westernization Movement from the perspective of China's modernization, the modernization program is considered the main issue studied, which enables exploring new areas of study and provides a new perspective of and ideas regarding issues (nature, reasons for failure, and historical position of the Westernization Movement) that have long been intensively studied.

As many areas studied in this book are new attempts, the author inevitably encountered some difficulties regarding the issues addressed in this book. However, there are also achievements and breakthroughs by virtue of the study's depth and improvements. The limitations of the study reported in this book are equally valuable. The author will certainly become a mature researcher who is good at seeking new ways of studying historical issues through an historical materialism and economic methodology.

Zhao Jing

About This Book

As the earliest modernization movement in China, the Westernization Movement has become the focus of scholars in the modern era. The earliest study of the Westernization Movement was implemented by the reformers led by Kang Youwei and Liang Qichao. Thereafter, academia had three major study climaxes in the 1930s, 1960s, and 1980s. As the politics and social environment of the periods are different, the focuses of studies also differ. However, the research can be delineated as focusing on the following five key issues. The first is the confrontation of ideas between westernizationists and conservatives, which are the three common controversies in the textbook of modern Chinese history. Second, the thoughts of high officials in the Westernization Movement, such as Li Hongzhang, Zeng Guofan, Zuo Zongtang, and Zhang Zhidong differ from those of the earliest reformers, namely Zheng Guanying, Ma Jianzhong, Wang Tao, and Guo Songtao (the aides and friends of the high officials). The third issue is the evaluation of the westernizationists' principal of "Confucianism leads the basics, while western science leads the techniques." The fourth is the criticism of enterprises operated by merchants and supervised by the government. Finally, the fifth is the relationship between the failure of the Westernization Movement, foreign capitalism, and domestic feudal rulers. Essentially, previous studies emphasize the exploration of the causes, nature, and reasons for the failure of the Westernization Movement, rather than the design of the Chinese modernization program. Specifically, we do not know westernizationists' visions for the improvement of enterprises at the micro level and development of the various departments of modern economics at the macro level. In the author's opinion, the microscopic productive base of society (construction of the enterprise system) is vitally important, as society's stability is not possible without the proper construction thereof. Therefore, China strives to construct the micro productive base of modern society through the current reform of its state-owned enterprises. Thus, the author believes that it is of great academic and realistic significance to study the Westernization Movement from a business perspective. This book focuses on the Westernization Movement from the perspective of the history of economic thought under the guide of Marxism and reference to modern economic theories.

Before examining Westernization thought, two issues must be explained.

The first is the ending time of the Westernization Movement, which academia regards as the Sino-Japanese War, as it marks the failure of the movement. However, scholars with different views think that the new policies of the late Qing Dynasty signify the ending of the Westernization Movement. The author supports the second view, as he thinks the mark of failure of a movement is different from the ending of the policies that support that movement. The Sino-Japanese War marked the failure of the Westernization Movement, not the changed policy of Westernization. After the Sino-Japanese War, Zhang Zhidong substituted Li Hongzhang to become the leader of the late Westernization Movement, spurring its advancement. The failure of the war made more people realize that China could only be saved by learning from the West. This strengthened the call that "Confucianism leads the basics, while western science leads the techniques" to the extent that the later reformation movement led by Kang Youwei and Liang Qichao kept the slogan. However, after the Sino-Japanese War, modern policies of Westernization changed. On one hand, voices for the reform of the political system were stronger and turned into practice. On the other, the policy of state-owned industries was gradually replaced by that for private-owned ones in the reform of the economic system. All these aspects laid a solid foundation for the policies of learning from the west in all respects.

Although the endeavor of learning from the west was not going well in this period and stagnated because of the failure of the reform movement of 1898, the Yihetuan Movement manifested the powerful will to learn from the west. Faced with the crisis of extinction, high officials of the Westernization Movement such as Zhang Zhidong and Liu Kunyi changed their standpoints of not mentioning constitutionalism and establishing parliament. Furthermore, they made breakthroughs in the dominating principal of "Confucianism leads the basics" mentioned in the book *Exhortation to Learning*, and demanded comprehensive learning from the west. The supreme ruler also realized that the regime would collapse either because of western powers or domestic rebellion, while the conservatives who curbed the westernizationists were accused or demoted. These conditions contributed to further reform and new policies, and deeper measures than the Reform Movement of 1898 were carried out. In summary, the Reform Movement of 1898 was an unsuccessful attempt to change the policies of westernization, while the new policies marked the change of the highest national policy of the Qing government. Therefore, the author contends that the introduction of the new policies of the Qing government marked the ending of the Westernization Movement.

The second issue needing explanation relates to the members of the Westernization Movement. Previous studies thereon considered as westernizationists the main government officials (e.g., Yi Xin, Wen Xiang, Li Hongzhang, Zeng Guofan, Zuo Zongtang, and Zhang Zhidong), while their aides, friends, and colleagues with slightly lower positions (e.g., Guo Songtao, Wang Tao, Xue Fucheng, Zheng Guanying, and Ma Jianzhong) were regarded the early reformers. These studies did not mention other members of the Westernization Movement like the entrepreneurs engaged in business and educators engaged in the new education. Thus, the author believes this cannot fully reflect the whole picture of the Westernization Movement. From the author's perspective, those who supported the "Confucianism leads the basics" principle advocated internal reform and opening up, and those actively engaged in the Westernization Movement are the members or participants of that movement. Westernizationists differed from the conservatives, who were opposed to western science in the early period, and from the reformers (in the Reform Movement of 1898), who advocated learning from the west in all respects. However, considering the influence of the academic tradition, this book defines all these people as participants in the Westernization Movement. Furthermore, to identify and research the ideological differences between the westernizationists more conveniently, this book defines the leaders and protectors of this movement, like Zeng, Li, Zuo, and Zhang, as the high officials of the westernizationists; those who are advocates, practitioners, and critics of the movement like Guo, Wang, Xue, Zheng, and Ma as the ideologists of the westernizationists; and those who adopt the ideologists as their spokesmen as general westernizationists including entrepreneurs, educators, and officials.

The writing strategy of this book must also be explained. In general, material that can reflect a person or a school of thought is primarily manifested through his (or its) words and then through his (or its) actions. Regarding the members of the Westernization Movement, knowledgeable officials and their aides have left a vast volume of written materials, which are the important historical materials used for the purposes of this study. On the other hand, the people who worked in enterprises have left few written materials based on the limitations of their occupations and knowledge. Thus, we must study the thoughts of westernization and enterprises' business notions through the materials of those enterprises at that time. This book uses a large number of materials regarding enterprises in the chapter on business.

The author thinks the following are the innovative points in this book. The first innovative point is considering enterprises as the object of study, as these have not yet been the focus of research in this regard. The second is using numerous materials that have not been used before in the creation of historical materials, particularly in the study of business thought. The third is the creation of ideas. For example, the offices of the main officials of the Westernization Movement prepared a batch of talents for the westernization and boosted the administrative agencies of the Westernization Movement. Again, this book discusses the development of modern strategic thinking, namely the establishment of a new industrial system with the military industry at the center, and "export substitution" and "import substitution" in the development of civil enterprises.

Contents

Part I Introduction

1 Change of Time and Formation of Westernization Thought 3

1.1 Victory of the Yi Xin Group in the Central Government of the Qing Dynasty 4

1.2 Rise of Local Governors and the Hunan and Anhui Military Groups 8

1.3 Voice of "Self-Strengthening" and Proposal of Westernization Thought 16

1.4 Participants in the Westernization Movement 20

2 Guiding Principles of the Westernization Movement 25

2.1 "Cementing Relations with Western Countries": The Prerequisite for Reform 25

2.2 The Principle of China's Internal Reforms: "Confucianism Leads the Basics, While Western Science Leads the Techniques" 28

3 Development Strategies of Westernizational Modernization 39

3.1 Establishment of the Military Industrial System 39

3.2 Civilian Industrial Development Strategy: Combination of Import Substitution and Export Promotion 47

4 **Social Reformative Thoughts of the Westernization Group** 55
- 4.1 *The Political Power Reformation Ideology of the Westernization Officials* 56
- 4.2 *The Political Reform Views of the Westernization Thinkers* 61
- 4.3 *Construction of Morality* 70

Part II Business

5 **Raising Capital** 79
- 5.1 *Rectifying the Traditional Tax System* 80
- 5.2 *Regulating Salt Tax* 85
- 5.3 *Taxing the Gambling Industry and Opium Trade* 87
- 5.4 *Selling Official Posts and Titles to Raise Money* 88
- 5.5 *Levying New Tax Categories* 88
- 5.6 *Attracting Foreign Capital* 94

6 **The Thought of Improving Technology** 103
- 6.1 *Introduction of Foreign Advanced Technology* 104
- 6.2 *Cultivation of Domestic Technical Personnel* 108

7 **Cultivating Personnel to Run Businesses** 117
- 7.1 *Selection of Entrepreneurs for Government-Run Enterprises (Including Government Commerce Enterprises)* 118
- 7.2 *Selecting Business Enterprise Entrepreneurs* 125
- 7.3 *Government's Role in Supporting the Growth of Entrepreneurs* 133
- 7.4 *Improvement of Entrepreneurs' Operation Capacity* 135

8 **Thoughts Regarding Waged Labor** 143
- 8.1 *Sources of Labor* 143
- 8.2 *Standards for Recruiting Workers* 145
- 8.3 *Wage Determination* 149
- 8.4 *Labor Management* 153

9 **Theories of the Operation and Management of Enterprises** 159
- 9.1 *Scientific Decision-Making* 159
- 9.2 *Personnel Management* 162

9.3	*Financial Management*	165
9.4	*Use Modern Management Means*	167
9.5	*Marketing Management*	170
10	**Views on the Enterprise Organization System Construction**	175
10.1	*Establishing a Joint-Stock Company*	175
10.2	*Notion of Merchant-Managed Enterprises*	185
10.3	*Government-Run Military and Civil Enterprises: Reform Recommendations and Practice*	194
10.4	*Government-Supervised and Merchant-Managed Enterprises: Reform Recommendations and Practice*	200
10.5	*Views on Government-Supervised and Merchant-Managed Enterprises*	213
Part III	**National Economy**	
11	**Views on Development of Modern Agriculture**	221
11.1	*Role and Status of Agriculture in the National Economy*	222
11.2	*Developing Modern Agriculture Using Western Methods*	226
11.3	*Paying Attention to Water Conservancy*	230
12	**The Thought to Develop Modern Industry**	233
12.1	*The Thought on Modern Mining and Metallurgical Industry*	233
12.2	*Development of Manufacturing*	245
13	**Ideology of Developing Modern Business**	253
13.1	*Ideology of Trade Relations with Foreign Countries*	253
13.2	*Methods to Develop Modern Business*	258
14	**The Thought of Developing Transportation and Communication**	265
14.1	*Developing Land Transportation*	265
14.2	*Significance of Developing Waterway Transportation*	274
14.3	*Significance of Developing Telecommunication*	277
15	**The Thought to Develop Modern Financial**	281
15.1	*Views Regarding the Making of Coins*	281
15.2	*Views Regarding the Issuing of Paper Money*	285

15.3 Views Regarding the Building of Banks 288

16 Thinking on Transferring the Surplus Workforce in an Agricultural Society 293
16.1 Machine Production Was the Solution to Transferring the Surplus Workforce 293
16.2 Transfer of the Surplus Population in Non-Production Departments in an Agricultural Society 300

Part IV Aftermath

17 The Origins of Westernization Thought 309
17.1 Influence of the Ideological Trends of Confucian Statecraft on Westernization Thought 309
17.2 Traditional Economic Thought and Conflicts Between Government-run and Merchant-managed Enterprises 320
17.3 The Westerners in China and the Formation of Modernization Thought 325
Western Diplomats in China and the Formation of Modern Thought 326
Missionaries in China and the Development of the Westernization Thinkers' Views on Modernization 328

18 Ideological Evaluation of the Westernization Movement 339
18.1 Acknowledging the Modern Economy 339
18.2 The Inevitability that Reformist Views Would Replace Westernization Thought 345

19 The Far-Reaching Impact of Westernization Movement 349
19.1 The Westernization Movement and the Progress of China's Economic Thought 349
19.2 The Connection Between the Westernization Movement in 1860 and the 1978 Reforms and Opening-up 352
19.3 The Restrictions on the Further Development of China's Economic Thought 353

19.4 *The Rise of Chinese Merchant Class and the Transformation of Ideology Accompanied by the Westernization Movement* 355

20 The Qing Government and Westernization 359
20.1 *Support from the Qing Government* 359
20.2 *The Inability of the Qing Dynasty to Complete Its Historical Mission* 362
20.3 *The Qing government's Inability to Contribute to the Establishment of a Modern Enterprise System* 366

Postscript 369

References 375

Index 381

PART I

Introduction

The Westernization Movement, also called the "Self-Strengthening Movement," is a well-known reform in the modern history of China. The movement aimed to improve national strength and strengthen the governance of the Qing government by learning from the West (transfer the learning of western advanced technology to politics, culture, education, and social ethics). In addition, leading groups with a firm resolution for reform, a series of leading agencies to advance the reform, and a guiding principle to increase cohesion were needed to lead the reform movement, which lasted several decades and greatly influenced society in the late Qing Dynasty. Furthermore, economic reform would influence politics and ethics, and produce the political, cultural, educational, and socially ethical thinking that conforms to the economic reform. In this chapter, to further explore the abovementioned issues, an overall grasp of westernization thought is needed before turning to the study of the construction of thought of enterprises in the Westernization Movement.

CHAPTER 1

Change of Time and Formation of Westernization Thought

In the process of the modernization of China and other developing countries, the basic premise of transforming the ideas of modernization into action is that modern elites with a modern stance obtain leadership positions.[1] The reason is that these countries are forced to make choices regarding their fates in the absence of modernization. The following outlines real and logical situations. First, most people cannot view their historical context from the perspective of the entire world; thus, only those in the upper class can consciously assume the responsibilities of a nation's fate. Second, as society is far from being aware of the whole context, the modern salvation of the nation is carried out by the upper class. Third, as traditional conservatives enjoy great power, they must rely on the modern power elites to obtain the forced input and support. Finally, as the power of civil society is weak and scattered, only political leaders with a modern inclination assume the roles of drivers and propellers.

In the process of China's modernization, 1860 is especially significant. In this period, a series of historical events occurred: a leading group embarked on the reform, a leading agency carried out the reform, and

[1] Kenichi, T. (1987). *Shehuixue Yuanli* (Principles of Sociology, 社会学原理). Beijing: Social Sciences Academic Press (China).

J. Zhou, *Westernization Movement and Early Thought of Modernization in China*, Palgrave Studies in Economic History,
https://doi.org/10.1007/978-3-030-86985-4_1

a principle mobilizing the reform emerged in China's political arena to initiate the Westernization Movement.

1.1 Victory of the Yi Xin Group in the Central Government of the Qing Dynasty

In August 1860, as the Anglo-French forces occupied Beijing, Emperor Xianfeng fled to the north, granting his half-brother Yi Xin "the entire discretionary right as an imperial envoy," and ordering the grand academicians of the grand council Gui Liang and Vice Minister of Revenue (Hubu) Wen Xiang to take "charge of the peaceful negotiation." Initially, Yi Xin shared the opinion of other bureaucratic literati, for he disdained the West and believed the Qing Dynasty could "put the westerners to death" as long as it persisted in war against them. However, in communication with the Westerners, he found they were gentle and polite, not "barbarous and uncivilized": the Westerners emphasized the agreement and "made requests according to the agreement instead of numerous peremptory demands."[2] As his new understanding of the West increased, he requested the Qing government to switched from the traditional policy of "appeasement or war" to "treat the West sincerely" to eliminate or alleviate the possibility of invasion and threat therefrom. Guided by his views, the *Convention of Peking* and *Treaty of Tientsin* were signed among China, Britain, and France. Different from the views of Duan Hua and Su Shun who strongly opposed the West, Yi Xin had an inclusive attitude toward the region. Thus, the West wanted Yi Xin to take office and supported the subsequent "Coup of 1861." As China was closely related to the West, support therefrom lent important weight to the competing of different political forces. As such, Yi Xin's political position was largely elevated as the first to garner this support. In addition, as Yi Xin resolved the conflict between China and the West through "not declaring war or losing dignity," he enjoyed the reputation of a "backbone minister" and

[2] *Chouban Yiwu Shimo, Xianfeng Chao, Juan Liushijiu* (History of Diplomatic Affairs in Late Qing Dynasty, Xianfeng, Vol. 69, 筹办夷务始末, 咸丰朝, 卷69). Beijing: Zhonghua Book Company, p. 2582.

"being more prestigious than Duan Hua and Su Shun,"[3] which laid a solid foundation for beating the group led by Su Shun.

Yi Xin gained reputation and honor and strengthened his political power in dealing with foreign affairs. He convened all the officials who stayed in Peking and established a political group led by him. This group included civil and military ministers such as Zhou Zupei and Weng Xincun, who were suppressed by the Su Shun group, and the grand academician Gui Liang, Vice Minister of Revenue (Hubu) Wen Xiang, and the Manchu and Han high-ranking officials Shen Zhaolin and Bao Jun etc., who held the same political views as Yi Xin. They also changed their traditional perception and vision regarding communication with Westerners. For example, the temporary Minister of Revenue Shen Zhaolin changed his political view of advocating war before signing the *Convention of Peking*. Before then, he was convinced that Westerners "focus on nothing but profit-making as they did not destroy the city after leaving."[4] Wen Xiang, the most capable of Yi Xin's assistants, further changed traditional political views toward the West. According to the *Draft History of Qing, Wen Xiang Bibliography*, in which his words are recorded, "Some people think that western countries are uncivilized and do not know politics, but in fact, as long as there are affairs in their countries, the monarchy will submit them to the House of Lords, and thus, the upper class has the right to participate in these affairs. Or the affairs will be submitted to the House of Commons, and thus, the commoner also have the right to participate. The implementation of affairs is based on the results of the discussions. All affairs should be tackled according to the interests of the people." As for China's national condition, Wen Xiang noted that "As China has a clear dividing line between the commoner and upper class, it is difficult to fully imitate the western political system, but we can learn from their method."[5] In his words, "being difficult to

[3] Qi, S. (1978). *Zhongguo Jindaishi Ziliao Congkan, Dierci Yapian Zhanzheng* (Materials on Modern Chinese History Series, the Second Opium War, Vol. 2, 中国近代史资料丛刊·第二次鸦片战争, 卷2). Shanghai: Shanghai Renmin Chubanshe, p. 146.

[4] Institute of Modern History, Academia Sinica. (1974). *Jindai Zhongguo dui Xifang ji Lieqiang Renshi Ziliao Huibian* (The Data Compilation of Modern China's Understanding on the West and Mighty Powers, Vol. 1, 1, 近代中国对西方及列强认识资料汇编, 第1辑第1分册, 第743页). Taiwan: Institute of Modern History, Academia Sinica (Tai Bei), p. 743.

[5] (1977). *Qingshi Gao, Juan Sanbaliu* (Journal of Qing History, Vol. 386, 清史稿, 卷386). Beijing: Zhonghua Book Company, p. 11,691.

imitate" is the feeling for reality, while "learning from the West" implies his ambition for reform.

Yi Xin, Gui Liang, and Wen Xiang proposed the *Six Regulations of the Comprehensive Arrangement of the Westernization Movement* in December 1860. His memorial indicates that he thought China should "seek self-strengthening" after being seriously invaded by the Anglo-French forces. Detailed measures of its self-strengthening were reportedly as follows: "establishing the Ministry of Foreign Affairs in Peking to focus on foreign affairs" and "establishing government agencies in northern and southern China to make their communications more convenient." Furthermore, "the central government should appoint local officials with impartiality and integrity to manage the tariffs of the ports near them"; "generals and governors should tackle foreign affairs together to avoid misunderstanding"; "Guangdong and Shanghai should dispatch two people who know foreign characters and foreign languages, respectively, to Peking to prepare for the inquiry from the central government"; and "The Ministry of Foreign Affairs is in charge of domestic and foreign businesses in all the ports and newspapers of all the countries." On December 21, Yi Xin proposed Emperor Xianfeng to purchase and manufacture western guns and cannons and to hire French craftsmen to impart the manufacturing technology to China. Three days later, Emperor Xianfeng published the first "imperial edict" to learn and implement the advanced technology of the West: "Since the French accept to sell guns and cannons to us and send craftsmen to teach us how to use and make these weapons, I appoint Zeng Guofan and Xue Huan to contact them."[6] Thus, the Westernization Movement began.

In short, the rise of the Yi Xin group broke the previous circular pattern of the vested interests and spearheaded the transformation from traditional rulers to modern drivers. The critical step for Westernization was that the Westernizationists presided over the policies of the central government and carried out top-down modernization reform. After the Coup of 1861, the Yi Xin group substituted the Su Shun group and seized central power. While the supreme power of the Qing dynasty was controlled by the empresses, in the early period of the Westernization

[6] *Chouban Yiwu Shimo, Xianfeng Chao, Juan Qishier* (History of Diplomatic Affairs in Late Qing Dynasty, Xianfeng, Vol. 72, 筹办夷务始末, 咸丰朝, 卷72). As cited in Xu, T. (1986). *Yangwu Yundong Xinlun* (New Statements on Westernization Movement, 洋务运动新论). Changsha: Hunan People's Publishing House, pp. 15–16.

Movement, "It was difficult for the two empresses to tackle the complex affairs of the early period. Thus, the official Council of State was in charge of all western affairs."[7] These words precisely portray the historical fact that Yi Xin held the real power while the empresses merely upheld their undeserved reputation. Having the facilitators of Westernization preside over the central power was the prerequisite of the start of Westernization. The rise of the Yi Xin group and the subsequent Coup of 1861 were also important parts of this process.

Although modern leadership provides the basic premise for the start of Westernization, authority outside the traditional ruling system had to also be established to lead the modernization movement. Here, the Ministry of Foreign Affairs was this authority, which was in charge of diplomacy (diplomatic negotiations such as cases of religion and diplomatic missions) and aspects related to foreign affairs including finance, military, education, manufacturing, transportation, coastal defense, and frontier affairs. It was also called the "translation department" or "head department," and engaged in all aspects pertaining to foreign affairs. Since the Ministry "fully imitated the official Council of State" at the beginning of its establishment and was led by the prince, its status and influence surpassed that of the six traditional ministries and were similar to those of the official Council of State. Together with the School of Combined Learning (Tongwen Guan), the Inspector General of Customs, and the Beiyang and Nanyang ministers in Shanghai and Tianjin, it formed a new system outside the traditional bureaucracy. Although a temporary agency that originally aimed at coping with the current situation, the Ministry of Foreign Affairs finally transformed into the "headquarters" of the new policies with the expansion of its powers. Therefore, Shen Ruilin, the official of the Ministry of Justice, believed it had great power, stating: "The Ministry of Foreign Affairs is in charge of all affairs relating to our national prosperity. Its affairs are more complicated than those of the traditional six ministries. Previously, the Ministry of Official Personnel Affairs was in charge of the qualifications of officials, and when the period of the ministers who go abroad expire now, the Ministry of Foreign Affairs should ask for a decree and put down its name through customs Circuit Intendants. High-ranking officials of the Ministry of Official Personnel Affairs

[7] He, G. (1996). *Kezuo Outan* (Guest Talk, 客座偶谈). As cited in Zhou, J. (1996). *Zuichu De Jiyuan* (The Beginning of the Era, 最初的纪元). Beijing: Higher Education Press, p. 108.

vouch for and register it. The financial expenditure and income belonging to the duty of the Ministry of Official Personnel Affairs is now considered customs duty to accumulate expenditure for going abroad, which is under the duty of the Ministry of Official Personnel Affairs, which is only in charge of controls. Since trading with the West, the Ministry of Foreign Affairs is in charge of the increasing number of diplomatic protocols, while the Ministry of Rites performs practically no function. The purchasing and establishment of Western weapons are overseen by the Ministry of Foreign Affairs, while the Ministry of War can be abolished. The Ministry of Justice was previously in charge of laws, while foreign affairs were handled according to international laws. The Ministry of Foreign Affairs has now substituted the Ministry of Justice and handles these types of laws. As western countries enjoy powerful weapons, we must engage in the building of railways and mineral affairs to defend them. The Ministry of Works can no longer manage these affairs, which are now dealt with by departments established by the Ministry of Foreign Affairs."[8] Although the central agency of this new policy has a strong sense of feudalism, its existence and proliferation are important signals of the start of Westernization and manifest the unprecedented changes to the traditional political system. From then to the early twentieth century, the Ministry of Foreign Affairs became another central agency of the Qing government and "headquarters" for new policies.

1.2 Rise of Local Governors and the Hunan and Anhui Military Groups

During the Xianfeng and Tongzhi Reigns, the rise of the powers driving Westernization was divided into two sections. In the central government, the Yi Xin group controlled central power through the prince, complementing the policy in the negotiation of the *Convention of Peking*. Peking was the center of their movement. In the local governments, powerfully elites with modern inclinations extended their powers through the local decentralization system in the suppression of the Taiping Rebellion. At the center of their movement was Shanghai.

[8] The Ming-Qing institution of National Archives Administration of China. (1958). *Wuxu Bianfa Dangan, Tianzaijigou ji Guanzhi Lizhi* (The reform movement of 1898 archives, The Reconstruction of Agencies and Bureaucracy, 戊戌变法档案·添载机构及官制吏治). Beijing: Zhonghua Book Company, p. 179.

Rong Hong (Yung Wing) remarked as follows on the relation between the Taiping Rebellion and Westernization Movement: "The positive result of the Taiping Rebellion is that the Chinese people have gradually wakened from the stagnant situation and are thinking of building a new type of country."[9] Therefore, the Taiping Rebellion exposed the weaknesses of the Qing Dynasty and expedited the emancipation of the Chinese people. Furthermore, it indirectly promoted the establishment of Westernizationists at the political level and served as the catalyst of Westernization thought at the intellectual level.

However, the feudal emperor did not show appreciation for the Hunan Army led by Zeng Guofan for some time. This is because Emperor Xianfeng considered an army trained by landowners unorthodox and unable to be as honest as the nation's regular army. The weakening military camps in the northern and southern areas of the Yangtze River shouldered more of the central government's expectations than the rising Hunan Army. However, the failure of the military camps in the southern areas of the Yangtze River in 1860 destroyed the central government's hopes and thus, military affairs in southeast China were transferred to the Hunan Army. As such, the Hunan Army dismantled barriers and made great strides in terms of its position. According to history, after the failure of the military camps in the southern areas of the Yangtze River, "Zuo Zongtang heard the news and sighed that God wills it!" Some asked him the reason, to which he replied: "So many generals and soldiers of the Hunan Army were not powerful enough to resist the Taiping Rebellion, while the Hunan Army rose to combat the rebellion. If people are asked who can shoulder the responsibility of combat against the rebellion, Hu Linyi answered that the military affairs in southern China should be handed to Zeng Guofan."[10] The remarks of Zuo Zongtang and Hu Linyi clearly exposed the discharge of their long-time depression and depicted the ambition of the Hunan Army.

With the rise of the Hunan Army, its leaders demonstrated a strong desire to administer the affairs of China's political arena. The book,

[9] Rong, H. (1998). *Xixue Dongjian Ji* (My Life in China and America, 西学东渐记). Zhengzhou: Zhongzhou Ancient Books Publishing House, p. 125.

[10] Lu, F., Gao, S. & Wu, R. *Zhongxing Jiangshuai Biezhuan, Sibu Beiyao Ben, Juanyi* (The Biography of The Meritorious Ministers Since the Period of the Emperor Xianfeng, Vol. 1, The Four Major Books, 四部备要·史部·中兴将帅别传, 卷1). Shanghai: Shanghai Zhonghua Book Company, p. 7.

The Story of Hunan Army, published in 1889, recorded the history in this regard. According to Luo Ju, "Since the rebellion occurred in Guangxi province, the whole country shook, and the soldiers were mobilized to combat the rebellion. Wang Xin, Luo Zenan, Li Xubin, Hu Linyi, Zuo Zongtang, Liu Changyou, Jiang Yili, Governor-general Zeng Guoquan, Minister Peng Yulin, Governor-general Yang Yuebin, and Governor Liu Jintang went on a punitive expedition around 18 provinces. The leaders of Hunan Army who demonstrated superior performance in battles were rewarded, including Governors-general Liu Yuezhao, Liu Gongrong, Tang Xunfang, and Chen Shijie. Provincial commanders-in-chief who also took charge of the rights of grand coordinators were Tian Xingshu and Jiang Zhongyi. However, though Lao Chongguang, assistant Vice Minister Guo Songtao, Governor-general Tan Zhonglin, and the Governor Li Peijing were members of the Imperial Academy, they engaged in military affairs. Many other officials were also prestigious because of their excellent performance in various battles."[11] Excepting the "people of Hunan," prominent officials who had a relationship with the Hunan Army included Shen Baozhen, Li Hongzhang, Yan Shusen, Li Hanzhang, Li Zongxi, Yan Jingming, and Xu Zhenqi, who were famous celebrities at the time. When Li Hongzhang led the Anhui Army, the Anhui group, which opposed the Hunan Army and the people following it were Zhang Shusheng, Pan Dingxin, Liu Mingchuan, Liu Bingzhang, Ding Richang, Qian Dingming, Guo Baiyin, Wang Kaitai, Liu Huangao, and Zhou Fu. In the subsequent Tongzhi and Guangxu Reigns, they dominated half of China for a long time. When China was at the turn of its traditional feudal time and the new modern time, the minds and footprints of these people were left in the ups and downs of the national destiny.

The Hunan-Anhui groups led by Zeng, Zuo, and Li were the emerging political forces in the political arena of the late Qing Dynasty. Their experiences in suppressing the Taiping Rebellion rendered these leaders' more capable and aware of advanced western military power and its threats. According to Taiwanese scholars, the Taiping Army began to purchase

[11] Wang, A. (1983). *Xiangjun Ji* (A History of Hunan Army, 湘军记). Changsha: Yuelu Press, pp. 1–2.

a large number of western guns from western merchants[12] and had a "foreign rifle detachment." After being seriously attacked by the Taiping Army, the Hunan and Anhui armies admitted the "thrilling power" of "the western cannons." Li Hongzhang wrote to Zeng Guoquan, complaining that "the Taiping Army used the guns to attack us, and each attack was fierce with thousands of people."[13] To win the battle, Zeng Guofan and Li Hongzhang had to purchase western weapons to combat the Taiping Army. However, only in 1862 were the Hunan and Anhui armies equipped with western weapons, the Anhui Army first.[14] In March that year, Li Hongzhang took the foreign ships in Anqing to support the forces in Shanghai and was shocked by the western ships and armament. He wrote to Zeng Guofan on April 2: "Thousands of western soldiers equipped with guns and cannons were invincible and their explosive shells were powerful."[15] The same year, he wrote to Zeng Guofan, emphasizing his feeling on December 15: "I have been to the French and British ships and felt that the cannons, bullets, apparatuses, and armies were much more powerful than those of China."[16] He added that it would be regrettable if the army stayed in Shanghai without learning the advanced weapons of the Westerners. In 1862, Zeng Guofan "established the Armory of Court and made western weapons for the armies."[17] Thereafter, the Westernization Movement entered the stage of production of great machines.

Pioneered by the power elites with modern thinking patterns, the duration, and achievements of the Westernization movement that proceeded

[12] Wang, E. (1963). *Qingji Binggongye De Xingqi* (The Rise of Military Industry in the Qing Dynasty, 清季兵工业的兴起). Taiwan: Institute of Modern History, Academia Sinica (Tai Bei), pp. 28–29.

[13] Li, H. *Liwenzhong Gong Quanshu, Pengliao Hangao, Juaner* (Complete Works of Li Wenzhong, Letters of Li Wenzhong, Vol. 2, 李文忠公全书·朋僚函稿, 卷2), p. 15.

[14] Wang, E. (1987). *Huaijun Zhi* (A History of Anhui Army, 淮军志). Beijing: Zhonghua Book Company, p. 92.

[15] *Yangwu Yundong, Juaner* (The Westernization Movement, Vol. 2, 洋务运动, 卷2), p. 407.

[16] Wang, Z. (1985). *Fangjiayuan Zayong, Jindai Baihai, Diyiji* (Fang Homestead, The Collection of Modern China Vol. 1, 方家园杂咏, 近代稗海, 第1辑). Chengdu: Sichuan People's Publishing House, p. 2.

[17] Wang, Z. (1985). *Fangjiayuan Zayong, Jindai Baihai, Diyiji* (Fang Homestead, The Collection of Modern China Vol. 1, 方家园杂咏, 近代稗海, 第1辑). Chengdu: Sichuan People's Publishing House, p. 2.

in the military environment depended not only on social needs but also on the amount of social resources dominated by the power elite. The Taiping Rebellion broke the traditional political pattern of centralization, and political and military power began to transit from being centrally led to locally oriented. Local governors mastered a variety of power their predecessors were not able to conceive of. They not only took over power of civil administration, the military, finance, and the judiciary, but also owned independent armed forces. Furthermore, they controlled financial and logistic systems including schools to cultivate people, councils to reserve human resources, and arsenals to manufacture guns and ammunition. Responding to the situation, Kang Youwei said, "From civil to military administration, the court hands over all rights belonging to the governors. Governors hold the power under the name of defending our country, which sounds reasonable."[18] In short, the 18 provinces were like 18 small countries and were in a free relationship with the central government. This devolution made it easier for the Westernization power elite to carry out various operations within their own area of domination. At that time, social thinking was pedantic, and there was still strong opposition to the Westernization Movement in the feudal ruling group. However, the Taiping Rebellion generated a small fissure in the feudal system, which benefited the growth of a new mode of production.

However, regarding the pioneering work of Westernizationists to "learn technology from foreign forces to restrict those foreign forces," traditional government agencies had neither the capacity nor talent to manage it. Therefore, it is difficult to naturally separate Westernization affairs from the central and local governments. The Private Secretariats System is full of tension, which provides the driver enabling them to connect with the Chinese community.

First, outstanding talent was accumulated in the private secretariats of the Hunan and Anhui armies. It attracted bureaucrat scholars, who noted that "Zeng pursued and cherished talent with an earnest heart" and "Zeng's moral prestige contributes to his great achievements."[19] The ambitious joined Zeng's council in succession "as a host of dimmer lights around the brightest one." Rong Hong (Yung Wing) met Zeng

[18] Kang, Y. *Kangnan Haiguan Zhiyi, Juanliu* (The Political Thoughts of Kang Youwei, Vol. 6, 康南海官制议, 卷6). Taiwan: Wen Hai Press Company.

[19] Li, D. (1985). *Zengguofan Jiqi Mufu Renwu* (Zeng Guofan and the figures in his council, 曾国藩及其幕府人物). Changsha: Yuelu Press, p. 4.

in Anqing in 1863, where he witnessed the many social figures gathered there, which left a deep impression on him: "The number of officers assembling in Zeng's private secretariats were more than 200 at that time. Most had their own purpose. There were about 100 people in Zeng's private secretariats, and still many candidates out there. Talented people and experts of law, mathematics, astronomy, and machinery all assembled there. The essence of talent across the country all converged there. Zeng's moral prestige and achievements were outstanding enough to attract these recruits."[20] Since Li Hongzhang created the Anhui Army and later became governor of Jiangsu, he followed Zeng in opening a private secretariat to attract talent. Following this, his private secretariats recruited mostly celebrity talent in Shanghai. The secretariats also included many traditional scholars, the more active of which was the elite with modern inclinations such as Feng Guifen, Zhao liewen, Xu Shou, Hua Hengfang, Xue Fucheng, Guo Songtao, and Li Shanlan, and these people constituted the backbone of this group. The ideological and scientific elite with modern inclinations entered the councils of Zeng and Li, denoting that the original situation of scattered modernization power was for the first time aggregated through the medium of the private secretariats. Zeng's private secretariats was compared to "the junction of the rivers" and "sowing areas" by Xue Fucheng, manifesting an important trace of the early advancement of the modernization process in China. The trend also helped to promote changes in the way of thinking of Zeng, Li, and other people. In Li Dingfen's book, *Zeng Guofan and the Figures in His Private Secretariats*, he wrote that "Zeng's thought has a great influence on many people and in turn, Zeng is also influenced by them. This is why he finally becomes such a figure." His comments highlight the key point here. For example, Feng Guifen, a theorist in the early Westernization Movement, proved that communication with high officials was taken in private secretariats for the first time in his work *Reform Proposals Written in Jiaoban Cabin*. The book *Guo Songtao Diary* mentions the communications between Zeng and Feng in the chapter *April 18, 1862*. Before *Reform Proposals Written in Jiaoban Cabin* was finished, Feng Guifen sent his *Defeating Foreigners by Knowing Them* to Zeng. Once completed, he again sent it to Zeng, who he invited to write the preface. Zeng applauded the work, saying it sufficiently settled problems that were

[20] Rong, H. (1998). *Xixue Dongjian Ji* (My Life in China and America, 西学东渐记). Zhengzhou: Zhongzhou Ancient Books Publishing House, p. 135.

difficult to resolve. To Feng he said, "The number of people copying your book has increased since putting your brilliant work here."[21] Though many actions were taken during the Westernization Movement, the gist thereof was generally guided by Feng's thinking, which established the tenets of communication between officials advocating Westernization and the ideological elites.

Second, officials of the private secretariats of Hunan and Anhui also laid the institutional foundation for the Westernization Movement. The prolonged war strengthened the power of military officers, which enabled them to integrate the power scattered in the council, consequently forging their private secretariats into government offices. Zeng was appointed as the "governor-general of Jiangnan and Jiangxi" in 1860. In a document sent to the emperor, he wrote: "I set up a new office in southern Anhui, and the former one is still located at Shuici in Anqing city. Their operation system is the same as that of the provincial government. The work file over the years will be kept in the Shuici office and I have designated an officer there. He is responsible for regular events, but important events will be sent to me. This is the flexible way in which I perform my associated duties."[22] The "new" and "former" offices are actually the private secretariats. The scale of the former office was similar to that of the government, showing that the private secretariats became a government in the civil war. Therefore, the "designated officer" was not appointed by the imperial court, just transferred from one office to another affiliated with the private secretariats. The unprecedented advancement of the Westernization Movement originally started with the private secretariats system. In 1861, Zeng "established the Armory of Court to produce western style guns and cannons"[23] in Anqing, which historians heralded as "the beginning of the military industry run by the Qing government in modern times."[24] However, the "Armory of Court" was like "the

[21] Zeng, G. *Zeng Wenzheng Gong Quanji, Shuzha Si, Zhi Feng Jingyu* (Complete Works of Zeng Wenzheng, Vol. 4, To Feng Jingyu, 曾文正公全集·书扎四·致冯敬宇), p. 1514.

[22] Li, S. (1986). *Zeng Guofan Nianpu* (The Chronicle of Zeng Guofan, 曾国藩年谱). Changsha: Yuelu Press, pp. 117–118.

[23] Li, S. (1986). *Zeng Guofan Nianpu* (The Chronicle of Zeng Guofan, 曾国藩年谱). Changsha: Yuelu Press, p. 142.

[24] Sun, Y. (1957). *Zhongguo Jindai Gongyeshi Ziliao Diyiji Shangce* (Materials of Chinese Modern Industrial History, Vol. 1, I, 中国近代工业史资料第1辑上册). Beijing: Science Press, p. 249.

arsenal," a department of the private secretariat at that time; thus, the director of the departments Xu Shou and Hua Hengfang was directly charged by Zeng Guofan.

These departments had become the "hottest" Westernization governments and their affairs became the emphasis of politics in the next 30 years. Thus, the supervisor's status was exalted, obtaining him a higher rank than that of the former officials in the bureaucracy. However, these "department"-named agencies could not be part of the national government system. They were neither charged within the scope of the six leading departments of the central government nor within the local administration unit. Since the identity of these departments was too obscure to figure out, the subsequent people who wrote the history of the Qing Dynasty erased the names of the officials in the book. This apparent asymmetry reflected the trait that the producing department evolved from the private secretariats and was still in charge of officials advocating Westernization. The director who managed production affairs was not a member of the staff of the government institution. Nie Qigui, son-in-law of Zeng Guofan, became a member of Zuo Zongtang's private secretariat and worked in the arsenal. The director of the arsenal was concerned that Nie was too young and "dandy." Zuo Zongtang wrote back, contending that "the management system in the arsenal is not the same as in the government. Nie should be promoted only if he has the ability and dismissed if deemed incompetent."[25] For Zuo, the affairs of the arsenal belonged to the private secretariats. However, the private secretariats belonged to his master during the Xianfeng Reign, and the arsenal could not be transferred elsewhere. When Zuo Zongtang left office, he handed over the arsenal to the next governor. The producing department was then under the charge of both the government and private secretariats. This particular administrative structure promoted the development of the Westernization Movement.

[25] As cited in *Lingxiao Hange Biji, Guowen Zhoubao, Juanshi* (Notes written in Linxiaohan Pavilion, Guowenzhoubao, Vol. 10, 凌霄汉阁笔记, 国闻周报, 卷10), Issue 9.

1.3 Voice of "Self-Strengthening" and Proposal of Westernization Thought

Alongside the rise of modernization and establishment of Zongli Yamen (the Ministry of Foreign Affairs in the Qing Dynasty), "self-strengthening" appeared frequently in official books, anthologies, and diaries. Unlike the scene after the First Opium War, "the ruling group seemed like they had already forgotten the pain caused by the war, and the capital recovered in a peaceful and joyful atmosphere." They were deeply shocked by the Second Opium War as numerous documents had been sent to the emperor concerning the "Turmoil of 1860." Zhou Jiamei, a scholar of bureaucracy, said, "the Turmoil of 1860 caused huge pain... Everyone has the ambition of self-strengthening; thus, everyone talked about self-strengthening."[26] This indicates the social trend and highly diffused concept of self-strengthening. In his book *China Wakes From Deep Sleep* published in 1885, Zeng Jize, who experienced the process, pointed out that "since British and French troops captured Beijing and burned the Summer Palace in 1860, China has been roused." The proposal for self-strengthening in this period signaled China's awakening.

To review the discussion on self-strengthening from government officials to civilians throughout the 1860s, the basic intent can be summarized as the following four points:

> First, the throes of the Turmoil of 1860 exposed China's backwardness and weakness. Self-Strengthening was the pivot to advancing from being backward and weak to being strong. According to Feng Guifen, "To realize the shame can help us take actions. If we want to humiliate them in turn, there is nothing better than relying on self strengthening."[27]
>
> Second, the Qing government was forced to sign the *Beijing Treaty*. To change the situation of being controlled by others, they had to "seek the way to self-strengthening."

[26] Suozhuoluo, B. *Chouban Yiwu Shimo, Tongzhi Chao, Juan Jiushiba* (History of Diplomatic Affairs in Late Qing Dynasty (Tongzhi), Vol. 98, 筹办夷务始末 同治朝, 卷98).

[27] Feng, G. (1998). *Xiaobinlu Kangyi* (Reform Proposals written in Jiaoban Cabin, 校邠庐抗议). Zhengzhou: Zhongzhou Ancient Books Publishing House, p. 197.

Third, after the *Beijing Treaty* was signed, the peaceful situation between China and foreign countries "could not be kept by the treaties, especially not by appeasement." In addition, whether the colonlist powers would invade again or not "depends on China's strength." Thus, Self-Strengthening is the only effective means of resisting foreign aggression.

Fourth, in the competitive and changing international environment, self-strengthening was an important way for China to improve its international status. Li Hongzhang explains, "Today's Japan was pirates in the Ming dynasty. Far from the western countries and near to China, Japan always chooses to attach itself to the more powerful of the two. Self-Strengthening is necessary for us, or even little Japan will gang up with the western countries to bully us."[28]

Simply put, the support for Self-Strengthening in the 1860s was centered on seeking independence and strength before foreign aggression.

Although the necessity of Self-Strengthening was widely approved by all, from government officials to civilians, in the 1860s, how to take actions to Self-Strengthening became the focus of a dispute among feudal bureaucrats. To achieve the goal of defending the country and the Confucian Norm theory, two opinions existed in the Qing court:

Wo Ren and his adherents believed the foundation of a country is "etiquette and the support of the civilians, not diplomatic tactics and modern technologies." Therefore, "if we want to defeat the foreigners, we shall seek the faithful man. If we want to pursue Self-Strengthening, we shall seek the scholar with good manners."[29] Wo Ren outlined his idea about how to achieve self-strengthening in *The Secret Memorial*: "The main method to completely defeat foreigners depends on how to choose officials. The road to self-strengthening is nothing more than keeping the

[28] As cited in Jiang, T. (1934). *Zhongguo Waijiaoshi Ziliao Jiyao* (The Abstract of Chinese diplomatic history, 中国外交史资料辑要). Shanghai: The Shanghai Commercial Press, p. 351.

[29] Suozhuoluo, B. *Chouban Yiwu Shimo, Tongzhi Chao, Juan Sishiqi & Sishiba* (History of Diplomatic Affairs in Late Qing Dynasty (Tongzhi), Vol. 47–48, 筹办夷务始末 同治朝, 卷47–48).

Confucian ethical code."[30] His citations regarding the personnel mechanism and administration method in the ruling group were essentially disciplines advocated by Confucianism, such as academic rectification, the cultivation of personnel, upright expostulation, division of labor, and downsizing of redundant personnel. He also advocated encouraging agriculture rather than trade and emphasizing substance rather than the superficially clever.

Yi Xin, Zeng Guofan, and other reformists leapt from the circle of traditional Confucianism to seek the road to prosperity by advocating as the foundation of Self-Strengthening the adoption of "Western learning to compete with foreign weapons." Yi Xin repeatedly stressed, "When it comes to Self-Strengthening, we should attach importance to troop training. Creating weapons should be prioritized."[31] He continued that "in addition to learning the military science of foreigners, we should seriously study methods to create weapons. We have to get their core technology… to make our country stronger."[32] Zeng also believed that "the road to Self-Strengthening begins with making guns, boats, and other tools."[33]

Wo Ren and Yi Xin represented different Self-Strengthening routes, which reflected the contradiction behind the doctrine that learning is both sound in theory and practice. Confucianism tended to pay attention to ethics and learning, and developed, respectively, along the two aspects. Wo Ren and his colleagues adopted the Neo-Confucianism of the Song and Ming Dynasties (a Confucian school of idealist philosophy of the Song and Ming Dynasties). They over-valued morality rather than material things and stuck to an unchanging system rather than the pursuit of reform. However, they never considered whether moralism and unchanging systems would prove effective. Yi Xin and Zeng Guofan

[30] Suozhuoluo, B. *Chouban Yiwu Shimo, Tongzhi Chao, Juan Sishiba* (History of Diplomatic Affairs in Late Qing Dynasty (Tongzhi), Vol. 48, 筹办夷务始末 同治朝, 卷48).

[31] Suozhuoluo, B. *Chouban Yiwu Shimo, Tongzhi Chao, Juan Ershiwu* (History of Diplomatic Affairs in Late Qing Dynasty (Tongzhi), Vol. 25, 筹办夷务始末 同治朝, 卷25), p. 2475.

[32] Suozhuoluo, B. *Chouban Yiwu Shimo, Tongzhi Chao, Juan Ershiwu* (History of Diplomatic Affairs in Late Qing Dynasty (Tongzhi), Vol. 25, 筹办夷务始末 同治朝, 卷25), p. 1027.

[33] Zeng, G. (1909). *Zeng Guofan Shoushu Riji* (The Handwritten Diary of Zeng Guofan, 曾国藩手书日记). Shanghai: China Printing Company.

were enlightened by a practical ideology, which emphasizes using practical knowledge to manage state affairs, rather than boasting. The Yi Xin faction pointed out that he held the same view as Wo Ren before they started the reform. After the Second Opium War, his mind changed: "People can view honesty and etiquette as armor and weapons. It is powerful enough to defeat the enemy by conducting diplomatic negotiations." However, he argued that "I do not believe such views." At the forefront of the reform camp, Li Hongzhang expressed these beliefs in a clearer way: "Suffering the foreign aggression that put our country into such a difficult situation, we are not facing a problem that can be resolved only through negotiation. Since we confronted a turbulent situation such as has not been witnessed for thousands of years, we should implement pioneering work that has not been done before. If we stick to convention, I worry that our country will weaken and never achieve self-strengthening."[34]

Confronting the turbulent situation not witnessed for thousands of years, the Westernization group called for reform to strengthen the country to achieve the same aim, namely to protect the Qing Dynasty and prevent the overbearing aggression of other countries. The conservatives clung to bygone values and wishful thinking to defeat capitalism with feudalism, defeat guns with ethics, and defend the Confucian ethical code. The author believes that the differences between the Westernization group and conservatives exceeded the scope of the traditional debate on inner sage and external domain. Rather, it became a conflict between the dynamic and hindering factors of modernization during the period China was transitioning from a traditional to modern society.

In short, the rise of the notion of Self-Strengthening in the 1860s helped to propel the reform in two aspects. First, "everyone has the aspiration of Self-Strengthening, and Self-Strengthening is widely mentioned." Such notions offered a sound atmosphere for public opinion regarding modern reform, as the promoters of modernization viewed self-strengthening as "the road to ruling the country," which helped establish the principles of the Westernization Movement. With the establishment of the Ministry of Foreign Affairs in the Qing Dynasty and the rise of

[34] Li, H. (1880). *Guangxu Liunian Shieryue Chuyiri Zhili Zongdu Li Hongzhang Zou, Yangwuyundong Juanliu* (The Memorial by Li Hongzhang on Dec 1st, 1880, Westernization Movement, Vol. 6, 光绪六年十二月初一日直隶总督李鸿章奏, 洋务运动 卷6). Shanghai: Shanghai People's Publishing House (SPPH).

modern leadership, China began to learn from the West with initiative rather than instinctive reactions after facing the challenges of the Western world. Although the ruling group was forced to take action and what they learned was preliminary, it was the first step toward modernization.

1.4 Participants in the Westernization Movement

The traditional view of participants in the Westernization Movement is that high officials such as Zeng Guofan and Li Hongzhang constituted the group, while advocators and practitioners were considered early stage Reformists. The author does not agree with this stance, because those guided by notions of absorbing Western technology based on the Chinese traditional system, and those who advocated learning from the West and implementing domestic reform to seek prosperity all belonged to the Westernization group, regardless of their social status in the second half of the nineteenth century and irrespective of the ruling and opposition parties, who can also be considered to represent Westernization. Of course, there were important officials among the Westernization group such as Zeng Guofan, Li Hongzhang, Zuo Zongtang, and Zhang Zhidong, but additional people including theorists and practitioners were attached to the officials, who can be called general members of the group. Their propositions were embodied in the thinking of participants such as Feng Guifen, Zheng Guanying, Guo Songtao, Xue Fucheng, Wang Tao, Ma Jianzhong, and Rong Hong (Yung Wing). Therefore, this book takes these thinkers in the Westernization Movement and presents their interests and propositions. With the passage of time and changes in social structure, the constitution of the Westernization group changed accordingly. Specifically, the participants of the Westernization Movement were primarily composed of the following groups:

1. A group divided from the central ruling group in the Qing court, which was represented by Yi Xin, Gui Liang, and Wen Xiang. When Anglo-French forces captured Beijing in 1860, they were ordered to leave to negotiate peace with Britain, France, and other countries. Thus, they encountered the material and spiritual civilization of the Western capitalist world. Consequently, they advocated the importance of maintaining amicable relationships with Western countries and sought self-strengthening through methods developed abroad.

They presided over Zongli Yamen, the headquarters of the Westernization Movement, which guided the size and direction of its development.

2. The rise of the local Han (ethnic group, compared Manchu) groups in the suppression of the Taiping Rebellion, which were represented by Zeng Guofan, Li Hongzhang, and Zuo Zongtang. Because they fought with the Taiping Army in the southeastern coastal areas, they encountered foreign invaders and personally experienced the great power of the Western ships and armament after stationing in Shanghai. Consequently, they advocated learning from the West in the pursuit of self-strengthening. They were the leaders and shields in the cause of the Westernization Movement.
3. A group of bureaucrats and intellectuals who advocated learning from the West and reforming: A number of intellectuals in the landlord class fled to Shanghai during the Taiping Rebellion. The lifestyle of the Shanghai Concession district and prosperity of its trading port promoted their observations, enabling them to ponder the changes of the times and identify new problems accompanying traditional culture from a different perspective to that of the traditional gentry. Feng Guifen and Zhao Liewen were typical representatives of this group. Feng's book *Reform Proposals written in Jiaoban Cabin* reflected that the dividing landlords were absorbing Western thought. Other important thinkers such as Guo Songtao, Xue Fucheng, Wang Tao, Ma Jianzhong, and Yung Wing experienced great changes in their way of thinking after encountering Western capitalist civilization in different ways, and they had a strong desire to learn from the West in the pursuit of self-strengthening. Since many had joined the Private Secretariats of Zeng or Li, their theoretical works enriched and deepened the modern ideas of the Westernization Movement. These works included Guo Songtao's *Diary of West Europe*, Xue Fucheng's *My Humble Opinions about the Westernization Movement*, Wang Taos' *Tao Yuan's Letter* and *Tao Yuan's Works of Foreign Affairs*, Ma Jianzhong's *Political Proposals Written in Shike Study*, and Rong Hong's *My Life in China and America*. These people were not only thinkers with empty ideas, but also practitioners directly involved in many of the organizations and operations in the cause of the Westernization Movement who became the right hands of the officials. Without them advocating the theory and participating in the planning and operations of the

Movement, the development of self-strengthening would have been difficult to imagine.

4. A number of comprador businessmen and traditional merchants aspired to develop the national industry and commerce. Most came from the southeastern coastal areas where they were first influenced by foreign cultures. Their earlier access to Western capitalist civilization and familiarity with the business management of modern industry and commerce enabled them to become pioneers of China's development of modern industry and commerce and the earliest national entrepreneurs in China. People like Tang Tingshu, Xu Run, and Zheng Guanying, from Xiangshan (now Zhongshan) in Guangdong province, were the typical type of compradors who transformed into national entrepreneurs, while those including Jing Yuanshan and Ye Chengzhong, from Jiangsu and Zhejiang province, were representative of traditional merchants who became national entrepreneurs. Because they had the unique experience of the long-term management of modern enterprises (that others did not have) and had obtained a better understanding of the operation of foreign companies and political reality after entering the upper class, they could observe problems that were difficult for ordinary people to notice and had unique opinions thereon. Based on his long experience in industry and commerce, Zheng Guanying wrote books such as *Jiushi Jieyao*, *Yi Yan*, and *Warning in the Blooming Age* to advocate a business war against foreigners. Regarding his life experience, he wrote, "I first learnt how to conduct a business war from the West, and now, I conduct a business war against them." Jing Yuanshan's book *A Collection of Ju Yichu* summarized his experience working in industry and commerce and provides important material for us to research the modern thoughts of the Westernization Movement.
5. People who separated to form the Qing group: This group was in the central ruling class and headed by the Grand Minister of State, Li Hongzao. Thanks to its publicity, the group enjoyed a great reputation. They satirized current politics, impeached corrupt officials, and advocated resisting foreign aggression. They were feudal gentries, but were not conservative. Many advocated learning from the West to establish affairs in the Western style. For example, Li Hongzhang asked Liu Mingchuan to invite Chen Baochen to write memorials that would declare the importance of building the railway in 1880.

Before the Sino-French War, the main character of the Qing group suggested training the navy to aid Vietnam and resist France to consolidate the frontier. Stating that "the most urgent task we must do is to conduct western-style affairs," he suggested learning from the West and advocated manufacturing military equipment: "It is better to test the skills of using firearms."[35] Since the majority of the members of this group lived in Beijing, they were seldom directly involved in Western-style affairs. As a result, they retained their relatively strong traditional way of thinking. On one hand, they viewed the Westernization Movement as a necessary affair, but on the other, were anxious to achieve quick success and obtain instant benefits. Thus, they often attacked the Westernization group. After the 1880s, with important members of the Qing group such as Zhang Zhidong, Zhang Peilun, Wu Dacheng, and Chen Baochen sent to be local officials, they were forced to amend their previous views under the rigorous social reality. Based on this, they turned to join the Westernization group. Among the members, Zhang Zhidong, as famous as Li Hongzhang, was an important representative of the late Self-Strengthening movement who became one of the leaders of the Westernization group. Because they enjoyed a great reputation in society, they promoted the popularity of the Self-Strengthening movement and helped improve its overall quality after joining the group.

6. Westerners in China: During the period of the Westernization Movement, a group of Westerners was deeply involved in China's social life. Some had mastered the power of tax; some were military advisers and instructors; some worked on Westernization projects such as building ships and manufacturing machinery or as railway, telegraph, and other engineering and technical personnel; and others were active in the cultural and educational fields, working as missionaries. They spread modern Western civilization and played an important role in providing guidance and other aspects of China's modernization.
7. A group of feudal officials who turned to learn from the West after the Sino-Japanese war: Japan's defeat of China greatly impacted feudal officials loyal to the country. At that time, "everybody talks

[35] Zhang, P. (1973). *Jianyuji* (Diaries in Jian Yu, 涧于集). Taiwan: Wen Hai Press Company, p. 471, p. 488.

> about learning from the West,"[36] "from the court to the people, everyone talks about reform."[37] Thus, a more enthusiastic appeal for "absorbing western technology based on the Chinese traditional system" and a tendency that officials abandoned their official career to go into business emerged. Even the Champion (title conferred on the one who came first in the highest imperial examination) ventured into business. Many other gentries also abandoned their official career for business. Some broke through the shackles of the traditional thought absorbing Western technology based on the Chinese traditional system, although most stuck to it.

In summary, the participants of the Westernization Movement included people from various levels of society who advocated absorbing western technology based on the Chinese traditional system. The advocators and decision makers were the officials in the central ruling group and local officials. The advisers and agitators who joined the private secretariats gave advice and campaigned for the cause. According to the progress of technology, the officials hired technicians to manage arising affairs. Theory propagandists spread the theory of the Westernization Movement by writing books. Finally, foreign guests became advisers. With the contributions of these five main players, the Westernization Movement became the main theme of that era.

[36] Ou, J. *Lun Zhengbian Yu Zhongguo Buwang Zhi Guanxi, Zhongguo Jindaishi Ziliaocongkan, Wuxu Bianfa, Juansan* (The Relationship between Coup and China's Undeath, Materials on Modern Chinese History Series· The Reform movement of 1898, Vol. 3, 论政变与中国不亡之关系, 中国近代史资料丛刊·戊戌变法, 卷3). Shanghai: Shanghai People's Publishing House (SPPH), p. 156.

[37] Liang, Q. *Wuxu Zhengbian Ji* (The 1898 Coup, 戊戌政变记). As cited in Zhou, J. (1996). *Zuichu de Jiyuan* (The Beginning of the Era, 最初的纪元). Beijing: Higher Education Press, p. 16.

CHAPTER 2

Guiding Principles of the Westernization Movement

A question worth discussing is: What are the guiding principles of the Westernization Movement? In the author's opinion, the guiding principles are "cementing relations with western countries, conducting domestic reform," and "Confucianism leads the basics, while western science leads the techniques." The first two principles tell us to improve the external environment to create a favorable condition for internal reform, while the latter indicates how to conduct internal reform, namely what should be changed and to what extent. Every reform needs to address these questions. Regarding the modernization thought of the Westernization Movement, the question arises as to how to deal with the relationship between traditional Chinese culture and the introduction of Western learning.

2.1 "Cementing Relations with Western Countries": The Prerequisite for Reform

Li Hongzhang proposed the guiding principle. He said, "In such a terrible situation, we should cement relations with western countries and conduct domestic reform... Other countries became stronger through reformation, but we stick to old rules and refuse to make progress. We

J. Zhou, *Westernization Movement and Early Thought of Modernization in China*, Palgrave Studies in Economic History,
https://doi.org/10.1007/978-3-030-86985-4_2

will ultimately pay for our stubbornness."[1] Li Hongzhang proposed this principle based on the situation at the time. Since the Second Opium War, those who advocated reform realized that China was facing a turbulent situation. According to Wang Tao, "It is an earth-shaking change and we need to undertake pioneering work."[2] Xue Fucheng sent a proposal to Zeng Guofan, stating that "the situation between China and other countries is facing a challenge never seen before."[3] Li Hongzhang was highly concerned about the destiny of China, and thus put forward the guiding principle.

Why did they choose "cementing relations with western countries" as a guiding principle? First, foreign armies were stronger than the those of Qing Dynasty. The Westernization Movement found that China had signed a series of unequal treaties with foreign countries since the Opium War. Thus, "Given that various treaties have been signed, the situation is impossible to change. Many trading ports were forced to open... We are too weak to defend ourselves, so the foreigners can bully us whenever they want." Once the war broke out, China "was not able to defeat the western countries with primitive weapons."[4] Thus, it had to make lean peace. Second, officials advocating the Westernization Movement had not acknowledged the essence of the foreign invaders. Guo Songtao said, "The foreigners want to establish trade relations with us. They do not mean to occupy our land."[5] Similarly, Yi Xin noted that "since the treaties were signed, the invaders returned to Tianjin and complied with the stipulations therein."[6] Thus, "they do not mean to invade our country. We can look over them and seek Self-Strengthening." As such,

[1] Li, H. *Liwenzhong Gong Quanshu, Pengliao Hangao, Juanshijiu* (Complete Works of Li Wenzhong, Letters of Li Wenzhong, Vol. 19, 李文忠公全书, 卷19), p. 43.

[2] Wang, T. (Year). *Tao Yuan Chidu, Daishang Sufu Ligongbao Shu, Juanqi* (Tao Yuan's letters, the letters to Li Gongbao, Vol. 7, 弢园尺牍·代上苏抚李宫保书, 卷7).

[3] Xue, F. (1987). *Xue Fucheng Xuanji* (Selected Works of Xue Fucheng, 薛福成选集). Shanghai: Shanghai People's Publishing House (SPPH), p. 22.

[4] Li, H. *Liwenzhong Gong Quanshu, Pengliao Hangao, Juanshijiu* (Complete Works of Li Wenzhong, Letters of Li Wenzhong, Vol. 19, 李文忠公全书·朋僚函稿, 卷19), p. 43.

[5] Guo, S. (1880). *Fujian Anchashi Gao Songtao Tiaoyi Haifang Shiyi, Yangwu Yundong, Juanyi* (Westernization Movement, Vol. 1, 福建按察使郭嵩焘条议海防事宜, 洋务运动 卷1). Shanghai: Shanghai People's Publishing House (SPPH), p. 140.

[6] (1979). *Chouban Yiwu Shimo, Xianfeng Chao, Juanqishiyi* (History of Diplomatic Affairs in Late Qing Dynasty, Xianfeng, Vol. 71, 筹办夷务始末, 咸丰朝, 卷71). Beijing: Zhonghua Book Company, Vol. 71, p. 2674.

he stood for lean peace. Third, the Westernizationists inherited the Mollification Policy under traditional suzerain-vassal diplomacy. According to Li Hongzhang, "As for policies for dealing with foreign countries after the Zhou and Qing Dynasties, countries that resorted to force failed to survive for long, while others adopting a suzerain-vassal policy survived for a long time. Does it not apply to countries at the present time?"[7] Zeng Guofan agreed that "adopting the Mollification Policy as the main policy is honestly the dictum." The Mollification Policy, called westernization, intended to seek peaceful relationships with foreign countries through empowering trading rights to coax foreigners. Ding Baozhen elaborated that "we adopt the Mollification Policy with foreigners through trading affairs, and they temporarily do not trigger conflicts because of the trade benefits."[8] Fourth, influenced by Confucian moral thoughts, they lacked modern diplomatic awareness. Zeng Guofan instructed Li Hongzhang that "Confucius' Loyalty, Belief, Earnestness, and Respectfulness should run through affairs relating to Self-Strengthening."[9] Li Hongzhang strictly observed his teacher's words and was committed to the principle, and "under the guidance of my teacher's four words: Loyalty, Belief, Earnestness, and Respectfulness, I strived to obtain a peaceful relationship with foreign countries by dealing with affairs."[10] Yi Xin also strove "for a peaceful relationship with foreign countries." It can be seen that Confucian values heavily limited the mindsets of the Westernizationists.

Note that maintaining externally peaceful relationships with foreign countries played a positive role under the circumstances. Furthermore, the international situation at that time provided a good opportunity to strive for a relatively peaceful international environment to focus on reforms and Self-Strengthening affairs. Moreover, the "peaceful foreign relationships" called for by the Qing government provided the obvious nationalism, meaning these relationships would be based on strength.

[7] Li, H. *Liwenzhong Gong Quanshu, Pengliao Hangao, Juanshijiu* (Complete Works of Li Wenzhong, Letters of Li Wenzhong, Vol. 19, 李文忠公全书 朋僚函稿 卷19), p. 43.

[8] Ding, B. (1875). *Chouyi Haifang Yingban Shiyi Zhe, Yangwu Yundong, Juanyi* (Westernization Movement, Vol. 1, 筹议海防应办事宜折, 洋务运动, 卷1), p. 100.

[9] Zeng, G. *Zeng Wenzheng Shuzha, Juanshiba* (The Letters of Zeng Wenzheng, Vol. 18, 曾文正书札, 卷18), p. 15.

[10] Li, H. *Liwenzhong Gong Quanshu, Pengliao Hangao, Juanyi* (Complete Works of Li Wenzhong, Letters of Li Wenzhong, Vol. 1, 李文忠公全书 朋僚函稿, 卷1), p. 26.

Realizing that foreign countries' supposedly obvious pursuit of a peaceful relationship occurred while they privately planned to dominate China, it was acknowledged that China must ostensibly maintain peaceful relationships and secretly prepare for war. Only in that way would the country's peaceful environment endure and be sustainable.[11] The Qing government considered maintaining a peaceful relationship with Western countries as a temporary expedient, considering this relationship a makeshift plan and warfare and dependence a long-term affair. This means that they did not necessarily disagree with the war. Thus, their conception was to some extent reasonable and strategic.

However, the notion of "cementing relations with western countries" proposed by the Westernizationists largely tended toward compromise. A weak country that strives for a peaceful relationship has to sacrifice certain national rights and interests, and unwillingly please the foreign invaders. This will, on one hand, make foreign invaders more aggressive, and on the other, make the weaker country worship foreign things and toady to foreign powers. Thus, in contrast, a peaceful relationship cannot be easily maintained, which is why Li Hongzhang implemented compromise diplomacy.

2.2 The Principle of China's Internal Reforms: "Confucianism Leads the Basics, While Western Science Leads the Techniques"

"Conducting domestic reform" is the general principle by which the Westernizationists handled internal affairs, which was supplemented by "cementing relations with western countries." Westernizationists believed that "China faced a special situation unseen for thousands of years. Thus, the country should establish special undertakings that had not existed for thousands of years. If China is limited by existing rules and laws in any situation, it is likely the country will gradually become weaker and not achieve Self-Strengthening."[12] They were enlightened by examples of how reforms rendered western countries prosperous and powerful,

[11] Li, H. *Liwenzhong Gong Quanshu, Zougao, Juanershisi* (Complete works of Li Wenzhong, Vol. 24, 李文忠公全书, 奏稿, 卷24).

[12] Li, H. *Liwenzhong Gong Quanshu, Zougao, Juansanshijiu* (Complete works of Li Wenzhong, Vol. 39, 李文忠公全书, 奏稿, 卷39), p. 28.

and realized that reforms should be carried out before achieving Self-Strengthening. Therefore, the Westernization school of thought with Self-Strengthening as the slogan and reforms as the content began to forge ahead.

How were the reforms to be implemented? The Westernizationists clung to the slogan "Confucianism leads the basics, while western science leads the techniques," which had two meanings. The first was that Western learning aimed to consolidate the feudal regime was carried out to "guard the feudal regime." The second meaning was that when Western learning conflicted with traditional "Chinese learning," the former should be halted to safeguard the latter. The author believes this is why the Westernization Movement succeeded in being carried out and why it developed slowly and arduously. On one hand, Western learning was carried out in China to "guard the feudal regime," providing a new conception of feudalistic ideology. As the national crisis deepened, more new conceptions of feudalistic ideology emerged. On the other hand, Western learning with capitalism and Chinese learning with feudalism were incompatible; thus, the exported Western learning was bound to conflict with Chinese learning. However, according to the "Confucianism leads the basics, while western science leads the techniques" principle, Chinese learning should be safeguarded, which resulted in the slow development of the spread of Western learning in China. The Westernization Movement process shows that the export of Western learning largely depended on external problems. When the external problems were serious, China would expedite the export of Western learning, and when less severe, the country would slow the process. The points above sufficiently show that the country's reform was passively carried out through the oppression of external forces. Fundamentally, the force for China's reform depended on external problems. The country could only follow a sound development path if its reform was actively rather than passively carried out through constant external oppression. In modern China, the sign of this change was the emergence of reformists led by Kang Youwei and Liang Qichao.

1. The rising and spread of this school of thought

In 1860, Feng Guifen noted that "Chinese ethics aided with foreign countries' methods to ensure prosperity and strength" in his work *Reform*

Proposals Written in Jiaoban Cabin, which first comparatively expressed the "Confucianism leads the basics" principle in terms of core–subsidiary relationships. From then, self-strengthening reformists delivered various speeches on this principle on various occasions. Wang Tao said, "China metaphysically exists because of ethics, and western countries physically exist because of technology. Technology should be learned from western countries, and our ethics should remain unchanged." Furthermore, according to Zheng Guanying, "Chinese learning should remain the main part and western learning supplement the less important part. Chinese learning should be aided by western learning."[13] Others including Li Hongzhang agreed that because of "the fine artilleries and machines of western countries, China will not defeat them. The advantages of China lie in ethics, righteousness, the three cardinal guides, and five constant virtues… So, it will leave western countries far behind." Thus, it is reasonable that Chinese and Western learning should be combined, and the former or Chinese ethics should retain its core principles. As such, for the people, the abovementioned statement meant that Chinese learning represents the body, root, and ethics, while Western learning is less important and a tool for application. The Self-Strengthening movement prospered over the next few decades guided by the "Confucianism leads the basics" principle, which was adopted by the reformists and considered the standard and principle by its leaders. It also became the dominating ideology in the school of thought and was widely accepted by various circles of society.

Why would the Self-Strengthening reformists propose the "Confucianism leads the basics, while western science leads the techniques" model of thought?

First, it was restricted by the values of the Self-Strengthening reformists, especially in the early time of the Movement, and by their level of cognition of western countries. Leaders of the Self-Strengthening movement such as Zeng Guofan and Li Hongzhang fought desperately with the armies comprising uprising peasants to guard the royal families and Confucian code of ethics, gaining success and fame. Furthermore, they realized the advantages of western weapons in the fierce war against the Taiping Rebellion, and understood the importance of western science

[13] Zheng, G. (1982). *Zheng Guanying Ji Xixue Shangce* (Zheng Guanying Works, Western Learning, Vol. I, 郑观应集·西学, 上册). Shanghai: Shanghai People's Publishing House (SPPH), p. 276.

including arithmetic and astronomy. They certainly did not understand why China's laws and ethics should be supplemented with learning from Western countries. Therefore, the notion of "using western learning to make up for the disadvantages of Chinese learning" arose.

Second, the Self-Strengthening reformists used it as a strategy. In the early time of the Westernization Movement, the conservatives fiercely opposed Western learning, considering it "diabolic tricks and wicked crafts" and an extremely harmful alternative. To relieve the pressure from the conservatives, the Self-Strengthening reformists aimed to prove a mutual connection and complement between Chinese and Western learning when dealing with the relationship between the two. In so doing, they sought a way for the legal introduction of Western learning and study from Western countries. They used the prevailing thought in society that "Western learning originated in China" (reportedly, modern Western learning had existed in ancient China and spread to the western countries) to oppose the conservatives. Guo Songtao noted, "The origin of Western learning teaches western countries from generation to generation."[14] Chen Qiu added that "the governance of western countries originates from the six classics and hundred schools of thought on which they rely for prosperity and strength, which proves that Chinese sages instructed western countries."[15] From their viewpoint, learning from the western countries meant seeking the cultural heritage lost by their ancestors at that time. Thus, the Self-Strengthening reformists were able to confidently oppose the conservatives.

2. The development of this school of thought

As a social thought, "Confucianism leads the basics, while western science leads the techniques" changed as society developed. Based on the development direction of the westernization school of thought, the principle developed as follows:

First, the focus developed from "Self-Strengthening" to "pursuing wealth," and from the corresponding "weapons-oriented war" to "commerce-oriented war." The Westernization Movement first proposed

[14] Guo, S. (1984). *Guo Songtao Shiwen Ji* (Guo Songtao Anthology, 郭嵩焘诗文集). Changsha: Yuelu Press, p. 68.

[15] Chen, Q. *Jingshi Boyi, Xu* (Jingshi Boyi, Preface, 经世博议·序).

the term self-strengthening, which is ultimately based on the manufacture of weapons, meaning they focused on a weapons-oriented war. However, as the Westernization Movement developed, many theoretical and practical problems arose, forcing the movement to learn and explore. Through self-examination, they doubted that simply focusing on manufacturing weapons and training soldiers would lead to Self-Strengthening. Li Zongxi contended that "the Self-Strengthening of China cannot depend on only manufacturing firearms."[16] The Self-Strengthening movement then turned its focus to the economy, using the slogan, "seek wealth." The reform spread to every aspect of the economy. Xue Fucheng said that "the reform should be carried out in commerce, politics, and the mines; otherwise, China cannot avoid being poor and foreign countries will remain rich. Industry and weapons should be finely directed, or those in China will remain awkward and remain ingenious in foreign countries. Reform should be implemented for trains, boats, and telegrams, or transportation in China will remain slow but be quick in foreign countries. The advantages and disadvantages of the rules and regulations are closely related with the merits and demerits of talent, and the military system and embattled arms should be reformed; otherwise, the arms of foreign countries will be coordinated and strong while those of the Chinese armed forces will be uncoordinated and weak."[17] Therefore, the Self-Strengthening reformists widened their vision, discussing not only military and economic affairs but also rules and regulations. *Wealthiness* by Ma Jianzhong, *The Policy for Enriching the Country Sequel* by Chen Chi, and the term "commerce-oriented war" coined by Zheng Guanying endowed the "Westernization Movement and Early Thought of Modernization in China" with obvious features concerning mercantilism and wealth, which possessed stronger national cohesion for reviving China.

Second, it developed from learning about Western "artifacts" to admiring and pursuing its "politics, religion, and argumentation." In the early time of the Westernization Movement, the reformists proposed the manufacture of cannons and ships, focusing on learning Western

[16] Li, Z. (1880). *Fuzou Zongli Yamen Liutiaoshu, Yangwu Yundong* (Westernization Movement, Vol. 1, 复奏总理衙门六条疏, 洋务运动 卷1). Shanghai: Shanghai People's Publishing House (SPPH), p. 71.

[17] Xue, F. (1987). *Xue Fucheng Xuanji* (Selected Works of Xue Fucheng, 薛福成选集). Shanghai: Shanghai People's Publishing House (SPPH), p. 556.

artifacts and technology. After the 1870s, as China and foreign countries witnessed increasingly frequent exchanges, the reformists gradually recognized Western rules and regulations. In 1875, Guo Songtao acknowledged China's pursuit of "Self-Strengthening and wealth after learning from western countries, which should be based on studying their gains and losses in national and military policies, and the advantages and disadvantages of the commerce situation before China learned from them how to design the military system and make weapons."[18] Zeng Jize was then sent as an envoy to Europe, where he noted "the politics and religion of Europe were orderly and he admired the roots of their prosperity and strength."[19] In 1882, Ma Jianzhong was sent on a diplomatic mission to Korea for the second time, after which he wrote *Second Record on the Journey to Korea*. He believed that "anyone who cares for the social situation could understand the fundamentals of politics. As the border is so longer banned in China, it is suitable for the country to establish schools and cultivate talent. The reform concerning official positions could be carried out after obtaining talent."[20] Politics were regarded as "fundamentals" and reforms concerning politics and regimes were on the agenda. Therefore, after the mid-term of the Westernization Movement, the reformists developed from learning western military and economic technology to becoming enthusiastic in discussing western politics, religion, and argumentation. This signaled the deepening of Self-Strengthening reform into high-level field politics and making the necessary preparations for the reformist school of thought.

The Westernization Movement was continuously complemented and developed, which is aimed to consolidate the feudal regime related with the "The Tongzhi Restoration" promoted by the Qing government. In *The Tongzhi Restoration*, Rui Mali wrote, "Not only a Dynasty has collapsed, but also a civilization has crashed. But the extraordinary efforts

[18] Guo, S. (1983), *Guo Songtao Zougao* (Memorials of Guo Songtao, 郭嵩焘奏稿). Changsha: Yuelu Press, p. 344.

[19] Zeng, J. (1983). *Zeng Jize Yiji* (Works of Zeng Jize, 曾纪泽遗集). Changsha: Yuelu Press, p. 171.

[20] Ma, J. (1967). *Dongxing Xulu, Dongxing Sanlu* (Second Record on the Journey to Korea, Third Record on the Journey to Korea, 东行续录, 东行三录). Taiwan: Kwangwen Book Company, p. 48.

made by excellent men mean they survived for another 60 years."[21] This clarified the relationship between "Restoration" and the Westernization Movement. Certainly, the main content of the Restoration was implementing the Westernization Movement and new policies, and the "Confucianism leads the basics" principle became the spirit backbone of this Restoration. Therefore, the Qing Dynasty had to agree with the self-strengthening mindset. The reformists could converse with each other in court and have discussions with ordinary people. Over time, the reform leaders including Zeng Guofan and Li Hongzhong became increasingly powerful and influential, and were honored as "famous courtiers of the Restoration." Second, as books from Western countries were translated, the people's vision widened, and their thinking and conceptions changed. Liang Qichao confirmed, "After people including Li Shanlan and Hua Hengfang translated several decades of books concerning science and politics, the Chinese people started to know that apart from the powerful ships and cannons manufactured by the western people, the reasons for that were becoming clear, and their opinions toward Western learning was gradually changing."[22] Furthermore, as the Westernization Movement deepened, its theories were continuously tested in practice, forcing people to explore the process of the alternate development of knowledge and practice. Essentially, the development of Westernization thought was closely related to the pulse of the times and represents the direction of that stage onward.

Although the reform views proposed by the self-strengthening reformists involved side issues instead of the feudal regime, they followed the development of world capitalism and pursued Self-Strengthening through reform. The reformists learned from foreigners to complement China's advantages, and unwilling to lag behind other countries, coincided with the general development of the country's history.

3. The disintegration and recession of this school of thought

[21] Fairbank, K. J. (1985). *Jianqiao Zhongguo Wanqing Shi Shangjuan* (The Cambridge History of China, Vol. 10, Late Ch'ing, 剑桥中国晚清史). Beijing: China Social Sciences Press, p. 517.

[22] Liang, Q. (1985). *Zhongguo Jindai Sanbainian Xueshu Shi, Liang Qichao Lun Qingxueshi Erzhong* (China's Academic History in Recent Almost Three Hundred Years, 中国近代三百年学术史). Shanghai: Fudan University press, p. 27.

According to Liang Qichao, the transformation of any great school of thought can be divided into four phases: the enlightenment phase, heyday phase, disintegration phase, and recession phase. He said: "Whatever country and Dynasty the thought belongs to, its development always abides by the rule."[23] The development of Westernization thought is no exception. In the early time, the Westernization Movement was considered taboo among the people, and some would be considered "crazy" if talking about it. Gradually, people became interested in discussing it, especially after the Sino-Japanese War. From then, provoked by the national crisis, the Chinese people's interest in Western learning increased. Thus, the "Confucianism leads the basics" philosophy peaked, and "knowing Westernization affairs was honored as talent both in the court and among the common people."[24] "Almost everyone talked about affairs related to Self-Strengthening." In 1896, Sun Jianai wrote in a memorial to the throne for reconsideration, "Now, when China established the Imperial University of Peking, Chinese learning should be the main content and western learning supplementary. Chinese learning should be the body, and western learning the subsidiary. Shortcomings should be supplemented by western learning. Chinese learning without inheritors should be complemented by western learning. Chinese learning covers western learning, and the former should not be overridden by the latter."[25] This became the tenet for all places establishing schools and Learning Societies. In 1898, when the Hundred Day's Reform was approaching its heyday, the leader of the Westernization Movement during its later period, Zhang Zhidong, wrote *Exhortation to Learning*. The book upheld the golden mean to "grasp Western and Chinese learning, and weigh between the reformists and conservatives." It painstakingly advocated arousing "loyalty and love, pursuing prosperity

[23] Liang, Q. (1985). *Qingdai Xueshu Gailun, Liang Qichao Lun Qingxueshi Erzhong* (Academic Introduction of Qing Dynasty, 清代学术概论). Shanghai: Fudan University press, p. 2. As cited in Li, R. (1996). *Jindai Zhongguo Shehui Sichao* (The Ideological Trend of Modern China, 近代中国社会思潮). Zhengzhou: Henan People's Publishing House, p. 101.

[24] Zhang, D. & Wang, R. (1960). *Xinghai Geming Qian Shinian Shilun Wenji, Juanyi, Xiace* (Essays in the First Decade of 1911, Vol. 1, Part II, *辛亥革命前十年时论文集，第1卷，下册*)). Shanghai: SDX Joint Publishing Company, p. 741.

[25] (1972). *Wuxu Bianfa, Juaner* (Wuxu Reform, Vol. 2, 戊戌变法, 卷2). Shanghai: Shanghai People's Publishing House (SPPH), p. 426.

and strength, respecting the court, and defending the country," instilling the same strong feeling in the school of thought and garnering the appreciation of Emperor Guangxu and Empress Dowager Cixi. Emperor Guangxu thought the book's "arguments are complete and smooth, and brings great benefits to the academy and public feeling." He ordered royal edicts for the second round of its publication. The book thus diffused rapidly at home and abroad because of the efforts of the court.[26] Even foreigners supported the book, thinking that "Chinese people, accustomed to the platitudes of Confucius, had become lifeless, but finally revived when facing the reality in this period."[27] In the 26th year (the year 1900) after Emperor Guangxu's ascension to the throne, the English version of *Exhortation to Learning* was published in New York, where they added the title: "China's Only Hope."

However, the law of development comprises a wane after a zenith. The "Confucianism leads the basics" principle spurred both the peak and turning point of the self-strengthening movement. Although the philosophy had become a commonly received theory by society, different people used it based on different standpoints. Some emphasized the "western science leads the techniques" part, while others preferred the "Confucianism leads the basics" part. For example, The Chinese learning proposed by the Westernization reformists differed from the views of high-ranking Westernization officers. Zeng Guofan, Li Hongzhang, and Zhang Zhidong considered themselves the guardians of the Confucian code of ethics. The Chinese learning they advocated focused on safeguarding the absolutism system and culture, with the "three cardinal guides" as the guiding principle. However, the reformists including Feng Guifen, Wang Tao, and Zheng Guanying despised the study (the absolutism culture of Qin and Han Dynasties) in the period "from the Song Dynasty to the middle of the 19th century," and advocated study (the culture across three generations including Yao, Shun, and Yu) in the period "before the Song Dynasty" when explaining Chinese learning. They adopted the stance of "returning to the origin and developing new ideas," and the Chinese learning they proposed referred to the original spirit of Chinese culture such as consciousness of worrying, flexibility,

[26] (1972). *Wuxu Bianfa, Juaner* (Wuxu Reform, Vol. 2, 戊戌变法, 卷2). Shanghai: Shanghai People's Publishing House (SPPH), p. 17.

[27] Woodbridge. Exhortation to Learning, preface, *Academic Journal*. As cited in Feng Tianyu, He Xiaoming: Zhang Zhidong.

endless Self-Strengthening, and people orientation. They advocated organizing Parliament and appealed for civil rights, which relied on Western learning and was testified by scholars in the pre-Qin period.

As the new type of Chinese economy developed, the people further realized that while the "western science leads the techniques" philosophy had been adopted, the "Confucianism leads the basics" approach would likely disappear, and should therefore inevitably be replaced. Here, an increasing number of people criticized the "Confucianism leads the basics, while western science leads the techniques" philosophy. The philosophy was mainly opposed by the conservatives in the early time of the Westernization Movement, and by the reformists after the Hundreds Days' Reform, especially after the Incident of 1900. Zhang Zhidong's attack from both sides is disclosed in *Zhang Zhidong's Governance in Hubei Province*: "In the early time when Zhang Zhidong came to Hubei Province, he was busy purchasing machines and manufacturing weapons. As a result, he was humiliated by bureaucrats and the conservatives, and therefore compared to Wang Anshi who had carried out reforms. After the Incident of 1900, the reform was widely discussed in the court and different opinions arose. The reformists vilified Zhang Zhidong for he did not have comprehensive views regarding western learning. So during the two decades in Hubei Province, Zhang Zhidong was constantly questioned and slandered."[28]

The situation Zhang Zhidong's "Confucianism leads the basics, while western science leads the techniques" encountered indicates that after the Sino-Japanese War, especially after the Incident of 1900, the philosophy could not unite the nation. Thus, as history developed, it transformed into the reformist mindset advocating that China be saved through Western ways.

Being a social thought and cultural value, "Confucianism leads the basics, while western science leads the techniques" was popular among Chinese modern schools of thought for more than half a century. Its role in the Westernization Movement period was embodied in the following two aspects:

[28] Zhang, J. (1947). *Zhang Wenxiang Zhie Ji* (Zhang Zhidong's Governance in Hubei Province, 张文襄治鄂记), p. 54.

1. In the name of safeguarding feudal cardinal guides and the Confucian code of ethics, it guided public opinion and reduced resistance toward importing Western culture.
2. As the traditional standard culture, it contained the national emotional worship of national cultural relics. When foreign countries invaded China, national self-esteem and sense of pride intensified. Because of its strong national consciousness, it was commonly supported by people at all levels of society and contributed to national cohesion.

Essentially, at that time, it was the best modern theory for reducing resistance to reform, reducing reform costs, and bringing maximum benefits to the reform. It included new viewpoints on a culture that advocated learning from western countries and opposing stubborn conservatives. It was the culture chosen by the ruling class including open-minded scholars and bureaucrats, who after Chinese and Western culture severely clashed, said they were unwilling and unable to discard the old things and intended to pursue new things in the difficult situation.

CHAPTER 3

Development Strategies of Westernizational Modernization

The development strategies of Westernizational Modernization had two characteristics. The first is that the government was eager to promote a completed military industry. In other words, the government gave priority to the military industry during the modernization. The second is that the national industry and commerce were developed through the combination of "import substitution" and "export substitution" (export processing).

3.1 Establishment of the Military Industrial System

As mentioned, the development of Westernizational Modernization was forced to initiate by the "powerful ships and cannons" of foreign countries. Under the circumstances that China would be invaded at any time due to its weak military power, the reformists considered the construction of ships and cannons the first step in defending China and pursuing Self-Strengthening. Li Hongzhang noted, "As long as China had cannons and ships, westerners would be astringent."[1] After hearing and seeing that

[1] As cited in Li, Z. (1947). *Zhongguo Jinbainian Zhengzhi Shi, Shangce* (The Political History of China in the Past 100 years, Part 1, 中国近百年政治史). Beijing: The Commercial Press, p. 29.

J. Zhou, *Westernization Movement and Early Thought of Modernization in China*, Palgrave Studies in Economic History,
https://doi.org/10.1007/978-3-030-86985-4_3

Britain, France, and other countries acted on their own will, Prince Yi Xin proposed that "Self-Strengthening focus on training troops, which should be based on the production of weapons," adding that "we should study the strength of various kinds of machines and weapons to grasp the core essence thereof. Thus, when there is war, these can be used to defend ourselves, and when there is none, they can be used to demonstrate our power."[2]

The British columnist Gundry commented: "Maybe because China was forced to open the door and trade with foreign countries, the western things that China initially adopted naturally fell on the weapon. China thought that their failure resulted from the superiority of the foreign weapons and naval ships, so the country spontaneously wished to keep up with their modern enemies in this way. Based on this evaluation, China aimed to obtain the value of western weapons, and ship plants and arsenals were constructed."[3]

With its strong military characteristics, Liang Qichao commented that "(the Westernization Movement) is bound to have two things: one concerns the military such as purchasing and manufacturing ships and machines, building gun emplacements, and repairing dockyards; the other refers to commercial affairs such as building railways and setting up Merchants Holdings, the Textile Bureau, the Kaiping Mines, and Mohe Mines. During that time, schools were built, and students were sent to foreign countries to prevent invasion by western countries."[4] This accords with the cognition logic of the Self-Strengthening reformists in the social transformation process and China's logic in response to invasion from western countries.

The Westernization Movement stemmed from the military, which conformed to law. At the beginning of the nineteenth century, the reform implemented by Mohamed Ali and the Meiji Restoration also started in the military industry. When the Westernization Movement began, on

[2] Suochuoluo, B. *Chouban Yiwu Shimo, Tongzhi Chao, Juan Ershiwu* (History of Diplomatic Affairs in Late Qing Dynasty (Tongzhi), Vol. 25, 筹办夷务始末 同治朝, 卷25).

[3] *Yangwu Yundong, Juanba* (Westernization Movement, Vol. 8, 洋务运动, 卷8).

[4] Liang, Q. *Yinbingshi Heji, Zhuanji, Li Hongzhang Zhuan* (Yinbing Mansion Compilations, Li Hongzhang, 饮冰室合集, 专集, 李鸿章传). As cited in Zhou, J. (1996). *Zuichu De Jiyuan* (The Beginning of the Era, 最初的纪元). Beijing: Higher Education Press, p. 133.

September 25, 1857, Marx wrote in his letter to Friedrich Engels, "In general, armed forces played an important role in economic development. For example, originally, salary grows from the ancient armed forces. Also, Roman's peculium castrense (property in the military camp) is the first law recognizing non-parent portable property. The fabric union (working crew or craftsmen for military affairs, a guiding person) is the start of the guild system. Machines were also initiated for use in the armed forces. Even the special value of the metal and its currency usage is based on its function in military affairs at the beginning of time (after the Greek Stone Age). The inner division of the department was first put into practice in the armed forces. Moreover, the whole history of citizens' society is obviously summarized by the history of the armed forces history."[5] The strength of the armed forces is related to the destiny of a country, nation, and society. Thus, the importance and urgency of wars mean every country and nation will put their best human and material resources in their armed forces to improve the organization of the army and develop the most advantageous weapons. Every creation and invention in favor of improving the effectiveness of battle is bound to be used in the armed forces.

How can the achievements and limitations of the modern military industry be evaluated?

Learning from "western science" created an advantaged situation for China to use "the privileges of persons who do not keep up with history" and to narrow the gap between Chinese and Western productivity. For example, guns and cannons were manufactured by hand in China when they were already manufactured by machines in western countries. The gap in technological facilities between China and Western countries lasted for the period of the industrial revolution. After establishing the military industry in the Westernization Movement, the gap rapidly narrowed after introducing western technology and equipment. For cannons, the Jiangnan Manufacturing Bureau produced a breechloader, adding a steel pipe wrought iron hoop and all-steel breechloader. Breechloaders with an 8-inch caliber and weighing 180 pounds were manufactured in the Western European countries 24 years ago. Regarding guns, muzzleloader rifles were reproduced by the Jiangnan Manufacturing Bureau in the 6th

[5] Marx, K. & Engels, F. (1972). *Makesi Engesi Xuanji, Juansi* (Selected Works of Karl Marx and Frederick Engels, Vol. 4, 马克思恩格斯选集, 卷4). Beijing: People's Publishing House, pp. 335–336.

year (the year 1867) after Emperor Tongzhi's ascension to the throne, and in Western Europe just 37 years ago. Furthermore, American-type Remington Breech Needle-guns were reproduced by the Jiangnan Manufacturing Bureau, and made in Western Europe just 20 years ago. In the 19th year (the year 1893) after Emperor Guangxu's ascension to the throne, rapid-fire guns that could shoot 22–25 targets per minute were manufactured. Similar guns were made in Western countries 13 years ago. In addition, portable small caliber rifles that can shoot accurately were used in Western countries in the 16th year (the year 1890) after Emperor Guangxu's ascension to the throne. Small caliber rifles were also successfully made by Jiangnan Manufacturing Bureau in the 24th year after Emperor Guangxu's ascension to the throne, which were made by western countries just 8 years ago.[6] All their advanced weapons were used to equip the ground forces and navy of the Qing government to suppress the Taiping Rebellion and other uprisings in other areas and played a role in resisting foreign invasion.

Although the military industry had been implemented for several decades during the Westernization Movement, China had just become a follower of powerful foreign countries and not kept up with them. Because of the low quality and high price of the products, Li Hongzhang argued that "making ships is inferior to purchasing them." However, once the Qing government resorted to arms, they would have to purchase weapons from foreign countries. Thus, it was heavily criticized by the court of public opinion. Regardless of how hard high-ranking officials including Li Hongzhang tried, the military industry during the Westernization Movement could not match the achievements of Western countries, because the modernization of national defense was out of line with society and the economy. Familiar with military affairs, Friedrich Engels analyzed the economic factors concerning the success and failure of wars: "The victory of violence is based on the production of weapons, and the production of weapons is based on the whole production. So it is based on 'economic strength' and material goods."[7] He continues, "The

[6] As cited in Xu, D. & Wu, C. (1990). *Zhongguo Ziben Zhuyi Fazhanshi, Dierjuan* (The History of Chinese Capitalism, Vol. 2, 中国资本主义发展史, 第二卷). Beijing: People's Publishing House, pp. 346–348.

[7] Marx, K. & Engels, F. (1972). *Makesi Engesi Xuanji, Juansan* (Selected Works of Karl Marx and Frederick Engels, Vol. 3, 马克思恩格斯选集, 卷3). Beijing: People's Publishing House, pp. 205–206.

ground forces and navy, to the greatest extent, depend on the economy as its prerequisite. Equipment, organization, war tactics, and war strategies firstly depend on the production level and traffic conditions at that time."[8] After the outbreak of the Revolution of 1911, Yan Fu recalled his conversation with Hart, the inspector of general customs. Hart had told him that "the relationship between the navy and a country is like the trees with flowers. The trunk and branches must be flourishing and adapt to the surrounding environment before the flowers blossom. If flowers are flourishing, the trees will live for a long time. Now, many people in your navy disagreed with me. It will bring no benefit to the navy if it is blamed rather than searching for the fundamental reason."[9] Hart's words are a sharp criticism of the high officials of the Westernization Movement who prioritized the military industry.

The priority development of the military industry significantly influenced China's industrialization. In western countries, the time-sequence pattern of early industrialization generally started with the textile industry, extended to other light industry sectors, and then shifted to the heavy industry. However, China's early industrialization began with the military industry, then extended to the civilian sectors including the heavy and light industries. In fact, from the perspective of China's comparative advantage in the world market system at that time, it was helpful to develop the labor-intensive textile industry to foster strengths and circumvent weaknesses. However, in contrast, the development of the capital-intensive heavy industry, especially the technology-intensive military sector, does not bring many advantages because of the low labor costs and high cost of capital (caused by the underdeveloped economy and insufficient supply of funds). The actual situation was the same. Light industry is a short-term low investment with quick effects that can generate accumulation for the industrialization of the country. The heavy industry is, however, long-term high investment with slow effects. China's Westernization industrialization started with the military industry

[8] Marx, K. & Engels, F. (1972). *Makesi Engesi Xuanji, Juansan* (Selected Works of Karl Marx and Frederick Engels, Vol. 3, 马克思恩格斯选集, 卷3). Beijing: People's Publishing House, p. 12.

[9] Yan, Fu. (1986). *Yanfuji, Haijun Dashiji, Banyan Dierce* (Yan Fu Collection • (Navy memorabilia) Preamble, Vol. 2, 严复集, 海军大事记 弁言). Beijing: Zhonghua Book Company, pp. 352–353.

with its associated high costs, slow effects, and heavy burden. This exacerbated the already problematic economic conditions and delayed the entire development process of industrialization.

However, regarding the time-sequence pattern of the Westernization of industrialization development, the Westernization Group inevitably chose to put the military before civilian industry, and heavy industry before lighter sectors, which should not be criticized. Developing countries such as nineteenth-century Japan and Egypt followed the same route to modernization. Problems emerged after the start of industrialization, when the Westernization Group should have adjusted the layout of industrial development in time, and further developed the civil industry, which was related to the national economy and the people's livelihood, especially the textile industry, to achieve balanced and stable development in national economic sectors. However, they responded poorly to this situation. After the 1870s, government-run civil industries were still mostly concentrated in fuel mining and other heavy industries. By 1880 (the 6th Year of the Guangxu Reign), the textile industry had begun when Zuo Zongtang founded the Lanzhou Textile Bureau. In the process of development of the light and textile industries, the Qing government advanced two controversial measures. First, to protect the newborn Shanghai Mechanical Textile Bureau, the government claimed that within 10 years, "neither the Chinese nor foreigners" shall seek the personal interest to "open another Textile Bureau." Second, according to regulations, the Shanghai Bureau and Hubei Bureau were provided with 400,000 spindles and 5,000 textile machines. This would not be supplemented within 10 years, confining the national textile industry to a narrow pattern. The administrator made these decisions only because the Westernization Group was concerned that private and foreign capital would "compete for profit" with government enterprises, and thus affect the most important goal, namely the development of the military industry.

Early modernization in Japan also began with the priority development of the military and civil heavy industries. However, the Meiji government soon realized that "the one who makes profit for the country will pay attention to the heavy industry, especially the textile industry."[10] Guided by this recognition, they adjusted the strategy in a timely way, founded and expanded a number of textile factories, and sold 10 sets of 2,000

[10] *Huilan Shiji, Diwubian* (Returning to Histroy, Vol. 5, 回览实记), p. 220. As cited in (1983). *Lishi Yanjiu* (History Studies, Vol. 6, 历史研究, 第6期), p. 129.

spindle textile machines bought from Britain to private capitalists at a low price, thus contributing to the rapid development of the textile industry and the country's industrialization.

Priority development of the military industry also drove China's modernization to development with government rather than private investment as the mainstay. Since the cost of the military industry and its subsidiary civil industry were high based on their complex technology and strict management requirements, civilian businessmen could not afford to invest, leading to the state's necessary investment in these enterprises. According to the statistics, from the 1860s to the Sino-Japanese War, the Qing government's industrial investment totaled approximately 27,966,000 silver dollars: 12.509 million silver dollars in the transportation industry; 12.08 million in the manufacturing industry; and 3.376 million in the mining industry. Investments in each company were approximately 200,000 silver dollars, although this was up to 6 million silver dollars in some companies.[11] The total investment accounted for 70.48% of domestic industry capital in that period.[12] As a leading role, national capital decided that enterprises founded during the Westernization Movement period would not take the non-monopoly capitalist private enterprise form that emerged in the European Modernization Movement. Instead, they took the form of state-capitalist government-run or government-supervised and merchant-managed enterprises. In addition, for high-ranking officials, the mining, transportation, steel-making, and textile industries guaranteed the development of the military industry. To avoid the impact of competition between foreign and domestic capital on the development of the military industry, officials used state political power to restrict foreign or domestic private capital into these areas through patents or other systems, which suppressed the enthusiasm of private capital investment. If private capital could not be used to invest in industry, the capitalist mode of production could not be adopted.

[11] Wu, C. (1985). *Zhongguo Ziben Zhuyi Yu Guonei Shichang* (The Chinese Capitalism and Its Domestic Market, 中国资本主义与国内市场). Beijing: China Social Sciences Press, p. 114.

[12] Wu, C. (1991). *Zhongguo Jindai Zibenjicheng He Gongnongye Ji Jiaotongyunshuye Chanzhi Guji* (China's modern capital integration and industrial and agricultural and transportation industry output value estimate, 中国近代资本集成和工农业及交通运输业产值估计). Researches in Chinese Economic History, No. 4.

The modernization route to developing the military industry did not singularly conform to the national economy's balance requirement, which hindered China's new economic development. Thus, Westernization thinkers including Guo Songtao and Zheng Guanying proposed changing the route. Visiting Britain and France, Guo wrote a letter to Li Hongzhang with two suggestions. One was that students dispatched to study military manufacturing and driving abroad should instead study civil technology. The other was that as the Japanese government did, the Qing government could first learn about the fundamental Western systems in politics, economics, society, and legislation. Zheng Guanying held similar views, advocating the development of the civil industry with national defense expenditure. He said, "Our country has prioritized military power for decades, and the costs spent on defense by purchasing firearms, ships, and cannons, and setting up artillery batteries are too high to count. It is more possible for a country with much money instead of many weapons to win in the long-term war, and it injures fewer common people and soldiers."[13]

However, the Westernization officials rejected their opinions. Li Hongzhang outright refused Guo's ideas, believing this would delay the realization of the modernization strategy based on the military industry. He argued, "I was in charge of the military department, and had to emphasize the military. Military power is a country's root; anyone who tries to develop the big and far instead of this will fail."[14] Unfortunately, the Westernization officials failed to see the true relationship between the civil and military industries, namely that military development also depends on the level of the civil industry. Therefore, coordinated and balanced development among departments of the national economy is important in planning a country's development strategy. Of course, this does not mean developing all departments along the same lines. As far as this author is concerned, development should occur at a key time point. Generally and strategically, all departments must develop equally in a coordinated way. Otherwise, a "bottleneck" will occur, which will impact the national economy.

[13] Zheng, G. (1982). *Zheng Guanying Ji,Shangzhan Shang, Shangce* (Zheng Guanying Works, Commercial War, Vol. I, 郑观应集·商战上, 上册). Shanghai: Shanghai People's Publishing House (SPPH), p. 590.

[14] Li, H. *Liwenzhong Gong Quanshu, Pengliao Hangao, Juanshiqi* (Complete Works of Li Wenzhong, Letters of Li Wenzhong, Vol. 17, 李文忠公全书, 朋僚函稿, 卷17), p. 14.

3.2 Civilian Industrial Development Strategy: Combination of Import Substitution and Export Promotion

Civil industry was also developed under the influence of the military industry. At that time, similar foreign enterprises were the greatest competitors; thus, a problem was that to improve the competitiveness of China's civil industries, "foreigners had to be prevented from sharing more business profits." In the long-term practice of Westernization, the Westernizationists proposed an economic development strategy that combined import substitution and export substitution.

In 1865, to establish the ironworks, Li Hongzhang highlighted the situation in the memorial to the throne: "Currently, the cloth from Britain shipped to China costs more than 30 million silver dollars a year, and copper, iron, plumbum [lead], and stannum [tin] also cost millions of silver dollars, dampening the interest of many Chinese artisans. Since we cannot stop the influx of foreign goods and cannot forbid Chinese people from using them, why not make machines, ships, and railroads by ourselves?" Here, Li Hongzhang was referring to a modernization strategy similar to import substitution.[15]

During the Tongzhi Reign and Guangxu Reign, many people advanced a similar import substitution modern vision. In 1875, once Guo Songtao was appointed Surveillance Commissioner in Fujian, he proposed "shipbuilding, machine-making, and learning from foreigners to make a profit for civilians," enabling coastal merchants to open the Machinery Bureau. He thought there were many benefits for doing this. For transportation, since ships from outside came into the area of the Chinese coast, companies like Yangtze River, Shanghai large junks, Ningbo line fishing boats, and Guangdong Hongdan ships were losing market shares, and more than half the ships were abandoned downstream below the Hankou. Therefore, if merchants could "make profits off preparing ships, the nation would benefit more. One more Chinese ship means more profits. One more ship on each coast means more security."[16]

[15] Li, H. *Liwenzhong Gong Quanshu, Chouyi Haifang Zhe, Juan Ershisi* (Complete Works of Li Wenzhong, Coast Defense, Vol. 24, 李文忠公全书, 筹议海防折, 卷24).

[16] *Yangwu Yundong, Juaner* (Westernization Movement, Vol. 2, 洋务运动, 卷2). Shanghai: Shanghai Renmin Chubanshe, p. 138.

In 1878, Li Fan, the investigating censor of Huguangdao, further advanced Li Hongzhang and Guo Songtao's idea of import substitution, proposing a more comprehensive strategy that organically combined import and export substitution. He claimed in a memorial to the throne: "According to the current situation, China cannot re-close the gates of the country and cut it off from foreigners. The only way is to use commerce as a weapon to encourage coastal people raising funds to establish companies like the foreigners did: Make trade, make a profit." Li Fan believed that using commerce as a weapon entailed two aspects: Foreigners should transport the goods they want by themselves, and China should make the goods the Chinese needed by themselves.[17] This signifies the simplest generalization of a modernization strategy of import and export substitution from the 1950s to the 1960s in many developing countries.

In 1879, Luo Yingliu, an official in Guizhou province, proposed the same idea as Li Fan when he delivered his memorial to the throne. He highlighted that China must take two countermeasures to retain its economic rights. First, "the underground treasures that Westerners coveted should be exploited by the Chinese." This means exploiting our own gold, silver, coal, and iron to make the country prosperous and strong, and to avoid being coveted. Second, "we should make the goods the Chinese need from abroad. Foreigners should transport the goods they want by themselves." For him, the advantage of import substitution was that "in the future, everything we added could reduce the interest of foreigners, and our country would generally become rich and prosper." The advantage of export substitution was that "no one can dampen our interests."[18] Therefore, he stressed that the products foreigners required, such as silk, tea, and rheum, should be self-processed to attract investment, and then transported overseas by China.

In 1890, Ma Jianzhong, who had followed Li Hongzhang engagement in Westernization, theoretically summarized these ideas. He pointed out that "to rule, a country should be built on a prosperous and strong base, and wealth is the first thing countries need to be strong." He proposed three ways to become wealthy: One is to expand exports by ensuring

[17] *Yangwu Yundong, Juanyi* (Westernization Movement, Vol. 1, 洋务运动, 卷1). Shanghai: Shanghai People's Publishing House (SPPH), pp. 166–167.

[18] *Yangwu Yundong, Juanyi* (Westernization Movement, Vol. 1, 洋务运动, 卷1). Shanghai: Shanghai People's Publishing House (SPPH), p. 179.

"the high quality of Chinese inherent goods to position them as best-selling products." The second is to reduce imports by "reproducing their products to use against their market." The third is to develop the mining industry, enabling the accumulation of wealth, and to ensure it will not disappear or be dispersed.

How can programs that benefit import and export substitution be developed? The Westernization Group contended that any Chinese products foreigners needed, such as silk, tea, rhubarb, and other objects, were all self-production and enterprise-establishing: "No one can dampen our interests." Particularly important was developing the silk and tea industry, which constituted the bulk of Chinese exports. Regarding substitute imports, Zhong Tianwei proposed a comprehensive production program: "The textile machine made the kitchen without felt. Textile machines rendered camlets unsellable. Soaps, perfumes, indigos, and western candles were easily manufactured with chemical knowledge. We could produce strong acid, rubber, kerosene, and cement if we grasp the procedures. Industrious planting can yield an abundance of grapes, wine, carrots, sugar, cigars, cigarettes, and coffee. Properly raising livestock can ensure cattle, junkets, lobsters, and yellow grasshoppers as our foodstuffs. Fine manufacture made us produce our own needles, umbrellas, ribbons, and flags to block their products."[19]

However, achieving import or export substitution required certain conditions, particularly technology. Therefore, the Westernization Group repeatedly emphasized the importance of using western new technology and new equipment to transform traditional industries. Regarding China's disadvantages in foreign trade, Zheng Guanying noted, "China is located in a variable zone. While things from here are better than those of the Western countries, China's manufacturing ability does not compare to that of the Westerners. Things we consider useless, such as feathers, wool, and camel, are all purchased and turned into something new and useful by the foreigners. Once the materials are processed, they sell them to the Chinese and make huge profits from it."[20] Chen Chi also mentioned that according to the foreigners, "Chinese exports were raw materials

[19] Zhong, T. *Yuezu Ji, Wanhui Zhongguo Gongshang Shengji Liquan Lun Er* (Zhong's Righteous Words, Save the China industrial and commercial livelihood economic rights theory II, *刖足集, 挽回中国工商生计利权论二)*.

[20] Zheng, G. (1982). *Zheng Guanying Ji, Shangwu Wu* (Zheng Guanying Works, Trade V, *郑观应集 • 商务五)*. Shanghai: Shanghai Renmin Chubanshe, p. 627.

to be processed, although the imports from the Western countries were finished products. The goods are worked on, and processed into elegant and useful products. Chinese exports of raw materials could be tallied by cases, shi, bags, or thousands of kilograms, but prices were cheap with only marginal profits. The foreign ships were usually filled with goods before they left. However, the finished products of imports were counted by pieces, bolts, bottles, and boxes. While the amounts were small, each product was worth a thousand dollars, and the goods of a whole ship were worth billions of dollars."[21] Here, Chen Chi presented the notion of increasing the technical contents and additional value through technological improvement.

The Westernization Group tended to be optimistic in terms of China's prospects of using business against the enemy for two reasons:

First, China has the cost advantage. They believed that China's low labor costs, thrifty tradition, domestic market, and low transportation costs would render Chinese products more competitive than foreign ones. According to Chen Chi, "the labor force in China is cheaper than in Western countries. For the same product, our costs must be lower than theirs, which is vital to ensure China's business thrives."[22] Li Hongzhang added that as long as the quality of national industrial products reached the standards of foreign goods, the foreign goods "certainly cannot be compared to homemade products." Regarding expensive freight, he added that "our interests grew as theirs gradually declined."[23] Thus, the future of domestic goods seemed optimistic.

Second, it is a natural law that something turns into its opposite if pushed too far. China is highly developed in terms of dialectic thought. Our ancestors developed a David and Goliath theory based on this mindset, which is the treasure of traditional Chinese philosophy. In modern times, Chinese business was left behind. While the Westernization Group was hopeful for the future, the writer thought the idea of David and Goliath played a considerable role therein. In this regard, Li Fan's remarks are considered typical: "In the middle period of the Ming

[21] Chen, C. (1997). *Chenchi Ji, Qiyong Zhigong Shuo* (Chen Chi Works, Meachine, 陈炽集·器用之工说). Beijing: Zhonghua Book Company, pp. 218–219.

[22] Chen, C. (1997). *Chenchi Ji, Zhizuo Zhigong* (Chen Chi Works, Textile Industry, 陈炽集·织作之工). Beijing: Zhonghua Book Company, p. 215.

[23] Li, H. *Liwenzhong Gong Quanshu, Chouyi Haifang Zhe, Juan Ershisi* (Complete Works of Li Wenzhong, Coast Defense, Vol. 24, 李文忠公全书, 筹议海防折, 卷24).

dynasty, commerce in Portugal was the most developed and the country was the wealthiest. The United Kingdom coveted and conquered the continent for 200–300 years, while Portugal gradually declined. God's way is cyclical: Things will develop in the opposite direction when they become extreme. China could be the next strong country after the United Kingdom."[24] Based on this, he was highly confident about China's economic prospects. He took the China Merchants Steamship Navigation Company as an example, and pointed out that the wharves in Southeast Asia were dominated by foreign traders. In the recent 10 years, they had been fully controlled by Chinese businessmen. Therefore, he believed in ocean commerce, and that China could compete with foreign businessmen and their luxury and expensiveness.

However, traditional Chinese dialectic thought believes that the conversion of things is conditional. For the weak to overcome the strong, two preconditions are required: First, the weaker party must be in the "sorrow" (sharing a bitter hatred of the enemy rather than sadness) position, as an army burning with righteous indignation is bound to win. Second, the weaker party must make good use of force to "avoid the solid and strike the weak." The Westernization Group believed that if Chinese business was to improve, although the objective advantages of a low-cost approach would work, it must actively and subjectively create conditions such as tariffs protection to reward industry and commerce, and reduce tax to improve merchant status. Luo Yingliu believed that implementing these methods would enable "conducting the power of the government and public" and increase the country's wealth and might.[25]

The author considered Westernization thought reasonable. Indeed, compared to developed countries, the advantage of a developing country was the low labor costs. If the developing country could organize production according to the principle of comparative advantage during the modernization period, positively develop foreign trade, use foreign currency to introduce advanced Western technology, and constantly adjust the production structure, it would reduce the disparity gap in a relatively short period. From the perspective of developed countries, production efficiency would certainly lead to rising labor costs. Therefore,

[24] Li, F. *Yangwu Yundong, Juanyi* (Westernization Movement, Vol. 1, 洋务运动, 卷1). Shanghai: Shanghai Renmin Chubanshe, pp. 166–167.

[25] *Yangwu Yundong, Juanyi* (Westernization Movement, Vol. 1, 洋务运动, 卷1). Shanghai: Shanghai People's Publishing House (SPPH), p. 181.

it should not be engaged in producing the same products as developing countries, which requires continuous scientific and technological innovation. However, significant innovation cannot be accomplished in a short time; thus, developing countries could possibly catch up with developed countries, which is consistent with the internal laws of economic development. In world economic history, in the eighteenth century, England surpassed the Netherlands; in the nineteenth century, Germany and the United States surpassed Britain; and in the twentieth century, Japan caught up with the United States and the Four Asian Tigers" caught up with developed Western countries. These are typical examples of backward countries catching up with developed ones.

However, if developing countries wanted to complete this "leap," aside from the active support of the regime, they also need an appropriate development strategy that focuses on science and technology to catch up with developed countries. Regarding phenomena, the differences between developed and underdeveloped countries are the different degrees of economic prosperity and different level of science and technology. Developed countries can produce high-quality and high value-added products based on their high technological level, while underdeveloped countries can only engage in the low-tech production of commodities and semi-finished products because of their low level of science and technology. Therefore, improving science and technology is the only way underdeveloped countries can catch up with developed ones. The simplest way to achieve this was to introduce advanced Western science and technology. This required much foreign exchange; thus, processed products had to be developed and exported, higher-quality and more value-added products had to be produced, and foreign currency had to be relied on.

According to the statement above, to achieve the purposes of import substitution, processed products must be produced for export. Improving technology was the only way to produce products to substitute imported goods. Without technological improvement, producing import substitution products could still be put into practice in a closed age, but this is not possible in the era of global economic integration. After World War Two, many developing countries replaced the import strategy to develop their national economies, but this was not usually successful. However, one successful example is the export-oriented strategy of the "Asian Tigers."

The Westernization Group focused on an import substitution rather than an export processing strategy. The guiding ideology of the military industry was "learning from foreign technological strengths to restrict foreign dominance." The civil industry was guided by the ideology based on "preventing foreigners from sharing more business profits," which was essentially an import substitution strategy. Although they realized the importance of technical issues, advanced technology paid the price. Much capital was used to develop substitute import products, which on one hand, led to the intermittent production of export processing goods such as traditional export goods including silk and tea, which also demonstrated a shrinking trend as tea from India and Japan became more popular. On the other hand, the decline of exports made it more difficult to introduce advanced western technology, which led to the inferior quality and high prices of substitute import goods, ultimately decreasing competitive market power. Unable to meet the target of selling abroad, the domestic market was also increasingly occupied by foreign products, rendering the goal of keeping pace with the Westerners impossible.

CHAPTER 4

Social Reformative Thoughts of the Westernization Group

As a society transitions from farming to modern industrial and commercial society, the function of the state government should also change accordingly. During the period of the Westernization Movement, relevant reformers discussed issues pertaining to how to promote the development of the new economy, transform existing national regimes, and construct social ethics. However, the discussion on the Westernization bureaucracy differed from that of the Westernization ideologues. Although the bureaucracy saw serious conflicts between existing national regimes and new production methods, they appealed to learn from the West and carried out political reform. In general, they held the position of the *ancient regime* in considering the problem, and while they were progressing with the development of the times, their way of thinking was behind the times. After the 1901 Treaty was signed, the severe national crisis extended Westernization officials' thoughts beyond the boundary set in Zhang Zhidong's work *Exhortation to Learning*, namely of no civil rights and no parliament. This indicates the maturation of the comprehensive study of the new Western capitalist policy. In contrast, the Westernization ideologues purported a radical reformation program that highlighted "enriching the people and paying attention to commerce," and "vigorously developing commercial affairs." Earlier, they had proposed the reformation of the political system, established a parliament, broke through the space capacity of the "Westernized

J. Zhou, *Westernization Movement and Early Thought of Modernization in China*, Palgrave Studies in Economic History,
https://doi.org/10.1007/978-3-030-86985-4_4

Chinese style," exceeded the acceptable range of the farming community established earlier in the political reform bureaucracy, and advocated its establishment, which constituted a form of transition to reformist thoughts.

4.1 The Political Power Reformation Ideology of the Westernization Officials

At the beginning of the Westernization Movement, Zeng Guofan, Li Hongzhang, and other officials repeatedly claimed that "everything in the Chinese civil and military system was better than that of the Westerners, except the firearms."[1] Furthermore, the "Chinese civil and military system differed from the brutal foreign regime to ensure the country's security, so that the huge estate can exist for a long time."[2] However, after the 1870s, the new mode of production was severely restricted by the old regime. Consequently, they began to criticize the corrupt nature of the old system, pointing out that "(Chinese) talent is not only weaker than that in the West, but also weaker than that in Japan. Japan has its own monarch, and officials and civilians stand on the same side. Thus, there is a constant stream of wealth and talent in Japan. In China, several officials preside, politics are inconsistent, and no one believes it will endure."[3]

Li Hongzhang's writing on the political reformation did not include clear definitions or systematic statements; thus, historians today have different inductive understanding thereof. However, his memorials and letters indicate that he had thought about "altering the established laws" to facilitate Self-Strengthening. This would mean changing traditional systems including the imperial examination system, the military system, and bureaucracy. This author discusses Li's Bureaucracy Reform views in this book.

[1] Suochuoluo, B. *Chouban Yiwu Shimo, Tongzhi Chao, Juan Ershiwu* (History of Diplomatic Affairs in Late Qing Dynasty (Tongzhi), Vol. 25, 筹办夷务始末·同治朝, 卷25), pp. 9–10.

[2] Li, H. *Li Wenzhonggong Quanshu, Zhiban Waiguo Tiechang Jiqi Zhe, Juanjiu* (Complete Works of Li Wenzhong: Purchase Foreign Steel Industry, Vol. 9, 李文忠公全书·置办外国铁厂机器折, 卷9).

[3] Li, H. *Li Wenzhonggong Quanshu, Pengliao Hangao, Juanshiqi* (Complete Works of Li Wenzhong: Letter with Friends, Vol. 17, 李文忠公全书·朋僚函稿, 卷17).

Li Hongzhang knew that "using the right person in a crucial position" would be very important in the Westernization Movement. He also equated "employment" with "reform" as the "starting point" of Self-Strengthening. He expressed his serious dissatisfaction with the widespread abuse and corruption evident in the institutions of the Qing Dynasty (e.g., more personnel than work available, decentralization, corrupt officials), attributing the causes thereof to bureaucracy. He believed that "the disadvantages of the law became obvious over time, and implementing reform was inevitable. The system of six codes in the Tang Dynasty included self-appointing officials, but after the middle period, commissioners held half the power. Until the Northern Song Dynasty, this was attributed to the servants, while real officers had only an inflated reputation. Thus, things in the past were different from those of the present. Some people thought that many officials set out to cheat the civilians, and were not engaged in any business."[4] Li Shuchang, Embassador to Japan, had sent him a list of newly appointed officials drafted by the Japanese government. In his letter of response to Li Shuchang, he complimented the Japanese: "The army, navy, agriculture, and commerce of every province in Japan learnt from the West. In general, one official engages in one business, and senior officials are lower than junior officials. This is the best way." In the letter, he also recalled the reformation of the Chinese official system, and illustrated the relationship between a good system ensuring the prosperity of the dynasty and a bad one. He said: "Since the official table of the Han Dynasty, a system like the *Twenty-Four Histories* (official dynastic histories from remote antiquity until the Ming Dynasty) no longer exists. Therefore, the Western Han Dynasty was the most prosperous period. Since then, the system has declined, and today, more than half the officials who expected to be promoted were employed with a high salary. How can such a country be governed?" In this statement, he argued that the "bureaucracy must be changed before reformation."[5]

[4] Li, H. *Li Wenzhonggong Chidu, Fu Liangjiang Zongdu Zeng Yuanweng, Dishiliu Ce* (Letters of Li Wenzhong: Reply to the Governor Zeng Yuanweng, Vol. 16, 李文忠公尺牍·复两江总督曾沅翁, 第16册).

[5] Li, H. *Li Wenzhonggong Chidu, Fuchushi Riben Dachen Li Chunzhai, Diqi Ce* (Letters of Li Wenzhong: Reply to the Japan Ambassdor Li Chunzhai, Vol. 7, 李文忠公尺牍·复出使日本大臣黎莼斋, 第7册).

In his recommendations for the reformation of the bureaucracy, Li Hongzhang had two major points. First, the government must accept the military and political unity of local governors that formed after the war with the Taiping Rebellion, and give it legal status. For him, "only frontier officials can direct military affairs."[6] This notion represents the interests and aspirations of the bureaucracy mainly in Hunan and Anhui. This group formed the backbone of the Westernization Movement. Second, he advocated for the opposite of the Yanguan System (a Censorate system), which he wanted to abolish. According to him, the "Yanguan System easily causes problems," because officials would "speak carelessly and loudly, like the outflow of river water, when expressing their ideas to attract people's attention, but they had obstructed many national affairs." In addition, "there would be problems if they did not implement measures to deal with these issues."[7] Despite the advantages and disadvantages, the Yanguan system was a tool for the traditional rulers. Li Hongzhang was disgusted with it because the Imperial Censors faced the diversionary power of local strength groups, and their indoctrination opposed the Westernization group's propositions. Furthermore, their object of attack tended to be Li Hongzhang.

Li Hongzhang also criticized the subscription system, considering it a maladministration that should be abolished.

Li Hongzhang's writings on the reformation indicate that he wanted to change the maladministration of the Qing Dynasty. His purpose was to make the traditional bureaucracy more efficient without involving the issue of the reformation of the traditional bureaucracy. In fact, in his view, the traditional bureaucracy was in general good, and therefore, he was opposed to fundamental reform. His attitude was clearly manifested in the debate with Mori Arinori, the Japanese Minister, in 1875. Very dissatisfied that the Japanese government had changed the calendar, costumes, and "Ancestor's routine," he emphasized that "we will never have this kind of reformation, but only reform the military, railways, telecommunications,

[6] Li, H. *Li Wenzhonggong Quanshu, Pengliao Hangao, Juanshisan* (Letters of Li Wenzhong: Letter with Friends, Vol. 13, 李文忠公全书·朋僚函稿, 卷13), p. 2.

[7] Wu, Y. (1984). *Gengzi Xishou Congtan* (Works about the Flee of the Emperor in 1900, 庚子西狩丛谈). Changsha: Yuelu Press, pp. 107–108.

and other necessary equipment. To gain the advantages of the West, we must adopt foreign ways."[8]

Zhang Shusheng went further than Li Hongzhang. He asked for the adoption of constitutional politics, which has been related to the core of the traditional bureaucracy. According to records, Cui Guoyin, a former ambassador to the United States, Spain, and Peru, was the first to directly tender a proposal to the government to establish parliament. In 1883, he claimed in his memorial: "A parliament that best uses the circumstances is key to achieving self-improvement." In October 1884, Zhang Shusheng, the Westernization official and former governor of Guangdong and Guangxi provinces, was dying. He gave his oral testament from his deathbed, stressing that it is not enough to save the country from peril without reformation and that political reformation should be based on constitutionalism. He noted, "Westerners founded the state based on their own principles. While their education and history is younger than that of China, they armed the body and limbs of the country to make it prosperous and wealthy. People studied at school and discussed politics in parliament. The leadership and the rank and file are of one mind: pragmatic and prepared. These constitute the body." He added that "naval mines, the railways, and electrical cables are their applications. China cares only about their applications, not their nature. With the long-term traditional system, China will not adapt to current society, regardless of the efforts made." Zhang Shusheng urgently called to "adopt the Western system to implement their applications."

Among the government officials supporting the Westernization Movement, others such as Wenxiang concurred with Zhang Shusheng. In winter, 1874, Wenxiang, a Qing government official of the Westernization Movement, mentioned the House of Commons system in the Western world, stating, "It is necessary to implement such a system however difficult it may be during this process." Yi Xin had further ideas regarding such a system. After the First Sino-Japanese War (1894–1895), summarizing the failure of the Qing government, Yi Xin noted, "the only reason for this failure is that we have not adopted the Western system; It is not

[8] As cited in Wang, X. (1987). *Jindai Zhongri Qishi Lu* (Revelation of Modern China and Japan, 近代中日启示录). Beijing: Beijing Publishing House, p. 74.

the fault of Li Hongzhang."[9] While this conclusion might not be accurate, it highlighted that the root cause for China's failure was rooted in the reformation of the whole social system, not specific reforms in machine manufacturing or new education, for example.

The high officials' discussions demonstrated that their ideas had improved through practice and self-reflectivity. After the Sino-Japanese War in 1894–1895, China's urgent survival crisis forced officials of the Westernization Movement to accelerate the learning from the Western world. Based on summarizing previous knowledge on Western learning by advocates of the Westernization Movement, Zhang Zhidong, a leader in the late Westernization Movement, widened the range thereof to "Western systems, Western technologies, and Western history," which he considered "the new knowledge we need to learn."[10] He further expounded the meaning of "Western systems" and "Western technologies" as follows: "Western systems refer to schools, geography, budget, tax, weapons and equipment, laws and rules, and industrial and commercial systems. Western technologies refer to mathematics, drawing and measuring, mining, medical technology, acoustics, optical technology. and electricity."[11] Except for the system of the House of Commons, Zhang Zhidong included all aspects proposed previously in connection with contemporary civilizations that China should adopt and imitate to "apply Western learning," including science and technology, laws and systems, and administrative measures. However, Zhang Zhidong opposed the establishment of the House system and promotion of civil rights, excluding democratic politics outside the scope of "Western learning for application." His aim was to maintain the last defense line of the Chinese system.

With the start of the twentieth century, which heralded China's national crisis, the ideas of officials of the Westernization Movement had improved, and important changes included a leaning toward the views of the reformists. Liu Kunyi had "an abhorrence of civil rights" in 1898.

[9] Huang, Z. *Maguan Jishi* (About Treaty of Shimonoseki, 马关纪事).

[10] Zhang, Z. (1998). *QuanxuePian, Shexuedisan* (Exhortation to Learning, Setting School-Third, 劝学篇·设学第三). Zhengzhou: Zhongzhou Ancient Books Publishing House, p. 121.

[11] Zhang, Z. (1998). *QuanxuePian, Shexuedisan* (Exhortation to Learning, Setting School-Third, 劝学篇·设学第三). Zhengzhou: Zhongzhou Ancient Books Publishing House, p. 121.

Three years later, he shifted his stance, admitting that the House of Commons system in Western countries was an "effective method in good faith" and the best Western system. He noted that it was not implemented in China because "too many other affairs had impeded the process."[12] In 1898, Zhang Zhidong rebuked proposals regarding civil rights and the House of Commons system as "nothing but hundreds of harms." However, in a telegraph sent to eight governors including Liu Kunyi on February 16, 1901, Zhang Zhidong stated: "There is one urgent and vital issue for reform, which is also the root cause thereof. The best Western system is related to the two Houses. However, common citizens in China have no idea about local or domestic affairs, let alone foreign affairs. Thus, the House of Commons is not currently applicable to China. However, we can establish a similar House of Lords."[13] In the "Jiang Chu Hui Zou Bian Fa San Zhe," Zhang Zhidong and Liu Kunyi emphasized that the "political system, knowledge, and technologies" of Western countries "are generally formed after many years of research and modified by thousands of people. Since such systems, knowledge, and technologies have had some effects, they are quickly learned by others. America learnt them from Europe, and the Eastern world learnt them from the Western world." China could use these effective "political systems, knowledge, and technologies" to cure diseases. These ideas, which had much in common with those of the reformists, demonstrated that the power of a situation can change tradition and that transformation to capitalistic production was a rule not changed by human will.

4.2 The Political Reform Views of the Westernization Thinkers

Compared to the Westernization officials, thinkers supporting the Westernization Movement including Guo Songtao, Ma Jianzhong, Wang Tao, Xue Fucheng, and Zheng Guanying had wider insights. Advocates for the theory of Westernization reform, were also the first to find severe problems related to the Westernization Movement that brought about

[12] Sheng, X. (1901). *Yuzhai Cungao, Juansiba, Liu Xianshuai Laidian* (Memorials of Sheng Xuanhuai, Vol. 48, Telegraph from Liu Xianshuai, 愚斋存稿, 卷48, 刘岘帅来电).

[13] Zhang, Z. (1875). *Zhang Wenxianggong Quanji, Diandu, Juanshi* (Collected Works of Zhang Wenxiang ·Telegraph Memorials to the Throne, Vol. 10, 张文襄公全集·电牍, 卷10).

its poor practical effects. Wang Tao expressed the people's perspective in that period: "We have built factories to manufacture machines and established new schools for education, but why does China remain as weak as before?"[14] Therefore, these thinkers' plans for political system reform were closely related to their reflections on the Westernization Movement.

1. In terms of the government system, recommendations including establishing a commercial ministry and House of Commons system, and rewarding persons who conduct their business well were proposed.

Since the Westernization thinkers supported "re-building China on industry and commerce," it was essential to change the country's social situation in which "the government and businessmen did not trust or cooperate with each other" to "bridge the government and commercial industry." They had learned that in western countries, "businessmen are involved in any major political issue." However, in China, businessmen were completely separate from the government. Therefore, Chinese merchants would rather be protected by foreign counterparts, and "dared not respond to" official government measures. Thus, "developing commerce" became the purpose of Westernization political system reform.

First, they proposed establishing a Ministry of Commerce. China's central government, which was constructed on an agricultural society, only included Ministries of Rites, Revenue, Personnel, War, Justice, and Works. With the transition from an agricultural to modern industrial and commercial society, commercial tax accounted for an increasing portion of the national revenue, and thus, industry and commerce played an increasingly important part in the national economy. In this environment, it was necessary to establish the Ministry of Commerce to ensure the sound development of a social economy. In China, Wang Yuan, a member of the Yan-Li school in the mid-seventeenth century, first proposed establishing the Department of Commerce. He recommended "installing a Da Sijun (minster of commerce)." However, this seemed like an illusory idea of landocracy theorists to contend with the social status of

[14] Wang, T. (1998). *Taoyuan Wenlu Waibian, Bianfa Ziqiang Xia* (Tao Yuan's Works of Foreign Affairs, Reforms, Vol. II, 弢园文录外编·变法自强下). Zhengzhou: Zhongzhou Ancient Books Publishing House, p. 91.

early citizens (merchants). After the Westernization Movement's crisis, as "people shifted to a new social type" (persons engaging in new industrial and commercial trades) inside China, Westernization thinkers such as Ma Jianzhong, Chen Chi, and Zheng Guanying conceived of the establishment of Ministry of Commerce. For Chen Chi, the solution to the problem was combining the revenues of the Qing government and merchants' interest. At that time, the revenues of the Qing government were mainly from commercial tax, tariffs, and salt tax, which were all filed by merchants. Land tax revenue was less important. Therefore, according to him, "No commerce means no taxation, which will lead to no country. Therefore, commerce and country are closely related and independent, which is different from the situation in old times."[15]

How could a Ministry of Commerce be established? Zheng Guanying proposed that "the central government appoint an official familiar with commercial affairs who has been overseas, and who understood both Chinese and Western languages to take charge of commercial affairs (and to be referred to as Minister of Commerce)." He further recommended "approving the establishment of a general commercial administration in the provincial capital for each province. Furthermore, the commercial trades can choose to establish branch administrations as they see fit. The general or branch administration should have one commercial director selected by all trades. Of the commercial directors, one general director should be elected that exhibits the standards of equality, justice, sophistication, and reputation. The general director would take charge of all commercial affairs within each province. Important issues pertaining to commerce and laws for rewards and funding should be delivered to Ministry of Commerce by the general director." This meant that except for the minister of commerce, "the general director in each provincial commercial administration and commercial director in each trade were to be appointed by election. The minister of commerce candidate should satisfy the following conditions: (i) The candidate shall be good at both Chinese and Western languages and have travelled overseas.[16] (ii) Any

[15] Chen, C. (1997). *Chenchiji, Chuangli Shangdu Shuo* (Chen Chi Works, on Commerce Ministry Establishment, 陈炽集·创立商都说). Beijing: Zhonghua Book Company, p. 233.

[16] Zheng, G. (1982). *Zheng Guanying Ji Shangwuyi Shangce* (Zheng Guanying Works, Commercial Affairs I, Vol. I, *郑观应集 • 商务一，上册*). Shanghai: Shanghai People's Publishing House (SPPH), pp. 605–606.

person out of the imperial examination system who is not familiar with commerce is not allowed."[17] Consequently, almost all members from the traditional bureaucratic system were excluded from the commercial system, and a new "independent realm" dominated by the new merchant class would be generated. Zheng Guanying proposed that the scope governed by the Ministry of Commerce include "planting, manufacturing, and selling, such as planting tea, trees, and cotton; sericulture and textiles; and establishing companies specializing in opium, coal, iron, and china. The final purpose is to ensure China can manufacture any foreign products it needs and can transport and sell any products foreign countries need from China."[18] Therefore, the so-called Ministry of Commerce he envisioned was actually an administrative body that governed both light and heavy industries. Nevertheless, establishing a central administrative institution out of the traditional bureaucratic system was an illusion. However, it did demonstrate the first capitalist political demand of the new industrial and commercial class of that age.

Zheng Guanying's views were based on the history of the United Kingdom. According to him, foreign trading had rendered the United Kingdom the wealthiest country worldwide. The British government "feared political order was not good for commerce, so it released an order that anyone who wanted to have a place to discuss political issues must have travelled at least three times for commercial affairs. Therefore, all members in government were here for business affairs, which would make commerce stand first among national issues. If China wants to develop its commerce and make a profit, it must adopt and transform the British methods to remove previous disadvantages."[19]

Second, they advised establishing the House system. The first problem in terms of developing commerce knew the demands of merchants, as

[17] Zheng, G. (1982). *Zheng Guanying Ji Shangzhanxia Shangce* (Zheng Guanying Works, Commercial War II, Vol. I, *郑观应集・商战下，上册*). Shanghai: Shanghai People's Publishing House (SPPH), p. 596.

[18] Zheng, G. (1982). *Zheng Guanying Ji Shangwusan Shangce* (Zheng Guanying Works, Commercial Affairs III, Vol. I, *郑观应集・商务三，上册*). Shanghai: Shanghai People's Publishing House (SPPH), p. 616.

[19] Zheng, G. (1982). *Zheng Guanying Ji Shangwusan Shangce* (Zheng Guanying Works, Commercial Affairs III, Vol. I, *郑观应集・商务三，上册*). Shanghai: Shanghai People's Publishing House (SPPH), p. 616.

satisfying them would motivate them. Investigating the Western capitalistic House system, thinkers of the Westernization Movement found it was the best method to meet the requirement of "satisfying the demands" of the industrial and commercial class. Zheng Guanying pointed out, "The primary issue for country development is to win people's support, for people's support is to know their demands, for knowing their demands is to set up Houses."[20] In simple terms, the advantages of setting up Houses were to "harmonize people and strengthen their morale," and "undisciplined emperors would have no leeway for outlandish acts, undisciplined officials would have no way to abuse their powers, all government members would have no way to shirk their responsibilities, and common people would have no reason for complaint."[21] They believed this system would ensure that western countries remain "strong." The people's "support" and "demands" they referred to were the support and demands of the bourgeoisie. In addition, Zheng Guanying demanded that since merchants in western countries could take the places of "members of parliament," it should also be possible in China to choose "just and fair merchants as members of parliament." Here, he explicitly called for the rights of the new bourgeoisie. Thinkers of the Westernization Movement also recommended that merchants be directly selected as government officials to manage and cope with relations between China and Western countries. Although these voices were weak, they outlined the basic direction of reforming despotism and the requirements for the economic development of industry and commerce, becoming the blueprint for the new industrial and commercial bourgeoisie to share political power.

Third, they proposed enacting commercial laws and rules to build a sense of law and instill the concept of respecting others' interests in society. Unlike the self-containing economic structure in an agricultural society, a modern economy based on socialized mass production is an exchange economy. The two trade parties must exchange products they produce to obtain the expected profits, with which they can purchase what they need. To prevent the exchange chain from breaking, which would affect production and society, government powers are necessary to

[20] Zheng, G. (1982). *Zheng Guanying Ji Yiyuanshang Shangce* (Zheng Guanying Works, The House System I, Vol. I, *郑观应集 • 议院上，上册*). Shanghai: Shanghai Renmin Chubanshe, p. 314.

[21] (1953). *Wuxu Bianfa Diyice* (Materials about Reform Movement of 1898, Vol. 1, 戊戌变法资料丛刊, 第1册). Shanghai: Shenzhou Guoguang She, p. 56.

regulate each member's behaviors through laws. This is the reason the modern economy is also known as the legal economy. The modern legal system, centered on property rights, has the basic connotation of the non-violation of private property rights. An important reason for the failure of enterprises established in the Westernization period was that awareness of private property rights was not established throughout society, whose traditional tradition penetrated the normal operation of enterprises. Ultimately, a series of shortcomings meant that "anyone with surplus money fears companies."[22]

Westernization thinkers strongly reprimanded the phenomenon of not respecting private ownership. Zheng Guanying angrily revealed behaviors that violated external company interests, stating that "Government officials cannot do anything but violate the interest of merchants. They envy merchants like the Qin people treated the Yue. Even if government officials gain enough personal profits, their acts have greatly blocked the sources of profit, which is the most severe malpractice."[23] Regarding officials, namely national investment representatives that damaged merchants' interest from the inside, Chen Chi disclosed: "I have received a telegraph from the Merchant Group that each year, the total revenues can reach millions of sales. However, merchants can only get 8% interest from the official interest. Everyone knows that the capital interest rate is 20–30%, not 8%, which is the abuse of public money for someone's own benefit."[24] Poor legal awareness meant that common merchants often violated each other's interest. In this regard, Zheng Guanying emphasized, "Most merchants engaged in fraudulent acts pursued small rather than long-term interest, and treated themselves better than others." Therefore, it was expected that "a subscription for shares will lead to the loss of capital share, and establishing the company will lead to its bankruptcy."[25]

[22] Xue, F. (1987). *Xue Fucheng Xuanji, Lun Gongsi Buju Zhibing* (Selected Works of Xue Fucheng, One the Fatal Disease of Companies, 薛福成选集·论公司不举之病). Shanghai: Shanghai People's Publishing House (SPPH), p. 480.

[23] Zheng, G. (1982). *Zheng Guanying Ji Shangwusan Shangce* (Zheng Guanying Works, Commercial Affairs III, Vol. I, *郑观应集 • 商务三，上册*). Shanghai: ShanghaiPeople's Publishing House (SPPH), p. 615.

[24] Chen, C. (1997). *Chenchiji, Jiuji Gongsi Shuo* (Chen Chi Works, On Company, 陈炽集·纠集公司说). Beijing: Zhonghua Book Company, p. 235.

[25] Zheng, G. (1982). *Zheng Guanying Ji Shangwusan Shangce* (Zheng Guanying works, Commercial Affairs III, Vol. I, *郑观应集 • 商务三，上册*). Shanghai: Shanghai Renmin Chubanshe, p. 615.

The only method to solve this problem was to enact commercial laws by the only legal user for national violence. Chen Chi pointed out that "the important articles of corporations from Western countries had to be selected to publish and circulate among people. Merchants should learn their principles, and government officials should ensure the normal application of such articles and evaluate the effects."[26] This may supply legal protection for commercial activities and a legal basis for settling commercial proceedings, which was beneficial in terms of eradicating problems like "government rights suppressing merchants' rights" and "shareholders caring only for their personal interests." In addition, they required that persons managing company affairs obtain legal awareness and safeguard investors' interest. Because company managers rather than official representatives acted on behalf of shareholders, they must oppose the government's irrational requirements by "rather speaking to the whole world than colleagues, and rather losing personal money than that of colleagues."[27] Regarding the popular phenomenon that people in charge of companies abused shareholders' subscriptions to operate their personal businesses (e.g., the major managers of the China Merchants Steamship Navigation Company, Tang Tingshu and Xu Run, used shareholders' money to operate their own businesses), Westernization thinkers angrily revealed and demanded that company managers improve their self-cultivation so there would be "no cheating and no malpractice, only the maintenance and improvement of companies' profits."[28] They thought it possible and permitted having businesses supervised or established by the government if the managers in charge of these enterprises could follow these rules. In contrast, if any company including a private one was not able to follow these rules, that company should be reformed. Otherwise, the only result of such a company would be a failure.

2. To better develop the new economy, the Westernization thinkers advocated changes to the traditional financial ideas based on an agricultural society.

[26] Chen, C. (1997). *Chenchiji, Jiuji Gongsi Shuo* (Chen Chi Works, On Company, 陈炽集·纠集公司说). Beijing: Zhonghua Book Company, p. 236.

[27] Chen, C. (1997). *Chenchiji, Jiuji Gongsi Shuo* (Chen Chi Works, On Company, 陈炽集·纠集公司说). Beijing: Zhonghua Book Company, p. 234.

[28] Chen, C. (1997). *Chenchiji, Jiuji Gongsi Shuo* (Chen Chi Works, On Company, 陈炽集·纠集公司说). Beijing: Zhonghua Book Company, p. 236.

First, they demanded establishing a budget system. With the increase of cultural exchange between China and Western countries, the Western budget system was known in China. In *Annals of Japan: National Issues*, Huang Zunxian praised Japan, which by adopting the budget system from the Western world, could guarantee that all taxation and expenditures were made in accordance with plans to prevent fiscal deficit or abuse. Considering this the best method in finance, he recommended that the Qing government use it. He said, currently, "Our revenues are not sufficient for all the expenditures. Government officials have no other method but levying people, while common people work very hard to file various types of taxes. However, they have no idea of the applications of such money. Therefore, they doubt the government. Why not publish all applications of this money for the people?This reform is urgent in this critical environment."[29]

Zheng Guanying also mentioned the budget issue in *Crisis Awareness in Millenium: On Revenues and Expenditures*: "Persons in charge of revenues should develop a budget for national expenditures. In Western Europe, revenues and expenditures are rationed and cannot be exceeded… For military needs, funds should be collected separately. Records should be kept of all revenues and expenditures, and published for the public at the end of the year. Thus, while foreign countries levy too many taxes on people, these people have no complaints."[30] He advised the Qing government to imitate the case of Western Europe by discussing and fixing a budget for one year, and to investigate all taxations. "All expenditures and revenues should be recorded and compared comprehensively. If the expenditure exceeds the budget, then such expenditure should be limited to prevent it from gradually eroding the budget. If revenue exceeds the expectation, then it should be reserved to prevent it from being wasted. This is the usual method of financial management in the provinces of our country." Zheng Guanying also paid attention to the revenue from customs tariffs. He highlighted the importance of "knowing about the money flow between China to foreign countries and that from foreign countries to China. By comparing the two, we can roughly obtain

[29] Huang, Z. *Riben Guozhi Guojipian* (Annals of Japan, National Issues, 日本国志·国计篇).

[30] Zheng, G. (1982). *Zheng Guanying Ji Duzhi Shangce* (Zheng Guanying Works, Revenues and Expenditures, Vol. I, 郑观应集·度支, 上册). Shanghai: Shanghai Renmin Chubanshe, p. 578.

the total net proceeds of the tariffs. If the two are generally equal, we do not need to manage it for now. If money out is more than the money in, we must investigate the reasons and find methods to compensate for it. If money in exceeds money out, we must investigate the reasons and develop methods to encourage such acts. This is the general method by which to manage the finances of China and other countries."[31]

Second, the Westernization thinkers discussed the differences between the financial principles of China and Western countries. Xue Fucheng pointed out that "the traditional Chinese financial principle is to formulate an expenditure plan according to revenue. Currently, the Western financial principle is to develop an annual budget and try to generate revenue according to expenditure plans."[32] However, Xue Fucheng did not further analyze the reasons underlying the principles applicable to China. On one hand, he agreed that the traditional Chinese principle to "formulate an expenditure plan according to revenue" was the "common principle from ancient times until now."[33] On the other, he appreciated the making of "revenue according to expenditure plans" approach of Western countries.[34] Regarding practices in Western countries, "if additional expenditure is proposed in one year, such money will be collected on different items. In the case of war, merchants' subscriptions or contributions are possible, which is identical to the likin tax (a type of taxation system used in the late Qing dynasty) except in name." Obviously, Xue Fucheng incorrectly regarded the likin(lijin) tax of the late Qing government as the additional goods tax levied under special occasions in western countries, indicating that he did not comprehensively understand Western financial principles.

[31] Zheng, G. (1982). *Zheng Guanying Ji Duzhi Shangce* (Zheng Guanying Works, Revenues and Expenditures, Vol. I, 郑观应集·度支, 上册). Shanghai: Shanghai Renmin Chubanshe, p. 578.

[32] Xue, F. (1987). *Xue Fucheng Xuanji, Xiyang Zhuguo Weimin Licai Shuo* (Selected Works of Xue Fucheng, On Financial Issues in Western Countries, 薛福成选集·西洋诸国为民理财说). Shanghai: Shanghai Renmin Chubanshe, p. 416.

[33] Xue, F. (1987). *Xue Fucheng Xuanji, Chouyang Chuyi* (Selected Works of Xue Fucheng, My Humble Opinions about the Westernization Movement 薛福成选集·筹洋刍议). Shanghai: Shanghai Renmin Chubanshe, p. 547.

[34] Xue, F. (1987). *Xue Fucheng Xuanji, Chouyang Chuyi* (Selected Works of Xue Fucheng, My Humble Opinions about the Westernization Movement 薛福成选集·筹洋刍议). Shanghai: Shanghai Renmin Chubanshe, p. 549.

In terms of the relation between financial revenue and expenditure, Xue Fucheng thought that all revenues should be expensed immediately, and all expenditures should immediately be made up by revenues.[35] Therefore, he appraised the revenue–expenditure principle used by Western countries, namely "collection from people to be used for people." For him, this principle complied with the ancient attitude of supporting all people. He said, "I found that among the expenditures made by Western countries, army and navy military expenditure ranks first, which is to safeguard people domestically. Expenditure related to pension and the elimination of poverty and to education for people from poor families exceeds 10 or 20 million taels per year. Expenditure related to death benefits for soldiers and pensions for retired officials exceeds ten or twenty million tales per year. All the money is used for the people."[36] Because of this expenditure system, even under a heavier taxation system, people in Western countries "do not think too badly about it." Finally, he considered as wrong practices the traditionally appreciated stories of Emperor Wen in the Sui Dynasty, who "stored grains in warehouses" and Emperor Chan in the Ming Dynasty, who "amassed gold in a warehouse."[37]

4.3 Construction of Morality

To develop a modern industrial civilization and "build a country based on industry and commerce," not only western scientific and technological knowledge was needed, but also the values of modern industrial civilization. Establishing these values, moralities, and thinking methods could contribute to commercial development.

[35] Xue, F. (1987). *Xue Fucheng Xuanji, Xiyang Zhuguo Weimin Licai Shuo* (Selected Works of Xue Fucheng, On Financial Issues in Western Countries, 薛福成选集·西洋诸国为民理财说). Shanghai: Shanghai Renmin Chubanshe, p. 416.

[36] Xue, F. (1987). *Xue Fucheng Xuanji, Xiyang Zhuguo Weimin Licai Shuo* (Selected Works of Xue Fucheng, On Financial Issues in Western Countries, 薛福成选集·西洋诸国为民理财说). Shanghai: Shanghai Renmin Chubanshe, p. 416.

[37] Xue, F. (1987). *Xue Fucheng Xuanji, Xiyang Zhuguo Weimin Licai Shuo* (Selected Works of Xue Fucheng, On Financial Issues in Western Countries, 薛福成选集·西洋诸国为民理财说). Shanghai: Shanghai Renmin Chubanshe, p. 416.

In a traditional agricultural society, produced goods cannot meet the people's demands because of the long-term poor condition of the production force. Therefore, the principle of relative equal consumption based on the rank system had to be adopted to promote "thinking highly of morality rather than interests" to strengthen peoples' ranked consumption ideology. In contrast, in an industrial society, advanced science and technology has meant that product supply can satisfy and exceed people's demands. Under this condition, society can only function through the motivation of consumption to increase social demands. Thus, during the period of transition from an agricultural to an industrial society, product supply gradually increased, and the "thinking highly of morality rather than interests" approach had to be reconsidered. As mentioned, Westernization thinkers advocated "building a country based on industry and commerce," which made it important to argue for merchants' "pursuit of interest."

1. Westernization thinkers' criticism of "thinking highly of morality rather than interest"

In 1879, Xue Fucheng noted that "not all merchants in the current market can make a profit, but countless people are trying to invest, because everyone wants to earn interest. As long as everyone wants to get rich, the national fund will not be damaged and profits will eventually be gained by the country."[38] After being the ambassador overseas, he further evaluated that Confucius and Mencius only refused the pursuit of profit for "people who wanted all the money for himself/his family." "Nearly half the chapter "Pacifying the World" in *Great Learning* discussed financial issues, and it is known hereby that saints do not avoid talking about profits. Later learners did not understand their meaning of criticizing anyone pursuing interest regardless of public or personal interest. Therefore, discussion on and methods to gain profit in China have been abandoned for a long time." He considered the sum of private interest

[38] Xue, F. (1987). *Xue Fucheng Xuanji, Chouyang Chuyi* (Selected Works of Xue Fucheng, My Humble Opinions about the Westernization Movement 薛福成选集·筹洋刍议). Shanghai: Shanghai Renmin Chubanshe, p. 541.

as public interest as long as "everyone can meet their private interest requirement."[39]

Chen Chi also discussed the relationship between interest and morality. He pointed out in *Continuation of On Nation Wealth · About Building Schools* that the majority of people were average in terms of wisdom and talent and would like to pursue their personal interest. "People can only learn morality after obtaining interest, but only with morality can people obtain future interest." "Saints" required themselves to "live and sacrifice their life for morality." However, the objectives of national governance should focus on average people. Thus, it was not enough to "dare to say interest." Rather, it required thinking about "every method to gain a profit every day," which was the "morality and mercy of saints. Therefore, saints were the best people to talk about making a profit." This meant that common people should make profits for themselves and "saints" should try to make profits for the common people. Both common people and "saints" talk about profits.[40] In *About the Gold Industry*, Chen Chi agreed that morality had positive effects on pacifying disputes: "As long as people pursue profit, disputes may arise, which will produce disorder. However, morality can stop such disputes." This did not mean that not making a profit should be promoted. He said that people should differentiate between public and private interests: "If all interests can be concealed, then men with evil ideas will dare to do anything. If all interests can be disclosed to the public, gentlemen will be moderate." He also noted that someone who opposed discussing interests actually pursued profits to a greater extent than others, using methods others were not aware of. Furthermore, others had no bad motivations, but did not comply with the standards of "saints that self-cultivate treat people with compassion and treat everything with love." Both types of people did not understand that "ancient saints did not avoid talking about profits or make anyone lose profit by avoiding discussing profit."[41] While Chen Chi positively evaluated morality, he focused on defending the validity of

[39] (1892). *Chushi Siguo Riji Xuke* (Continuation on Journals about Ambassador life in Four Countries, 出使四国日记续刻).

[40] Chen, C. (1997). Chenchiji, Fenjian Xuetang Shuo (Chen Chi Works, about Building Schools, 陈炽集·分建学堂说). Beijing: Zhonghua Book Company, p. 273.

[41] Chen, C. (1997). *Chenchiji, Gongjin Zhigong Shuo* (Chen Chi Works, about Gold Industry, 陈炽集·攻金之工说). Beijing: Zhonghua Book Company, p. 212.

obtaining market interest and criticized the hypocrites who pretended to oppose profit but pursued it more than others.

In 1895, He Qi and Hu Liyuan pointed out: "In Chinese people's eyes, all merchants are cheaters. They do not know that pursuing profit is in the nature of human beings. Thus, those who pursue profit will not be forbidden by a country, which only requires them to have valid methods of doing so. If so, the government will be willing to help them." For them, helping others should be based on helping themselves. "Anyone who is not economically independent will become the burden of society. Anyone who has surplus assets can help others with these assets. Merchants using valid channels to gain profit will try to help others by first being wealthy themselves."[42] They further proposed that "everyone's private assets are private, and everyone can gain profit from a common place, which should be regarded as public assets. Everyone has his own private interest, but not everyone will deprive others for his own private profit, and will not lose his own for others' private profit. If so, then the whole country will be wealthy."[43] This meant that everyone has a private profit. As long as no one impedes others to make such private profit, it will be beneficial and the sum of such private profit is public profit.

2. Westernization officials' opinions on interests and morality

Over time, Li Hongzhang and Zuo Zongtang experienced the evolution of the proponents of "valuing loyalty over money" to the criticism thereof. According to history, Li Hongzhang liked to "drive others by interests." Zuo Zongtang disdained the hypocrisy of the traditional "shamed to discuss interests explicitly" preaching, thinking that making money will not be hindered as long as it is done legally and "is suitable for supporting oneself through your own efforts." Zuo Zongtang had been writing a text, saying that people worldwide pursue two purposes: wealth and fame. "How does fame act without benefit?" In his opinion, the purpose of social activities is nothing more than wealth. Fame is

[42] He, Q. & Hu, L. (1994). Xinzheng Zhenquan, Xinzheng Lunyi (The Real Interpretation of the New Policy, Discussion on New Policies, 新政真诠·新政论议). Liaoning: Liaoning People's Publishing House, pp. 131–132.

[43] He, Q. & Hu, L. (1994). Xinzheng Zhenquan, Quanxuepian Shuhou (The Real Interpretation of the New Policy, Continuation on the Only Hope of China, 新政真诠·劝学篇书后). Liaoning: Liaoning People's Publishing House, p. 413.

merely a means of wealth. He further emphasized three pursuits of wealth: morality, knowledge, and skill.[44] At that time, he thought that those famous for morality or knowledge were far from reality: "Because of morality, people should obey the rules, and because the upper like to read sophisticated speech, some have written it for them."[45] Zuo Zongtang appreciated skillful people, believing they relied on their own ability to survive. Although the literati and officialdom looked down on them, artisans were self-reliant and contributed to society.

Zuo Zongtang also advocated "reasonable" means to obtain wealth, namely money and power: "The farmer and merchant are discontented with those who use despicable means to obtain wealth."[46] He cited from the *Book of Songs· Fatan* to criticize the shameless plundering of corrupt officials and gentry of the people.

Clearly, Zuo Zongtang's concept of fame aims to prove the rationality that middle and small landlords, farmers, businessmen, and craftsmen can become wealthy. He considers their activities reasonable events based on private property and personal intelligence, and opposes those using shameful means to obtain wealth.

The change of attitude of Li Hongzhang and Zuo Zongtang reflects the pursuit of profit and wealth from the clandestine to the public following the Chinese Opium War. Obviously, the pursuit of wealth enabled the Westernization Movement to recruit a large number of talented people and establish a large industry. Without admitting the rationality of the pursuit of wealth, Westernization would be unable to cooperate with the new industrialists and businessmen who adopt the means of production of the Western world.

The basic values pursued by the modern capitalist society are as follows: Everyone is equal in wealth regardless of class: the hero can make money. Personal value comes first: everyone can be self-seeking and the government cannot intervene. That the Westernization thinkers evolved around the debate of justice and benefit was an attempt to use modern utilitarian values to replace traditional ethics, which is of positive significance to the

[44] Zuo, Z. *Zuo Wenxianggong Quanji Wenji* (Complete Works of Zuo Wenxiang, Corpus, Vol. 1, 左文襄公全集·文集), p. 1.

[45] Zuo, Z. *Zuo Wenxianggong Quanji Wenji* (Complete Works of Zuo Wenxiang, Corpus, Vol. 1, 左文襄公全集·文集), p. 1.

[46] Zuo, Z. *Zuo Wenxianggong Quanji Wenji* (Complete Works of Zuo Wenxiang, Corpus, Vol. 1, 左文襄公全集·文集), p. 1.

development of the market economy and represents the demands of a new era.

Although the Westernization thinkers also explored the relationship between righteousness and benefit in the new period, they focused on the traditional ideological criticism that "righteousness is more important than benefit." They defended interests-driven behavior, but did not consider how to construct a view of the new period. The author believes that righteousness and benefit are a unity of opposites, and both are indispensable. The gain is not equal to the sum of public benefits and denying or neglecting the benefit is bad for the development of the market economy.

To establish a capitalist mode of production in a state in the leading position, the key is to establish a sound and clear factory system, which is the micro foundation of capitalism. While constructing a sound and clear factory system, it is necessary to establish a capitalist production development outlook. Because of the huge scale of modern enterprises, the complex division of labor, and multi-level trust in the relationship between agents, a real and efficient system can be established only through morality and loyalty. Clearly, Zuo Zongtang's concept of fame aims to prove the rationality that middle and small landlords, farmers, businessmen, and craftsmen can become wealthy. He considers their activities reasonable events based on private property and personal intelligence, but opposes those who use shameful means to become rich.

PART II

Business

Different from a traditional family management mode, modern production is socialized and the enterprise is the basis of modern society. The Westernization Movement focused on six aspects of constructing a modern enterprise system: financing, improving technology, free labor employment, selection and training of business personnel, definition of enterprise internal property rights, and management technology.

CHAPTER 5

Raising Capital

Capital plays an important role in the development of modern enterprises. The Westernization Movement needed great wealth to train the army, build ships, and manufacture tools according to the Western method to pay the "salaries of instructors in addition to the amount of the purchase of ships, rations, shipbuilding, and ship reparations, as well as the operations of weapons, guns, and gunpowder."[1] However, China was in a period of social transformation and faced a shortage of funds; thus, how could it provide money for modern enterprises? According to Zhang Zhidong, "Who wants to gain money, should first invest money,"[2] as "spending money usually comes before managing it."[3] In general, the Westernization Movement focused on rectifying the traditional tax system, collecting the new commercial tax, and attracting foreign investment.

[1] (1874). *Fuzou Zongli Yamen Liutiaoshu, Yangwu Yundong, Juanyi* (Westernization Movement, Vol. 1, 复奏总理衙门六条疏, 洋务运动 卷1). Shanghai: Shanghai Renmin Chubanshe, p. 29.

[2] Zhang, Z. *Zhang Wenxianggong Quanji Zouyi Juanwushisi* (Collected Works of Zhang Wenxiang・Memorials, Vol. 54, 张文襄公全集·奏议, 卷54).

[3] Zhang, Z. *Zhang Wenxianggong Quanji Diandu Juanerbai* (Collected Works of Zhang Wenxiang・Telegraph Memorials to the Throne, Vol. 200, 张文襄公全集·电牍, 卷200).

J. Zhou, *Westernization Movement and Early Thought of Modernization in China*, Palgrave Studies in Economic History,
https://doi.org/10.1007/978-3-030-86985-4_5

5.1 Rectifying the Traditional Tax System

In theory, only agriculture has a surplus, people can invest in other industries, and raw materials and a sales market can be provided for those industries. Therefore, world modernization without funds drawn from traditional agriculture is not possible. In the early stage of a country's economic development, traditional agriculture bears more financial burdens. To rectify the traditional tax system, the Westernization Movement focused on two aspects: traditional land tax and salt tax.

1. Traditional land (including violet and tribute rice) tax reform.

Violet contributed a significant portion to the finances of the Qing Dynasty. The tax rate was not based on the production of the land or land price, but on the area of land around the reference environment and land with different conditions. Tax rates could differ by three to nine levies. In this regard, the period of the Westernization Movement brought many disadvantages, first, because the tax on violet could not be changed with the land price or productivity, and second, because in the ancestral system, "violet tax cannot be increased." On one hand, the land price changed quickly. Due to the pull of foreign trade, the coastal areas and those on the verge of modern industrial and commercial cities, towns, and regions could produce more products, thus increasing the land productivity and the corresponding rise in prices. Under these circumstances, the set of long-term differential tax collection measures were unreasonable and needed urgent remedy. On the other, modern social expenditure greatly increased. In the late Qing Dynasty, military supplies, river labor, relief, and repayments of debt were pushed into the government. However, the dynasty, restricted by the ancestral system, could not raise the taxes. Thus, the shortage of funds could only be resolved through donations, likin(lijin), and opium tax. However, relying on these taxes is like drinking poison to quench the thirst, and seriously affected the development of modern industry and commerce. Furthermore, these were worth thousands of times more than land tax. At that time, Western financial theory was brought to China, and the government first considered increasing the tax.

In this regard, the items to be taxed had to be increased. In the early years of the Guangxu reign period, Huang Zunxian noted that tax in Japan and Europe was higher than in China: "People only know that

Britain, Russia, France, and the United States are very wealthy, but not that their taxes total seventy million pounds. If the Chinese people pay as much taxes as in those countries, which is five or six times more than today, our country can be strong and wealthy. What difficulties can we face? Because taxes are lacking, foreign and government affairs are perfunctory. Are the taxes too light?" However, Huang Zunxian also advocated the national expansion of income with some conditions, namely that "what they earn from the people they should use for the people." He said, "All people have the same desire to make money, while money is necessary to political affairs. Using the money on only one person is not feasible. In contrast, if the money from people can do things for those people with officials' sincerity, the nation can benefit from the total wealth and not worry about a shortage of funds."[4]

Xue Fucheng served as the minister of four countries successively, namely Britain, France, Italy, and Belgium. He knew much about the Western tax system and advocated increasing the tax in China. Regarding the western countries that managed money for their people, he said, "The island countries, Britain, France, Germany, and other countries, only have the area of two provinces of China, but their taxes from the people are almost 100 times more than that of China. Everything in those countries is taxed, such as feeding a dog, wearing a ring, even housing." If the Chinese people will bear heavier tax, they may live a miserable life. However, Western people can live with the heavier tax because "they collect tax from the people with which they do things for the people."[5]

How should governments raise taxes? He Qi and Hu Liyuan thought that "it would cost much money in the case of the new political system." If the government wanted to own enough wealth to mobilize, it needed to collect more money. Thus, how should this money be collected? The main way is to raise money from housing tax, such as one-tenth or one-twentieth of the housing rent. Finally, the funds raised would be to construct the nation, such as infrastructure for a water conservancy facility, lighting, fire protection, roads, and so on. They believed that the people would support their activities because "if the people do that for themselves, they must shoulder a big burden, while if they

[4] *Huang, Z. Riben Guozhi Zushuihouxu* (Annals of Japan · Tax, 日本国志·租税后序).

[5] Xue, F. (1987). *Xue Fucheng Xuanji, Xiyang Zhuguo Weimin Licai Shuo* (Selected Works of Xue Fucheng · On Financial Issues in Western Countries, 薛福成选集·西洋诸国为民理财说). Shanghai: Shanghai Renmin Chubanshe, p. 416.

put money together for construction, that burden might be lightened." Not everyone would agree. As an example, they explained, "If the land is affected by flooding, the government provides an irrigation machine, minimizing flooding of the land. Without the flooding, it will yield a harvest. Thus, is taxation wrong?".[6]

Zhang Zhidong, the governor of the Self-Strengthening movement, conducted a lot of business. It is therefore certain that he mobilized a large amount of funds. To raise funds for the enterprise, he advocated changing the traditional light tax system, and increased the tax appropriately. In 1901, Zhang Zhidong and Liu Kunyi wrote a letter named Recommendations of the Governor-general of Hubei and Hunan and the Governor-general of Jiangnan and Jiangxi, which is also known as the threefold reform. In the section on stamp tax, he noted that in Britain, the government collects money from inheritance tax. The Chinese industry is poor and inherited by descendants, so it is difficult to gain much tax in this regard. However, if the government can gain more tax (at least 5% of that in Britain)—i.e., 5–6 million taels, things will improve. He therefore recommended learning each country's political system as soon as possible and taking action. Zhang Zhidong did as he said. He introduced new taxes in Hubei, including school tax, pawnshop tax, estate tax, and other taxes. Essentially, everything was taxed. According to history, when Zhang Zhidong worked as Hu-guang Governor from 1889–1906, he increased provincial tax from 7 million taels to 15 million taels. People commented that "the tax collected in Hubei is higher than anywhere else in China."[7]

Second, taxation measures had to be reformed. Before the Opium War, the Qing government firmly ruled the country, but it was difficult to collect violet tax because of the many disadvantages of taxation by local officials. After the Opium War, the authority of the Qing government waned, and local officials become more corrupt, deepening an already bad situation. Therefore, the Self-Strengthening movement proposed taxation reform.

Feng Guifen and Zheng Guanying contended that first, to maximize the collection of tax on violet, the land area should be calculated to eliminate unequal tax rates. According to Feng Guifen, "the inequality

[6] He, Q. & Hu, L. (1994). *Xinzheng Zhenquan, Xinzheng Lunyi* (The Real Interpretation of the New Policy · Discussion on New Policies, 新政真诠·新政论议). Liaoning: Liaoning People's Publishing House, p. 143.

[7] Jiang, J. *Jingcao Tang Biji* (Notes written in Jincaotang, 劲草堂笔记), p. 99.

of taxation that resulted from the land calculation has a long history."[8] To calculate the correct land area, Zheng Guanying suggested that "each province measure the land area with measurement instruments and levy the tax according to that area." The specific actions were to "first draw and then confirm the area." In this way, "each county is responsible for its own land area and accompanying levy tax. This does not impose on the young and old, and affords no partiality to the strong and rich."[9]

He Qi and Hu Liyuan proposed specific operational measures to prevent officials from cheating: "A good way to collect taxes is to ensure those taxes do not disappear." For this, four main points were described: First, strengthen the supervision of public opinion: "Tax funds are held only by a few officials who are unknown to other officials. Thus, how can ordinary people know the money, which is the evil, begins?" Only in this way would "the correct amount of tax be collected. What has been spent and what remains should be recorded." This would eliminate current flaws. The second step is executing the guarantee of the law: "All money paid to the employed public should be accompanied by a signed note and guarantee of two rich families. Once there is a deficit, the guarantor should compensate for the loss. Thus, both the employed and the guarantor will not cheat each other." "Third, competition law should be executed." "Construction in places like mountains, swamps, livestock, plains, mineral resources, and houses, where no-one lives, can only be carried out by someone the government permits to do so. Regardless of the amount that person pays (even if nothing), the government should encourage them to carry out the construction. If a place is popular among some people, officials can sell it on auction. The place will be sold to the highest bidder. This news must be published, and the money from the auction should be taxed by the government." "Fourth, increase the wages of accountants to help support their families." "An accountant's wage should be high. Currently, some people are employed for levying tax and paid a wage of 15 *yuan*. This will ensure employees take their jobs seriously and work hard. After one year, their salaries should be increased

[8] Feng, G. (1998). *Xiaobinlu Kangyi, Jun Fushui Yi* (Reform Proposals Written in Xiaobin Cabin, Equal Tax, 校邠庐抗议·均赋税议). Zhengzhou: Zhongzhou Ancient Books Publishing House, p. 108.

[9] Zheng, G. (1982). *Zheng Guanying Ji, Ge Bi, Shangce* (Zheng Guanying Works • To Reform the Misgovernment, Vol. 1, 郑观应集·革弊, 上册). Shanghai: Shanghai Renmin Chubanshe, p. 465.

without disadvantage. However, a person with a wage of 3 *yuan* will not perform as well as the one mentioned earlier. Because the latter can reduce taxation by levying less tax from a renter, the total tax will be reduced and employers' real income will not decrease. Thus, there are many disadvantages to a lower wage. However, it is unavoidable because families need to be supported. Governors should consider that employees' support their families and implement appropriate policies to deal with their taxation to ensure the state treasury is rich enough."[10]

Tribute rice was also levied directly from the land and is part of the land tax. However, in the tax system, tribute rice was under an independent system.

Tribute rice came from places with abundant food production, such as Shandong, Henan, Jiangsu, Zhejiang, Anhui, Jiangxi, Hubei, and Hunan. From the eight provinces, the government took rice, beans, and other grains. The government instilled the Governor-general to control all aspects, and each province set up a route for providing foodstuff. In addition, a garrison was stationed along the river to protect the transportation of tribute rice by reclaiming wasteland in a province with tribute rice to support the army. This system was put in place to ensure food supply, and increased the prosperity of regions directly under central control. However, from an economic viewpoint, the transportation of tribute rice was a highly irrational system, because every year, 4 million *shi* had to be transported from the provinces to the capital city. The total income from the upper to lower level was uncountable. Sometimes, one *shi* of rice could be worth 18 taels because of the transfer fee; thus, the total amount of rice could be worth 70 million taels, despite that one *shi* of rice was only valued at 1 tael in the capital. During the Jiaqing period (1796–1820), Assistant Grand Secretary Liu Quan co-organized this team. He suggested that one *shi* of rice be sold for 1 tael 4 *qian*. After the Opium War, Feng Guifen reignited this view, pointing out the proverb that "price attracts business far away, but each province is different from the capital."[11] He further claimed that it was unnecessary to transfer food

[10] He, Q. & Hu, L. (1994). *Xinzheng Zhenquan, Xinzheng Lunyi* (The Real Interpretation of the New Policy · Discussion on New Policies, 新政真诠·新政论议). Liaoning: Liaoning People's Publishing House, pp. 144–145.

[11] Feng, G. (1998). *Xiaobinlu Kangyi, Zhenan Caoyi* (Reform Proposals Written in Xiaobin Cabin, South Grain Waterway Transport, 校邠庐抗议·折南漕议). Zhengzhou: Zhongzhou Ancient Books Publishing House, p. 128.

from southern China, and that provinces with tribute rice should pay tax according to the land area. Cities such as Beijing and Tianjin could attract enterprises to sell rice, which the government could purchase with the money paid from southern China. Similarly, Zheng Guanying also proposed halting the transfer of tribute rice, and purchasing rice with the tax paid from southern China. Thus, he thought "the government could save more money than before."[12] According to the author, "As the number of ships is increasing, it is unnecessary for the government to fund shipping enterprises." The opinions of Zheng Guanying and others reflect the development of the commodity-money relationship.

While stopping the transfer of tribute rice would be acceptable for the economy, "officials would consider the disadvantages thereof and other staff would lose their jobs, bringing much turmoil. Thus, it was difficult to stop the transfer of tribute rice."[13] As such, Zheng Guanying had to seek another method to avoid the over-levying of tax: "Many types of items can be taxed, making it difficult to calculate the total tax."[14]

5.2 Regulating Salt Tax

As a necessity good in daily life, salt was consumed in the Qing Dynasty. Thanks to the natural characteristics mentioned above, salt tax revenue became an important financial source supporting the economy of the empire. Since the Spring and Autumn Period, the central government had adopted an exclusive operation system for salt, and had been attempting to increase the tax to earn more money, especially when a financial deficit occurred. Such was the case in the late Qing Dynasty. It had been defeated and humiliated by European allies in the Opium Wars, and had to mobilize its fragile army to suppress domestic rebels. This deteriorated the Qing regime's financial situation. Thus, the government bet its

[12] Zheng, G. (1982). *Zheng Guanying Ji, Ting Cao, Shangce* (Zheng Guanying Works • Stop the Grain Transportation, Vol. 1, 郑观应集·停漕, 上册). Shanghai: Shanghai Renmin Chubanshe, p. 569.

[13] Zheng, G. (1982). *Zheng Guanying Ji, Ting Cao, Shangce* (Zheng Guanying Works • Stop the Grain Transportation, Vol. 1, 郑观应集·停漕, 上册). Shanghai: Shanghai Renmin Chubanshe, p. 569.

[14] Zheng, G. (1982). *Zheng Guanying Ji, Ge Bi, Shangce* (Zheng Guanying Works • To Reform the Misgovernment, Vol. 1, 郑观应集·革弊, 上册). Shanghai: Shanghai Renmin Chubanshe, p. 465.

fortune on taxing salt. This was a wise decision, because, at that time, the emperor's law enforcement was weakened by lax salt trade regulations and salt smuggling, which decreased tax revenue. To solve the salt problem, some liberal officials who advocated national Westernization urged the central government to regulate salt tax to raise money for the great cause of the empire's re-prosperity work. Consequently, officials proposed the following three recommendations.

First, "we should collect salt tax according to the number of people," which could not only reduce the cost of salt tax collection, but also greatly increase the salt tax revenue. He Qi and Hu Liyuan gave the most detailed description here. They pointed out their opinion in the article "The Beginning of the New Deal." To strengthen their theory, they quoted national demographic data and predicted that if the government had implemented taxes according to the population, the empire would have earned much more money.[15]

Second, reformed the salt management method, changed the former official business management to private business management, which is, "the state should properly negotiate new regulations, collect a certain amount of money in each well every year, then cheating would over." Tang Shouqian believed that the advantage of doing so can not only master the salt tax through the number of people but also reduce the cost of collection, finally appeared "all the officials and business would observe law and discipline".[16]

Third, reduce marketing costs. Zheng Guanying believed that salt was unsalable, which was caused by the rise of illegal salt. High price of official salt promoted the birth of illegal salt, while the high price came from high cost. So he concluded that the only way to increase salt production was to reduce costs. But how? Zheng's method was: (1) reducing the salt tax collection. Zheng Guanying believed that the key to the high cost of official salt was the salt tax. (2) making more ships to carry salt. It on the one hand can lower salt price through reducing the transport cost of salt, on the other hand can reduce smuggling of salt. (3) building more salt

[15] He, Q. & Hu, L. (1994). *Xinzheng Zhenquan, Xinzheng Shiji* (The Real Interpretation of the New Policy · The Fundamental of New Policies, 新政真诠·新政始基). Liaoning: Liaoning People's Publishing House, p. 223.

[16] Tang, S. *Tangshi Weiyan, Yanjuan* (Warnings from Tang, Salt Tax, 汤氏危言•盐捐).

warehouses for the purpose of reducing transport costs as well as playing a price leveling role.[17]

Tang Shouqian held a different opinion about salt tax reform. He insisted that the government cooperate with civil private capital. The government signed a contract with private capital enterprises about gross sales and the tax rate, and authorized private sellers. He strongly believed the private sector would be more efficient in regulating salt and managing anti-smuggling operations than government officials and branches. If adopted by the authority, he added that government branches would employ fewer workers and establish a stable tax source from the salt trade.

5.3 Taxing the Gambling Industry and Opium Trade

To fill the great financial gap caused by the wars, liberal officials suggested the government adopt a new tax on the gambling industry and opium trade, which counter traditional Chinese morality and regulations.

For example, when Zhang Zhidong took office in Guangdong and Guangxi, he acquiesced to illegal gambling called "Weixing"[18] and taxed it. At first, gambling was secretly operated and illegal; thus, the gamblers took their business to casinos in Macau (a colony of Portugal at the time), which greatly benefited from their move. Consequently, a great amount of money flowed from the mainland to Macau. To stop this flow, Zhang had to cooperate with these illegal activities. The taxes from the illegal trade were mostly spent on purchasing ships, shipyards, looms, and the reinforcement of dams. In his memorial to the throne, he stated the facts and appealed for the emperor's permission.[19]

Opium trade was another profitable industry in the Qing Dynasty. Traditionally, Britain exported thousands of boxes of opium to China, making a huge profit from this trade. To prevent the outflow of money, Li Hongzhang suggested that the government ban opium trade with British dealers and sell homemade opium to addicts as an alternative,

[17] Zheng, G. (1982). *Zheng Guanying Ji, Yanwu, Shangce* (Zheng Guanying Works, Vol. 1, 郑观应集·停漕, 上册). Shanghai: Shanghai Renmin Chubanshe, pp. 567–570.

[18] Note: (in Chinese 闱姓: this is a type of gambling in which gamblers bet on the Imperial civil servant exams).

[19] Zhang, Z. *Zhang Wenxianggong Quanji, Chioushe Liantiechang Zhe, Juanershiqi* (Collected Works of Zhang Wenxiang, 张文襄公全集·筹设炼铁厂折, 卷27, 奏议27).

which would also greatly benefit tax.[20] Regarding the money from the opium trade, Chen Chi argued that "drug addicts will be less supportive of heavy taxation, and the tax money will be used as the initial capital for China's modernization or national defense."[21]

5.4 Selling Official Posts and Titles to Raise Money

Selling official posts and titles was another way to raise money. This practice has a long history in China, especially when the government faced a severe financial crisis. To raise more money, the authority simplified related procedures and auctioned off the posts to the highest bidders.

In the short term, this was a quick way to raise money; however, in the long term, the practice negatively affected the empire's mechanisms. For one, the money could not long support the empire's modernization, and for another, this practice fueled corruption. Consequently, its positive effects declined. Thus, to realize modernization, liberal officials recommended that the authority permit the rich to establish companies and invest in industry and business. As a return, the government could award these pioneers with nominal titles. Feng Guifen and Zheng Guanying were proponents of these ideas. Furthermore, officials such as Zhang Zhidong called on the rich to donate for public welfare. His appeal was answered and many rich businessmen-built academies, schools, and steelworks.

5.5 Levying New Tax Categories

To ensure the sustainable development of the economy, innovationists suggested that the authority levy new tax categories (tariffs and likin (lijin) tax). This would save the economy and issue national debt to raise money from the people.

1. **Tariffs**

[20] *Yangwu Yundong, Juanyi* (The Westernization Movement, Vol. 1,洋务运动, 卷1), p. 51.

[21] Chen, C. (1997). *Chenchi Ji, Yanshui* (Chen Chi Works, 陈炽集·烟税). Beijing: Zhonghua Book Company, p. 68.

Before the Opium Wars, China was less connected with the global market. However, after the war, China had to open its doors and import industrial goods and opium from Britain and export its handiworks and agricultural products. This increased the tariffs tax, which thanks to prosperous international trade, played an important role in government fiscal revenue. In 1849, the tariffs revenue was 2,210,000 taels of silver, and in 1871, the value soared over 10,000,000 taels. The great increase was significant to the authority and businessmen. The authority had more money to spend on investing in industry and modernization, while businessmen, especially those who were foreign, were pleased with the booming international trade. At that time, China's tariffs taxing system was designed under the guidance of Robert Hart, a Qing tax officer of British origin.

The tariffs tax was used as follows: 40% of the tax income was handed to Beijing's national revenues, 20% was for the war indemnity, and the remainder was earmarked for modernization. According to the statistics, tariffs accounted for 83.7% of the entire volume invested in improving the military industry.

2. Likin (Lijin) Tax

To crush the rebels, the Qing government adopted likin (lijin) tax to raise money, promising that this taxation would stop once the rebels had been defeated. However, with the influence of the war and the decline of field tax, the government needed an alternative to address the money gap, and selected tariff and likin tax to do so. As tariffs were not under the control of Qing government, the government had to rely on likin tax.

The officials did not reach a consensus regarding likin tax: some were for the proposal, while others vetoed it. Guan Wen, Guo Songtao and Li Hongzhang thought it was a supplement for the national fiscal revenue; meanwhile, Li Hongzhang was concerned that the high tax would increase the price of commodities, which would consequently enable cheaper foreign imported goods to occupy the domestic market. To resolve these issues, the liberal officials proposed several plans:

The first, proposed by Ma Jianzhong, was to halt likin tax and increase the tax rate. Ma argued the policy would serve two purposes. Businessmen would pay less because of the absence of likin tax, and foreign businessmen would pay for the increased tariffs, even if they got revenue from likin tax.[22]

Zheng Guanying contended that likin tax was bad for business. He suggested that the authority stop likin tax and levies the tariffs on imported foreign goods, while taxing exported goods once.[23]

Tang Shouqian proposed a third solution, namely that the government should tax fixed sellers, not street vendors.[24]

Finally, Li Hongzhang suggested that the government construct more railways to boost the economy and decrease the exorbitant taxes. He argued that the traditional tax system was inefficient and could lead to corruption. He further predicted that once the railway was built, the transport network would link all the cities of the country, and eventually, all goods could be distributed via train transportation.[25]

As seen, officials' views regarding the issue of tax varied based on their personal experience and understanding. As a high-ranking official of the emperor, Li Hongzhang was conservative and cautious, and deeply relied on the adjustment of the emperor, not fierce reform. Like other conservative officials, he was critical of commerce. For example, when asked why he taxed the businessmen, he explained that while increasing the tax would be controversial, taxing businesses was not a bad idea.[26] To strengthen his argument on taxing businesses, he criticized opponents who supported commerce as "attending to trifles and neglecting the essentials."[27]

3. Domestic Debts

[22] Ma, J. *Lun Yanghuo Ru Neidi Mianli, Huangchao Jingshiwen Xinbian, Juanshier* (New Edition of Royal Classic, Vol. 12, 皇朝经世文新编, 论洋货入内地免厘, 卷12).

[23] Zheng, G. (1982). *Zheng Guanying Ji, Li Juan, Shangce* (Zheng Guanying Works, Vol. 1, 郑观应集·厘捐, 上册). Shanghai: Shanghai Renmin Chubanshe, pp. 558–559.

[24] Tang, S. *Tangshi Weiyan, Bao Li* (Warnings from Tang, 汤氏危言·包厘).

[25] Zhong, S. (1986). *Li Hongzhang Lipin Oumei Ji* (李鸿章历聘欧美记), Changsha: Yuelu Press, p. 227.

[26] *Li, H. Liwenzhong Gong Quanshu, Pengliao Hangao, Juanliu* (Complete Works of Li Wenzhong, Letters of Li Wenzhong, Vol. 6, 李文忠公全书·朋僚函稿, 卷6), p. 45.

[27] *Li, H. Liwenzhong Gong Quanshu, Pengliao Hangao, Juanliu* (Complete Works of Li Wenzhong, Letters of Li Wenzhong, Vol. 6, 李文忠公全书·朋僚函稿, 卷6), p. 37.

In ancient China, the central government did not borrow money from its citizens, although this was common in the Western world to support large-scale construction projects or a war, with the national debt amortized over a few years. Using the money, the country could finish great projects, and the people benefited from its interest: a win–win situation. In the late Qing Dynasty, some businessmen became rich from the tea trade, but the government's fiscal situation was worsening because of the reparation in the Opium Wars. The liberal officials began to copy the idea and suggested that the government issue national debt to wealthy businessmen to raise money for the empire's modernization cause. However, a major problem was that the businessmen did not trust the government, and it was difficult to raise internal debt through this system during this period. People distrusted the government because of the tradition of economic control in Chinese society. According to Tang Shouqian, "Chinese merchants do not always trust the imperial court, and they regard officers with abhorrence. Will they be willing to put their hard-earned money into the court's pocket?"[28] To address this contradiction, the Westernization Group proposed three projects.

First, Tang Shouqian advocated changing the treasury into an official bank. This was to ensure that national debt would not pass through the government, and would be beneficial in regaining civilians' trust in officials. It would also lead to a situation in which "people will rely on the official bank and willingly deposit their money there, a win–win situation for both the court and merchants."[29] The author considers Tang's methods reasonable, but not suitable for the situation at that time, as changing the official treasury into an official bank would be a change in name only and not lead to fundamental changes in the government's function. In other words, the proposed method was a change in form but not in content.

Second, Zheng Guanying proposed adopting the methods of the Western world and borrowing money from the people. He believed that in China, "there are a large number of wealthy men in the 21 provinces. If Ministry of Revenue and treasuries of other vassal states provide shares as in the Western countries, and each share contains 100

[28] Tang, S. *Tang Shi Wei Yan, Guo Zhai* (Tang's Righteous Words · National Debt, 汤氏危言·国债).

[29] Tang, S. *Tang Shi Wei Yan, Guo Zhai* (Tang's Righteous Words · National Debt, 汤氏危言·国债).

gold pieces, then these financial departments will return money within a fixed period including yearly interest without fraud. The merchants will then have more trust in the banks than in the Ministry of Revenue, and more trust in China than in foreign countries."[30] Zheng's proposal reflected the Western economic principles that had been disseminated into China. Moreover, it indicated his long work experience in industry and commerce. However, this was not practically applied at the time because of China's backward political system.

Third, Zhong Tianwei thought that internal debt should be managed by customs, which had fixed incomes. He said that if people bought the national debt, they would obtain a certain interest managed by customs. Customs would provide bills as vouchers and be responsible for the interest. Therefore, common people and merchants would withdraw their savings to buy national debt for interest, which would bolster the circulation of money.[31]

4. Raise Private Capital to Invest in the Enterprises of the Westernization Group

At the time, the social legal system was not sound and competition between Chinese and foreign businessmen was not equal. In that social environment, many Chinese businessmen were attached to foreign companies, hoping to achieve the desired interest in their investment. A few Chinese businessmen even pretended to be foreign traders to evade taxes. To attract these Chinese businessmen to invest their funds in the enterprises of the Westernization group, the group proposed organizing a "stock company"—operated by enterprises and supervised by the government—to protect the interests of businessmen through state power. However, shareholders' benefits were negatively affected because it was difficult to coordinate the relationship between the government and businessmen. A situation arose in which "all the people complained and

[30] Zheng, G. (1982). *Zheng Guanying Ji, Guozhai, Shangce* (Zheng Guanying Works • National Debt, Vol. 1, 郑观应集·国债, 上册). Shanghai: Shanghai Renmin Chubanshe, p. 583.

[31] *Zhong, T. Yuezu Ji, Waipian* (Zhong's Righteous Words • Foreign Affairs, 刖足集·外篇).

regretted these actions, from which he took warning." To attract businessmen to continue to invest in the enterprises of the Westernization group, it proposed a measure to reform the joint-stock method.

The article "Establishment of the Railway in China," written by Zhong Tianwei to refute Liu Xihong, said, "As for the joint-stock method, the first important thing is that government should ensure benefits. Both earnings and losses belong to the state. In other words, the government ensures benefits. Whether gains or losses, the government must pay the interest on time. Customs are responsible for recruiting shareholders and paying interest every year. The people will then depend on and trust the government, making it easier to raise funds."[32] In one of his later articles, namely "How to Choose Routes for the Chinese Railway," he suggested "ensuring the government's benefits and recruiting shareholders through funds." He explained that if China could follow the Western policy of the "government ensuring people's benefits and paying out the interest every year, people will trust the government and raise funds by themselves."[33] Zheng made a similar claim. He believed that Chinese businessmen considered companies a "dangerous way" because while "the government was initially responsible for recruiting shareholders, when the company was dismissed, the government turned its back. As such, no-one dared become a shareholder." He added that in Western countries, "if the government wanted to hold a large event but lacked the funds to do so, it would recruit shareholders and ensure they made a profit. Whether making losses or gains, the government would be liable for the consequences. Thus, a great deal of money was easily raised."[34] A special system that guarantees the interests by the government was formed in Chinese modern industrial history. The "government's interests," generally 7–10%, had two uses. On one hand, it helped reduce merchants' risk and encouraged them to invest. As per Zhang Jian, "the development of Chinese industry was dependent on that, or the capitalists' businesses

[32] Zhong, T. *Yuezu Ji Waipian* (Outer Chapters of Zhong's Righteous Works, 刖足集·外篇).

[33] Zhong, T. *Yuezu Ji Waipian* (Outer Chapters of Zhong's Righteous Works, 刖足集·外篇).

[34] Zheng, G. (1982). *Zheng Guanying Ji, Yinhang Xia, Shangce* (Zheng Guanying Works • Banks II, Vol. 1, 郑观应集· 银行下, 上册). Shanghai: Shanghai Renmin Chubanshe, pp. 686–687.

would be limited and China would have no industry."[35] However, on the other, the government benefit policy negatively influenced the opening and management of enterprises. One example is the establishment of Dasheng Cotton Mill, which was influenced by the policy. At the time of these financial difficulties, the mill spent 17,000 taels of the government by selling cotton.

Zhang Zhidong positively carried out the government-supervised and merchant-managed enterprises. Finding it difficult to attract investment, he put forward two alternatives regarding the financing strategy for the Luhan Railway Company. One was "attracting investment by borrowing money." He said that "by borrowing, everyone would know the railway project would be completed on time and benefits would be ensured. People could get their interest if they invested in advance." The government would pay back their capital stock once the project was completed. The second alternative was to "collect business stock and pay the principal back." Wealthy people like business chiefs would be selected, and shareholders attracted according to the needs of the railway project, and only 20% cash would be collected. "Until a company is established, if the business stocks are insufficient, the company should be responsible for borrowing and paying back. For example, if the company borrowed 80% capital, which had to be repaid in 30 years, the company only needed to pay a little money back each year and the procedure would be easier."[36]

5.6 Attracting Foreign Capital

Facing a lack of modern capital, Western countries were concerned about searching for profitable fields of investment, which created the condition for the Westernization Group to use foreign capital. There were two ways in which to use foreign capital: foreign indirect investment and foreign direct investment.

1. Foreign indirect investment

[35] Zhang, J. (1932). *Zhang Jizi Jiulu, Shiye Lu, Juanwu* (Nine Chapters of Zhang Jian · Industry, Vol. 5, 张季子九录·实业录, 卷5). Beijing: Zhonghua Book Company.

[36] Zhang, Z. *Zhang Wenxianggong Quanji, Luhan Tielu Shangban Nancheng Lingchou Banfazhe Juansishishi* (Collected Works of Zhang Wenxiang · Another Way to Solve the Difficulties in Merchant-Operated Luhan Railway, Vol. 44, 张文襄公全集·卢汉铁路商办难成另筹办法折, 卷44).

In 1879, Ma Jianzhong put forward his articles "The Railway" and "Building the Railway through Foreign Debts," in which he proposed that China build its railway using foreign debt. In "The Railway," he refuted the argument that it was shameful to borrow foreign debt, which would lead to China's control by other countries. He stated, "most Western countries had foreign debt, but Britain, France, Germany, and Russia continued to rule the roost as before."[37] In 1890, he recommended that the government borrow foreign debt to develop domestic industries, copy western products and exploit minerals, and set up Ministry of Commerce following Western countries as a specialized agency that would borrow this foreign debt. Ministry of Commerce was responsible for borrowing about 25 million taels from Western countries, and established a head office for Chinese businessmen to draft a contract with these countries to use the debt within 10 years. The annual interest was about 4–5%, and the debt would be repaid within 20 years in installments. If not, interest would be added up to 6.5%. Every year, China needed to repay the interest, rather than the capital, for about 55 years. At that time, the debt should be fully repaid.[38] After borrowing the debt, Ministry of Commerce needed to arrange Westernization affairs according to the level of difficulty. Ma Jianzhong repeated that the Chinese government should personally borrow foreign debt and deliver it to Chinese companies. The interest should be a little higher to compensate for the loss of exchange and other losses, because Chinese and foreign merchants looked down on each other and the government could gain the trust of foreign countries.

Zhang Zhidong firmly advocated borrowing foreign debt. In 1880, he suggested that to "raise vast sums, foreign debt must be borrowed."[39] In 1885, as the Governor-general of Guangdong and Guangxi provinces, he requested 1 million taels of foreign debts from the court to develop a school, gun factory, and mine factory. He also used 1 million taels of the debts borrowed from Fujian province for the Fuzhou Arsenal to produce

[37] Ma J. (1960). *Shikezhai Jiyan* (Political Proposals Written in Shike Study, 适可斋记言). Beijing: Zhonghua Book Company, p. 17.

[38] Ma J. (1960). *Shikezhai Jiyan* (Political Proposals Written in Shike Study, 适可斋记言). Beijing: Zhonghua Book Company, p. 8.

[39] Zhang, Z. (1880). *Zhang Wenxianggong Quanji, Haijing Ripo Jichou Zhanbei Zhe Juansan* (Collected Works of Zhang Wenxiang · Vol. 3, 张文襄公全集·海警日迫急筹战备折, 卷3).

cannons. In 1895, he asked the premier government to borrow around 25 million taels from Britain. He "could use Taiwan as the guarantee" and "permit Britain to open a mine within 15 years." He thought this would convince Britain to send their army to protect Taiwan "from Japanese pirates," and "when the debt was repaid, Britain would have no right to covet Taiwan. As such, Taiwan would forever belong to our country."[40] While not unreasonable, this suggestion was not practical in the era of monopoly capitalism.

After the signing of the Treaty of Shimonoseki, many requests to borrow foreign debt were proposed in Zhang Zhidong's memorial by Zhang Jian: "He thought China could create an opportunity for Self-Strengthening by borrowing foreign debt, so that China did not need to worry about the repayment." In 1898, in the article of his book *Encourage Learning—Railway*, Zhang Zhidong further supported building the railway by borrowing debt, stating: "Borrowing foreign debts needs a collateral, while building the railway can only take the railway as the collateral. It is a benefit to our nation."[41]

However, it also posed some risk, and could lead to a debt crisis. Thus, some objected to the borrowing of foreign debts. Zheng Guanying pointed out that some foreign countries such as Turkey and Persia had become very weak because of foreign debt and being controlled by other nations; therefore, China should also not borrow foreign debt.[42] He then contended that China should stop borrowing foreign debt altogether.[43] In the book *Annals of Japan—A Record of Food and Commodities*, Huang Zunxian emphasized that foreign debt could benefit China in the short term; however, in the long term, it would harm the nation and benefit

[40] Zhang, Z. (1895). *Zhang Wenxianggong Quanji, Zhi Zongdu Juanqishiqi* (Collected Works of Zhang Wenxiang, Vol. 77, 张文襄公全集·致总督, 卷77).

[41] Zhang, Z. (1895). *Zhang Wenxianggong Quanji, Yuqing Xiubei Chucai Zhe Juansanshiqi* (Collected Works of Zhang Wenxiang, Vol. 37, 张文襄公全集·吁请修备储才折, 卷37).

[42] Zheng, G. (1982). *Zheng Guanying Ji, Lun Jiekuan Shangce* (Zheng Guanying Works • Debts, Vol. 1, 郑观应集·论借款, 上册). Shanghai: Shanghai Renmin Chubanshe, p. 160.

[43] Zheng, G. (1982). *Zheng Guanying Ji, Guozhai, Shangce* (Zheng Guanying Works • National Debt, Vol. 1, 郑观应集·国债, 上册). Shanghai: Shanghai Renmin Chubanshe, p. 583.

neighboring countries. He also pointed out that foreign debt had weakened Turkey and Egypt, and that China could learn something from that.

However, as Zhong Tianwei noted, at that time, China was not able to construct the railway without foreign debt, which would have negative influences. Foreign debt posed both advantages and disadvantages. How could China draw on the advantages and avoid the disadvantages? The Westernization Group claimed the following in this regard:

First, they considered the purpose of foreign debt. Ma Jianzhong thought it could be used in production rather than for consumption. Xue Fucheng held the same view. In one of his articles, he supported Liu Mingchuan's proposal to construct the railway using foreign debt.[44]

Second, they considered the method by which to borrow foreign debt. In the paper "Building the Railway through Foreign Debt," he mentioned that to prevent the few foreign banks acting in collusion and monopolizing the market, the government should send especially assigned people to Britain and France to enter into face-to-face discussions with officials and private banks. Foreign private lending could also be considered for a lower interest. However, this method also had disadvantages, because it may not be possible to raise enough money on time through private lending. Therefore, the manager should work hard to ensure the foreigners know that China would use the money for the construction of the railway.[45]

Xue Fucheng highlighted three points of consideration regarding foreign debt: The first was that to prevent foreigners from holding the rights to the railway, it needed to be clearly written that they had no right to interfere in China's affairs and all things related to the railway; for example, China would control employment issues and the purchasing of materials. Second, foreigners could not buy stocks or take the railway as a mortgage in the case of insufficient capital and interest. The third point of consideration was that the debt had no relation with customs. These three points of consideration were the prerequisites for foreign debt. He

[44] Xue, F. (1987). *Xue Fucheng Xuanji, Dai Liboxiang Yiqing Shiban Tielu Shu* (Selected Works of Xue Fucheng, Li Hongzhang's Proposal of Building Railway, 薛福成选集·代李伯相议请试办铁路疏). Shanghai: Shanghai Renmin Chubanshe, p. 139.

[45] Ma J. (1960). *Shikezhai Jiyan* (Political Proposals Written in Shike Study, 适可斋记言). Beijing: Zhonghua Book Company, pp. 22–23.

warned that the parties should not be so anxious for success that they regret it in the future.[46]

Although Zheng Guanying objected to borrowing foreign debts, once this action was decided, he actively thought about methods to ensure the disadvantages would be avoided. He emphasized that China should not use customs as a collateral, which would give the rights to and benefit corrupt foreign businessmen and not the wealthy foreign people. For him, it was not necessarily better to borrow from Britain, Russia, and France than from the United States, because "Britain, Russia, and France are on the border with China. Our country is liable to blackmail, should we have disagreements. Exchange with the United States presents no such concerns." He also thought that "borrowing several 10 billion taels was much better than borrowing a billion taels" because "the former had a lower interest." Zheng suggested that the government borrow a huge sum with lower interest. As such, China could repay the loans from other countries and use the funds to develop the country in a holistic way. He added that "borrowing silver was much better than pounds in case of exchange loss."[47]

2. Foreign Direct Investment

Before the 1894–1895Sino-Japanese War, the court and common people were open to foreign debt, but objected to "attracting foreign stocks." Ma Jianzhong said that borrowing and participating were different. Participating could make a profit every year, while parties who borrowed money could only rely on annual interest. China established the railway that stretches into the hinterland. How could they encourage foreigners to participate in stocks? Using some foreign countries as an example, he noted that when Turkey built the railway, the wealthy people of Britain, France, and Austria-Hungary participated in the stocks. When Egypt dug the Suez Canal, people from France participated in the stocks,

[46] Xue, F. (1987). *Xue Fucheng Xuanji, Dai Liboxiang Yiqing Shiban Tielu Shu* (Selected Works of Xue Fucheng, Li Hongzhang's Proposal of Building Railway, 薛福成选集·代李伯相议请试办铁路疏). Shanghai: Shanghai Renmin Chubanshe, p. 139.

[47] Zheng, G. (1982). *Zheng Guanying Ji, Guozhai, Shangce* (Zheng Guanying Works • National Debt, Vol. 1, 郑观应集·国债, 上册). Shanghai: Shanghai Renmin Chubanshe, pp. 584–585.

which afforded the French privileged rights.[48] Later, the stocks belonged to the British. The treaty then concluded and the canal was used by all nations.

However, Taiwan's Governor Liu Mingchuan approved of foreign direct investment, and actively carried it out. When he established the Taipei Telegraph Administration in 1886, he recruited foreign contractors to install the undersea cables. In 1889, the government-run Jilong Badou Coal Mine continuously operated at a loss, which the government was unable to cover. At that time, an English businessman wanted to pay to run the mine. Liu Mingchuan immediately submitted the request to the court for approval.[49] Making use of Foreign direct investment not only changes the situation of deficit but also learn the management from the foreigner.

As indicated by the above, Liu Mingchuan believed the advantages of recruiting foreign merchants were that it could resolve the government's financial difficulties, exploit Taiwan's natural resources, reform the customs of government-run enterprises, earn back capital, reduce the losses caused by government-run enterprises, add income from tariffs, bolster transportation and business, and boost the employment rate. However, the Qing government rejected his suggestion, as it worried other countries would make the same requests.

After the 1894–1895 Sino-Japanese War, the Great Powers obtained the rights to set up factories in China, and it became impossible to oppose foreign direct investment. The Westernization Group began considering the new situation in a more active way.

In 1898, He Qi and Hu Liyuan in the article "The Origin of the New Policy" described four inappropriate methods for China to build the railway. One was not participating in foreign debt and another was borrowing foreign debt. In other words, they opposed borrowing foreign debt and proposed participating in foreign stocks. This was because they believed borrowing foreign debt would not be discounted and would increase the gold price. However, these reasons differed from those of others. They also believed that if the Chinese could buy foreign shares

[48] Ma J. (1960). *Shikezhai Jiyan* (Political Proposals Written in Shike Study, 适可斋记言). Beijing: Zhonghua Book Company, p. 22.

[49] Liu, M. *Liu Zhuangsugong Zouyi, Yingshang Chengban Jilong Meikuang Dingni Hetong Zhe, Juanba* (Memorials of Liu Zhuangsu, Vol. 8, 刘壮肃公奏议·英商承办基隆煤矿订拟合同折, 卷8).

when China was constructing the railway, they would be able to actively participate because the foreigners were beyond the control of the government. This would ensure that the common people would not be exploited by officers. They stated that if China wanted to construct the railway by pooling everyone's efforts, people had to buy foreign shares.[50] Here, He Qi and Hu Liyuan focused on the function that foreign shares could promote Chinese investment.

Zhang Zhidong strongly supported foreign direct investment in the late Qing Dynasty. In 1897, he said that if foreigners set up factories in China, all materials and the labor force had to be obtained from China. Thus, when foreign businesses acquired benefits, China could also benefit. While the benefits for Chinese businessmen would decrease, the peasants and workers in the country would benefit. In addition to the benefits, they would also have an opportunity to learn the technology. As such, it was beneficial for Chinese businessmen to set up factories.[51]

In 1901, he continued that China would also benefit from setting up foreign factories in the country.[52] In this view, the advantages of foreign direct investment in China far outweighed its disadvantages. First, it could create employment. Second, it was beneficial in enabling selling Chinese products. Third, Chinese businessmen could set up factories by learning advanced technology and management experience. Fourth, it could add revenue and improve the financial condition of the government. However, he opposed the idea that foreigners set up factories throughout China.

In 1898, Zhang Zhidong said in an article in his book *Encouraging Learning* that Chinese businessmen were not able to run the mining industry well because they lacked funds and knowledge about mining. He suggested sending a delegate abroad to learn about mines, who would return to China and exploit this new knowledge. However, learning

[50] He, Q. & Hu, L. (1994). *Xinzheng Zhenquan, Xinzheng Shiji* (The Real Interpretation of the New Policy · The Fundamental of New Policies, 新政真诠·新政始基). Liaoning: Liaoning People's Publishing House, p. 195.

[51] Zhang, Z. *Zhang Wenxianggong Quanji, Huashang Yong Jiqi Zhihuo Qing Conghuan Jiashui Bing Qing Gaicun Chuguan Zhanzhang Chengzhe, Juansishiwu* (Collected Works of Zhang Wenxiang, Vol. 45, 张文襄公全集·华商用机器制货请从缓加税并请改存储关栈章程折, 卷45).

[52] Zhang, Z. (1880). *Zhang Wenxianggong Quanji, Zhi Jiangning Liu Zhitai Shanghai Sheng Dachen, Juanyiqiwu* (Collected Works of Zhang Wenxiang Vol. 175, 张文襄公全集·致江宁刘制台上海盛大臣, 卷175).

required much time. Thus, he suggested that alternatively, each province choose a mine and recruit Western people with experience as contractors for the mine factory. If the foreigners exploited the mine, the government would reward them. If they were unable to do so before the deadline, they would be punished. In this way, Chinese students, committee members, and craftsmen could also learn the technology. He further proposed a method that would exploit Westerners according to shares. Foreigners would only be able to hold shares of 30–40% (less than half).[53] Exploitation in partnership with Westerners was an unprecedented approach initially proposed by Zhang Zhidong, who discussed Sino-foreign joint ventures in the early days.

[53] Zhang, Z. (1998). *QuanxuePian, Kuangxue Dishiyi* (Exhortation to Learning Mining science XI, 劝学篇· 矿学第十一). Zhengzhou: Zhongzhou Ancient Books Publishing House, p. 155.

CHAPTER 6

The Thought of Improving Technology

The successful experience of the world's modern countries in economic development indicates that the fundamental approach toward ensuring enterprises' progress and development is technology dependent. Enterprises improve by selecting and fully using advanced technology. Once its operation becomes increasingly scientific and standardized, "great efficiency" can be realized, namely the imbalanced combination of direct working time and output. Marx referred to this as "motive power" or "science strength".[1] Enterprises in developing countries must strengthen scientific and technological innovation to catch up with developed countries in a short time. The first way to do this is to learn the technology of developed countries and introduce advanced equipment and proprietary technologies. The second is to cultivate domestic technology to innovate based on the original technology, which will enable becoming as strong as the Western powers.

[1] Marx, K. & Engels, F. (1979). *Makesi Engesi Quanji, Di Sishiliu Juan, Xiace* (Collected Works of Karl Marx and Friedrich Engels, Vol. 46, II, 马克思恩格斯全集, 第46卷, 下册). Beijing: People's Publishing House, pp. 217–218

J. Zhou, *Westernization Movement and Early Thought of Modernization in China*, Palgrave Studies in Economic History,
https://doi.org/10.1007/978-3-030-86985-4_6

6.1 Introduction of Foreign Advanced Technology

The introduction of foreign advanced technology includes the application of hard and soft technology. To introduce foreign advanced technology, Li Hongzhang proposed that first, western machines had to be introduced, and second, western craftsmen had to be employed.[2]

For example, Jiangnan Manufacturing Bureau was established using the machines and equipment left by American businessmen purchased abroad. Until 1891, as a large-scale military factory, it had been expanded into 13 factories including machines, wrought iron, and steamships. Moreover, it had 662 machine tools including lathes and drilling machines of different sizes, and 361 steam-powered machines. The equipment of the Hanyang Iron Works, founded by Zhang Zhidong, was bought by Liu Ruifen, who was entrusted by Zhang at a British company. The Works was "the first in Asia" in terms of its large scale and vast investment. The US Ambassador to Hankou noted, "that was the most advanced movement for China to make weapons, steel rails, and machines thus far, because the factory was efficient and large scaled. It would take hours to walk around with a hurried glance."[3]

General Private Capital enterprises restricted by capital had a lower level of mechanization than Westernization enterprises, and fierce market competition forced them to continually update their equipment. For example, the printers established through private capital in Shanghai introduced lithographic machines abroad to compete with foreign-invested enterprises. This was popular in China based on excellent technology.[4]

Economics states that for both sides of the supply and demand chain to reach a satisfactory equilibrium in terms of price and quantity, it should be based on the premise of complete information. The demand side would

[2] *Haifang Dang, Bing, Jiqiju Yi* (Coast Defense Files IV, Machinery Bureau (a), 海防档, 丙, 机器局). Taiwan: Institute of Modern History, Academia Sinica, p. 5.

[3] *Yangwu Yundong Juanba* (Westernization Movement, Vol. 8, 洋务运动, 卷8). Shanghai: Shanghai Renmin Chubanshe, p. 462.

[4] (1893). *North China Daily News*. *Shanghai Jinxi Guan* (Shanghai's Today and Yesterday, 上海今昔观), p. 11. As cited in Sun, Y. (1957). *Zhongguo Jindai Gongyeshi Ziliao, Diyiji, Shangce* (Materials for the Modern History of Industry in China, Vol. 1, 中国近代工业史资料, 第1辑上册). Beijing: Science Press, p. 74.

be cheated if they lacked knowledge on the products. This may result in buyers purchasing low-quality products at a high price. During the Westernization Movement, this phenomenon was universal. For example, sellers sold used items at the best quality prices, and buyers were oblivious as they lacked the knowledge to realize this. As another example, the first chief of the China Merchants Steamship Navigation Company, Zhu Qi-ang, was repeatedly cheated in the process of buying advanced western equipment because of his lack of shipping knowledge. The same was true for Zhang Zhidong.[5] When ordering the Steel-making facilities from English company, Zhang Zhidong refused suggests doing some investigations to choose ideal sets. This was the bitter cost paid by the Westernization Group for the introduction of technology.[6]

1. Employing western craftsmen

Based on the theory, the introduction of soft technology includes introducing "intelligence" and foreign proprietary technology. During the Westernization Movement, Chinese enterprises did not buy too many foreign patents, as they were mainly limited by the introduction of intelligence by employing foreign experts. At that time, foreign experts had been working in the Westernization military enterprises throughout the year. The military factory founded by Li Hongzhang employed many famous foreign experts such as Macartney Halliday, James Stewart, Robert Mcllwraith, and Zuo Zongtang's military factory included renowned foreign experts like Prosper Giquel, Paul-Alexandre Neveue d'Aiguebelle.

While foreign experts improved the manufacturing technology and management practices, they also gave rise to numerous problems. One was their high payment, which increased the cost of the products. Sheng Xuanhuai said to Li Hongzhang that every year, the China Merchants

[5] Liu, G. (1995). *Li Hongzhang Pingzhuan, Zhongguo Jindaihua De Qishi* (Biography of Li Hongzhang: The Beginning of Chinese Modernization, 李鸿章评传——中国近代化的起始). Shanghai: Shanghai Classics Publishing House, pp. 109–110.

[6] Ye, J. *Han Yeping Chansheng Zhi Lishi, Yangwu Yundong, Juanba* (Comment on History of the Origin of Han Yeping Steel Company, Westernization Movement, Vol. 8, 洋务运动·汉冶萍产生之历史, 卷8), pp. 526–528.

Steamship Company had to pay much money for Westerners.[7] However, many people did not actively work. According to him, it was difficult to recruit a western employee rather than raise money.[8] His words reflect that on one hand, technology played an important role in modern enterprises. On the other, it was difficult to search for a foreign specialist. Furthermore, the monopoly of foreign experts would threaten national security. At that time, most foreign experts worked in the official enterprises that played an important role in people's livelihood and national defense. The Westernization Group was concerned about the situation, believing that once the war broke out, these people would likely resign, and the Chinese people would not be able to assume their heavy responsibilities. This was a very dangerous situation. They, therefore, suggested opening a school and cultivating their own talent.

Of course, the Westernization officials were not willing to hire foreign experts over the long term. In their view, the long-term policy was to cultivate their technical personnel. Li Hongzhang said that if craftsmen could learn to use the equipment and master the skills required, they might use them on their own and learn from each other.[9] However, Chinese society could not enrich itself by learning from Western countries. Moreover, officials of the Westernization Group lacked new industry technology and management experience. The group's own administrative system excluded the possibility of selecting and cultivating officials. Therefore, their military factories had to employ foreign experts for a long time, from which stemmed serious disadvantages.

Thus, how should the most capable foreign experts be selected? The Westernizationists suggested the following in this regard:

> First, experts had to be paid a high wage. Hu Yufen stated, "Fewer experts are specialized in mining in China; thus, most are reluctant

[7] Sheng, X. (1889). *Shengdang: Shang Li Hongzhang Zoutie* (The petition to Li Hongzhang, 盛档: 上李鸿章奏贴). As cited in Xia, D. (1998). *Sheng Xuanhuai Zhuan* (The Biography of Sheng Xuanhuai, 盛宣怀传). Tianjin: Nankai University Press, p. 248.

[8] Sheng, X. (1876). *Shengdang: Sheng Xuanhuai Zhi 000 Han* (Archives Materials for Sheng Xuanhuai: Sheng Xuanhuai "To 000", 盛档: 盛宣怀致000函). As cited in Xia, D. (1998). *Sheng Xuanhuai Zhuan* (The Biography of Sheng Xuanhuai, 盛宣怀传). Tianjin: Nankai University Press, p. 188.

[9] *Yangwu Yundong, Juansi* (Westernization Movement, Vol. 4, 洋务运动, 卷4). Shanghai: Shanghai Renmin Chubanshe, p. 244.

to come to the country. Anyone willing to come to China is not a real expert. All he wants is the profit. Therefore, if we want to develop mining enterprises, we must first hire experts, and to do so, we need to pay them a high wage." To what extent should they have been paid? The Westernizationists had no clear answer, but the wage had to be higher than that in their own country. Only in this way, would foreign experts be willing to come to China, despite its faraway location.

Second, the warrant of a foreign consular officer was essential. In 1885, Zhong Tianwei proposed his idea in *How to Eliminate Drawbacks in the Telegraph Ship II*, that in Western countries, a captain had credentials issued by the state. "Captains employed by us also have credentials. The environment plays an important role for humans. While foreigners once enjoyed the Chinese food and pension, they soon revert to their native habits. They gamble and engage with prostitutes, get drunk, and shy away from work. As a result, they are careless when sailing. According to Western rules, if an accident happens, the captain is imprisoned for like or his license is revoked." However, in China, the inequality of the consular jurisdiction meant they got away with their actions and were not charged for the loss they caused. In view of this situation, Zhong Tianwei advocated that "hiring foreign captains should be warranted by a consular officer from their own country, who should be asked to pay 10,000 taels as a cash deposit. All that is prohibited should be indicated in the contract, and the penalty/fine for prostitution and alcoholism prescribed. If an accident occurs, the whole penalty will be confiscated, and the person responsible punished for the crime. This will ensure that foreigners and merchants are wary of unscrupulous behavior."[10]

Third, the minister in foreign countries must pay close attention to the dynamics of foreign technology markets, get to know the level of foreign technical experts and position of these experts in his country, and what they did in effective projects should be determined. Zheng Guanying proposed that the "general administration should send

[10] Zhong, T. *Yuezu Ji, Waipian* (Outer Chapters of Zhong's Righteous Words, 刖足集.外篇).

ministers to visit renowned ore mining engineers with mining experience in other countries. They should be appointed regardless of expense to ensure we employ foreign talent."[11]

Moreover, for technological advancement, some Westernizationists pointed out the importance of novelty when employing foreign experts. In 1873, Sheng Xuanhuai, returning from the Fuzhou Arsenal, told Li that as the foreign experts had long been in China, they no longer possessed knowledge of the newest technology of recent years.[12] As such, Sheng proposed paying attention to updating the knowledge structure when hiring foreign experts.

6.2 Cultivation of Domestic Technical Personnel

The Westernization Group understood that relying on foreign craftsmen would be preliminary in the bid to revive the nation through foreign skills. It would be more important to cultivate domestic talent. The measures the Westernizationists used to cultivate domestic talent can be categorized as follows:

1. Chinese learners should be dispatched to learn from the foreign experts who visit China

After the Second Opium War, Wei Yuan proposed an idea of "learning the advanced technologies in the West to resist the invasion of the Western powers." He also discussed how to learn foreign skills. It was suggested a dockyard and firearm factory to be established in Guangdong, and Western technicians and experts hired to master the construction of the ships and machines. Furthermore, Western captains should be recruited to teach us how to sail, and artisans selected to teach casting skills. Soldiers

[11] Zheng, G. *Zheng Guanying Ji, Kaikuang Xia, Shangce* (Zheng Guanying Works Mining II, Vol. 1, 郑观应集·开矿下·上册). Shanghai: Shanghai Renmin Chubanshe, p. 711.

[12] Sheng, X. (1873). *Sheng Xuanhuai Shang Li Hongzhang Bing, Shiye Han Dian'gao, Shangce* (Official report to Li Hongzhang form Sheng Xuanhuai,Business Correspondence, Vol. 1, 盛宣怀上李鸿章禀, 实业函电稿, 上册), p. 4. As cited in Xia, D. (1998). *Sheng Xuanhuai Zhuan* (The Biography of Sheng Xuanhuai, 盛宣怀传). Tianjin: Nankai University Press, p. 249.

should be selected to learn how to attack when sailing, so that over time, we will master the technology and no longer rely on foreigners. Over time, we will be able to keep improving our skills and manufacture our own ships and firearms. After reaching this level, "we will be able to forge ahead overseas and fight the foreign barbarians at sea."[13] When Zuo Zongtang and Shen Baoczhen established Fuzhou Arsenal, they applied the theory of Wei Yuan to practice. To ensure Chinese technicians could master the shipbuilding technology, Shen Baozhen, the Minister of Vessel Administration, asked both parties to enter into a contract when hiring experts to ensure the Chinese technicians were trained to the level of operating the ship independently. In 1873, Shen submitted a memorial to the throne: "Initially, we are focusing on studying, not manufacturing. The foreign experts must leave China without the excuse that the students have not graduated."[14]

2. Establish a new system for schools and cultivate Westernization talent

Zuo Zongtang believed there was a big difference between China and foreign countries in the training of talent: "China's knowledge lies in the empty, while the wisdom of foreign countries lies in the real. China centers on beliefs first and technology last, while foreign countries are the opposite;"[15] "Chinese talent is better than foreign talent; however, they concentrate on morality rather than technology. Thus, they sometimes present their shortcomings."[16] To change this situation, Li Hongzhang suggested imitating the educational system in Western countries and established Tianjin Naval Academy, Wubei Academy, Weihai Naval Academy, Lushun Torpedo School, the Telegraph School in Tianjin, and Tianjin Western Medicine Academy.

[13] Wei, Y. *Haiguo Tuzhi, Chouhai Pian, Yizhan, Juaner* (海国图志·筹海篇·议站, 卷2), p. 11.

[14] Shen, B. *Sheng Wensugong Zhengshu, Xuchen Gechang Gongcheng Bing Tiaoyan Jiangtu Ling Fangshou Zizao Zhe, Juansi* (Memorials of Shen Wensu, Vol. 4, 沈文肃公政书·续陈各厂工程并挑验匠徒试令放手自造折, 卷4), pp. 59–60.

[15] Zuo, Z. *Zuo Wenxanggong Quanji, Zougao* (Complete Works of Zuo Wenxiang · Memorials, Vol. 18, 左文襄公全集·奏稿, 卷18), p. 4.

[16] Zuo, Z. *Zuo Wenxanggong Quanji, Shudu* (Complete Works of Zuo Wenxiang · Letters, Vol. 9, 左文襄公全集·书牍, 卷9), p. 59.

However, Li Hongzhang only established military schools, which was likely inevitable as the military industry was at the center of the modernization development strategy of the Westernizationists. However, this did not meet the need for talent for the increasing number of Westernization civilian enterprises. Thus, at that time, some Westernization officials who supported these enterprises were concerned about the lack of talent available for them. Zhang Zhidong, who was appointed Governor-general of Hubei and Hunan, had presided over the handling of a series of civilian industrial enterprises in Hubei Province. At the time, it was difficult to select the right professionals to shoulder the responsibility of the production technology and management of each enterprise, which posed challenges. To address the dilemma, Zhang Zhidong noted, "Talent is rare, especially regarding those specialized in foreign affairs and familiar with machines, guns, iron, and the cloth factories open in Hubei Province. However, there was not enough talent available to shoulder the responsibility of the management of these enterprises."[17] Thus, entering the 1890s, Zhang Zhidong focused more on industrial education, establishing in Hubei the Ziqiang Academy and Language Academy, as well as schools for mathematics, agriculture, technical skills, mining, dialectical business, as well as an East Railway School. For a time, these new types of schools in Hubei Province ranked first countrywide. In the long process of handling the Westernization enterprises, Sheng Xuanhuai realized that new talent was sorely needed to staff them. Thus, in the process of running the business, he launched training classes with an academic character, which he attached to the enterprise. Establishing the telegraph office, he founded the Telegraph Academy in Tianjin, Shanghai, and other places. Alongside supervising the construction of Hanyang Iron Factory, he also established academies attached to the factory. However, these short-term training courses focused on practical issues in the educational system, curriculum, and other aspects. As such, the theories and basic knowledge were not systematic enough, and could not be adapted to meet the needs of the further development of enterprises. Thus, in the early 1890s, he highlighted the importance of establishing a regular academy for the merchant marine and mining industries. After the Sino-Japanese War, with the support of Zhili Governor Wang Wenshao and Governor-general of Jiangnan and Jiangxi Liu Kunyi,

[17] *Yangwu Yundong Juanqi* (Westernization Movement, Vol. 7, 洋务运动, 卷7). Shanghai: Shanghai Renmin Chubanshe, p. 212.

Sheng founded Beiyang University and Nanyang University. The former is the predecessor of today's Tianjin University, and focused on training senior technical talent adapted to development. The latter is the predecessor of Shanghai Jiaotong University, which focused on cultivating talent to adapt to the development of policy, the economy, diplomacy, and other aspects.

3. Send students abroad

The best way for the Westernizationists to realize Self-Strengthening by learning Western technology was to send students abroad. The first to initiate this was Rong Hong, who devoted his life to the Westernization Movement. As early as 1868, he suggested to Jiangsu Governor Ding Richang that the government select outstanding young talent to study abroad to cultivate talents for China. Two years later, he asked Ding Richang to recommend this approach to Zeng Guofan. Zeng Guofan considered this appropriate. Thus, he and Li Hongzhang presented memorials to the court explaining the importance of sending talent abroad to acquire skills and technology with 12 terms. As part of their efforts, in 1872, the first group of students was sent to the United States under the leadership of Rong Hong, who established this precedent in modern China. Thereafter, the Fuzhou Arsenal also sent students to study in Britain and France to learn manufacturing and sailing technology, military navy and mining science, chemistry, and public law negotiation. Zuo Zongtang appreciated the policy of sending students to study abroad, considering it essential that the Chinese people do so to widen their horizons. He also proposed sending students to the United States, not only to Britain and France, and emphasized considering sending students to any country with advanced technology. He further advocated that this be done at no cost to the students.

Zhang Zhidong, leader of the Westernization Group in the last stage, continued the project of sending students abroad. During his governorship of Hubei and Hunan, he was keen to send students aboard. An *Exhortation to Learning*, he said that going abroad for one year was better than reading Western books for five years, which was the truth of Zhao Yingping: "Studying in a foreign academy for a year is better than studying in a Chinese one for three years.[18] After the coup of Gengzi, Zhang was saddened by stubborn bureaucrats' role in endangering the country, and contended again that "to strengthen the nation, sending more scholars abroad to study is the most important."[19]

Regarding the study major and destination, Zhang believed that Japan was better than the Western countries in various ways. The first was that Japan was nearer to China than Western countries, meaning it would be easier to monitor students' situations. The second was the lower fees. The third was that the Japanese language was close to the Chinese system, which made the Japanese easy to understand. The fourth was that the Japanese had abridged versions of Western books, which were easier to learn from. Therefore, in the late nineteenth and early twentieth centuries, a large number of students from Hubei were selected to study in Japan. According to rough statistics, this amounted to many thousands of students, putting Hubei Province at the forefront of sending students abroad to Japan.

In addition to selecting students to go abroad, the Westernizationists also advocated sending personnel abroad to further cultivate their knowledge in diplomacy, the military, and economics. In the 6th year of Tongzhi Reign (1867), Zuo Zongtang submitted a statement to Western-style Foreign Office, asking that the governors and Ministers of Vessel Administration in the coastal provinces of Jiangsu, Zhejiang, Fujian, Guangdong, and other provinces to be proficient in foreign languages. He also stated that the Westernizationists should determine the quota for the number of people, and send them abroad to study. This would enable selecting talent in diplomacy from this group.[20] Zhang also strongly supported sending officials abroad to study. After the Sino-Japanese War, in July 1895, he submitted a memorial to Guangxu that while Westernization had been progressing for several decades, few officials knew much about the domestic and foreign situation and no effort was spared in the reform. "We do not know the advantages of countries overseas; thus, we

[18] Zhang, Z. (1998). *Quanxue Pian, Youxue Dier* (Exhortation to Learning·Study Tour, 劝学篇·游学第二). Zhengzhou: Zhongzhou Ancient Books Publishing House, p. 116.

[19] Zhang, Z. *Zhang Wenxianggong Quanji, Zouyi, Juanwushi* (Collected Works of Zhang Wenxiang · Memorials, Vol. 50, 张文襄公全集·奏议, 卷50).

[20] Zuo, Z. *Zuo Wenxanggong Quanji, Shudu, Juanjiu* (Complete Works of Zuo Wenxiang · Letters, Vol. 9, 左文襄公全集·书牍, 卷9), p. 54.

do not realize their hostility. We should send officials to study abroad to solve these problems."[21]

Given that the officials sent to other countries did not understand foreign languages, Zhang advocated selecting talented scholars and dispatching them to various countries. He added that they should be provided with sufficient funds and that they study for one year. Furthermore, officials should be provided with a translator to ensure a better understanding of other countries and their industry, agriculture, military, gunboat battleships, and law cases, all of which had to be extensively studied. Zhang sent officials abroad and strengthened the management of the students to ensure that both officials and students were familiar with each other and able to distinguish who was talented and who was not.[22]

Given the financial difficulties of the Qing government, it was impossible to send more officials abroad. Thus, to improve efficiency, Zheng Guanying advocated sending ministers to study abroad to improve the quality and efficiency of the decision-making of the highest authorities. He explained that "the Chinese system and limited funding made it possible for us all to travel abroad as Westerners. Thus, we should select princes and ministers to travel abroad, as they know more about the ancient world and modernization. The young, who have not shouldered the responsibility of the country, should be sent abroad to learn about the pros and cons, and to improve them and ensure they cooperate with our envoys. All good ministers were once young, and they should obtain the skills and knowledge to ensure they rise above mediocrity."[23]

4. Reform the Imperial examination system

Saying that several measures were implemented to cultivate talent in foreign affairs outside the traditional education system, the reform of the Imperial examination system was the breakthrough in that system. In 1861, an early theorist of Westernization, Feng Guifen, published

[21] Zhang, Z. *Zhang Wenxianggong Quanji Zouyi, Juanershisi* (Collected Works of Zhang Wenxiang · Memorials, Vol. 24, 张文襄公全集·奏议, 卷24).

[22] Zhang, Z. *Zhang Wenxianggong Quanji Zouyi, Juansanshiqi* (Collected Works of Zhang Wenxiang · Memorials, Vol. 37, 张文襄公全集·奏议, 卷37).

[23] Zheng, G. (1982). *Zheng Guanying Ji, Youli Shangce* (Zheng Guanying Works • Journey, Vol. 1, 郑观应集·游历, 上册). Shanghai: Shanghai Renmin Chubanshe, p. 382.

Reform of the Imperial Examination System, *Manufacturing of Exotic Devices*, and other essays, becoming a pioneer of the education system reform in the 1860s. Soon after, Wang Tao, Zheng Guanying, and other Westernizationists continued the reform, publishing *Statement to Minister Ding*; *Reform and Self-improvement*; *On Examination*, *Western Culture*, and other works. Echoing this, Li Hongzhang and a number of Westernization officers submitted statements to the throne in an attempt to obtain Imperial support to put the ideal alternative examination system into practice. This triggered a wave of propaganda regarding the Imperial examination system in society.

The Westernizationists realized that the capitalist powers had come to China. After the two opium wars, China's isolation from the outside world was over. The new era required talent well versed in the world and in technology, and the military and translation. However, the traditional education system only guided scholars to focus on literature, which they could not apply to practice. To cultivate the relevant talent for the new era, the Imperial examination system had to be reformed.

However, people generally agreed that the traditional Imperial examination system would be difficult to transform; thus, they realized they should not attempt a complete transformation. The government should reform the content of the Imperial examination on one hand, and on the other, include courses in addition to the major subjects to test Western knowledge. The Western course would complement the subject, and its name would not be changed to that used in Western learning. This would reduce the resistance to implementing the reform. However, the Qing government did not accept this type of modest reform, and the traditional education system remained unchanged. In this situation, the Westernizationists could only establish more schools and select more students to study abroad to meet the demand of the new era. However, the existence of the Imperial examination system directly impacted the source and quality of students. Li Hongzhang said that other than school and ship training, there was no real place to cultivate students. Furthermore, the government and Ministry paid less attention to Westernization, and noble families refused to learn about it. This worried him, and he tried to fight for the benefits of affording school personnel with Western learning the appropriate status to reverse this unfavorable situation. In 1885, the Qing government made a decision to strengthen the navy. Li stated that talent for the navy should be selected. He recommended elevating the rank of school personnel, and that the government adopts stricter measures in assessing the law, which would enable them to dismiss those not performing appropriately.[24] Based on Li's efforts, in 1888, instructors and students of Tianjin Naval Military Academy, and students at the Shanghai Language School (*Shanghai Guangfangyan Guan*) and the School of Combined Learning (*Tongwen Guan*) undertook the Shuntian Provincial Examination. The provincial examination was the first implementation of Western and Chinese history to break through the barriers of traditional education.

After the Sino-Japanese war, more people became aware of the disadvantages of the Imperial examination system. At the time, the mainstream of Chinese intellectuals was no longer the reformation of the Imperial examination system, but its abolition. After Li returned from Europe, he wrote to a friend, exposing the shortcomings of the Imperial examination system. He stated that as it had been deeply rooted in China for centuries, reform could not undo the system's negative effects. Thus, he encouraged removing officials who advocated the Imperial system and canceling the spring and autumn examinations. He emphasized that the academy of classical learning had to change to a college and that students had to be taught specific courses each year and granted an official title after their graduation. In addition, he suggested canceling other ways of promotion, contending that after two decades, the environment would change and appropriate talent would by then have been cultivated. However, the Qing government did not think about changing the old system, and an aging Li had lost his political power. As such, his views were dismissed as utopian.[25]

In *Exhortation to Learning*, Zhang Zhidong did not propose abolishing the Imperial examination system, but highlighted the disadvantages thereof. He held the view that self-help begins with political reform, and political reform starts with educational reform. In the twentieth century, Zhang proposed the gradual abolition of the Imperial examination system. He noted that there existed much plagiarism in the system, and that homework tasks should focus more on reality. He considered the Imperial examination system as merely demonstrating one day

[24] *Yangwu Yundong Juaner* (Westernization Movement, Vol. 2, 洋务运动, 卷2). Shanghai: Shanghai Renmin Chubanshe, pp. 565–566.

[25] Li, H. *Li Wenzhonggong Chidu, Fu Yuanmu Chenyuqiao, Diershijiu Ce* (Letters of Li Wenzhong: Reply to the Governor Chen Yuqiao, Vol. 29, 李文忠公尺牍·复院幕陈雨樵, 第29册).

of performance, although school should instill the pursuit of life-long learning. "The Imperial examination system focused on the expression of words, but we were unable to see their moral standing. School learning focused on the cultivation of manners so that we could see their moral standing." In short, the school had absorbed the advantages of the Imperial examination system and eliminated the disadvantages thereof; nevertheless, to be feasible, Zhang recommended terminating the system within 10 years by diminishing posts to alleviate the resistance against the new education system by the social forces with traditional values. He also emphasized that the Imperial examination system was not being destroyed, but combined with the schooling system.[26] However, the situation worldwide and in China was developing rapidly, and a few years later, Zhang and Yuan Shikai petitioned to the throne that China abolish the Imperial examination system and build schools. The Qing government adopted their recommendations and announced the abolition of the Imperial examination system from 1906, which symbolized the death of medieval culture.

[26] Zhang, Z. Zhang Wenxianggong Quanji, Qing Shibian Dijian Keju Zhe, Juan Liushiyi (Collected Works of Zhang Wenxiang Official Report to Diminish Imperial Examination, Vol. 61, 张文襄公全集·请试边递减科举折, 卷61).

CHAPTER 7

Cultivating Personnel to Run Businesses

In the history of Economics, Marshall was the first to examine entrepreneurs as a factor of production. He believed that the role of the entrepreneur was to coordinate various factors of production organically and considered him a scarce social resource. Since then, Western economists have focused on entrepreneurs as the research object, proposing the concept of entrepreneurship to encompass the activities of business units (including decision-making) for the purpose of producing and selling goods either privately or in groups to engage in the economy and generate, maintain, or expand profit. Schumpeter discussed the entrepreneurial spirit in terms of adventure and innovation, and the role thereof in the development and progress of a society.

The Westernizationists wanted to apply Western methods to realize self-improvement, in which the selection and training of entrepreneurs specialized in modern business management was very important. The British and French bourgeoisie were mainly private businessmen and the traditional aristocracy who invested in new industries. Modernization in China was carried out through external forces, and Chinese entrepreneurs tended to be compradors or overseas Chinese.

J. Zhou, *Westernization Movement and Early Thought of Modernization in China*, Palgrave Studies in Economic History,
https://doi.org/10.1007/978-3-030-86985-4_7

7.1 Selection of Entrepreneurs for Government-Run Enterprises (Including Government Commerce Enterprises)

Based on who invested in enterprises in modern China, two types can be discerned: government-run enterprises (including government commerce enterprises) and commercial enterprises. The former was involved in investing in heavy industry and some light industry related to the military and involved large-scale investment, complex technology, and a high management standard. The latter was involved in light industry not related to the military and involved small-scale investment and simple technology and management requirements. The Westernization ministers were concerned about the selection and training of entrepreneurs in government-run enterprises, while the Westernization thinkers were worried about the selection and training of those in private enterprises. Here, the entrepreneurs were important in terms of building the micro-foundation of a new means of production. However, the Westernizationists were not knowledgeable of problems pertaining to entrepreneurs, although they had engaged in some communications on business.

The content of this book was extracted from numerous documents and historical materials relating to business, which also describe the selection and training of entrepreneurs. First, as mentioned, government-run enterprises (including government commerce enterprises) involved large-scale investment, complex technology, and high management standards, for which the Westernization ministers had certain requirements regarding entrepreneurs. These included the capacity to raise funds, personal wealth, and management capability, namely a "no shell fortune." Among the Chinese people at that time, only the compradors had these qualities; thus, they became the first generation of entrepreneurs in China in the 1870s. Tang Tingshu, Xu Run, Zheng Guanying, and other compradors took charge of the wheel, electricity, coal, textile, and other major companies of the Northern system, and operated metal, mining, and other enterprises in Guichi, Tianhua, Pingquan, and Sanshan in which they actively engaged. In addition, some officials in Li Hongzhang's Private Secretariat, such as Sheng Xuanhuai and Li Jinyong, mastered knowledge on modern enterprise management through a period of Westernization practice. After 1880, they successfully joined the enterprise business, playing an important role among Chinese entrepreneurs.

The selection of entrepreneurs for government-run enterprises was carried out by the Private Secretariats. Ten years of the Taiping Rebellion filled the Private Secretariats of the Hunan and Anhui armies with those specialized in Western technology to ensure it was capable of employing talent in modern industry and commerce during the Westernization process. The Private Secretariats comprised businessmen such as Zhu Qi-ang and Zhu Qizhao, who worked in junk shipping, and Ding Richang and Xu Run, who had compradorial family backgrounds. They worked as Li's aides and staff. Furthermore, some non-merchant staff had accumulated much experience in engaging in foreign affairs, such as Sheng Xuanhuai and Li Jinyong, who all became well-known entrepreneurs at that time. A third method of selection was based on introductions to business talent for government-run enterprises stemming from the extensive contact between staff and commerce. Introduced by Sheng Xuanhuai, Tang Tingshu and Xu Run became leaders of the China Merchants Steamship Navigation Company. These three men also introduced Zheng Guanying, who was employed in the Company as well.

1. Compradors attract the attention of the Westernization ministers

The compradors were a special class that arose with the penetration of Western capitalism in China's economy when the commodity-selling network was established for foreign investors. The compradors had accumulated considerable wealth in a surprisingly short time and ultimately became the *nouveau riche* of modern China. Because of their close contact with foreign businessmen, they realized the importance and attraction of new businesses earlier than others. Thus, they became the main force of business investment in China. For example, in 1873–1874, compradors' capital played an important role in the establishment of the China Merchants Steamship Navigation Company (investment of 476 thousand taels, accounting for 78% of paid-venture capital). Compradors' proportion of investment was also impressive in key industries of Chinese early modernization, such as mining, textiles, and the manufacturing of machinery.

The management capacity of the comprador businessmen was crucial for early modernization in China. They had close and long-term contact with foreign merchants as intermediaries and became experts in new business operation modes. This expertise was essential for China's early modernization, but out of reach of most other people at the time.

Wealth aside, the comprador businessmen also had a good knowledge of foreign languages and the Western commercial system. As such, they were respected by the Westernization ministers who were eager to apply Western methods to realize Self-Strengthening. The Westernization ministers had long considered that the only way to establish modern enterprises was to hire foreign experts, buy foreign machinery, and apply foreign technology. Compradors had become a bridge for them to contact Western countries. As such, the Westernization ministers hoped to achieve self-improvement through the relationship between compradors (and their vast wealth) and foreign merchants. Thus, in the 1860s, which signaled the rise of the Westernization Movement, compradors became the sweet pastry of local governors and Westernization ministers. In 1863, when Zeng Guofan and Li Hongzhang set up the machinery office, seeking Westernization talent, they found Rong Hong and Ding Richang. Rong Hong was the first student to graduate from Yale University, and after returning to his motherland, he became the comprador of Augustine Heard Co and Dent & Co. In 1863, he became a member of the staff of Zeng Guofan. Working there, he traveled to the United States in November that year to buy machinery. After returning to China in 1865, he acted as an interpreter of a qualified candidate commander, earning a monthly wage of 250 *Jin*. Ding Richang was also a comprador with scholar status. In 1864, Li Hongzhang appointed him Circuit Intendant of Susongtai, and the following year, he became responsible for funding the biggest military enterprise, namely the Jiangnan Manufacture General Bureau. He was soon promoted to governor of Jiangsu Province and became a Westernization minister. The China Merchants Steamship Navigation Company—China's first large-scale private enterprise in the modern capitalist period—was run by the compradors Tang Tingshu and Xu Run. In 1876, Li Hongzhang delegated Tang Tingshu to organize and operate the Kaiping Coal Mine, a large-scale Westernization enterprise. After contact with them, Li spoke highly of Tang Tingshu's proficiency in Westernization. Li also respected Xu Run in that he was familiar with the business. He praised Zheng Guanying for his elaboration. When Zheng Guanying was funding the Shanghai Mechanical Textile Bureau, he argued with his boss Peng Zongru and resigned. Li approved his resignation and repeatedly invited him to work with him, indicating Li's focus on Guanying's work.

The first effect of having compradors in Westernization enterprises was successful fundraising. Before Tang Tingshu and Xu Run worked for China Merchants, prospecting work in the Steamship Company was difficult. Li Hongzhang was concerned that if the shares were too small, the relationship may be affected. Once Tang Tingshu and Xu Run joined China Merchants, their popularity in the business sector helped them raise 1 million taels of capital. According to Li Hongzhang, "The shares have increased to nearly 1 million taels in two months, and it seems the Steamship Company can now be expanded."[1]

The second effect of compradors in Westernization enterprises was their successful management of large-scale modern enterprises. Before Tang Tingshu and Xu Run joined China Merchants Steamship Navigation Company, Li Hongzhang commissioned the Zhu Qi-ang, a junk shipping magnate, to take charge of the company. While known for his sound knowledge of the shipping industry, his business practice at China Merchants Steamship Navigation Company indicated that he did not have the ability to manage a modern enterprise. Tang Tingshu, considered the most experienced in the industry in China, found running the shipping business easy. To start with, he had his own ship. Second, as a director, he had conducted business with numerous foreign shipping companies. Third, and most important, he was a comprador to Jardine Matheson in Shanghai, where he worked for 10 years and had responsibilities related to the shipping business. Thus, in terms of business, Tang Tingshu was knowledgeable of shipping management. China Merchants thrived after Tang Tingshu and Xu Run joined. According to Li Hongzhang, "in the past 40 years, the attraction of investing in the steamship industry has been most successful."[2] Ding Richang also praised Tang Tingshu: "He is well known worldwide and in China, is good in foreign languages, and has acquired profound insight through his experience."[3]

[1] Li, H. *Li Wenzhonggong Quanshu, Pengliao Hangao, Juanshisan* (Works of Li Hongzhang, Letters from/to Friends and Colleagues, Vol. 13, 李文忠公全书·朋僚函稿, 卷13).

[2] Li, H. *Li Wenzhonggong Quanshu, Pengliao Hangao, Juanshisan* (Works of Li Hongzhang, Letters from/to Friends and Colleagues, Vol. 13, 李文忠公全书·朋僚函稿, 卷13).

[3] Institute of Modern History, Academia Sinica. (1957). *Haifang Dang, Yi, Fuzhou Chuanchang, Er* (Coast Defense Files II, Fuzhou Arsenal, Two, 海防档, 乙, 福州船厂二). Taiwan: Institute of Modern History, Academia Sinica, p. 686.

2. Entrepreneurs emerge from among officials

When China was transitioning from a traditional to modern society, many entrepreneurs emerged from among the officials because of the unstable market. Business development also requires strong government support. Since the country was involved in business development, some officials were included in the process. Thus, this group of entrepreneurs, the first official type, understood the economy and was good at managing officials. Because Li Hongzhang was engaged in the Westernization Movement from its earliest time, the early influential entrepreneurs were mostly from his Private Secretariat. Well-known entrepreneurs included Sheng Xuanhuai, an agent in Li Hongzhang's foreign trade office; Li Jinyong, a supervisor at Mohe Gold Ore; the brothers Yang Zonghan and Yang Zonglian, supervisors at the Shanghai Mechanical Textile Bureau; and Li Zongdai, a gold supervisor at Shandong Pingdu. They all worked in Li Hongzhang's Private Secretariat, mainly in military work and the supply of logistics. This work often sent them to conduct business between Tianjin and Shanghai and other places, and the purchasing of munitions and other items. As such, they had access to new things, new ideas, and new technology, helping them become potential entrepreneurs in Li Hongzhang's Private Secretariat.

Between the compradors and official entrepreneurs, the officials tended to pay more attention to official business. This is because comprador entrepreneurs approached business from a merchant perspective, focusing on profit. In contrast, the official entrepreneurs approached it from an official viewpoint, which was more conducive to achieving national goals. This preference for official entrepreneurs is evident in Li Hongzhang's praise of Sheng Xuanhuai, who he said had great talent and an attentive mind, and whose familiarity with foreign affairs he respected. Li said, "now that people are familiar with Westernization, there has been a separation of officialdom, the livelihood of the people, and officials. Westernization and the officials should not be divided, and Sheng Xuanhuai's measures have solved this problem. Second, because of this, when the province establishes a business, they first consider whether any shogunate officials have business experience." For example, for China Merchants Steamship Navigation Company, the first person Li Hongzhang considered was the junk shipping businessman Zhu Qi-ang. In the middle of the 1870s, with the domestic mining boom in China, the Qing government intended to open three mineral mines in Taiwan, Hubei, and Kaiping in

Hebei. Li Hongzhang handled mining products from Hubei, which for Sheng Xuanhuai, had the best environment for personnel. (At that time, Li Hanzhang, Li Hongzhang's brother, was Governor-general of Hubei and Hunan; the Huai Army comprised the local officials in charge of mines.) Li Hongzhang hoped Sheng Xuanhuai would succeed and serve as a model for places elsewhere. (Kaiping Coal Mine was hosted by the famous businessman Tang Tingshu.) However, subjective desire could not replace objective reality, and these officials had little knowledge of how to manage a modern enterprise. Thus, officials' first attempts often ended in failure. Unsuccessful endeavors include Zhu Qi-ang's tenure at China Merchants Steamship Navigation Company, and Sheng Xuanhuai and Li Jinyong's management at Hubei Coal Mine. Thus, Sheng Xuanhuai was criticized by Li Hongzhang for his "ridiculousness."[4] However, these failures also taught the officials valuable lessons they could apply in the future of the mine and other undertakings, thus creating favorable conditions.

Li Hongzhang knew how to motivate his official entrepreneurs. Most had irregular backgrounds, and appeared in the political arena in the late Qing Dynasty. They were active in the suppression of the Taiping Rebellion, and met during the rise of the Westernization Movement. To gain an advantage in the competition with officials, they too had to be able to achieve great things.

In the late Qing Dynasty, great things had to do with Westernization, which while the officials had no interest in, was important to the Qing government. As such, as long as they were able to manage activities related to Westernization, their position as officials was safe. Li Hongzhang advised Sheng Xuanhuai to do great things and become an official. This was also an incentive for all staff who became official entrepreneurs.

In the late 1870s, when Sheng Xuanhuai ran the coal mine in Hubei, Li Hongzhang often wrote to him to remind him that "if this factory does not make a profit in Hubei for several years, other people will look down on you."[5] In 1886, Sheng Xuanhuai wanted to go to the Beiyang for

[4] Li, H. (1881). Shengdang: *Zha Sheng Xuanhuai* (Archives for Sheng Xuanhuai: Letter for Sheng Xuanhuai, 盛档: 札盛宣怀). As cited in Xia, D. (1998). *Sheng Xuanhuai Zhuan* (*The Biography of Sheng Xuanhuai*, 盛宣怀传). Tianjin: Nankai University Press, p. 61.

[5] Quoting from Xia, D. (1998). *Sheng Xuanhuai Zhuan* (*The Biography of Sheng Xuanhuai*, 盛宣怀传). Tianjin: Nankai University Press, pp. 138–139.

senior officials and no longer work at China Merchants Steamship Navigation Company. However, Li Hongzhang told him: "Like a key business transition, you should stay in Shanghai, and gradually this work will have an effect. Do not rush into being an official. Just wait for the right time."[6] He wanted Sheng Xuanhuai to know that it was not the time to become a Beiyang official. The time was right to complete the work of the Westernization Movement, and if successful, he would obtain a position satisfied as an officer. Essentially, ensuring the success of Westernization would ensure his success in becoming an official.

Compared to the compradors, the official entrepreneurs lacked experience in the management of modern enterprises. However, as Westernization progressed, this weakness was largely addressed. Furthermore, their close relationship with the government meant they had access to government capital and support, which was difficult for comprador entrepreneurs. When the steamship company acquired Qi Chang, it faced a shortage of funds. However, after obtaining a large sum of capital from the Governor-general of Jiangnan and Jiangxi Shen Baozhen, Sheng Xuanhuai earned newfound respect from Tang Tingshu and Xu Run. Therefore, until the 1880s, the number of entrepreneurs that emerged from among the officials increased, and they became an important part of the Westernization group's official business. The Westernization officials had much praise for the business acumen of the official entrepreneurs. In 1896, in a telegram to Wang Wenshao on the situation at Hanyang Iron Factory and the Luhan Railway, Zhang Zhidong praised Sheng Xuanhuai: "Look around. Officials know nothing about business, and businessmen know nothing of Westernization and disregard the situation in general. They have no knowledge of the Chinese regime, or are prone to being bullied by foreigners, or lack experience, or dare to deceive, but they are not able to achieve in practice".[7] Simply put, only Sheng Xuanhuai could take charge of the job.

The quality and performance of the state enterprise officials during the period of the Westernization of entrepreneurs indicate that many had the

[6] Quoting from Xia, D. (1998). *Sheng Xuanhuai Zhuan* (*The Biography of Sheng Xuanhuai*, 盛宣怀传). Tianjin: Nankai University Press, pp. 139–140.

[7] Sheng, X. (1894). *Yuzhai Cungao, Juan Bashijiu, Buyi Liushiliu* (Memorials of Sheng Xuanhuai, Vol. 89, Supplement 66 愚斋存稿, 卷89, 补遗66), p. 8. As cited in Xia, D. (1998). *Sheng Xuanhuai Zhuan* (The Biography of Sheng Xuanhuai, 盛宣怀传). Tianjin: Nankai University Press, p. 198.

ability to manage a modern enterprise, spirit beyond the profit motive, and career dedication. Illustrating this is the fire incident in Yang Zonghan and Yang Zonglian's Shanghai Mechanical Textile Bureau: "Hundreds of millions were lost in an instant and people had to jump to safety. The fire died thereafter."[8] As a business representative of Li Hongzhang's Westernization of Beiyang, Li Jinyong supervised the Mohe County Gold Mine: "All articles of association, quite properly.[9] In addition, the Mohe County Gold Deposit was a productive enterprise under President Li Jinyong. In the 21st Year of the Guangxu Reign, Li Jinyong died of exhaustion in Mohe County in December. People pitied him. After Li Jinyong died, people regard Li as the guardian of the Mohe Mining Factory."[10]

7.2 Selecting Business Enterprise Entrepreneurs

While the development of officials in the modern military industry was confined to economic issues, Westernization thinkers could consider the new economic future from a longer-term perspective. They paid much attention to the development of folk capital and the selection and cultivation of business operators.

Because business enterprises were characterized by smaller investments, and the technology and management thereof were relatively simple, the requirements for business entrepreneurs were not as high as those for official entrepreneurs. At that time, the Westernization thinkers selected business entrepreneurs from among traditional compradors, businessmen, officials, and overseas Chinese businessmen.

1. Compradors

The author has discussed in detail problems pertaining to the status of comprador entrepreneurs in modern China, focusing on the selection of entrepreneurs. Thus, it is not delved into here as well. Here, the only thing to emphasize is that the compradors were the first in modern China

[8] (1894, Jul 22). *Shenbao* (The Chinese Newspaper Shenbao, Shanghai News, 申报).

[9] (1889, May 21). *Shenbao* (The Chinese Newspaper Shenbao, Shanghai News, 申报).

[10] (1918). *Mohe Jinkuang Yan'geshilve* (Mohe County Gold History Biography, 漠河金矿沿革事略).

interested in investing in the new industrial era. As they also had the capital to invest, they played an important role among the earliest official business entrepreneurs and business enterprise entrepreneurs. Because of the low probability of being selected as an official in a large enterprise, most compradors acted as entrepreneurs in business enterprises.

2. Traditional businessmen investing in new industries

Mao Zedong said that the invasion of foreign capitalism "has not only played a role in breaking the foundation of China's traditional economy but has also brought about objective conditions and the possibility to develop capitalist production in China."[11] In Shanghai, Guangzhou, and other ports, because of foreign enterprises, state enterprises, and overseas Chinese compradors were stimulated by high business profits, the interest of traditional merchants in the new industrial era increased, and they mastered the technology and gained management experience, laying the foundation of self-built enterprises. For example, Jichanglong Silk Filature Factory, which produced silk through overseas Chinese businessman Chen Qiyuan, was founded in Guangzhou. The silk was "smoother and cleaner than that produced by hand, but the price more expensive."[12] Under his influence, many imitators appeared in the surrounding area, greatly promoting the development of Guangdong and its silk spinning industry. According to the *The South China Sea County Annal*, "in 3 to 4 years, Nanhai and Shunde now have up to 100 households." In 1901, "the whole province was using machinery for spinning. Thousands of women were hired to do this work. Silk exports now amount to over 40 million taels."[13] Guangdong had become the center of the Chinese silk spinning industry using modern machinery.

The Westernization Group predicted the utility model for the new industry and commerce. In early 1865, Li Hongzhang said upon building the iron factory, "Foreign machinery has benefited farming and weaving, printing, and pottery. It can also help in manufacturing and daily life.

[11] Mao, Z. (1991). *Mao Zedong Xuanji, Dierjuan* (Selected Works of Mao Zedong, Vol. 2, 毛泽东选集, 第2卷). Beijing: People's Publishing House, p. 626.

[12] Zheng, Y. (1910). *Nanhai Xianzhi Juanershiliu* (The South China Sea County Annal, Vol. 26, 南海县志, 第26卷).

[13] Zheng, Y. (1910). *Nanhai Xianzhi Juanershiyi* (The South China Sea County Annal, Vol. 21, 南海县志, 第21卷).

The original machinery was not designed for arms. The advantage in the power of the use of force is saving on labor costs." Therefore, he predicted that once the environment gradually opened after decades, "Wealthy Chinese entrepreneurs will copy Westernization machinery in the pursuit of benefits."[14] Wang Tao called on the government to comply with the people's pursuit of profit and allow them to open their own companies: "Wealthy men invest capital, but the poor work hard. All can benefit."[15]

From the 1860s to 1870s, traditional Chinese businessmen invested in the shares of foreign enterprises and those in the Westernization Movement. Since 1880s, private capital has been invested in independent modern industrial enterprises in the form of start-ups, a practice that peaked after the Sino-Japanese War. *The Chinese Newspaper Shenbao* described the private capital used to invest and establish factories as follows: "Today, Chinese culture has opened up. Chinese businessmen all know the importance of benefits, so they do not want to have shares in Western companies. They want to set up their own company with its own shares. Chinese business is moving toward achieving its potential."[16]

More traditional merchants began investing in start-up factories, strengthening the power of Chinese entrepreneurs and signaling the fruition of the modernization and growth of China. The Westernization thinkers were pleased that traditional merchants were investing in new industries. Wang Tao pointed out that "in the old times, Chinese entrepreneurs had to rely on Westerners. Chinese businesses had enough products, but did not know how to sell them overseas. They could only listen to the commands of the businessmen of the West. Over ten years, Chinese businesses have become good at running affairs with foreign countries, reducing the profits of Western businessmen in China. The Chinese businessmen were like those from Hong Kong who went to Annan and Siam to purchase rice. Because the Chinese labor force is very

[14] Li, H. *Li Wenzhonggong Quanshu, Zhiban Waiguo Tiechang Jiqi Zhe, Juanjiu* (Complete Works of Li Wenzhong: Purchase Foreign Steel Industry, Vol. 9, 李文忠公全书·置办外国铁厂机器折, 卷9).

[15] Wang, T. (1998). *Taoyuan Wenlu Waibian, Zhong Min Zhong* (Tao Yuan's Works of Foreign Affairs · People Foremost Two, 弢园文录外编·重民中). Zhengzhou: Zhongzhou Ancient Books Publishing House, p. 63.

[16] (1889, Jun 9). *Shenbao* (The Chinese Newspaper Shenbao, Shanghai News, 申报).

cheap, those in the southeastern ocean and the Chinese helped each other, while Western trade was reduced."[17]

3. Officials

The officials referred to here are not those working as Westernization staff in the Private Secretariats. These are Qing government officials at all levels. These officials completed the Imperial examination and were well versed in classical culture. Why did they join in the new economy? One reason was the economic stimulation of high profits, and the other was that they were motivated to do so under the pressure of patriotism. As early as in the Sino-Japanese War, many active or retired officials were already tempted to profit from the new industry by anonymously investing their capital therein: "These officials also did business with other people, gaining a huge profit and honorable titles. If someone bribed others, he was punished. Many people invested money to conduct business, and it seemed as though the officials and businessmen were working together."[18] Society had not yet begun honoring businessmen, so business officials "worked as officials but had no right to conduct business." Only those opening and legally operating new industry ventures had a legitimate business identity, such as Sheng Xuanhuai, Li Jinyong, Yang Zonghan, Yang Zonglian, and Li Zongdai.

With the outbreak of the Sino-Japanese War, the Qing government realized the importance of developing e-commerce. It encouraged officials to join businesses, stating, "Officials have always invested relatively big sums in businesses. However, accustomed to old habits, these officials may be too ashamed to include their names in the trade. They usually changed their names or hired others to conduct business directly. Ultimately, this created many barriers between the officials and businessmen. The government should now highlight the importance of official business to eliminate prejudices and attract businessmen from all fields."[19] In times of crisis, the Chinese traditional government sent officials to work

[17] Wang, T. (1998). *Taoyuan Wenlu Waibian, Xiren Jianji Huashang* (Tao Yuan's Works of Foreign Affairs, 弢园文录外编·西人渐忌华商). Zhengzhou: Zhongzhou Ancient Books Publishing House, pp. 155–157.

[18] (1883, Nov 3). *Shenbao* (The Chinese Newspaper Shenbao, Shanghai News, 申报).

[19] *Shangwu Guanbao* (商务官报 第3册 第19期).

for a landlord. For example, during the Taiping Rebellion, Zeng Guofan was ordered to join the militia to suppress the uprising of scholar identity. Thus, "eliminate officialdom but conduct business" became a trend, and even the traditional champion became a great businessman in this way. In 1895, the new champion Zhang Jian established a cotton mill north of the Yangtze River in Nantong, and then became a gentle merchant. In 1896, another Tongzhi champion, Lu Runxiang, set up the Sulun Cotton Mill to the south of the Yangtze River in Suzhou. The names of champions qualified to run a business were whispered in admiration. In addition, other classes of gentlemen from the officialdom also ran a business, and consequently, special official entrepreneurs appeared.

A 1957 book *China's Modern Industrial History* states that "aside from the capital in China's economy from merchants or squires, foreign capitalists cannot see who is an official through the smokescreen. In other countries, officials are not always wealthy. However, in China, many officials make a lot of money through business. Thus, Chinese people including officials became gradually richer. When they retired, they implicitly manipulated politics, and the villagers feared them. The second is the merchants. As they were ranked either as officials or businessmen, there was no great difference and they often worked in government. In reality, they were engaged in commerce."[20]

Official engagement in business reflected the further development of industrialization and contributed to transforming public opinion regarding business. However, those stuck in the old cultural age, instead of saying the officials had knowledge of administration, said they understood Confucian classics and had experience of traditional officialdom. This was not sufficient in terms of managing a modern enterprise, meaning that if they were to become real entrepreneurs, they needed practical experience. Zhang Jian founded Dasheng Cotton Mill; while its development was blessed by the state, it lacked scientific strength.

After Dasheng Cotton Mill was established, Zhang Jian faced many challenges in raising capital. In dealing with these, his first consideration was not the introduction of technical and management personnel, but to strengthen relations with the government. He explained, "businessmen and officials know the importance of responsibility, and of

[20] Wang, J. (1957). *Zhongguo Jindai Gongyeshi Ziliao, Dierji, Xiace* (Materials for the Modern History of Industry in China, Vol. 2, II, 中国近代工业史资料, 第2辑下册). Beijing: Science Press, pp. 925–926.

generating benefits to reduce disadvantages." This was also the strategic basis of Zhang Jian's activities. Furthermore, around six managers worked with Zhang Jian as high-level decision makers. While most were businessmen and experts on the purchasing of raw material and sales in the cotton yarn market, they knew little about the management of production and technology. Thus, for the operations of the Dasheng Cotton Mill, internal planning and the external environment were coordinated, and making a profit was strategically prioritized in planning and decision-making. Furthermore, the mill focused on progress and developing relations to enrich its professional technical and management personnel, the management system was reformed, and the overall quality and management ability of enterprise members were optimized as secondary tactical requirements. However, putting "the cart before the horse" in terms of strategy and tactics negatively influenced the development of the enterprise, leading to the need for crisis management.[21]

4. Overseas Chinese businessmen investing in new industries

The Chinese had been living overseas since the record began. However, the Chinese government did not consider this important. Rather, the government saw these people as "without the father or the Emperor." This attitude prevailed until the Opium War, especially changing after the progress of the Westernization Movement. The outbreak of the Opium War, close link between the Chinese and world market, and free flow of the global labor force became inevitable. In 1860, Britain and France signed the Treaty of Beijing with the Qing government, which stated, "if a Chinese man wants to go abroad, the Chinese government should offer no resistance." This originated from an international law that required the Qing government to change the policy of persecuting Chinese people overseas. After the rise of the Westernization Movement, to find the funds needed to support modernization, the Westernization Group turned to overseas Chinese businessmen. The diplomat Huang Zunxian highlighted that the Chinese overseas had enough capital to help the motherland. Furthermore, "despite living overseas for more than 100 years, they had retained their Chinese traditions including customs for weddings,

[21] Duan, B. & Shan, Q. (1987). Investment Environment and Countermeasures of Dasheng Yarn Mill (大生纱厂的投资环境与对策). *Jianghai Academic Journal, 6*.

funerals, hosting, and sacrifice. In recent years, overseas Chinese businessmen donated large sums of money to be rewarded titles." Another Chinese diplomat, Xue Fucheng, also called attention to the Chinese overseas: "overseas Chinese had made contributions for the prosperity of Britain and Netherlands. Although they emigrated from China to other countries, it is never too late to unified to seek their support."[22]

However, Chinese social culture is not open, and the Chinese overseas were frequently persecuted, decreasing their enthusiasm to invest. Huang Zunxian and Xue Fucheng pointed out that the Chinese overseas wanted to return to China, but that while "some Chinese overseas want to return to China, they are advised not to do so as they would be treated badly upon their return. If they were framed, they would not be able to protect their rights. Some businessmen claiming to be Dutch did many things to endanger society, but the government dare not punish them."

To solve this problem, the government needed to develop regulations to protect the Chinese overseas: "Ensure the Chinese overseas want to live in China. If something bad were to happen to them, the government must protect their rights." The Qing government approved their request, and the coastal governors instructed: "If businessmen with foreign marriage, interest, or willingness are given a passport by ministers or consular officers, return home and defraud those on the mainland, they will be treated according to the law of punishment."[23]

The change of policy in the late Qing Dynasty provided the conditions for Chinese businessmen overseas to invest. According to the data records, overseas Chinese enterprises were established in the early 1860s, and Mr. Li, a businessman in Peru, began operating the import and export trade in Guangzhou in 1862. In 1872, Nanyang Chen Qiyuan founded in Guangdong a silk spinning machinery factory with tons of silver from the trade across the South China Sea. This was the first industry to attract overseas Chinese investment. Zhang Bishi (Zhenxun), who is from Indonesia and was born in Dapu, Guangdong, established the Yantai

[22] Xue, F. (1987). *Xue Fucheng Xuanji, Qing Huochu JiuJin Zhaolai Huamin Shu* (Selected Works of Xue Fucheng, Please Exclude the Old Ban to Welcome Oversea Chinese, 薛福成选集·请豁除旧禁招徕华民疏). Shanghai: Shanghai Renmin Chubanshe, p. 494.

[23] Xue, F. (1987). *Xue Fucheng Xuanji, Qing Huochu JiuJin Zhaolai Huamin Shu* (Selected Works of Xue Fucheng, Please Exclude the Old Ban to Welcome Oversea Chinese, 薛福成选集·请豁除旧禁招徕华民疏). Shanghai: Shanghai Renmin Chubanshe, pp. 495–497.

Zhangyu Wine Co. Ltd. Because of its sufficient capital, it introduced the world's most advanced technology, which enabled producing high-quality wine and the wine of brandy, winning the gold prize in Paris before the First World War. As such, it became a source of national pride in modern China.

Why were the overseas Chinese businessmen an important part of the modern entrepreneurs in China? They founded the national capital machinery industry. In the decades after the Opium War, small production was dominant in society. Few people saw and knew about large capitalistic machinery production other than overseas Chinese businessmen who had witnessed the superiority thereof and accumulated monetary capital concurrently. Imitating what they saw, they returned to China and invested in establishing profitable factories. For example, Chen Qiyuan, who founded Jichanglong Silk-filature Factory, returned to China to invest because, "I saw the silk manufactured by French machinery was exquisite when I did business in Siam, so I wanted to imitate that out of admiration." According to the records, in 1872, Chen, a merchant operating across the South China Sea, returned from the South Asia and founded Jichanglong Silk-filature Factory in his hometown of Xiqiaojian Village. This factory "made silk with French machinery." In addition, "the factory employed 600–700 female workers and earned substantial profits from the exquisite silk it produced, which was marketed in Europe and America at a price twice as high as before." After the 1894–1895 Sino-Japanese War, the Qing government changed traditional government-run industry policies to encourage private capital investment to resist foreign capital investment in China. Based on the weak domestic capital, the Qing government anchored their hope on overseas Chinese businessmen, and sent officials to the coastal provinces to invite investment. The expectation was to attract wealthy overseas Chinese businessmen to take over the poorly managed official military industry. In an Imperial edict, Guangxu Emperor stated that "many wealthy Chinese merchants who live in the islands of southeast China including San Francisco must be willing to follow accept the government's invitation of investment. Bian Baoquan, Tan Zhonglin, and Ma Piyao are commanded to select clean and proper officials to send there to announce the will of the court and dispatch officials to manage recruitment. If a merchant is willing to invest, he can collect and charge the original factory or collect personal capital stock out of the official factory to build a new factory on a new site, all according to Western examples."[24]

However, the Chinese overseas did not have the ability to undertake the important task of modernizing China's Westernization. Overseas Chinese capital tended to be family-run and there is a close relationship between employers and employees. This characteristic was more suitable to managing small capital, short-term plans, and profitable operations, not intensive capital, and large-scale enterprises with complex or long-term planned operations. Apparently, this was inconsistent with the development strategy of China's Westernization, which prioritized the development of heavy industry. Thus, it was difficult to undertake the important task of the modernization of China's Westernization.

7.3 Government's Role in Supporting the Growth of Entrepreneurs

Entrepreneurs in early China faced considerable challenges including the invasion of official power of civil power, and barriers from traditional influences and concepts. Not only landlords were against them, but also craftsmen and farmers. Westerners reported the dilemma of mechanical sericulture in Guangzhou in June 1874: "Many people have objected to reeling silk with machines. Some criticisms are unreasonable, and others are simply horrible. People's main reason for objection is their belief that the machine power replacing manual operation will have evil consequences. The second reason is that having men and women work in the same workshop will breed immorality. The third reason is that craftsmen with poor skills can easily injure others when operating the machines. People are also against the noise of whistles and machines. Others think the chimneystack will harm fortune. A machine-operated silk-filature factory was recently established in Henan to which many people objected."[25]

The Westernization Group argued these difficulties could only be solved through government support. According to Zheng Guanying, "It

[24] As cited in (1895, Jun 21). *Wanguo Gong Bao* (The Review of the Times, 万国公报). August & September Issue, p. 27.

[25] (1874, Jun 3). *Jie Bao* (China Gazette, 捷报).

is difficult to raise a large amount of capital by only depending on official power. It will be much easier to raise commercial capital as well. If everything is brought about by merchants, local thugs may cause problems. In this case, relying on official power will cost much in terms of paying servants. Therefore, it must be government-supervised and merchant-managed: the merchant raises the capital to start construction with no practice favoritism and the government audits the operation to levy without extraordinary demand. The government and merchants working together will eliminate the two drawbacks."[26] Sheng Xuanhuai added that in China, "it is difficult to start a business and even harder to continue its operations. A business cannot be started without the support of government and continued without the operation of entrepreneurs."[27] Recognizing the significance of the *ancien regime* in supporting enterprise development, entrepreneurs of the time associated with government in the hope of obtaining some privileges in favor of their companies' development, and in turn, served the government greatly. For example, some private capital enterprises voluntarily branded their company as "government-supervised and merchant-managed" to ensure government protection.

However, with the growth of enterprise strength and ability to resist the external environment, enterprises no longer needed "protection" from the government. Thus, they became unwilling to pay the price for "protection," namely "favor" and other "contributions." They hoped the government would relinquish their microscopic management of enterprises and only regulate them at a macroscopic scale. In accordance with the development of the economies of western countries, which relied on merchants, thinkers of the Westernization Group expanded the market, and demanded the government exit the companies and merchants run their own business. The government's role would be only to protect and support merchants' activities by collecting tax. Zheng Guanying stressed that "revitalization of the business" must rely on private businessmen with

[26] Zheng, G. (1982). *Zheng Guanying Ji, Kaikuangshang, Shangce* (Zheng Guanying Works·Mining I, Vol. 1, 郑观应集・开矿上，上册). Shanghai: Shanghai Renmin Chubanshe, p. 704.

[27] Sheng, X. (1881). *Shengdang: Xiangding Dalue Zhangcheng Ershi Tiao* (Archives for Sheng Xuanhuai: Stipulation of Twenty Articles of General Regulations, 盛档: 详定大略章程二十条). As cited in Xia, D. (1998). *Sheng Xuanhuai Zhuan* (The Biography of Sheng Xuanhuai, 盛宣怀传). Tianjin: Nankai University Press, p. 75.

full autonomy in operation. He wrote: "To reorganize business, it must first follow business conditions that enable more easily doing things, not those beyond one's power and will. It will then be able to conduct business that generates a profit." He stressed that "in all treaty ports and central provinces where railways, steamships, mines, planting, weaving, and manufacturing should be constructed, it is generally permitted that these be opened by non-governmental organizations or people determined to raise equity or self-manage. Everything is in accordance with the principle of business without depending on an official system."[28] This was essentially the practice of "not relying on the power of officials or the gentry." Regarding the government's obligations in the process of modernization, Zheng said that "officers shall check tax collection and not engage in blackmail."[29] In other words, the duty of the government was only tariffs enactment to comfort merchants, and the internal management of an enterprise was independent, handled by the enterprise without government control or intervention. He believed that as long as this was done, the result would be "favorable and everything will flourish. Everything harmful will be abolished. I believe the benefits of Chinese business decades later will keep pace with the West."[30]

7.4 Improvement of Entrepreneurs' Operation Capacity

The Westernization Group realized that the prospect of the new economy in China depended on the operation capacity of Chinese entrepreneurs. For them, the lack of operational capacity of Chinese entrepreneurs could be attributed to the following:

[28] Zheng, G. (1982). *Zheng Guanying Ji, Shangwuer, Shangce* (Zheng Guanying Works·Commercial Affairs II, Vol. 1, 郑观应集·商务二, 上册). Shanghai: Shanghai Renmin Chubanshe, p. 617.

[29] Zheng, G. (1982). *Zheng Guanying Ji, Kaikuangshang, Shangce* (Zheng Guanying Works·Mining I, Vol. 1, *郑观应集・开矿上, 上册*). Shanghai: Shanghai Renmin Chubanshe, p. 704.

[30] Zheng, G. (1982). *Zheng Guanying Ji, Shangwusan, Shangce* (Zheng Guanying Works·Commercial Affairs III, Vol. 1, *郑观应集・商务三, 上册*). Shanghai: Shanghai Renmin Chubanshe, p. 612.

1. The narrow scope of candidates did not comply with the principle of the supremacy of power in a modern industrial and commercial society. For example, all kinds of modern enterprises, which first rose in treaty ports and then gradually formed a certain scale of industry, were developed at different levels with the aid of market conditions, producing a group of prominent tycoons worth hundreds of thousands or millions of taels, despite that the organization form and management means of these enterprises did not eliminate the formation of a trade association. Staff were always selected within the circle of kinsmen and countrymen. People were employed thanks to relatives and friends, and others were not considered at all. Ye Chengzhong, the leader of a Ningbo business group operating in Shanghai, reputed as a giant in business, was better at educating talent than other businessmen at the time. In his Laodeji Hardware Store, he "employed Western teachers to teach the gathered young talent languages, business, and taxation" by organizing night school every night.[31] However, Ye still failed to eliminate the relationship circle of the trade association in selecting and educating talent. People in the upper and middle management of his enterprises were mainly exceptional people from among his relatives and friends with the same census register as Ningbo, and based on the succession of teachings from a master or family. Ye's enterprises selected people in this way.

While businessmen were limited in terms of selecting talent from within the circle of kinsmen and countrymen, and could not recruit from society as a whole, the officials of the Westernization Group "chose talent based on official rank," which severely hindered the development of talent and harmed enterprises. This so-called "talent," selected based on official rank, was according to Jing Yuanshan, "men with the deepest official

[31] *Ye Gong Chengzhong Rongai Lu* (Records of Honored Ye Chengzhong, 叶公澄衷荣哀录). Shudetang self-published edition. As cited in Xu, D. (1995). *Zhongguo Jindai Qiye De Keji Liliang Yu Keji Xiaoying* (Technical Strength and Effects of China's Modern Enterprise, 中国近代企业的科技力量与科技效应). Shanghai: Shanghai Academy of Social Science Press, 1995, p. 7.

connections who called to obey the law, but sought private gain."[32] Thus, many average people with high ranks occupied major positions in Westernization enterprises, while those with low status and genuine talent went unrecognized. Some of those selected could not demonstrate their capacity under the constraints of the corrupt government management system. Moreover, the officials holding management power considered the enterprise their own property, and arbitrarily assigned and raised a private force to seek personal gain and exclude those with different views. This resulted in redundancy and chaotic management. At the time, a report of a foreign business delegation to China noted that "in factories operated by the Chinese, there is an astounding situation that in every department, there are several well-dressed but lazy gentlemen who rest or study Confucian classics. They are friends of the director. Although they know nothing about work, they get salaries and good titles as supervisors or administrators. The only thing these useless commanders do on time is to get a monthly wage." The result was that "the machine is not in charge and if it breaks down, nobody is responsible for repair. These supervisors do nothing there, so the workers do not receive adequate care and proper treatment. Accounts are not clear on most things, so the manager absolutely does not know the total amount of production per week."[33] Although the description above was slightly exaggerated, it was true that a significant number of Westernization official enterprises were harmed by ignorant bureaucrats.

2. Out-dated operations management did not conform to the principle of efficiency. At that time, to determine the actual situation of the competitor, namely Shanghai Xiechang Match Factory founded by Ye Chengzhong (a top-ranked emerging national match industry), a Japanese match-making merchant in Shanghai conducted an investigation and found that the management of this factory was in extreme disorder. When they "entered, they were surprised first by the uncleanness, untidiness, and indiscipline of the factory. Utensils and medicine were scattered everywhere. The bedboard was filled

[32] Jing, Y. (1901). *Ju Yichu Ji Juaner, Xiuxian Baoguo Fei Shance, Juaner* (A Collection of Ju Yichu: Lines Repairing for Defending Country is Not a Good Strategy, Vol. 2, 居易初集, 修线保国非善策, 卷2).

[33] *Yangwu Yundong Juanba* (Westernization movement, Vol. 8, 洋务运动, 卷8). Shanghai: Shanghai Renmin Chubanshe, pp. 426–427.

with soil. The whole house was damaged without any sign of repair. Later, they were more astonished by groups of female workers who were the mothers or sisters of those male workers, roaring, crying, laughing, and joking there, as if in a hall of millions of evils. As for the workshop, there were only several kinds of misplaced machines." The poor operations management of this factory made it impossible to produce high-quality matches. Based on the results of the investigation, the Japanese concluded that the "products were shoddy" in this factory and "could not match" the Japanese-made matches exported to China.[34] This was the fact. The matches produced by Xiechang factory had nearly no market in Shanghai, and the factory survived by selling to some inland provinces.

3. Enterprises suffered losses based on no distinction between public and private interest in the enterprise business process. Tang Tingshu and Xu Run, China's most prominent entrepreneurs at the time, still had the moral defects of disloyalty to the enterprise. After joining the China Merchants Steamship Navigation Company, they introduced the comprador system foreign firms employed in the semi-colony therein. The stacking and shipping department employed a comprador who was responsible for the compensation and profit relating to stack goods and cargo capacity. Second and third-level compradors were also installed, which resulted in nepotism and favoritism. The main managers of the bureau and stacking and shipping were assigned by the head comprador, Tang or Xu. These businessmen including Tang and Xu also engaged in their own businesses, "taking the bureau and ship for their own purposes to transport private goods."[35] For example, Tang Tingshu, who was in charge of shipping matters, canvassed the supply of goods based on his small attached shipping bureau, affecting the waterway transportation revenue of China Merchants Steamship Navigation

[34] (1908). *Zhongguo Jingji Quanshu, Diyiji, Guangxu Xushen Lianghu Dushu Cangban* (The Economy of China, Vol. 1, Collection Edition of the Supervising Department of Hunan and Hubei in 1908, 中国经济全书, 第1辑, 光绪戌申两湖督署藏版), p. 94. As cited in Xu, D. (1995). *Zhongguo Jindai Qiye De Kejiliang Yu Kejixiaoying* (Technical Strength and Effects of China's Modern Enterprise, 中国近代企业的科技力量与科技效应). Shanghai: Shanghai Academy of Social Sciences Press, p. 14.

[35] Ma, L. *Gailiang Zhaoshangju Jianyi, Yangwu Yundong Juanliu* (Proposals to Reform China Merchants Steamship Navigation Company, Westernization Movement, Vol. 6, 洋务运动·改革招商局建议, 卷6), p. 125.

> Company. Xu Run, who was in charge of silver money, arbitrarily embezzled huge sums thereof to undertake speculative real estate. When the stock price of China Merchants Steamship Navigation Company rose in the financial market, all staff borrowed money to hurriedly buy stocks. Once the stock price decreased, they would "retain their money as capital stock,"[36] and transfer all their losses to the Group. Such utterly confused operations management resulted in the decrease of water transportation revenue and an immense increase in expenditure, leading the transportation revenue of the Group to stagnate at around 2 million taels of silver for long time. Even in the years during which the number of ships increased, transportation revenue did not, although the cost of each ship also rose. Over many years, the expenditure of each ship accounted for more than 70% of the transport revenue, the highest for 84.8%. Based on the abovementioned corruption in the operations management of the enterprise, it is not hard to understand why the vast majority of the shipping income of China Merchants Steamship Navigation Company came to nothing.

How could these problems be solved? The Westernization Group advocated strengthening the cultivation of enterprise management personnel through education. However, they emphasized using modern education methods to cultivate entrepreneurial talent, not the traditional way of education.

"Without a bitter cold, how can a plum smell better," a maxim considered the norm by people in business, underscored the traditional way of cultivating business talent. During the Westernization Movement, Japanese in China once investigated the quality and knowledge status of Chinese businessmen, finding that in Chinese business, "masters only explained to students some basic concepts and provided them with general direction. As for every slight change or concrete action in operation, students were required to practice and understand by themselves. After long-time practice and experiencing numerous problems, they would master the skills and become outstanding leaders. This was

[36] As cited in Zhang, G. (1979). *Yangwu Yundong Yu Zongguo Jindai Qiye* (Westernization Movement and China's Modern Enterprises, 洋务运动与中国近代企业). Beijing: China Social Science Press, p. 175.

how Chinese businessmen acquired their knowledge of business."[37] This traditional development route from learning from masters to take office after finishing an apprenticeship, or obtaining finance to open a shop or establish a new business, did not conform to the training requirements needed for talent in modern China. Therefore, the Westernization Group argued that entrepreneurial talent be cultivated in accordance with the modern education method, namely school, to ensure the advantages of the economy of scale of education.

Zheng Guanying suggested starting "Institute of Science and Technology," "Institute of Arts and Crafts," "Business School," and other types of schools, employing "European or American scholars or official servants studying abroad" as teachers to reach the target of "promoting Chinese and Western education to widely open the road of progress and have people acquire knowledge and obtain practical skills."[38] To understand the reason for success, further aims were to educate businessmen about initiating intelligence, punishing the false and praising the truth, encouraging creation, pursuing the great, and starting from little. This would enable combining the separate, enhancing proficiency, enriching the poor, and turning waste into something useful."[39]

In the process of developing Westernization, Zhang Zhidong deeply realized the lack of industrial and foreign language talent. He said, "if education on agriculture, industry, and commerce is not promoted, China's territory and population, although of vast number, cannot be fully used."[40] When Sheng Xuanhuai advised the Qing government to

[37] (1908). *Zhongguo Jingji Quanshu, Dierji, Guangxu Xushen Lianghu Dushu Cangban* (The Economy of China, Vol. 2, Collection Edition of the Supervising Department of Hunan and Hubei in 1908, 中国经济全书, 第2辑, 光绪戌申两湖督署藏板), pp. 12–14. As cited in Xu, D. (1995) *Zhongguo Jindai Qiye De Kejiliang Yu Kejixiaoying* (Technical Strength and Effects of China's Modern Enterprise, 中国近代企业的科技力量与科技效应). Shanghai: Shanghai Academy of Social Sciences Press, p. 7.

[38] Zheng, G. (1982). *Zheng Guanying Ji, Lun Yangxue, Shangce* (Zheng Guanying Works · Discussion on Western Education, Vol. 1, 郑观应集·论洋学). Shanghai: Shanghai Renmin Chubanshe, p. 106.

[39] Zheng, G. (1982). *Zheng Guanying Ji, Shangwusan, Shangce* (Zheng Guanying works Commercial Affairs III, Vol. 1, *郑观应集 · 商务三, 上册*). Shanghai: Shanghai Renmin Chubanshe, pp. 616–617.

[40] Zhang, Z. (1998). *QuanxuePian, Nonggongshangxue Dijiu* (Exhortation to Learning Agriculture, Industry and Commerce IX, *劝学篇 · 农工商学第九*). Zhengzhou: Zhongzhou Ancient Books Publishing House, p. 143.

establish business schools, he noted that by "taking good faith as body and business accounting as usage, and stressing financial management, a galaxy of business talent will emerge a few years later, and the Customs Commissioner, banks, railways, and mining business will no longer worry about vacancies."[41]

Ye Chengzhong, Tang Tingshu, Zhang Zhidong, Jing Yuanshan, and Sheng Xuanhuai were known for founding industrial schools. In his later years, Ye Chengzhong bought land of 25 *mu* in Shanghai and sponsored 100,000 taels of silver to found Chengzhong School to educate poor students from Shanghai. Even when he was on his deathbed, he was still worried about his school, and said, "Poor and lonely in my childhood, I regret being absent from school. Every time I thought that talent needed to be fostered, I desired to build a school in Hongkou, Shanghai." However, "as construction on the school began, I caught a deadly disease. My desire has not yet been realized, but I will soon die." This remained a life-long regret for him. He entrusted his relatives and friends to continue to realize his desires by pushing ahead to construct schoolhouses, employ teachers, and "negotiate the best regulations possible." The school was opened shortly after Ye's death and admired through word-of-mouth in industrial and commercial circles in Shanghai. Therefore, until the beginning of the twentieth century, when recalling the achievements of Ye Chengzhong in terms of running a school, people still noted that "today's scholars who built business schools do not know of the first example built 20 years ago."[42] Tang Tingshu was also an entrepreneur active in running schools. In the 1870s, he sponsored Yinghu Shu Guan in Shanghai, a missionary school founded to address "the requirements of business people." Furthermore, he participated in initiating the establishment of Shanghai Gezhi Academy, where he held the post of director at the same time as Xu Run.

[41] Sheng, X. (1899). *Shangwu Shiyi Xiangxi Kaiju Qingdan, Yuzhai Cungao, Juansan* (Memorials of Sheng Xuanhuai, Detailed List of Business Matters, Vol. 3. 愚斋存稿·商务事宜详细开具清单, 卷3), p. 62. As cited in Xia, D. (1998). *Sheng Xuanhuai Zhuan* (The Biography of Sheng Xuanhuai, 盛宣怀传). Tianjin: Nankai University Press, p. 267.

[42] *Yegong Chengzhong Rongai Lu* (Records of Honored Ye Chengzhong, Huaidetang Self-Published Edition. 叶公澄衷荣哀录, 怀德堂自印本). As cited in Ding, R. & Shen, Z. (1994). *Shanghai Jindai Jingjishi Diyijuan* (Modern History of Economy in Shanghai, 上海近代经济史第一卷). Shanghai: Shanghai Renmin Chubanshe, p. 667.

CHAPTER 8

Thoughts Regarding Waged Labor

The labor force was an extremely important problem in the time of modern socialized mass production. Competent operators were needed to run the machinery to produce cheaper and higher-quality products. This would ensure industry remained unbeatable amid the fierce market competition and remained highly efficient in modern society. The Westernization Group had the following views regarding sources of labor, formulation of wage standards, and management of labor.

8.1 Sources of Labor

Influenced by the cheap machinery used in the West, the traditional modes of production of farming and weaving ended, and workers separated from the means of production appeared in society, creating the conditions for a new mode of production. The Westernization Group claimed to support the poor and refugees with machinery to ensure social stability. According to Chen Chi, "with factories in all Chinese provinces open, millions of poor men will get food and warmth immediately, and settle down with a wife and children. Craftsmen in the former

J. Zhou, *Westernization Movement and Early Thought of Modernization in China*, Palgrave Studies in Economic History,
https://doi.org/10.1007/978-3-030-86985-4_8

days were hard, hungry, and cold, and could not enjoy plentiful lives."[1] This presented the source of the early modern workers, namely vagrants without the means of production, including unemployed craftsmen and unemployed farmers.

For enterprises, craftsmen were recruited before farmers, as they were more aligned with the technical requirements of the factory. For example, the earliest workers at Jilong Coal Mine in Taiwan were 1300 craftsmen employed in local pits. Later, as the scale of the coal mine expanded, poor peasants near the mining area were recruited as mine workers. Helmsmen and sailors of the China Merchants Steamship Navigation Company were almost employed as battle-hardened windjammers. The majority of workers involved in the mechanical sericulture and machine-operated cotton spinning industry were supplemented by workers reeling by hand and manual cotton textile workers.

Another important source of modern workers was soldiers who transferred from the military to civil society. Numerous records showed that after the 1860s, many workers in the military industries, telecommunications, and railway enterprises were soldiers who transferred from the Qing army. They had been commanded by sergeants with military rank. Until around 1884, other records state that "most manufacturing workers in each camp were from Hunan province"[2] at the Jiangnan Manufacturing Bureau.

In his article "Prosperous Prophecy - Inmates," Zheng Guanying claimed that prisoners constituted another source of workers: "In western countries, work for prisoners can be conducted inside or outside prison. Work outside prison includes the manufacturing of goods for males, while females do weaving or embroidery. One can learn a skill when in prison or if a skill has already been mastered, the inmate can continue with his own work. Half the wages earned by inmates are theirs for personal use, and the other half goes to the jail for public use." Given the growth of the transportation industry at the time, Zheng advocated that prisoners be employed to repair the railroad and roads. He proposed that "local officials are required to dispatch and command the prisoners involved in

[1] Chen, C. (1997). *Chenchi Ji, Jinde Yangmin Shuo* (Chen Chi Works· On Nature Cultivation for Nourishing People, 陈炽集·进德养民说). Beijing: Zhonghua Book Company, pp. 228–229.

[2] *Zhong Fanggong Yishi* (Anecdotes of Nie Zhongfang, 仲芳公逸事). As cited in Gujin, Banyuekan (Ancient and Modern Semimonthly, Vol. 36, 古今半月刊, 第36期), p. 14.

construction work in their areas of jurisdiction." He thought this was good for the prisoners, first because "it would enable them to practice their thews, they would get their energy and blood flowing, and improve their spirit, which would help protect them from diseases from being confined in moist spaces." Second, "the jail keeps their wages, except the small amount given to them, and pays this out to them upon their release. They will then have enough money to make a living should they act recklessly again and be re-arrested." It was also good for the country, because it would "have broad plain roads everywhere from then on."[3] Similar to Zheng's proposition, Chen Chi said in *The Tactics of Enriching the Country · On Workers for Repairing Roads*: "The work of knocking stones and packing roads is allocated to criminals with misdemeanors and unemployed poor people."[4] This showed using prisoners to construct railroads was a fairly common notion in society. As such, quite a few workers repairing roads and highways were prisoners at the time.

8.2 Standards for Recruiting Workers

Since workers were required to operate the machines, standards for their recruitment were aligned with the specifications of the machinery. The requirements for workers based on the machinery differed between industries. For example, the technical requirements of workers based on the machinery to be operated were higher in capital-intensive industries and lower in labor-intensive light industries. At the time, China's national industry contained both capital-intensive industries in which high standards were set for workers' technical abilities, such as in the armament, iron and steel, mining, railway, telegraph, steamship and other transportation, and communications industries. Lower standards were set for workers' technical abilities in labor-intensive industries such as in the textile, oil manufacturing, brewery, and other light industries. That meant an industry could hire workers based on its own characteristics.

[3] Zheng, G. (1982). *Zheng Guanying Ji, Yuqiu, Shangce* (Zheng Guanying Works • Inmates, Vol. 1, 郑观应集·狱囚, 上册). Shanghai: Shanghai Renmin Chubanshe, pp. 505–507.

[4] Chen, C. (1997). *Chenchi Ji, Zhidao Zhigong Shuo* (Chen Chi Works· on Workers for Repairing Roads, 陈炽集·治道之工说). Beijing: Zhonghua Book Company, p. 227.

Because technical ability was highly demanded in capital-intensive industries, skilled craftsmen were needed. Wu Dacheng, the Vice Censor-in-chief of the Left handling Beiyang matters, said that "the head of the craftsmen is the most important for one factory, and machinery is the most important for all factories. Only skilled craftsmen could set up boilers and only eminent workers could assemble the machines."[5] These skilled craftsmen often came from the southeastern coastal provinces such as Guangdong, Fujian, Zhejiang, Jiangsu, and Shandong, especially Guangdong province. This was because, first, these places were originally developed in an economy that involved many craftsmen. Second, geographically, these places had borne the brunt of cheap foreign goods in earlier times, and their traditional economic structure had disintegrated earlier. Thus, numerous bankrupt craftsmen were waiting to be employed in these provinces. Third, these provinces were early trading ports; thus, many people who worked in the foreign-owned factories were more skillful in terms of foreign advanced technology. As Zhang Shusheng, the former Governor-general of Guangdong and Guangxi put it, "Based on abundant materials in eastern Guangdong, most people there learned from the Westerners and most products were made in a similar way to those in the West. The delicateness of our craftsmen and robust products are deeply praised by the Westerners."[6] As such, the skilled workers in the military industrial enterprises and mining industry founded by the Westernization officials mostly came from these places. Even the enterprises of Zuo Zongtang in Shaanxi, Ding Baozhen in Sichuan, and Li Jinyong in Mohe River in northeast China specifically recruited craftsmen from these provinces. In the 13th Year of the Tongzhi Reign, Zuo Zongtang, Governor-general of Shaanxi and Gansu, wrote a letter to the Western-style Foreign Office that Lanzhou Manufacturing Bureau had "selected craftsmen from Ningbo, Guangdong, and Fujian to engage in manufacturing, and appointed a commander-in-chief to supervise them."[7] On September 23 in the 5th Year of the Guangxu Reign, Ding Baozhen, Governor-general of Sichuan, also noted in "the Delayed Establishment

[5] (1885, Dec 24). *Jing Bao* (Peking Gazette, 京报).

[6] Zhang, S. (1899). *Zhang Jingdagong Zouyi, Juanwu* (Reform Proposals of Zhang Jingda, Vol.5, 张靖达公奏议, 卷5), p. 12.

[7] Zuo, Z. *Zuo Wenxianggong Shudu, Juanshisan* (Complete Works of Zuo Wenxiang, Letters, Vol. 13, 左文襄公书牍, 卷13), p. 40.

of Fuchen Machinery Bureau" that "at the onset of the bureau's establishment in Sichuan, Chinese people learning about the machinery and craftsmen, especially from Hunan, Jiangsu, and Shandong provinces, were primarily recruited to follow this idea at full steam."[8]

However, the experienced workers highly demanded in society were scarce. The Westernization officials solved this problem by announcing the government's orders. Many skilled craftsmen in an ordnance factory founded later were transferred from a similar enterprise established earlier. For example, the establishment of Tianjin Machinery Bureau was assisted by "the help of skilled and reliable craftsmen transferred from Shanghai Iron Works." Jiangnan Manufacturing Bureau, the first modern military enterprise in China, was honored as the father of the Chinese military industry because it transferred much technical talent to newer military factories. However, the changes in their place of work instead of the spontaneous adjustment of the market meant these skilled craftsmen were not highly motivated to work, especially when their new living conditions were poorer than those provided at the former factory. In the 11th Year of the Guangxu Reign, Wu Dacheng complained that the skilled craftsmen transferred to Jilin Machinery Bureau "have long worked in the bureau of Tianjin and Shanghai, where they enjoyed deep qualifications and abundant work meals. They viewed the bureau of Jilin and other cold areas as dangerous places and were not willing to be transferred there. Others who had already been transferred would return under the pretext of being ill after one or two months. It is difficult to recruit craftsmen."[9]

For work in a field with lower requirements for technical ability, businessmen commonly hired local people. According to the British Consul Business Report, in 1882, Kaiping Coal Mine hired 120 craftsmen from the South and about 400 local workers. The former were skilled, while the latter were not.

Labor-intensive light industries generally had lower requirements regarding technical ability, and it was thus easier for them to recruit and select workers.

[8] Ding, B. *Ding Wenchenggong Yiji, Zougao, Juanshiqi* (Drafts of Ding Wencheng,, Vol. 17, 丁文诚公遗集·奏稿, 卷17), p. 39.

[9] (1885, Dec 24). *Jing Bao* (China Gazette, 京报).

1. Proximity principle. Regarding Zhang Zhidong's practice at the Hubei Weaving Bureau, "about 2000–3000 weavers were needed and they are all local people."[10] Another example is the Shanghai Machine Weaving Bureau, where "the majority of the women weavers, young and old, are from Shanghai and live around the city."[11] The reason for this is that the businessmen hoped to decrease recruitment costs and better manage them by taking advantage of local officials and social power.
2. Recruitment of women workers and child labor. The Shanghai Silk Spinning Bureau employed hundreds of women workers. Their work often entailed cocoon stripping and picking, or they worked as drivers and so on.[12] According to the *China Gazette*, Entry November 24, 1893, "it is estimated that about 15,000–20,000 women are employed to work on cleaning the feathers of domestic poultry to be exported, cotton and silk picking, and match and cigarette production."[13] Why were women and children so widely employed in the newly established industry and commerce? Marx stated that women and child labor was prioritized by capitalists using machinery. That is because machinery simplifies the production procedure and requires less physical strength, meaning that the work only men could do is now suitable for women and children as well. Furthermore, using women and child labor is a good way to reduce production costs and increase the profits of businessmen. Therefore, in the second half of the nineteenth century, women and child labor was common in modern enterprises including in silk reeling, cotton weaving, and match and cigarette manufacturing. Many children also worked in the coal mines.

Hiring workers was restricted based on technical ability and by the political environment, social customs, and morality. In the transitioned society, the latter had the greatest influence. According to Zhang

[10] Zhang, Z. *Zhang Wenxianggong Quanji, Zouyi, Juansanshisan* (Collected Works of Zhang Wenxiang · Memorials, Vol. 33, 张文襄公全集·奏议, 卷33), p. 16.

[11] *Xinji Shiwu Huitong, Juanyilingsan* (The New Series of Huitong Times, Vol. 103, 新辑时务汇通, 卷103), p. 12.

[12] (1882, Nov 21). *Shen Bao* (The Chinese Newspaper Shenbao, 申报).

[13] *Jie Bao, Juanwushiyi* (China Gazette, Vol. 51, 捷报, 卷51), p. 822.

Zhidong, Governor-general of Hubei and Hunan, "it is an ancient rule that women should just deal with housework at home." For this reason, "Hubei Cloth Weaving Bureau hires men only as a preventive measure that benefits social decency."[14] A delegation from the British Chamber of Commerce stated in a report that "Hubei Cloth Weaving Bureau had many similarities with Shanghai's, except that Hubei only hired men as its governor thought unsuited for Confucius' code." Regarding child labor, many foreign businessmen and Chinese enterprises established with private capital paid more attention to the economic benefits; thus, they employed children aged around seven to eight years. Government-run enterprises also had some limitations. For instance, according to Rule 28 of the 33 coal pit rules at Kaiping Coal Mine, "all children aged less than 13 and women young and old cannot be recruited to work in the pit. Children aged between 13 and 18, though hired, must be kept under strict control."[15] The 15th rule of the pit regulations said, "children working in the pit must follow other adult workers and be brought out of the pit after duty."[16]

8.3 Wage Determination

Based on the practice at enterprises at the time, workers' wages were mainly determined by the following four principles:

1. The standard of productivity was the fundamental principle guiding wage determination. The *China Gazette* reported on November 15, 1881 that there were 700–800 workers at Jinling Manufacturing Bureau, of which "some earned 3 *yuan* per day, some earned 2, some earned 1, and children, who were apprentices,

[14] (1893, Jan 23). *Yi Wen Lu* (Yi Wen Lu, 益闻录).

[15] *Kaiping Kuangwu Chuangban Zhangcheng Anju Huibian* (Collection of Kaiping Mining Founding Regulations Basis, *开平矿物创办章程案据汇编*), p. 28. As cited in Sun, Y. (1957). *Zhongguo Jindai Gongyeshi Ziliao Diyiji Xiace* (Materials of Chinese Modern Industrial History, Vol. 1, Part II, *中国近代工业史资料第1辑下册*). Beijing: Science Press, p. 1233.

[16] *Kaiping Kuangwu Chuangban Zhangcheng Anju Huibian* (Collection of Kaiping Mining Founding Regulations Basis, *开平矿务创办章程案据汇编*), p. 41. As cited in Sun, Y. (1957). *Zhongguo Jindai Gongyeshi Ziliao Diyiji Xiace* (Materials of Chinese Modern Industrial History, Vol. 1, Part II, *中国近代工业史资料第1辑下册*). Beijing: Science Press, p. 1233.

made only several *cents* per day."[17] On September 23, 1872, Li Hongzhang explained in the "expenditure folder of the Machine Bureau" the wage disparity between workers: "The wage disparity between workers at home and abroad appear determined by a value judgment of their ability." "Measuring one's value to pay wages" means wages are paid according to a worker's productivity, in other words, the benefit he brings to the factory. Zhong Tianwei emphasized that wages for workers should be determined considering "one's skill and workmanship rather than seniority and prestige, or social relationship,"[18] which is similar to Li's view.

2. Living costs. Marx stated that once turned into a commodity, the labor force would achieve its value as other commodities do. This value is the sum of the labor needed in value production and workers' means of livelihood. Wages are a monetary expression of the value of those means of livelihood. According to a British Consulate business report in 1878 on the coal pits in Danshui and Jilong in Taiwan, "The wages for those coal mining workers, carpenters, iron workers, and unskilled laborers are very low because of officers' plundering, and those officers always find ways to exploit more, which finally results in problems in recruiting workers. Very few coal mine workers stay behind in the end with few unskilled workers."[19] As is shown here, the wages for coal mining workers must be kept at a level just high enough to support his family. If wages are too low to support a family, there will naturally be problems in hiring workers. Lin Zhidao, general director of Jiangnan Manufacturing Bureau, explained, "It is much more difficult for workers to make money when the prices of commodities are high. They have trouble resolving their living problems with a small wage, and if exploited and the wage cut off, they will have numerous complaints, which will

[17] *Jie Bao Juanershiqi* (China Gazette, Vol. 27, 捷报, 卷27), p. 516.

[18] Zhong, T. *Yuezu Ji, Dainibing Lijuexiang Caiche Jiqiju Tiaoyi* (Zhong's Righteous Words· Discussion on Dissolving Machine Bureau as Reported to Li Jue, 刖足集·代拟禀李爵相裁撤机器局条议).

[19] (1878). *Yinglingshi Shangwu Baogao* (Business Report of Britain Consul, 英领事商务报告), pp. 143–145, As cited in Sun, Y. (1957). *Zhongguo Jindai Gongyeshi Ziliao Diyiji Xiace* (Materials of Chinese Modern Industrial History, Vol. 1, *中国近代工业史资料第1辑下册*). Beijing: Science Press, pp. 1217–1218.

lead to work delays." In his opinion, problems will arise if "workers' wage is cut off too much to meet their living needs."[20] This indicates that the wages paid by military factories only retain a labor force through much effort. If those wages decreased, manufacturing may not have proceeded as usual because of work delays brought about by workers' dissatisfaction.

3. Social differentiation. In a traditionally agricultural society, the low level of science and technology meant that the physical power of man was important. The physical condition of men in this type of society was typically good and much needed to support their families.

Thus, the concept that men are the main body of a family while women are the necessary emerged, as embodied in the slogan, "the men plough and the women weave." However, upon entering a modern society, machine production largely substituted men's labor, providing an opportunity for women to step into fields once only occupied by men. If wages are based on productivity, men and women should get equal pay for equal work; however, this is not the case. While capitalist countries in the West gradually moved toward this principle over time, it is not well implemented in the real world. As such, how can this be applied in a country with a newly emerging modern society? The statistics show large differences between the wages of men and women. For example, at a cotton mill in Shanghai in 1894, men were paid 4–6 pennies per day, 1.5–2.5 times more than women, who only earned 1.5–4 pennies per day.[21] Another example is Xiechang Match Factory, "which employed around 800 workers. Men earned 20–30 cents per day, and women 10–15 cents. Men earned double what the women did."[22]

[20] *Jiangnan Zhizao Zongju Ji, Juansi* (Notes of Jiangnan Manufacturing Bureau, Vol. 4, 江南制造总局记, 卷4), pp. 20–21.

[21] Sha, J. (1895) *Zhongying Shangwu yu Maoyi* (Business and Trade between China and Britain, *中英商务与贸易*), p. 261. As cited in Sun, Y. (1957). *Zhongguo Jindai Gongyeshi Ziliao Diyiji Xiace* (Materials of Chinese Modern Industrial History, Vol. 1, Part II, *中国近代工业史资料第1辑下册*). Beijing: Science Press, p. 1206.

[22] *Qing Guo Shiqing, Juansan* (Things in Qing Dynasty, Vol. 3, *清国事情，卷3*), p. 566. As cited in Sun, Y. (1957). *Zhongguo Jindai Gongyeshi Ziliao Diyiji Xiace* (Materials of Chinese Modern Industrial History, Vol. 1, Part II, *中国近代工业史资料第1辑下册*). Beijing: Science Press, p. 1207.

Why is it impossible for society to achieve equal pay for equal work after the period of transition? The fundamental reason is the traditional notion that "men do farm work and women do the weaving." Men are viewed as being responsible for supporting their families. Thus, his wage must not only meet his own needs, but also those of his family. In contrast, a woman's wage need to meet only her needs alone.

4. The opportunity cost principle refers to the comparison between the wage a worker loses if he does not work in a place and the wage he earns if working in other places. In general, a rational worker has the motivation to change his job only if there is a job with a higher salary. Based on this, Yangwu enterprises followed the opportunity cost principle when setting wages standard; otherwise, they would have had difficulties in recruiting qualified workers. A tea factory that relocated from inland to Hankou had to increase its wages because its workers were mainly from remote areas. If they were to earn low wages that excluded transportation fees to visit their families and compensation for the mental distress experienced when leaving their families, they would not have relocated for work.[23] Furthermore, Hubei Guns Factory established by Zhang Zhidong "employed more than 260 workers, most of who were from the North and Guangdong. None were from Shanghai." This was because skilled craftsmen from Shanghai were paid well locally and did not like to work in other places where wages were lower. Thus, to motivate them, Zhang "set a new standard as reward for those who come."[24]

Wages were delineated as piece-meal wages and hourly wages at the time. The piece-meal wage was applied in light industries, which required lower technical abilities and relied more on independent work. As such, it was better to ensure workers' passion by paying them a piece wage.

[23] (1877). *Guan Ce Xiapian* (Guan Volume, Part 2, *关册，下篇*), pp. 14–15. As cited in Sun, Y. (1957). *Zhongguo Jindai Gongyeshi Ziliao Diyiji Xiace* (Materials of Chinese Modern Industrial History, Vol.1, Part II, *中国近代工业史资料第1辑下册*). Beijing: Science Press, p. 1207.

[24] Zhang, Z. *Zhang Wenxianggong Quanji, Diandu, Juanyibaisishi* (Collected Works of Zhang Wenxiang·Telegraph Memorials to the Throne, Vol. 140, 张文襄公全集·电牍，卷140).

For instance, Xiechang Match Factory paid workers according to pieces of goods: "10 cents for 1000 pasted boxes, 1 cent for 2 rows of match sticks, and 5 cents for 1000 packed match boxes."[25] Chongqing Match Factory "hires women and child labor to either work at the factory or at home for 40 wen for 100 boxes."[26] On the working conditions at Shanghai Bark Company, the *China Gazette* reported that the company "applies a piece-meal wage to almost all work, which seems to be working well. The company does a lot of work on the wage."[27] In capital-intensive heavy industries, the piece-meal wage was suitable for independent work, and hourly wages for dependent work. The coal mining industry is an example of the former, often paying for workers based on the size of the coal they cut. At Kaiping Coal Mine, if a coal miner cut a large piece of coal, he would get 45 cents, 30 cents for a medium-sized piece of coal, and 15 cents for a small piece of coal.[28] The firearms industry is a good example of the latter, as the achievements of work cannot be divided and the wage standard is often based on work property, labor intensity, and the technical ability required. There, workers were paid daily or monthly. Jiangnan Manufacturing Bureau stipulated that "apprentices should be paid based on their attendance."[29]

8.4 Labor Management

Labor management includes the management of wages, work, and daily life.

1. Wage management

Many enterprises at that time realized they should use wages as a lever to stimulate production. For example, in the third year of the reign of

[25] *Qingguo Shiqing, Juansan* (Things in Qing Dynasty, Vol. 3, 清国事情, 卷3), p. 566.

[26] *Qingguo Shiqing, Juansan* (Things in Qing Dynasty, Vol. 3, 清国事情, 卷3), p. 566.

[27] *Jie Bao, Juanershiba* (China Gazette, Vol. 28, 捷报, 卷28), pp. 599–600.

[28] (1882). *Yinglingshi Shangwu Baogao, Disanpian* (Business Report of Britain Consul, Vol. 3, *英领事商务报告，第三篇*), pp. 788–792, As cited in Sun, Y. (1957). *Zhongguo Jindai Gongyeshi Ziliao Diyiji Shangce* (Materials of Chinese Modern Industrial History, Vol. 1, Part II, *中国近代工业史资料第1辑下册*). Beijing: Science Press, p. 1214.

[29] Li, H. *Li Wenzhonggong Quanshu, Juanshiqi* (Memorials of Complete Works of Li Wenzhong, Vol. 17, 李文忠公全集·奏稿, 卷17), pp. 16–18.

Qing Dynasty emperor Guang Xu (1877), Tang Tingshu pointed out in the *Overall Accounting of Kaiping Mine Cost Pandect* that "every Chinese worker could have more than 1 copper for dinner per day if they dig 500 kg of coal, while if they were paid 2 coppers, they would dig 2.5 tons of coal."[30] Therefore, the wages workers earn gradually increases with improved production efficiency. Take the spinning mills in Shanghai for instance, "Workers could initially earn 16 cents per day. Now, working only for 11 h per day, they can make 40–45 cents."[31]

Aligned with the practical situation, all enterprises increased their profit mainly by lengthening the working time, i.e., the absolute surplus value. According to the *China Gazette* and Shun Pao, the working hours were more than 10 hours per day. In 1880, Tianjing Machine Bureau extended their working hours to 11.5 hours per day, and Shanghai Mechanical Textile Bureau made it 10 hours. In 1881, Fuzhou Arsenal increased their working hours from 10 to 11, while Hubei Textile Bureau extended that to 12 hours or even 13 hours in 1893.

Jing Yuanshan disagreed with the action of prolonging working hours, and thus proposed the Western six working days per week. He explained, "Sunday is suitable for resting. People have some home affairs to deal regardless of whether they are rich or poor. A day a week for rest can assure that workers can devote themselves to their work during the six working days. If not, there may eventually be thoughts of loafing on the job."[32]

2. Production management

[30] *Kaiping Kuangwu Zhaoshang Zhangcheng* (Investment Regulations of Kaiping Mining, 开平矿务招商章程), p. 33, As cited in Sun, Y. (1957). *Zhongguo Jindai Gongyeshi Ziliao Diyiji Shangce* (Materials of Chinese Modern Industrial History, Vol. 1, Part II, *中国近代工业史资料第1辑下册*). Beijing: Science Press, p. 1214.

[31] Mai, Z. *Huangchao Jingshiwen Xinbian, Juanshisan* (New Edition of Royal Classic, Vol. 13, 皇朝经世文新编, 卷13), p. 28.

[32] Jing, Y. *Juyi Chuji, Shangchudu Zhangzhifu Chuangban FangzhiJu Tiaochen, Juanyi* (Early Works of Juyi: Items of Founding Weaving Bureau by Director Zhang Zhifu, Vol. 1, 居易初集·上楚督张制府创办纺织局条陈, 卷1), p. 25.

To ensure workers work efficiently, the relevant administration and management should be considered. Over that period, people located nearby the factories would often be employed at those enterprises. The majority of coppersmiths in many factories in Shanghai were local people from Nanjing. Iron workers, rammers, and prefabrication workers were initially mainly Cantonese and later from Wuxi. Wood workers and wood pattern makers were mostly from Ningbo and Guangdong. Here, enterprises selected a craftsmen leader based on his capability to manage all workers and ensure they obey the commands of the traditional head.

However, managing workers in this way countered the principle of modern enterprise competence. Therefore, in the 1880s, some in the Westernization Group thought that the craftsmen leader should not only have potential leadership abilities, but also outstanding skills. "One who knows a foreign language and is put in a good position has no true ability. In that case, those affiliated with him will be unwilling to submit, becoming more intelligent each day. Sooner or later, the affairs of the manufacturing business will deteriorate."[33]

3. Daily life management

Household production was prevalent in the traditional agricultural society, and this production model contributed to individual production and consumption, constituting a picture of idyllic scenery. People rose up against oppression probably because of the excessive taxes and levies of officials. A stable regime, the traditional dynasty was most afraid of public gatherings. While a public gathering may not signify rebellion, it was closely related, as people had achieved self-sufficiency. Governors made their best efforts to avoid people gathering. If a gathering was discovered, it was immediately dispersed.

A modern mode of production is the right to mass production. Governors tried their utmost to manage the workers because they were concerned that something may happen to sway their governing position.

[33] Zhong, T. *Yuezu Ji, Dainibing Lijuexiang Caiche Jiqiju Tiaoyi* (Collected Works of Yue Zu: Discussion on Dissolving Machine Bureau as Reported to Li Jue, 刖足集·代拟禀李爵相裁撤机器局条议).

This was most evident in the government enterprises of the Westernization group. In 1867, Shen Baozhen, a manager of Fuzhou Arsenal, reported in "Current Situation of Dockyard Machines in Operation" that with 2000–3000 craftsmen employed by the Ship-building Bureau: "It is totally out of order, which can easily lead to problems and accidents. Thus, it is difficult to call upon these workers when they are lost." Therefore, they built two more residences for the workers, namely Dongkao Workers' House on the left and Xikao Workers' House on the right. "These workers were under the control of Yuanshen, going to work in the morning and returning home in the evening, thus avoiding chaos." Fuzhou Arsenal also had a rule that workers could only live in the factory and must be on and off duty under guard. The facilities and rules there were similar to those in barracks.[34]

Tang Tingshu from the executive office of the Kaiping Mine proposed using torture instruments: "Workers who have to be with shackles for a month or be free after three months or be given a lighter sentence face what is called interrogation." They would "ask for responsibility at the scene, and as long as workers know the law, the number of violations of that law will decrease."[35]

When dealing with workers' rebellion and strikes, the enterprises usually brutally suppressed them with the government. On April 25, 1895, Cai Xiyong from the executive office of Hubei Railway reported to Zhang Zhidong, "There are some workers from Guangdong causing trouble in the iron factory and being flogged by three translating committees including Zeng Hai. These workers are so unconvinced that they have led more than 200 workers to strike, and will not stop until the three committees are dismissed." In this event, the workers began to fight against persecution. Later, Cai Xiyong came to the scene to negotiate, and sent soldiers armed with guns to control the situation. The situation was finally diffused using both soft approaches and force. Nevertheless, several months later, some workers again walked around in Hankou after work

[34] Shen, B. *Sheng Wensugong Zhengshu, Juansi* (Memorials of Shen Wensu, Vol. 4, 沈文肃公政书, 卷4).

[35] *Kaiping Kuangwu Chuangban Zhangcheng Anju Huibian* (Collection of Kaiping Mining Founding Regulations Basis, *开平矿物创办章程案据汇编*), pp. 78–79. As cited in Sun, Y. (1957). *Zhongguo Jindai Gongyeshi Ziliao Diyiji Shangce* (Materials of Chinese Modern Industrial History, Vol. 1, Part II, *中国近代工业史资料第1辑下册*). Beijing: Science Press, pp. 1243–1244.

and caused a disturbance. Yun Zuyi and Cai Xiyong said in their reports that "those people are not afraid of anything. Only by force can we better tame them."[36]

[36] Zhang, Z. *Zhang Zhidong Dian'gao* (Zhang Zhidong's Electric Draft, 张之洞电稿), As cited in Feng, T. (1985). *Zhang Zhidong Pingzhuan* (Critical Biograph of Zhang Zhidong, 张之洞评传). Kaifeng: Henan Education Press, p. 137.

CHAPTER 9

Theories of the Operation and Management of Enterprises

According to economic theories, the production and supply of an enterprise or from society are determined by several productive factors: technique, capital, land, and the labor force. The right way to run an enterprise is to combine all these elements efficiently, open to the public, and achieve the highest profit. This involves two main aspects: how to motivate workers at the enterprise and how to decrease the number of mistakes workers make. With respect to business efficiency, the Westernization Group stressed the importance of enforcing management. Furthermore, they proposed the following regarding how to establish an appropriate enterprise management system in China.

9.1 Scientific Decision-Making

Sound decisions are vital in any enterprise. Simon, a well-known management expert considered "management a decision." Two types of decisions can be discerned. One is a purposeful decision related to an organizational goal to be achieved. The other is a decision on the means to reach organization goals. The former is a strategic decision that requires an environmental analysis. The enterprise should identify strategic elements in the dynamic environment and make decisions based on these. The latter is a tactical decision, which demands rational and replaceable methods for

J. Zhou, *Westernization Movement and Early Thought of Modernization in China*, Palgrave Studies in Economic History,
https://doi.org/10.1007/978-3-030-86985-4_9

some purpose to develop an optimized plan by which the enterprise can achieve its objectives.

Ideologues from the Westernization Group realized the role of decision-making in improving the operations of Chinese enterprises based on investigations of failed cases, and provided recommendations in this regard. They thought that decisions related to what product to manufacture should be based on the resources owned, following the practice of Westernization production systems. However, how should the enterprise be organized and arrange for production? For this, the Westernization Group had learnt a few lessons. In the 1870s, Zuo Zongtang was preparing to sell cashmere made of the abundant wool of the northWestern areas with funds raised through an official-merchant joint partnership. Some suggested that the factory be constructed in Hankou, which used raw materials transported nationwide and was responsible for production and sales. Hankou had a large population, was economically prosperous, and was convenient in terms of transportation. As such, it had the ability to transport goods countrywide and contribute to product sales. However, the area around Lanzhou House was the center of the wool production industry. Therefore, it had advantages in terms of obtaining raw material at a lower cost. However, it was difficult to sell the products there because of the small population, backward economy, and poor purchasing power. Furthermore, the people living in those areas preferred cotton to wool. Zuo Zongtang disagreed with the advice. After all, Gansu was in his charge and he intended to exploit the resources in this area. Therefore, he constructed the factory in Lanzhou.[1] When planning for the factory, the factory's need for water was ignored. Its location "lacked water resources, and the available water contained alkali that made it difficult to bleach and dye. Thus, the wool cloth looked dull." The scarcity of water also meant that the machines could only weave 10 wool cloths of 18 yards each day, despite having the capacity to produce much more. Obviously, this decreased the quality, and increased production and transportation costs, ultimately reducing the enterprise's competitive power with Western countries exporting wool cloth. From

[1] Sun, Y. (1957). *Zhongguo Jindai Gongyeshi Ziliao Diyiji Xiace* (Materials of Chinese Modern Industrial History, Vol.1, Part II, 中国近代工业史资料吗, 第1辑, 下册). Beijing: Science Press, p. 898, p. 905.

读秀: 孙毓棠编. 中国近代工业史资料第1辑 1840-1895年 下[M]. 北京: 科学出版社, 1957.04.

this perspective, Lanzhou Wool Cloth Bureau was destined to fail. Moreover, wool cloth made in China was not as good as that manufactured in South Africa, Australia, and Germany, and "as a result, it was inferior to that of the Westerners." The wool in the northWestern area "was rough, and about 40 people were employed to pick 2 pounds per day. As a result, the wool itself cost a lot before being woven into cloth."[2]

Sympathetic to the failure of achieving Zuo's ambition, Chen Chi, speaking about the Lanzhou Wool Cloth Bureau, stated, "Zuo Wenxiang also wanted to buy machines for weaving faux wool fabric; however, the pasture is still being constructed, making it difficult to operate and sell the product. This situation stems from a lack of overall planning in the beginning."[3] A similar example of faulty decision-making is the Hanyang Iron Factory established by Zhang Zhidong, which produced low-quality products at a high cost and lacked competitive power.

To avoid such mistakes, Zheng Guanying emphasized that "businesses should carefully consider the situation, plan accordingly, and implement the plan with certainty. This would ensure sufficiently knowing the market and goods first before making decisions regarding buying commodities while waiting for price increases." Following that, real action would ensue.[4] How could this be realized? The piece *Abridged Version of the Founding of Biangliang Business Company in Bianzhou* by Xu Run was a typical example of scientific decision-making in business operations.

In 1897, Xu Run investigated 14 prefectures and counties in Chengde and Yongping, and highlighted the value in exploiting the abundant local product resources including native silk, cotton, kaoliang liquor, white noodle, fur and feather, mulberry paper, tobacco leaf, and peanut and Thanakha flour. In addition, business operations were heavily dependent on external conditions such as whether transportation was convenient, the labor force sufficient, living expenses low, prices of raw material reasonable, and the potential of the market. Based on his analysis, he asserted

[2] Sun, Y. (1957). *Zhongguo Jindai Gongyeshi Ziliao Diyiji Xiace* (Materials of Chinese Modern Industrial History, Vol.1, Part II, 中国近代工业史资料第1辑下册). Beijing: Science Press, p. 899.

[3] Chen, C. (1997). *Chenchi Ji, Xumu Yangmin Shuo* (Chen Chi Works· Herdsmen Story, 陈炽集·畜牧养民说). Beijing: Zhonghua Book Company, p. 176.

[4] Zheng, G. (1982). *Zheng Guanying Ji Shangwusan Shangce* (Zheng Guanying works • Business (3), Vol. 1, 郑观应集·商务三, 上册). Shanghai: Shanghai Renmin Chubanshe, p. 621.

that this area met these standards, and optimistically stated, "Therefore, it could be the best option with its advantageous location, low product costs, and developed transportation." The writer believes that Xu Run's statement regarding the significance of the area was not a prediction for the future economy of specific regions, but a manifestation of a new approach of an early entrepreneur with a modern sensibility to social and economic problems. For the significance of setting up Luanzhou Bianliang Business Company, Xu Run gave five reasons from the perspective of a prosperous inland economy, including transportation, financing and taxes, and the livelihoods of poor people. He believed that if this plan could make a profit and gradually expand its influence, "the growth of inland business would come soon, the benefits and power of Western businesses would dissolve, commodities could be transported via the railway, and expenses related to maintaining the road would increase, as would the likin tax. More sales channels would be developed, more profits gained, and more jobs created, which was beneficial for poor people. As a result, we can say it is really to achieve many things in one stroke."[5]

9.2 Personnel Management

At the time, redundancy was widely prevalent in business circles in China, especially in government enterprises. This problem dramatically increased costs, reducing the market competitiveness of the enterprise. Zheng Guanying lamented, "Personnel management is the first important thing of any enterprise." Using the development of the banking industry as example, he noted, "Now that the bank has been established and branches opened everywhere, accountants, administration staff, people responsible for contractual agreements, and those to take charge of the market are needed. Big banks need hundreds of people, and small ones need many too. As there are so many people in the bank, they must meet to get together. People were employed based on stock recommendations, the recommendations of relatives and friends, and entrusting prominent officials. If negligence occurs, many problems will arise. The salaries and expenditure were excessive, and the bills and affected behaviors mixed. Even when there was no position for a recommendation, they gave gifts to avoid bad feelings, ranging from a few pieces of gold to tens of pieces

[5] Xu R. *Xu Yuzhai Zixu Nianpu* (The Chronicle of Xu Yuzhai, 徐愚斋自叙年谱). p. 91.

of gold. This loophole continued year on year. These practices were bad for the bank, but good for endless problems."[6]

How could these problems be solved? Zheng Guanying said, "It is better to imitate western countries," which meant learning their tradition of respecting private property, respecting shareholder benefits in business operations, and balancing shareholders' interests. He added that "the Westerners are superior to us because they can distance themselves from their emotions and feelings, and widely solicit talent without trusting officers and based on the recommendations of relatives and friends. Thus, the steward officers were not only familiar with affairs, but also exceptional at what they did. The shareholders elected the board, and if members did not come from commerce, they would not be used."[7] For this purpose, Westernization Group proposed three methods to solve the problem:

1. Stock traders present selected people they trust and maintain their interest in joining the board of directors. Zheng Guanying explained, "Everything that must be done is determined by a capable and well-experienced person with integrity who is selected from among the stock traders. In addition, 10 people who are stock directors will help them." To supervise the work of the board of directors and maintain the interest of stock traders, Zheng Guanying also pointed out paying attention to the powers of office, increasing payment, offering rewards for motivation, and penalizing bad behavior. This would ensure more benefits than problems. Chen Chi emphasized the level of morality of members of the board of directors, noting that those who oversee the affairs of a company should bear in mind that it is "better to break a promise to the world than to a colleague, and better to suffer from my own actions than from those of colleagues."[8] He emphasized the importance of maintaining the interest of the investor.

[6] Zheng, G. (1982). *Zheng Guanying Ji, Yinhangxia Shangce* (Zheng Guanying works • Bank, Vol. 1, 郑观应集·银行下, 上册). Shanghai: Shanghai Renmin Chubanshe, pp. 684–685.

[7] Zheng, G. (1982). *Zheng Guanying Ji Shangwusan Shangce* (Zheng Guanying works • Business (3), Vol. 1, 郑观应集·商务三, 上册). Shanghai: Shanghai Renmin Chubanshe, pp. 618–619.

[8] Chen, C. (1997). *Chenchi Ji, Jiuji Gongsi Shuo* (Chen Chi Works· On Company, 陈炽集·纠集公司说). Beijing: Zhonghua Book Company, p. 234.

2. The company implemented the Sponsor Responsibility System to supervise a sponsor to recruit exceptional talent. Zheng Guanying contended that if the sponsor was dishonest when selecting someone, he or she must be punished. For him, this meant supervising and judging everybody, which he believed would eliminate problems and maintain an appropriate ethos.[9] Note that these measures countered the principle of legality in a modern society. However, problems should be dealt with on a case-by-case basis. Sometimes, traditional disadvantages should be surmounted to achieve the goal of pursuing modern legal principles, and problems solved in traditional ways. This is the so-called national character of management.
3. The company should insist on ability first, and object to appointing people through nepotism. At that time, companies tended to employ managers from among their relatives and friends. This was fine for operations in a stable environment, but problems would arise once things became more competitive. Thus, this entrepreneur aimed to abolish these problems in his company and adopted a system of appointing personnel based on their abilities.

Appointed to manage the Shanghai Mechanical Textile Bureau, Zheng Guanying emphasized the importance of seeking "highly reputable people to forge connections with other people." This means employing those who were competent and confident. Later, he became the management assistant of China Merchants Steamship Navigation Company. He laid down 16 rules in the "Put Right Guideline" in an attempt to rectify the company's problems, emphasizing, "The rules must change when problems have been addressed. The emphasis is on recruiting and selecting personnel." He provided rules for the selection and employment of personnel. The first was appointing people based on abilities and assigning them work suited to these abilities. Once those with talent had been appointed, powers or authority of office were given. Relatives or friends of the manager who were found to be incompetent were to be dismissed immediately. The second rule was that specialized responsibilities be

[9] Zheng, G. (1982). *Zheng Guanying Ji, Yinhangxia Shangce* (Zheng Guanying works • Bank, Vol. 1, 郑观应集·银行下, 上册). Shanghai: Shanghai Renmin Chubanshe, p. 685.

clearly divided, and that rewards and punishments be given according to merit.[10]

9.3 Financial Management

The financial revenues of the government enterprises of the Westernization Group had no strict system; thus, excessive spending and various pretexts emerged arbitrarily therein. Even the Qing Dynasty admitted the phenomenon was irregular and surprising. Outside the company, aristocratic bureaucrats with power and influence got "served" by the company. Furthermore, officers who entered the company relying on the influence of the rich and powerful and controlled the company, and in turn they bribed their patrons using various names and did their utmost. On the Empress Dowager Cixi's birthday, four departmental officials in charge of the Kaiping Coal Mine paid 30,000 taels of silver in the name of the board of directors and shareholders. Beijing and Li Hongzhang praised them as loyal people.

How could financial management be improved? Ideologues of the Westernization Group proposed the following rules:

1. Establish the perfect financial system, and improve the cost of the party's mistakes

The constitution of Jiangnan Manufacturing General Bureau formulated by Zeng Guofan integrated each department. A manager was hired to handle the public affairs of the bureau, and two branch managers employed to help him. The "bargaining office, and revenue, expenditure, and final accounting office were established for the bureau, and several officials installed. The material was purchased as follows: first, the price was discussed with the merchant in the bargaining office. Second, this was ratified by the manager, and third, paid for in the revenue and expenditure office. Fourth, it was accounted for in the final accounting office. The process was precise to hinder embezzlement by those in charge. Three people were appointed to cover each other to ensure one person did

[10] Xia, D. (1981). *Zheng Guanying Zhuan* (郑观应传). Shanghai: East China Normal University Press, pp. 46–47.

not hold all the authority. Controlled by the manager, they were scrupulous and dared not cheat. The same applied to the manager. This is the so-called perfect rule."[11]

2. Improve the supervision system

Zheng Guanying thought that to improve, the company should be modeled based on cases from the West. He explained that if "the director is elected by shareholders, someone who has never worked in business cannot be employed. Selecting an expert in numbers means the accounts can be checked each month. When important things happen, the directors must call a meeting to discuss these. If nothing important has arisen, they should meet when settling the accounts. Every year, the manager records the accounts and business situation in a brochure, which is printed for everyone to see. The director expresses his views regarding selection as well." Simply put, "the director should do his best to maintain all that benefits the company."[12]

3. Strict and impartial financial management

When Zheng Guanying discussed exploiting the mine, he emphasized that the company should have a set of strict financial rules and regulations, and pointed out that after selecting a competent supervisor, the company should follow the following operational mechanisms: "The company should be constructed by adjusting measures to local conditions. This means the supervisor should consider the terrain, exit of the wells, costs, and the market. The company should not be mired by personnel abuse, ill treatment, extravagant situations, and wasted salaries." The amount of ore was calculated every year excepting the interest on tax and expenses. The surplus was divided: some was saved in the company, some divided equally, some presented to the manager, and some given as a reward to the mine. The settlement of accounts was clearly reported

[11] (1904, May 30, Jun. 2, 4, 8, 10). *Zhongwai Ribao, Lun Zhizaoju* (中外日报, 论制造局).

[12] Zheng, G. (1982). *Zheng Guanying Ji, Shangwusan Shangce* (Zheng Guanying works • Business (3), Vol. 1, 郑观应集·商务三, 上册). Shanghai: Shanghai Renmin Chubanshe, pp. 618–619.

and posted in the company for everyone to see. Zheng Guanying called this "management by law."[13]

4. Reduce the consumption of resources and focus on managing costs

Zheng Guanying analyzed the issues of reducing consumption, accelerating ship transfer, and increasing profits in the reform scheme implemented by the China Merchants Steamship Navigation Company. In terms of reducing consumption, his calculations included the ship's coal consumption when running. He pointed out that if a ship saved 1 ton of coal every day and night for 15 days per month, 180 tons of coal could be saved per year. Taking 30 vessel into account, this would save 5400 tons of coals annually. As "per ton of coal was valued 4 taels of silver, the total could be higher than 21,000." Therefore, "the burning of coal should be carefully monitored." He thought that another approach toward improving economic benefits was to dispatch the ship within a reasonable time and shorten the docking time. By docking a ship 1 day longer, in addition to needing more coal, a cost of 150 to 180 gold incurred. If stopping at every port for 1 day more a month, the cost of silver would increase by 600–700 as well. "Taking 30 vessel into account, this would save 200,000 gold annually," Zheng Guanying emphasized that the goods would be in enough demand to shorten the docking time, and that preparations should be made for the loading and unloading of cargo.[14]

9.4 Use Modern Management Means

At that time, official business enterprises largely implemented the means of traditional government in terms of management, as manifest in applying written instructions in a bureaucratic way, handling affairs without information, neglecting deadlines, and not paying attention to cost accounting. The management of modern enterprises must emphasize

[13] Zheng, G. (1982). *Zheng Guanying Ji, Kaikuangshang Shangce* (Zheng Guanying works, Vol. 1, 郑观应集·开矿上, 上册). Shanghai: Shanghai Renmin Chubanshe, p. 705.

[14] Zheng, G. (1988). *Zheng Guanying Ji, Shengshi Weiyan Houbian,Juanshi Xiace* (Zheng Guanying works, Vol. 10, 郑观应集·盛世危言后编, 下册). Shanghai: Shanghai Renmin Chubanshe, p. 786.

principles related to staving off problems, effort, finances, and material. With no regard for these principles, decisions were made at the leaders' volition. In the long days of managing the company, the Westernization Group realized the great differences between managing a modern company and small family business. Here, traditional management methods were essentially useless. In the progress of managing a modern company, they had to learn from Western managerial experience.

1. Managers must obtain specialized education and have knowledge on manufacturing. Hu Yufen noted that "the foremen and craftsmen of foreign companies come from college and learn from the origin. In addition, the people who supervise the mall are experts in technology and have knowledge of photoelectric effects. Thus, they can keep and create laws and keep improving. Right now, some managers in the bureau of China know nothing about these conditions. They cannot distinguish between the minerals or name the machinery. It is rare for them to not cheat on workmanship and materials."[15] According to Zheng Guanying, "If the managers of the steamship company are not familiar with the business, they will not be able to find able people and employ them in suitable posts. If they were fooled by other people and managed improperly, they suspect a lack of knowledge. When they demonstrate their disappointment, the company will suffer losses."[16] Zhong Tianwei added that at that time, while many Chinese companies bought the materials abroad at a high price, they could have bought the same material in China. While the prices were similar, they paid more when adding expenses related to transportation. This practice ensued because no one in the company understood the materials, thus putting everything under the command of foreigners.[17]
2. Managers should delve into the workings of machine production to research the production process and master site management. Using the steamship company as example, Zheng Guanying illustrated the

[15] *Guanxu Zhengyao* (Vol. 21, XVII, 光绪政要). pp. 17–18.

[16] Zheng, G. (1982). *Zheng Guanying Ji, Shangwusan Shangce* (Zheng Guanying works • Business (3), Vol. 1, 郑观应集·商务三, 上册). Shanghai: Shanghai Renmin Chubanshe, p. 619.

[17] Zhong, T. *Yuezu Ji, Daini Bing Lijuexiang Caiche Jiqiju Tiaoyi* (Zhong's Righteous Words, 刖足集·代拟禀李爵相裁撤机器局条议).

importance of site management, explaining, "The cargo should be received before the canvassing ship arrives. If it is not received first, the shipping schedule will be delayed. I see ships waiting for cargo everywhere, which increases the cost of waterway transportation." Once the cargo had been collected, he proposed "supervising the porter to advance the job rather than stay in dock. If we dock for a day every time, we will lose a lot of money. This is very important for those engaged in the shipping industry." Regarding the cargo on the ship an inn, he thought that "laborers should be supervised to stack it neatly to avoid wasting space, which will save on rent." As such, corrupt acts like smuggling cargo in the cabin, reporting an inferior seat, reporting higher hotel expenses, evading passengers, and collecting rent privately were easily abolished thanks to human effort.[18]

3. Introducing the competition system into the internal enterprise was not only good for reducing production costs, but also for eliminating corruption. In 1892, Zheng Guanying was appointed by Li Hongzhang for the second time to manage the China Merchants Steamship Navigation Company, where he was charged with fixing the company.
4. Strengthen internal oversight mechanisms of the construction of the company

Zheng Guanying stated that despite the dispersed business of the company, each ship operated dependently, which complicated supervision and enabled corruption from the ship owner and cabin. It is difficult to guard against natural disasters. To improve managerial effectiveness, Zheng Guanying proposed strengthening supervision. To do this, the first action should be introducing punishments to increase the anticipated cost of any transgressions or mistakes, which would decrease the costs associated with such mistakes.

5. Purchasing principle

[18] Zheng, G. (1982). *Zheng Guanying Ji, Shangwusan Shangce* (Zheng Guanying works, Business (3), Vol. 1, 郑观应集·商务三, 上册). Shanghai: Shanghai Renmin Chubanshe, p. 619.

Jing Yuanshan believed the manager of the company should pay attention to two principles when purchasing raw material, namely quality and price.

9.5 Marketing Management

At the beginning of Westernization, many people joined the new industry as they admired the high profits of foreign merchants. They believed that through machine production and adopting Western technology, they too would generate a profit and divide the interest of foreigners. However, they did not consider the issue of market demand, which was a mistake. A low price and good quality of production would certainly improve market appeal. However, the products could not be sold if the people did not have purchasing power and desire. At that time, many companies did not pay attention to the market and ultimately declared bankruptcy, leaving a stock of unsold products.

1. Paying attention to market investigation

In the discussion on scientific decision-making, we cited Zheng Guanying: "We must take the whole situation into account and plan accordingly in business, being confident before taking action. If we want to buy goods to be first, we must be familiar with the market situation and distribution of goods in this place." These words are also valuable in terms of market management. Zheng Guanying disagreed with the behavior of those not familiar with market conditions and anxious for success. He emphasized that "to start a business, one must first test to remain unbeaten, and then gradually expand to succeed."[19]

2. Paying attention to collecting information

At that time, the enterprise operating conditions in China were poor. One important reason for this was that no attention was paid to collecting business information. In China, the attitude toward business was one

[19] Zheng, G. (1982). *Zheng Guanying Ji, Shangwusan Shangce* (Zheng Guanying works, Business (3), Vol. 1, 郑观应集·商务三, 上册). Shanghai: Shanghai Renmin Chubanshe, p. 621.

of restraint and dislike, the rise and decline of businesses were not paid attention to, and the country was long closed to international exchange. Furthermore, there was little understanding of the external and internal business environment. When the ban on maritime trade lifted, more people spoke about developing a business, but ignored business information.

3. Paying attention to sales promotion

Foreign investors played a guiding role in this respect. In Shanghai, to promote products, foreign tradesmen struggled to place adverts for a few months. Newspapers became a major advertising media, which impacted China's entrepreneurs. For instance, Laoshunji Matheson was established by Ye Chengzhong, who placed an advert in *Shen Bao Newspaper* (*Shanghai News*) for 10 months to sell a ship in 1876–1877. Another example is the national entrepreneur Jing Yuanshan, who was in charge of soliciting stock for Shanghai Textile Bureau. He took measures to offer shares for public subscription in the newspaper to expand its social influence and relieve concerns related to the textile bureau. From October 13 to 15, 1888, Shanghai Mechanical Textile Bureau's invitation to invest and buy stocks of incorporation was published in Shen Bao Newspaper (Shanghai news). The article emphasized that although the officials caused problems, the essence is business control, a public construction project, and careful budgetary expenditure. The names of banks and commercial firms with stock and methods to buy a share were published. If the stock was not neat, the first 3% of silver income would be collected and the interest reimbursed as an amount. The article clearly explained that the extravagant habits of the officials would be eliminated, and stipulated that those who become directors of the company must be moral and familiar with the business conditions. Furthermore, the director would be elected by shareholders, who would be consulted on any major events. Methods to collect shares in public were rare at that time. The published content and practice respected the rights and interests of business stock in the bureau and ensured that stocks did not lose interest. This strengthened business enterprises and the move was welcomed by shareholders.[20]

Faced with fierce market competition, both foreign and domestic steamships failed to sell well. In this case, some entrepreneurs adopted flexible marketing methods. For example, Ye Chengzhong, founder of the Fachang Machine Factory, introduced a flexible operation mode, building steamships to "rent or buy" according to customers' demands.[21] Of course, this was advantageous for Fachang Machine Factory, reducing the overstock of funds and utilizing products to advertise activities. To overcome difficult situations, some private companies adjusted their scope of business to market needs. While the original main operation was steamship repair, both Dachang Machine Factory and Yongchang Machine Factory shifted operations to using Italian silk spinning machinery and copying professional silk manufacturers. They used small horsepower steam engines in the 1880s to oppress foreign steamships and the silk spinning industry emerged.[22] Realizing that the lack of a source of coal in the market and its high price led to the failure of coal-engine small steamships, some companies carried out reforms on the production process and successfully produced small non-coal pedal steamships and artificial small "push and move" steamships. For example, the bomb steamship designed and manufactured by Guangdechang Machine Factory in 1889 was equipped with tents and paddles in case "all the coal was used. In the absence of coal, the steamship can still move with the power of the wind or labor force." When the steamship launched, British-owned Xiangsheng Steamship Factory had much praise, stating, "This is the best China has produced since it started manufacturing steamships."[23] Therefore, the private invested steamship and machine with limited capital, and it developed relatively quickly after they adjusted the scope of operations, carried out reforms, and adopted a flexible operation mode based on the market.

[20] Jing, Y (时间). *Juyichu Ji, Juanyi* (A Collection of Juyi, Vol. 1, 居易初集, 卷1), p. 55.

[21] (1879, Nov 16). *Shen Bao* (the Chinese newspaper Shenpao, 申报).

[22] (1966). *Shanghai Minzu Jiqi Gongye, Juanyi* (Shanghai National Machinery Industry, Vol. 1, 上海民族机器工业, 上册). Beijing: Zhonghua Book Company, p. 91, p. 99.

[23] Sun, Y. (1957). *Zhongguo Jindai Gongyeshi Ziliao Diyiji Xiace* (Materials of Chinese Modern Industrial History, Vol. 1, Part II, 中国近代工业史资料, 第1辑, 下册). Beijing: Science Press, pp. 1032–1033.

4. Paying attention to the motivation and restrictions of marketing personnel

According to Zhong Tianwei, "the Chinese are less creative than the foreigners, but on imitating and pursuing personal gains, they are much better. From the royal court officials to the folk people, no one acts sincerely." With China Merchants Steamship Navigation Company as an example, he said their marketing staff (referring to the compradors searching for business for the China Merchants Steamship Navigation Company) "apply for more reimbursement or report less freight. When it comes to passengers, they will load as many as possible so they can charge additional shipping fees fee privately. They even carry forbidden goods to make personal profits. Thus, besides the annual wage of 1000 taels of silver, they often have extra gains."

In fact, this situation existed in both government-run (including government-supervised and merchant-managed enterprises) and merchant-run enterprises. How could this problem be solved? Zhong Tianwei proposed two approaches. First, he highlighted the importance of the appointment of marketing staff. He believed they were currently appointed based on being the relatives of the business executives or recommendations of others. Thus, Zhong required that the office chief of companies act justly, and "not bend the law for personal gains but implement enforcement and refuse bribes." Second, he suggested increasing the wage of marketing staff and steepening the penalties for their mistakes.[24]

He contended, "We should imitate foreign companies and increase their wage, make them improve their actions, and restrain their behaviors with regulations. They can then have the qualification of recommendation. Those who make no mistakes over a long period can enjoy lifelong public supply. If mistakes are discovered, their good reputation will be destroyed and other companies will not employ them." He believed that with such strict incentives, people would cherish their reputation, perform their duties, and not engage in malpractice. The author believes that the moral infidelity in business highlighted by Zhong Tianwei is correct, but doubts his solutions could address the problem. His perspective is

[24] Zhong, T. *Yuezu Ji, Waipian* (Outer Chapter of Zhong's Righteous Words, 刖足集·外篇).

less mature and pragmatic than that of Zheng Guanying. For example, his recommendation to limit the appointment authority of the office chief is undoubtedly correct, but no specific measure and moral requirements could be implemented. In addition, imitating foreign companies by improving material and political benefits to the marketers, and increasing the costs of mistakes through penalties and other measures are also good ideas. However, China was importing the market economy at that time and did not have the norms of professional ethics applied in Western countries. A marketer who had made mistakes could still find a job in other companies. Therefore, what Zhong Tianwei expected—everyone valued their reputations and dared not make mistakes—could not manifest in reality. In this regard, Zhong Tianwei's management approach is too idealistic. Management is a kind of culture. Only when we adjust it according to the Chinese pattern can we increase the costs of their mistakes and effectively improve management. Zheng Guanying's method was more effective because he combined Western management with Chinese conditions.

In addition, according to the ancient Chinese art of war strategies, Zheng Guanying proposed a marketing strategy of taking advantage of our strong points to compete with the rival's weak ones. He indicated: "If the rivals focus on the price, we pay attention to the value; if they focus on the quantity, we pay attention to the quality. We can live with or without the rivals' products, but they cannot live without our products. This strategy comes from *The Art of War*—using the best horse to compete with the second-best horse of the enemy and using our second-rate horse to compete with the more inferior horse of the enemy." This is the strategy of one loss and two wins.[25] This perspective, which is similar to the current notion of "producing things people do not have and improving it when other people also have it," reflects the Chinese characteristic of aiming for victory against foreign companies amid fierce market competition.

[25] Zheng, G. (1982). *Zheng Guanying Ji, Shangzhanshang Shangce* (Zheng Guanying works • Commercial War I, Vol. 1, 郑观应集·商战上, 上册). Shanghai: Shanghai Renmin Chubanshe, p. 590.

CHAPTER 10

Views on the Enterprise Organization System Construction

To raise enough capital for economic development, Western companies designed a joint-stock system of operations. Approving of this mode of operation, the Westernization Group thought that as "many a little makes a mickle," the approach would address the scarcity of capital in China's modernization attempts, and as such, should be promoted. However, the joint-stock company system was closely linked with advanced large-scale socialized production. Neglecting that the system was a management innovation, the Westernization Group honed in on its advantages in terms of funding but ignored its complex internal structure. Therefore, when the joint-stock company system was introduced in China, it was not adapted to the country's traditional heritage system, values, and customs. The Westernization Group explored this advanced approach further to ensure it took root in China. Their main assumptions are described below.

10.1 Establishing a Joint-Stock Company

Along with the gunboat diplomacy of Western colonizers, the joint-stock company system was introduced into China and attracted the interest of the progressing Chinese people. Wei Yuan favorably introduced this system in *Haiguo Tuzhi* (*Illustrated Annals of Overseas Countries*), writing, "Dozens of Western countries trade with Guangdong Province.

J. Zhou, *Westernization Movement and Early Thought of Modernization in China*, Palgrave Studies in Economic History,
https://doi.org/10.1007/978-3-030-86985-4_10

Among these countries, only Britain adopts the pattern of a joint-stock company rather than distributed traders. A joint-stock company is co-financed and co-operated by tens of distributed traders. Regarding funding, all the traders work together. As to the profits, the money is divided according to their investment. This model takes advantage of its scale."[1] Thereafter, many Chinese businessmen wanted to adopt this mode of operation and invest in new companies. In the Sixth Year of the Tongzhi Reign (1867), Rong Hong proposed four recommendations to Ding Richang, the governor of Jiangsu Province. The first was "to organize a joint-venture steamship company."[2] In the 11th year of the Tongzhi Reign (1872), Li Hongzhang cited in *Memorial: Steamship Construction Cannot be Dismissed* that "foreign traders have swept up all steamship trade in all ports." Thus, if Chinese businessmen wanted to regain the economic rights thereto, "we must have our own companies." Owing to his political power and influence, the Qing government quickly approved the request and set up China's first joint-stock company, the China Ship Business Soliciting Bureau. Based on the Western convention, the "bureau is established by an official to address national affairs, while the company is built by the merchants to manage business."[3] Thus, China Ship Business Soliciting Bureau did not name the company. Since then, Li Hongzhang, Zuo Zongtang, and other Westernization officials established a series of joint-stock companies based on the design of China Ship Business Soliciting Bureau.

The initial joint-stock companies in China were supervised by the government and managed by the merchants. The support of officials afforded these companies various privileges including industrial monopoly. As such, their external competitiveness was strengthened and the earning expectations of civil society improved. As a result, in treaty ports—particularly in Shanghai, the new economic stronghold of China—people were enthusiastic about this type of investment. In 1882, *Shanghai Pingzhun Voting Company Charter* noted: "Envious of the great gains of

[1] Wei, Y. *Haiguo Tuzhi, Chouhai Pian Si* (Haiguo Tuzhi: Chouhai Four, 海国图志·筹海篇四).

[2] Rong, H. (1998). *Xixue Dongjian Ji* (My Life in China and America, 西学东渐记). Zhengzhou: Zhongzhou Ancient Books Publishing House, p. 147.

[3] Zheng, G. (1982). *Zheng Guanying Ji, Shangwuer Shangce* (Zheng Guanying Works·Business Affairs II, Vol. 1, 郑观应集·商务二, 上册). Shanghai: Shanghai Renmin Chubanshe, p. 612.

the China Ship Business Soliciting Bureau and Kaiping Mine Company, people competed to invest in companies, and more than ten joint-stock companies were established in one year. Once a new company was established, thousands of people would rush to buy stock, so excited to gain a share that they cared little about its vicissitude."[4]

This highlights the new trend regarding companies from citizens' perspective. However, that same year, the Shanghai stock market plunged, sparking a financial crisis and wave of bankruptcies. Under this heavy blow, almost all small and medium-sized joint-stock companies collapsed. Only large-scale joint-stock companies survived with the help of officials. Significant in the history of China's joint-stock companies, this event clarified to advocators—the Westernization Group—that while a joint-stock company was convenient in terms of funding, there were potential dangers. Thus, to avoid the risks, the modern enterprise system had to be constructed and promoted.

1. A joint-stock company must be established in accordance with the law and tighter company quality reviews must be initiated. In 1883—during the time of the financial crisis—Zhong Tianwei wrote the article *Ten Items on Business Expansion*. In "Combining Companies," he detailed success stories of Western countries and emphasized the importance of law. He said, "Before establishing companies, Westerners must first report to the government. Then, the Ministry of Commerce assigns officials to conduct an investigation. Only those deemed to show potential and prospect obtain approval." Alternatively, in China, "People only report to the superior, and then summon investment and fabricate a charter and description." In other words, the hasty construction of China's joint-stock companies fueled the preceding crisis. Accordingly, Zhong Tianwei believed that to ensure that an advanced form of joint-stock company take root in China, we must "follow the Westerners and lay down laws." From now on, "an investigation by the Chamber of Commerce is a necessity for each company."[5] Only

[4] Shanghai City Archives. (1992). *Jiu Shanghai de Zhengquan Jiaoyisuo* (Stock Exchanges of Old Shanghai, 旧上海的证券交易所). Shanghai: Shanghai Classics Publishing House, p. 263.

[5] Zhong, T. *Yuezu Ji, Kuochong Shangwu Shitiao* (Zhong's Righteous Words • Ten Items on Business Expansion, 刖足集·扩充商务十条).

> those who conformed to the founding conditions were permitted to start a company. However, fueled by the corruption and incompetence of Qing government officials, the review merely provided them with opportunities to take bribes. Therefore, Zhong Tianwei transferred the power from the state to the Chamber of Commerce.

How was a quality review to be conducted? Zheng Guanying suggested, "Those who want to start a company must report the following details: Who will be the shareholders and chief executive? How many capital stocks do they have? What kind of business are they going to operate? After clarifying, they can go to the local official for the registration. Without this registration, should anything bad happen, the official will not take care of it. With registration, the company will be protected and no exploitation will take place. This foundation will halt corrupt practices."[6] Here, the conditions to establish a company were clear: Running a company needs an applicant and investors, registered capital, purposes, and the legal force of registration.

According to the Westernization Group, the purposes of a quality review was to ensure the company had the potential to grow, which would on one hand, strengthen company management and improve efficiency, and on the other, protect the interests of shareholders.

2. We must establish a sound internal organization system. Zhong Tianwei noted that "in western countries, except shareholders, all companies had 12 directors. The general director appoints a general and deputy executive. All possess many shares. The power of the general executive is restrained by the directors, and that of directors by shareholders. In that way, rights are strictly limited, and as a result, companies run in an orderly way and malpractice is avoided from the headstream." Zhong Tianwei further pointed out the most severe problem in Chinese companies, namely the unstable organization system. In this regard, Chinese companies merely simulated the form of Western companies, but ignored their essence. In his opinion, as joint-stock and traditional companies in China differed in terms of fundraising, joint-stock companies needed to adopt a

[6] Zheng, G. (1982). *Zheng Guanying Ji, Shangwuer Shangce* (Zheng Guanying Works, Business Affairs II, Vol. 1, 郑观应集·商务二, 上册). Shanghai: Shanghai Renmin Chubanshe, p. 613.

stable organization system that differed from that applied in traditional companies. He added that the Western Board System was an ideal way to prevent injustice in companies. He further advocated that Chinese joint-stock companies learn the Board System from the Westerners and include it in company review procedures: "When someone wants to establish a company, the Chamber of Commerce must examine its charter, ensuring that the shareholders, rather than the general executive, have the initiative of decision-making. Otherwise, in the railway, telegraph, mining, and manufacturing industries, any official will be able to start a company with the money of others."[7]

3. Government should utilize state power to support joint-stock companies. In 1893, Xue Fucheng, a Chinese ambassador to Europe, wrote *Reasons Companies Fail*. In the book, he noted, "Foreign companies succeed for the following reasons: common interest and common will, precise regulations, strict administration, and refined plans. However, in China, businessmen do not have common will and their actions do not accord with the regulations. In terms of the regulations, they are a mere scrap of paper, and furthermore, companies do not have a detailed plan. They are thus doomed to fail."[8] According to him, the government should be held responsible for this failure. Without its close attention, no commercial ethos would be formed. He emphasized, "According to Western custom, joint-stock companies are considered the lifeline of all countries. They are inspired by the government, and are thus more likely to have enough capital. With strict regulations added, they are more likely to succeed and affect the social commercial ethos. In China, joint-stock companies are set up in one night. People rush to run a company before understanding the essence thereof, and the government fails to comprehensively review these plans. How can commercial ethos take shape in China?" Xue Fucheng's viewpoint is convincing. On one hand, the government can advance the formation of a country's micro production through various incentives,

[7] Zhong, T. *Yuezu Ji, Kuochong Shangwu Shitiao* (Zhong's Righteous Words, Ten Items on Business Expansion, 刖足集·扩充商务十条).

[8] Xue, F. (1987). *Xue Fucheng Xuanji, Lun Gongsi Buju Zhibing* (Selected Works of Xue Fucheng, On the Fatal Disease of Companies, 薛福成选集·论公司不举之病). Shanghai: Shanghai Renmin Chubanshe, p. 480.

and in turn, establish its foundation. On the other, it can eliminate the negative effects that could hinder its development through violent power. As such, the Chinese government could help establishing joint-stock companies in China. Unfortunately, the late Qing government still focused on maintaining the traditional method of production. For the Chinese government, it was enough to not suppress the development of the new economy, let alone encouragement it. In this respect, Sheng Xuanhuai held the similar views as Xue Fucheng. He regarded government's unreasonable policy as an important factor in the struggle of joint-stock companies. In particular, he discussed the sacrifices from companies to the government, stating, "Mohe Company, steamship companies, wire companies, and Kaiping Mine Company all offer up sacrifices, which may hinder the operations of joint-stock companies." Thus, Sheng Xuanhuai proposed adopting the Western method and formulating regulations: "In Western countries, companies deliver taxes according to their incomes and there is no company sacrifice." He believed China should do the same: "If a joint-stock company runs with the help of the government, when gaining profits, it should offer up two tens of its profits. This sacrifice is called a contribution, an offering from the profits." Moreover, no more contribution was available. "If the joint-stock companies established by Chinese businessmen are not funded with the money of the officials and do not differ from other independent shops, they need not pay any sacrifice. The above mentioned should be included in the regulations to avoid the doubts and concerns of Chinese businessmen." He also proposed "making decisions on discretionary business law so that Chinese businessmen have a route to follow, and to avoid officials bending the law for personal gain. In other words, Chinese businessmen should not attach themselves to foreign businessmen, thus fostering the force of the enemy."[9]

In terms of governance, Zheng Guanying considered it important to "learn from Western law and lay down the business law of China as soon as possible. China only enacts criminal law, temperament theory, press

[9] Sheng, X. (1901). *Yuzhai Cungao Juansan* (Memorials of Sheng Xuanhuai, Vol. 3, Telegraph from Liu Xianshuai, 愚斋存稿, 卷3).

regulations, and navigation Acts; thus, there is no institution for business people to litigate." On one hand, this will invite "individual officials and the unjust treatment of businessmen." On the other, it would lead to "corruption between small tradesmen and porters. The fortunate ones may be able to avoid this, but the majority will not be able to survive. They may therefore consider a joint-stock company a risky method."[10] Adding that "without commercial law, the business of a country cannot flourish," he suggested that the imperial court "absorb the strong aspects of the laws of the western countries, and formulate and enact this law in China."[11] To ensure Chinese businessmen truly understood the details of the Western organization system, Zheng Guanying included the *British Company Ordinance* compiled by George Jamieson, the British consul general in Shanghai, in *Warnings in a Blooming Age,* adding, "Britain enacted the Company Ordinance and proved its effectiveness in practice. We can learn from them and avoid the fraudulent practices of corrupt merchants."

4. The importance of constructing internal morality in companies must be stressed. The Westernization Group believed that to root joint-stock companies in China, in addition to laws and regulations, internal morality or the cultural construction of companies was also needed. In *Reasons for Companies' Failure,* Xue Fucheng emphasized that one reason foreign companies succeeded was their "common interest and will" or common values and ethics. The main reason Chinese companies failed was that they lacked a unified set of values and ethics. He suggested that the government play its part in forming the appropriate social environment and help establish joint-stock companies through encouragement, regulation, and education. Sheng Xuanhuai agreed. In 1899, he submitted "Memorial: Statement on Training, Raising Military Expenditure, and Other Business Affairs." In the memorial, he attributed the failure in the promotion of joint-stock companies to the quality

[10] Zheng, G. (1982). *Zheng Guanying Ji Shangwusan Shangce* (Zheng Guanying Works·Business Affairs III, Vol. 1, 郑观应集·商务三, 上册). Shanghai: Shanghai Renmin Chubanshe, p. 622.

[11] Zheng, G. (1982). *Zheng Guanying Ji Shangwuer Shangce* (Zheng Guanying Works·Business Affairs II, Vol. 1, 郑观应集·商务二, 上册). Shanghai: Shanghai Renmin Chubanshe, p. 613.

> of Chinese merchants. He said, "Chinese businessmen are short-sighted. They care about nothing but the benefits for themselves. Those who invest in a company only care about their profits, not the development of the company. Some people cooperate to open a company, but it is not different from other shops. Other companies like western Joint-stock Company, fail to operate smoothly in China with local businessmen. It is eventually competed by foreigners for its balanced rights and interests and unified management, which is regrettable for Chinese."[12]

Discussing the development of a joint-stock company, Chen Chi emphasized that "the general executive of a company should devote himself to the public interest" and highlighted the importance of morality.

According to him, "Fair or unfair behavior determines whether a company succeeds or not. What is a company? It integrates justice into business affairs." Chen Chi explained the meaning of a company from an exegetical perspective; however, his views were too idealistic. He criticized the unfairness of Chinese companies, believing that a company's managers should "never lose trust among businessmen. They should rather endure losses than let colleagues suffer."[13] Essentially, businessmen should completely safeguard investors' interests. According to him, if managers can manage companies in this way, companies, whether government or merchant run, could succeed.

The opinions of Xue Fucheng, Sheng Xuanhuai, and Chen Chi are reasonable. Modern business is huge in scale in terms of staff and complex in terms of internal labor division. Thus, simply relying on the supervision of managers increases management costs and decreases company competitiveness. In this case, a company culture should be constructed and a set of unified ethics and values formulated, which would ensure the company embarks on a healthy road and decrease business costs. However, in China's government-run companies, this was difficult to achieve. To form unified values, companies must first form a centripetal force. To this end, companies should not only offer objective interest to shareholders, but

[12] Sheng, X. (1901). *Yuzhai Cungao Juansan* (Memorials of Sheng Xuanhuai, Vol. 3, Telegraph from Liu Xianshuai, 愚斋存稿, 卷3).

[13] Zheng, G. (1982). *Zheng Guanying Ji Shangwuer Shangce* (Zheng Guanying Works·Business Affairs II, Vol. 1, 郑观应集·商务二, 上册). Shanghai: Shanghai Renmin Chubanshe, p. 613.

also develop an interest mechanism based on varied contributions. Only in this way could colleagues feel comfortable and derive a sense of belonging to the company, which would enable them to cultivate shared values and morality. The pressure of foreign competition forced modern companies in China to face huge risk and rendered them unable to obtain a profit, which fueled the short-term opinions of shareholders. Moreover, the transformation of the modern society destroyed the traditional value of "justice benefit" and strengthened these short-term opinions. Thus, various types of corrupt practices emerged in companies. This further demonstrated that in modern China, while important, it was difficult to construct a company culture.

5. The securities market needed to be standardized. The Westernization Group realized that to maintain the healthy development of joint-stock companies, the securities market had to be standardized. In an earlier section of the chapter, it was noted that when the joint-stock company system arrived in China, business managers merely considered it an efficient new way to raise funds. Ordinary shareholders used its advantages to make a profit fast without considering the risks. At the end of 1882, a financial crisis erupted in Shanghai, highlighting the risks of the funding system to the Westernization Group: As long as the shareholders of a company had good expectations, they would invest capital into the company, expediting its development. In contrast, should their expectations be pessimistic, they would sell the stocks, worsening the situation. Therefore, how could people's investment behavior in the securities market be standardized and benefits delivered to the long-term interests of these companies?

In "Combining Companies" in *Ten Items on Business Expansion*, Zhong Tianwei analyzed the speculative notion of shareholders. He pointed out that China's shareholders tend to buy stocks blindly: "They did not intend to leave property to descendants, but speculated through the ups and downs of the stocks."[14] In 1888, he further pointed out in

[14] Zhong, T. *Yuezu Ji, Kuochong Shangwu Shitiao* (Zhong's Righteous Words • Ten Items on Business Expansion, 刖足集·扩充商务十条).

Restoring the Livelihoods of China's Industry and Commerce that "capital from the wealthy is meant to collect property to leave to the next generation. Capital from ordinary people is speculatory. If they do not gain profits immediately, they will abandon it without hesitation, leading companies to disintegrate. Thus, it is better to absorb larger stocks than dispersed small amounts of money."[15] He delineated individuals who invested in stocks as investors and speculators. Those who "want to leave property to their descendants" are investors, and those who "buy and sell" are speculators. According to him, most large stock buyers were investors and independent stock buyers were speculators. Thus, he noted that it would be better to absorb larger stock than small amounts of money. However, Zhong Tianwei's delineation was not scientific, as ordinary people who made speculatory investments could also purchase larger stock.

It is not good practice to welcome investors and oppose speculators when developing the stock market. In particular, it is inadvisable to attribute the failure of a joint-stock company to frequent stock turnover. In general, people select a stock because they want to gain a profit from it, not to invest in the development of a company. Therefore, most people were more interested in the stock prices than company performance. However, there were significant aspects in Zhong Tianwei's views. He considered that to stabilize companies, a group of long-term investors was needed. This is aligned with what we advocate today in joint-stock companies, hoping that each listed company has a number of relatively stable long-term investors. Indeed, only long-term investors who want to "leave property to their descendants" care about companies' management and exercise their rights, improving the efficiency of these businesses through the joint-stock system.

Chen Chi also believed that to ensure shareholders stayed in the stock market, the government should formulate laws to protect their rights. According to him, "Previously, many mining companies shut down and the founders took the remaining money. A negative effect was that people complained about the stocks. Based on this, the officials mistook the joint-stock approach as a risky method, and thus did not permit it. Therefore, people dared not respond to the appeal despite gently opposing

[15] Zhong, T. *Yuezu Ji, Wanhui Zhongguo Gongshang Shengji Liquan Lun* (Zhong's Righteous Words • Restoring Livelihoods of China's Industry and Commerce, 刖足集·挽回中国工商生计利权论).

the officials' stance."[16] This shows that Chen Chi's view was far-sighted. However, without relevant laws and regulations, and strict enforcement thereof, the problem could not be addressed. Unfortunately, it was difficult to enact these in the late Qing Dynasty, and it became difficult to reinvigorate Chinese businesses.

During this period, public opinion also showed that investors should be aware of the risks in investment and careful in stock selection. In the late 1870s and early 1880s, the Chinese tended to invest in minerals. Many small and medium-sized government-supervised and merchant-managed companies "such as Changle, Hefeng, Chizhou, Jinzhou, Jingmen, Chengde, and Xuzhou were established as soon as they obtained approval with hundreds of thousands in financing."[17] Zhong Tianwei was critical, stating that "shareholders do not care about the location and quality of mining resources."[18] They invested blindly, daring not to benefit anyone else. By 1882, China Ship Business Soliciting Bureau, Kaiping Mine Company, and other government-supervised and merchant-managed companies in Shanghai were able to operate smoothly. However, the rest were still in the planning phase and their profitability could not yet be predicted. However, the stocks they issued were speculatory, and the market prices were higher than the face value, some twice as much. Thus, to some extent, investors' blind investment gave rise to a stock market bubble. This false prosperity would undoubtedly discourage people's investment once the bubble burst. Therefore, until the 1890s, many people still feared any mention of a company. This phenomenon reflected the aspiration of private capital investment in the new economy, but was also a blind impulse in the development of capitalism in China.

10.2 Notion of Merchant-Managed Enterprises

At the onset of the launch of modern industry in the 1860s, a debate emerged among those of the Westernization Group in terms of government-run and merchant-managed companies. This debate gradually expanded, peaking in the 1880s–1890s. Consequently, the appeal of

[16] Chen, C. (1997). *Chenchi Ji, Chuangli Shangdu Shuo* (Chen Chi Works, Establishing Commerce Chamber, 陈炽集·创立商都说). Beijing: Zhonghua Book Company, p. 233.

[17] (1883, Jan 22). *Zilin Hubao* (Zilin Shanghai Gazette, 字林沪报).

[18] Zhong, T. *Yuezu Ji, Kuochong Shangwu Shitiao* (Zhong's Righteous Words, Ten Items on Business Expansion, 刖足集·扩充商务十条).

merchant-managed enterprises increasingly grew. After the 1894–1895 Sino-Japanese War, the Qing authorities officially encouraged private businessmen to invest in new industries, hoping they could take over government-run ammunitions companies running at a loss. Later, they also promoted investing private capital into the new industrial and commercial enterprises. This indicates the shift in the national policy toward permitting ordinary people to freely establish factories. In the twentieth century, the Qing government implemented the New Deal, a law confirming the legal status of ordinary people establishing factories. This signified the progress of merchant-managed enterprises from theory to practice.

Toward the end of the First Opium War (Britain's invasion of China, 1840–1842) at the end of 1842, Wei Yuan compiled the *Illustrated Treatise on the Maritime Kingdoms (Hai-guo tu zhi)*, which proposed measures to solve the problems faced by the Qing Dynasty. Discussing how to "learn technology from foreigners," he advocated strictly limiting officials' involvement in economic activities and the approach of prioritizing privately operated enterprises. The government-run handicraft industry has a long history in China, and as such, Wei Yuan had an in-depth understanding of the collapse of government-run enterprises in the Qing Dynasty and corrupt behavior of officials in economic activities. He stressed that "if coastal traders voluntarily construct shipbuilding and firearms factories, it will be permitted for both personal use and for sale. If officials build warships and firearms factories, they should be located in the east of Guangdong Province."[19] He further proposed that officials "not undertake shipbuilding." This reflected the policy of restricting government-run enterprises and freeing the development of the non-governmental economy.

At the beginning of the establishment of Fuzhou Arsenal in 1866, speaking to Zongli Yamen, Guo Songtao proposed that "to ensure China's steamships can compete with those of foreigners, it is not appropriate to only rely on the few steamships built by the government. We should allow merchants to build steamships to take the benefits from foreigners. If we can do so, we will certainly retain our competitiveness." He further advocated that official of the marine trade, elected by the merchants, manage the official steamships, "which should without

[19] Wei, Y. *Haiguo Tuzhi, Chouhai Pian San Juan Er* (Haiguo Tuzhi, Chouhai Four, Vol. 2, 海国图志·筹海篇三, 卷2), p. 46.

exception be used to ship goods on merchant steamships." However, this proposal, which depended on merchant shipbuilding and the development of domestic and foreign trade, was not adopted. Instead, "Zuo Zongtang, the governor-general of Fujian Province, implemented the Imperial court decision to set up a minister of Vessel Administration. Consequently, only one steamship was manufactured at a cost of more than millions taels of silver after more than 3 years." Guo Songtao had no choice but to lament, "Zuo Zongtang's proposal was adopted instead of mine, which is also the destiny of the country."[20]

After the 1870s, under the impact of Song Jin's proposal to stop manufacturing steamships and the Japanese invasion of Taiwan, the debate on how to develop China's economy emerged. Zheng Guanying, Guo Songtao, and others who clearly opposed the route of government-run enterprises, advocated developing the economy by using private businessmen.

In *Saving the Times*, issued in March 1873, Zheng Guanying pointed out there were difficulties hard to eliminate in governmental shipbuilding and insisted on replacing government-run enterprises with merchant-managed ones. He explained, "If merchants build ships, there will be a steady stream of funds and no need to worry about the quality, because this undertaking is closely related to their lives and family possessions even without supervision and punishment. As it is, the government need not raise funds, but will still be able to fill the sea with available ships. A few years later, as commerce gradually revives, the manufacturing process will also be improved." Therefore, he thought they should "advocate for long-term policies dealing with replacing government-run enterprises with merchant-managed ones.[21] Discussing the issue of coastal defense in 1875, Guo Songtao proposed a complete program for the development of private capitalism in his memorial "Proposals on Affairs Related to Coastal Defense." He stated, "The costal businessmen are the right people for manufacturing machines and equipment. Those who trade by sea will weigh gains and losses and have a plan to preserve life and possessions. Therefore, they learn lessons by reviewing why the foreigners failed

[20] Guo, S. (1981). *Guo Songtao Riji Juan Er* (郭嵩焘日记, 卷2). Changsha: Hunan People's Publishing House, p. 608, p. 609.

[21] Zheng, G. (1982). *Zheng Guanying Ji, Lun Zhongguo Lunchuan Jin Zhi Dalve Shangce* (Zheng Guanying Works, Vol. 1, 郑观应集·商务二, 上册). Shanghai: Shanghai Renmin Chubanshe, p. 55, p. 56.

or succeeded. If the government undertakes the business, it will cost more times and the treasury funds will gradually decrease. However, if the businessmen can share the benefits, there will be more steamships and a strong momentum along the ports. All this is apparent."[22] Zheng, Guo, and other people could clearly state the gains and losses of different choices for two reasons. First, they knew about the corruption of the traditional dynasty bureaucracy and in the government-run industry and commerce in China's history. Second, they roughly understood the economic and political system on which strong Western countries relied. They understood that the Western countries had developed the economy and expanded the market through businessmen, while the government merely collected taxes to preserve and support the economic activities of these businessmen. They hoped that China could learn this way from the West.

The shortcomings of government-run enterprises (including government-supervised and merchant-managed enterprises) were thoroughly exposed in the financial crisis (1883–1884). Small and medium government-supervised and merchant-managed enterprises discontinued their production one after another, while large government-supervised and merchant-managed enterprises survived through foreign debt. Therefore, it was considered risky to invest private capital in government-run enterprises, and it was instead invested into private factories. In this case, the advocators of merchant-managed enterprises shifted their view from why enterprises should be operated by merchants to how to create better conditions for developing merchant-managed enterprises. They first proposed abolishing the monopoly of government-supervised and merchant-managed enterprises, appealing that "all private industry must not be forbidden in all treaty ports and the hinterland suitable for the development of the railway, steamship, mining, cultivation, textile, and manufacturing industries. They can buy a share or open their own factories as they wish."[23] Second, they proposed transitioning government-supervised and merchant-managed enterprises to merchant-managed ones.

[22] Guo, S. (1983). *Guo Songtao Zougao* (郭嵩焘奏稿). Changsha: Yuelu Press, p. 342.

[23] Li, Hongzhang. *Beiyang Teke Chaodeng Diyiming Meipi, Gezhi Keyi Huihai* (北洋特课超等第一名眉批, 格致课艺汇海), p. 4.

In the 1890s, Chen Chi theoretically explored why government-run enterprises were less efficient than merchant-managed ones. He explained that "the government can only share benefits. If it freely spends the capital and fails in trying again, it will stop and be easily deterred by even a slight risk." However, the businessmen were different: "Now that they have raised the capital, they will not give up until they make a profit." Therefore, he concluded that "it is suitable for businessmen" to operate the enterprises.[24] Accordingly, he advocated that the government fade from the field of micro-management, and instead, let merchant-managed enterprises take its place.

Faced with inefficient government-run enterprises, major Westernization governors including Li Hongzhang and Zuo Zongtang had also warmed to the idea of developing the economy through merchant-managed enterprises after failing to think of another effective way. According to Li, "Companies that can be run by businessmen should not be run by the government. As stated in books on financial management, foreign enterprises were run by private businessmen without government interference. The higher was governmental expenditure, the lower was the people's profit. Those assigned to run the undertaking would gain their interest, but it was difficult to determine if they wanted to develop the economy."[25] Zuo Zongtang, another major Westernization governor, also admitted "it is difficult to avoid the shortcomings of government-run enterprises." When he governed Urumqi, a small metal fabrication plant for farm equipment production had to be constructed as a government-supervised and merchant-managed enterprise. He indicated that "It should be given to private businessmen to handle their companies and make profit. If operated by the government, there will be a lowered profit and increased shortcomings. Even worse, while the products will not be sophisticated, there will be less capital and more waste."[26]

In addition, Zuo Zongtang detailed the role of the government in the development of merchant-managed enterprises. He advocated that the government promote the development of those enterprises whose products "competed against Western products. They should also reduce tax

[24] Chen, C. (1997). *Chenchi Ji, Weichi Kuangzheng Shuo* (Chen Chi Works, 陈炽集·维持矿政说). Beijing: Zhonghua Book Company, p. 178.

[25] Li, Hongzhang. *Beiyang Teke Chaodeng Diyiming Meipi, Gezhi Keyi Huihai* (北洋特课超等第一名眉批, 格致课艺汇海), p. 4.

[26] Zuo, Z. *Zuo Wenxianggong Quanji, Pizha Juan Qi* (左文襄公全集·批札, 卷7). p. 7.

to attract those with sufficient private capital to invest." He explained, "If the tax is not reduced according to the circumstances, the cost of production will be higher, and it will be very difficult to compete against Western products." Therefore, he suggested that the Qing government "maintain the commercial foundation and stop the drain of national interest."[27] For enterprises lacking sufficient capital, he proposed following "the pattern of government-run enterprises at their early stage and merchant-managed enterprises at their later stage."[28] On February 7, 1885, Zuo Zongtang, in his memorial "Profit from a Pilot Project of Taisugar Corporation," emphasized the development of merchant-managed enterprises: "Guiding people to make a profit is better than competing against them for profit." He elaborated that "government-run enterprises cannot last for long. If the government advocates its interests, people will want to share its interests. If households have solid finances and do not hold shares in foreign enterprises, but want to hold shares in their capital bases, their capital should be allowed to serve as tax. If the governmental cost of investment is returned, we can end the tax and the assignment of officials to manage the factories, for example."[29] This indicated that first, Zuo thought government-run enterprises that "cannot last long" was not an appropriate way to develop. Second, he believed that private capital should be raised in these enterprises, which could shift enterprises from being government-run to government-merchant jointly managed. Thirdly, he stated that some measures including returning the governmental cost of investment and ending the assignment of officials to manage the factories were implemented to transform government-merchant jointly managed enterprises to merchant-managed ones.

Accordingly, Zuo's ideas favored the development of private capital and China's new economy. Unfortunately, these ideas were not implemented in his lifetime.

After the 1894–1895 Sino-Japanese War, an unprecedented national crisis made the Westernization Group realize that to save China, industry and commerce had to be developed. This could only be achieved through

[27] Zuo, Z. *Zuo Wenxianggong Quanji, Zougao Juan Wushijiu* (左文襄公全集·奏稿, 卷59). p. 72.

[28] Zuo, Z. *Zuo Wenxianggong Quanji, Shudu Juan Ershisan* (左文襄公全集·书犊, 卷23). p. 24.

[29] Zuo, Z. *Zuo Wenxianggong Quanji, Zougao Juan Liushisan* (左文襄公全集·奏稿, 卷63). p. 55.

the more efficient merchant-managed enterprises. Therefore, many officials at different levels, including Zhang Zhidong, Liu Kunyi, Hu Yufen, Chu Chengbo, and Wang Pengyun, asked the government to allow businessmen to establish various types of new enterprises and to lift bans not conducive to the development of merchant-managed enterprises. Faced with domestic strife and foreign aggression, the Qing government had to seek a way to implement "redress." In 1895, the Qing government ordered that the Bureau of Merchants in each province set up more agencies to weave silk and cloth to expand manufacturing and to allow small steamships to run in inland rivers. In 1896, it ordered all governor-generals and provincial governors to set up a Bureau of Commerce in each provincial capital. Squires and businessmen who were well off, steady, prudent, and prestigious were elected by each Chamber of Commerce to be the directors of each bureau and deal with any arising affairs. In 1898, the Qing government issued "Twelve Laws and Regulations to Reward Technological Inventions," according to which hereditary positions, nominal official titles and official titles, and patents or horizontal inscribed boards were awarded to businessmen who established factories and enterprises. To facilitate the turnover of capital between the industrial and commercial sectors, the Imperial Bank of China opened in Shanghai in 1897. Though these acts were not seriously implemented, they can be regarded as incentive measures for attracting private capital to invest in establishing factories and enterprises. Moreover, a movement of "setting up factories by self-help" appeared for the first time in the history of China, ushering in the first golden period in the history of the development of capitalism in the country.

However, it was conditional for major Westernization governors to promote the development of merchant-managed enterprises. They prevented the spread of the shortcomings of government-run enterprises by limiting their field to, according to Li, "those that can be run by businessmen should not be run by the government." However, this did not mean they had eliminated government-run enterprises. (After the 1894–1895 Sino-Japanese War, government-run military and civil industry continued to develop.) In the opinions of major Westernization governors, because government-run enterprises were less efficient than merchant-managed ones, those industries that could be operated by businessmen should not be run by the government. Conversely, the government was expected to run those that could not be operated by businessmen. The governors did not clarify what fields or industries businessmen could not enter. However, it is clear from their responsibility to defend the country and action of establishing the enterprises that industries closely related to people's livelihood failed to attract the interest of businessmen, were beyond the reach of private capital, and could not operate well because their focus was beyond that of the businessmen. Industries or fields outside this range were classified as being those of the businessmen. At the end of the Qing Dynasty, Zhang Zhidong launched a fierce debate with squires and businessmen from Hubei, Hunan, and Guangdong Provinces about the construction right of Guangzhou-Wuhan Railway. That debate clarifies the principles major Westernization governors used to delimit the boundary between government-run and merchant-managed enterprises.

Note that Zhang Zhidong was a very open-minded bureaucrat. He could clearly stand his ground regarding whether the enterprises should be operated by the government or businessmen. He thought businessmen could share the profits but not the power,[30] just as "the country can bring the profits to businessmen, farmers, and workers, but cannot let them have the power."[31] In his view, there was no need for the government to solely control the general business and trade that could be managed by private businessmen. "I heard we could get the profit as the people made a profit. However, we cannot make a profit by depriving the people of their profit. According to the report, the government established the market and built civil houses. They simply derived the profits of businessmen from buying and selling goods, holding the title deed for a house, and lending money. It was not the right way."[32] He also advocated that the Chamber of Commerce be established by businessmen themselves; thus, "the government does not need to invest." Furthermore, "the enterprises funded by the businessmen should not be operated by the government,

[30] Zhang, Z. *Zhang Wenxianggong Quanji, Zouyi 43, Juan 43* (Collected Works of Zhang Wenxiang, 张文襄公全集·奏议43, 卷43).

[31] Zhang, Z. *Zhang Wenxianggong Quanji, Diandu Juan 150* (Collected Works of Zhang Wenxiang, 张文襄公全集·电牍29, 卷150).

[32] Zhang, Z. *Zhang Wenxianggong Quanji, Gongdu Sanshi, Juan 115* (Collected Works of Zhang Wenxiang,张文襄公全集·公牍30, 卷115).

since businessmen dislike this way most."[33] However, for those industries (including railways) closely related to the national economy and the people's livelihood, Zhang asserted that the political power should be firmly grasped by the government without the meddling of the public. He said, "Though building railways is related to the important policy of making it easier for businessmen and making a large amount of money, it is very different and concerns the vein of the country, speed of implementation of government decree, power of weapons, people's livelihood, and channel of understanding between the government and common people. Therefore, there is no harm in raising capital by floating shares from businessmen. However, the government should hold the power to make overall plans and assess the pros and cons."[34] He clarified, "Because the construction of railways concerns the interests and power of the country, we are not willing to give up the profits to the businessmen, let alone the power."[35] Thus, he on one hand supported the requests of the squires and businessmen from Hubei, Hunan, and Guangdong Provinces to take back the construction rights of Guangzhou-Wuhan Railway, but on the other, firmly objected to handing the construction rights to the businessmen. He further refused their private capital and raised a loan from foreigners to construct the railway for fear that the squires and businessmen would grasp the interest and power, which would threaten the interests of the country. "The government obtained a loan and constructed the railway. Thus, all interests belong to the country. This is the best policy."[36]

[33] Zhang, Z. *Zhang Wenxianggong Quanji, Shuzha Ba, Juan 221* (Collected Works of Zhang Wenxiang, 张文襄公全集·书札8, 卷221).

[34] Zhang, Z. *Zhang Wenxianggong Quanji, Zouyi Liushiba, Juan 68* (Collected Works of Zhang Wenxiang, 张文襄公全集·奏议68, 卷68).

[35] Zhang, Z. *Zhang Wenxianggong Quanji, Zouyi Sishier, Juan 42* (Collected Works of Zhang Wenxiang, 张文襄公全集·奏议42, 卷42).

[36] Zhang, Z. *Zhang Wenxianggong Quanji, Zouyi Sishisi, Juan 44* (Collected Works of Zhang Wenxiang, 张文襄公全集·奏议44, 卷44).

10.3 Government-Run Military and Civil Enterprises: Reform Recommendations and Practice

Government-run enterprises in the late Qing Dynasty were either government-run military or government-run civil enterprises. Military enterprises were operated from the 1860s to the time of the Qing government's collapse. Military enterprises should only be operated by the government to avoid ordinary people's involvement in the production of ammunition. Government-run civil enterprises, established by businessmen as factories, appeared in the mid-1880s when the reputation of government-supervised and merchant-managed companies was in tatters. In this case, the government had to take over civil enterprises that needed large-scale investment established by major Westernization governors. At the time, the government had no solid finance and had to approach foreigners for loans. After the 1894–1895 Sino-Japanese War, the Qing government encouraged the development of merchant-managed enterprises and supported the government-run enterprises in each province to raise funds, ensuring their continued development. However, less efficient government-run enterprises were replaced by merchant-managed ones or operated according to commercial principles.

The inefficiency of government-run enterprises remained a continued problem throughout history. Long criticized, these problems remained unresolved as all the dynasties were constrained by the limitations of agricultural dominance. Alongside these problems, salt administration, the water transport of grain to the capital (in traditional times), river engineering projects, and administration of officials were considered incurable "diseases." After the spread of Western learning to the East, the Westernization Group enlightened by the Western experience of developing economies, tried to solve these problems by running the enterprises according to commercial principles.

In the 1880s, the Westernization Group's exploration of reform issues pertaining to government-run enterprises was launched with a focus on the government-run military industry. The main points were as follows:

1. Idea of contracting contractors: In "setting up private factories" in *Ten Proposals on the Expansion of Business*, Zhong Tianwei was critical of the "tortuous course to set up government-run enterprises

> with little effect." He said that more Western ships and ammunition were manufactured by private factories. Several government-run ammunitions factories were adopting the method of contracting contractors, rendering them similar to private factories. He thought this practice could help "avoid redundant workers and the abuse of food to achieve high-quality work." In his view, all the shortcomings resulted from too many miscellaneous craftsmen, a lazy working attitude, and unwillingness to "do hard work inducing others' dislike." Thus, "every finished product was more expensive but less refined than foreign products. All the products looked impressive, but lacked real worth. Moreover, the craftsmen and officials teased the foreigners and became ignorant and arrogant. As a result, nothing could be achieved, even after 100 years."[37] To solve the inefficiency of government-run factories, he proposed following the foreigners' method of contracting contractors. Contractors could be categorized as workers in these factories and private businessmen. If the contractors were workers, they would be assigned specific projects according to the principle of internal competition and earn their income according to their work. If the contractors were private businessmen, some long-term projects of components and parts with no comparative advantage could be contracted to them according to the principle of competition. Thus, they could be the processing plants of machine fittings for factories. Of the government-run ammunitions factories in that period, Zhong pointed out that only those in Guangdong Province had been contracting contractors, increasing their efficiency.

In addition, for highly inefficient government-run factories, Zhong proposed "getting rental income annually by leasing government-run factories to businessmen to pay the manufacturing fees."

In Zhong's opinion, the good prospect of an "upward atmosphere, increased talent. and progressive skills" would emerge "with no need to promote country" if government-run ammunitions factories were reorganized in this way. He was confident government-run enterprises would perform well if operated according to commercial principles.

[37] Zhong, T. *Yuezu Ji, Waipian* (Outer Chapter of Zhong's Righteous Words, 刖足集·外篇).

2. Notion of specialized production: Some in the Westernization Group criticized the repeated construction of ammunitions factories and asked to continue with specialized production. On May 19, 1877 (the 3rd year of the Guangxu Reign of the Qing Dynasty), Li Hongzhang wrote, "Tianjin Arsenal and Shanghai Arsenal prove too costly. Recently, Guangdong, Shangzuo (now Shangdong), and Hunan Provinces followed in its footsteps. The officials were complacent, and it was like looking at the sky from the bottom of a well. The arsenals established in every province may expand the scale, but this is equal only to a small part of those of the Westerners. The more arsenals there will be, the more difficult it will be for us to do it well. Therefore, it is better to merge all arsenals to form one large-scale one."[38] Zhong Tianwei also argued that each arsenal only concentrated on scale and quantity, not on quality, and recommended that they adopt the method of specialized production. He asked all arsenals to produce a suitable variety of products according to local conditions to "play to their strengths and perform their own functions."[39] While sound, these recommendations were difficult to implement because the activities of the Westernization Movement were conducted by each governor-general and provincial governor without country-level unified planning, alongside the impact of political factions.
3. Change government-run enterprises into merchant-managed ones: At that time, some in the Westernization Group lost confidence in inefficient government-run industries. They suggested changing the mode of operation of ammunitions enterprises and allowing businessmen to operate these enterprises. In 1884, Zhu Yixin, the editor and compiler at the Hanlin Academy, proposed learning from the foreigners and allowing squires and businessmen to operate ammunitions enterprises. In 1895, Hu Yufen, chief administrator of the Beijing area, and Chu Chengbo, the court-admonisher, presented memorials to the emperor criticizing the corruption and waste of government-run ammunitions enterprises. Therein, they advised that a merchant-run mode of production be adopted. According

[38] Li, H. *Li Wenzhonggong Quanshu, Pengliao Hangao Juan 17* (Works of Li Hongzhang, Letters from/to Friends and Colleagues, 李文忠公全书·朋僚函稿, 卷17).

[39] Zhong, T. *Yuezu Ji, Daini Bing Lijuexiang Caiche Jiqiju Tiaoyi* (Zhong's Righteous Words, 刖足集·代拟禀李爵相裁撤机器局条议).

to the memorials, Emperor Guangxu indicated, "The old mode should be urgently changed to contract government-run enterprises out to private businessmen." He assigned major officials to attract wealthy overseas Chinese businessmen in Nanyang (an old name for Southeast Asia) to undertake the operations of the ammunition's enterprises. This was eventually not implemented based on the tradition that ordinary people should not be involved in the production of ammunitions.

After the 1894–1895 Sino-Japanese War1895, the development of and changes in the mode of operation of government-run ammunitions enterprises, especially in the twentieth century, were aligned with the ideas of the Westernization Group, namely to operate the enterprises according to commercial principles.

1. The previous free allocation of arms products was paid according to the price at the time. The budget of Hubei Arsenal was never enough to support its daily operations. As Zhang Zhidong's proposal that "the arms from Hubei Arsenal be charged at 20% of the foreign purchase price to ensure revolving funds" was approved, and other provinces, including Shaanxi, Gansu, Xinjiang, Yunnan, Guizhou, and Shanxi, ordered and paid for the arms based on the price after 1895.
2. Operations for military purposes adapted for civil use: In 1903, when Zhang Zhidong planned to move the Jiangnan Manufacturing Center inland, one proposal was to operate the old factory for civil use. He explained, "The steel produced in the steel mill of Jiangnan Manufacturing Center can not only provide for itself, but can also be sold to foreign firms to manufacture machines and ships. The old dock can be used to repair the official and merchant ships of locals and foreigners. Its arms factory, the machinery of which could be appropriately changed, can manufacture various machines to sell. In this way, we can raise a colossal sum of money to finance the factory."[40] In 1905, the dock was separated from the Jiangnan Manufacturing Center. The previous primary purpose of

[40] *Jiangnan Zhizaoju Yishe Wuhu Gezougao* (江南制造局移设芜湖各奏稿). As sited in Huang, Y. (1992). *Jindai Zhongguo Jingji Bianqian* (近代中国经济变迁). Shanghai: Shanghai Renmin Chubanshe, p. 396.

building naval vessels for the Qing Dynasty was gradually shifted to a civil enterprise to conduct business and serve the naval vessels and merchant ships of locals and foreigners. Until April 1907, its net profit totaled 130,000 taels of silver.

3. Implementation of the contracting system: In 1897, when the French Doyere was hired as the supervisor of Fuzhou Arsenal, "all the much-needed machine elements could be contracted to the craftsmen team after negotiating the price with the contractor in charge."[41] Recorded in the *Zhongwai Daily* on May 6, 1904, Jiangnan Manufacturing Center also implemented the contracting system. If the project was contracted to the contractor with the valuation of 10 workers' wages and the contractor finished the project at the cost of 8 workers' wages, the contractor would be paid the primary price. "Since then, they frequently operated in this way, which became common practice" and "other factories followed this example."[42] The Englishman R.B. Mauchan, was hired as the chief engineer of Jiangnan Shipyard in 1907, and actively promoted the contracting system of foreign shipyards. He implemented a contracting system for migrant workers for work including cold working, carpenters, and painters. The contractor employed temporary workers to complete the project and dismissed them immediately after its completion, after which those workers would look for another job.

The reform of government-run civil industry was mainly carried out after the 1894–1895 Sino-Japanese War. After the war, Qing government agencies at all levels established many large and small-scale government-run civil enterprises; however, their inefficiency was soon revealed. At the time, operating enterprises had been the mainstream of public opinion. As such, enterprises that could be saved—excluding those that went bankrupt—conducted the reform according to commercial principles.

1. Lease the operation to the private businessmen: For example, through innumerable trial and error, Zhang Zhidong founded

[41] (1904, Jan 16). *Hui Bao* (汇报).

[42] As sited in Huang, Y. (1992). *Jindai Zhongguo Jingji Bianqian* (近代中国经济变迁). Shanghai: Shanghai Renmin Chubanshe, p. 396.

Hubei Spinning Company, Hubei Weaving Company, Hubei Silk Reeling Company, and Hubei Hemp-Making Company. Good as their operation projects were, they soon faced yearly losses because of the inefficiency of government-run enterprises. Despite much capital invested in the company and the replacement of general managers numerous times, the enterprise remained in difficulty. Furthermore, debt of 510,000 taels owed to German businessman Arnhold Karberg & Co. was due for payment. Even worse, the government was unable to raise much money. Therefore, Zhang Zhidong was forced to lease the four companies to Yingchang Company, run by Deng Jichang, the comprador of the Hong Kong and Shanghai Banking Corporation (HSBC), and other people. The rent term was 20 years and yearly rent was 110,000 taels, which would be used to pay off the debt of Arnhold Karberg & Co. in monthly installments. As a result, Yingchang Company made a profit of more than 1,500,000 taels within 3 years.[43]

2. Shift of the government and businessmen to joint-steering enterprises: In these enterprises, the government and private investment would have shares and jointly steer the company. These enterprises would also get the profit and share the loss based on their share. This type of enterprise, rare after the 1894–1895 Sino-Japanese War, appeared after the New Deal. These enterprises were operated according to the Qing commerce law and company rules. The board of directors was organized in line with the requirements of the law. However, the government appointed many of the people in charge of these enterprises, and operations, personnel, and finance were still controlled by the government or people assigned by the government. This led to the inefficient operation of these enterprises. Later, some of these enterprises transformed into merchant-run companies and were jointly steered according to commercial principles.
3. A shift to merchant-managed enterprises: At the time, many government-run civil enterprises founded by the provincial government were forced to invite private businessmen to take over operations to improve their efficiency. These were transformed into merchant-managed enterprises. After the Hanyang Iron Works, founded by Zhang Zhidong, was taken over by Sheng Xuanhuai,

[43] Chen, Z. (1961). *Zhongguo Jindai Gongyeshi Ziliao, Disanji* (中国近代工业史资料, 第3辑). Beijing: SDX Joint Publishing Company, pp. 287–288.

it became a government-supervised and merchant-managed enterprise. Remaining inefficient, Zhang invited more private investment in 1908, and then founded Hanyeping Company. It was registered at the Ministry of Works and reformed as a merchant-managed enterprise. Zhang planned to set up Hubei South Pinning Factory, but ultimately failed in this endeavor. Half the 40,000 spinning machines of the factory, which had been stored in Yangshupu huts in Shanghai for many years, were used to establish the Dasheng Mill by Zhang Jian in 1899. The rest were again put into operation by Zhang Jian in 1902.

10.4 Government-Supervised and Merchant-Managed Enterprises: Reform Recommendations and Practice

Government-supervised and merchant-managed enterprises appeared in the 1870s, prevailed at the beginning of the 1880s, and deteriorated after the financial crisis of 1883–1884. In 1872, Secretary of the Grand Secretariat Song Jin presented his memorial requesting that the construction of Fuzhou Arsenal be stopped for its high cost and small effect. However, construction continued through the efforts of Li Hongzhang, Zuo Zongtang, Shen Baozhen, and others. To find a marketing channel for the ships of the factory and advance the Westernization cause, major Westernization governors, bored with the lack of capital, conceptualized a government-supervised and merchant-managed approach to enterprises. The establishment of China Merchants Steamship Company was the initial trial of this type of enterprise.

Government-supervised and merchant-managed enterprises were joint-stock companies based on government-businessmen cooperation. It had the following features: First, in terms of the relationship of investment, before private businessmen raised the entire capital amount, the government would make up the balance, which would be gradually returned later. Second, for the division of power between the two parties, "the government would make the overall plans, assess the pros and cons, and listen to the proposals of the businessmen directors to appease and persuade them."[44] Furthermore, the "businessmen undertake the operation and the government presides over the overall situation."[45] This was why the term "government-supervised and merchant-managed" was coined. These enterprises aimed to make ends meet and play to their strengths. However, the relationship between the managing merchants and supervising government was important.

As a form of enterprise organization, government supervision and merchant operation reflected the cooperation between government capital and private capital. It solved the problem of lacking start-up capital faced by the government of the traditional agrarian country when it started establishing enterprises of new type industries, and contributed to developing the early modernization of China. However, because of the chaotic property relations within the companies, this type of joint-stock company failed to meet the founders' expectation that the government and businessmen could play to their strengths and cooperate. Instead, they faced a deep contradiction. From an investment perspective, the government, as the creditor, invested in and could get fixed interest income. The businessmen's investment was the venture capital; thus, they got unfixed risky income, namely the income after removing all expenditure (including the interest of the government). According to the modern enterprise's property rights theory, when the enterprise is in a state of operation (not bankrupt), the businessman who undertakes the risk, not the creditor, should enjoy the control of power of the enterprise. Only when the enterprise is facing bankruptcy and the creditor's interests are threatened should the creditor take control of the enterprise. If the enterprise returns the creditor's capital, the creditor will no longer have any form of control over the enterprise. However, the division of power in government-supervised and merchant-managed enterprises did not confirm to this principle. When the enterprises were in a state of operation, the government, not businessmen, took power. Furthermore, if an enterprise returned the government's capital, it did not mean businessmen could take control of an enterprise. As Governor Liu Kunyi stated, "When the government's capital was paid off, the capital to fund the enterprise belonged to the businessmen. Even if there was a loss, it

[44] Li, H. *Li Wenzhonggong Quanshu, Shiban Lunchuan Zhaoshangju Zhe* (Works of Li Hongzhang, Vol. 20. 李文忠公全书·试办轮船招商局折, 卷20).

[45] Li, H. *Li Wenzhonggong Quanshu, Zhengdun Zhaoshangju Shiyi Zhe* (Works of Li Hongzhang, Vol. 30. 李文忠公全书·整顿招商局事宜折, 卷30).

had nothing to do with the government's capital. Furthermore, there was no intention to grasp power over the enterprise. In fact, the government still controlled the personnel and inspection of accounts, which indicated that businessmen undertook the operation while the government maintained the main power."[46] As such, the enterprise was still controlled by the government, decreasing the zeal of businessmen stockholders, and rendering business inefficiency inevitable. According to Zheng Guanying, "The government grasped the power in the government-supervised and merchant-managed enterprises,"[47] decreasing the power of businessmen in those establishments. Tang Tingshu, the long-time general comprador of the Bureau of Merchants and Kaiping Mining Administration, explained the business relationship between Li Hongzhang and himself: "Governor-general Li led me, and I carried out his orders."[48]

In those enterprises, the reversed relationship between the government and businessmen was reflected in the title of the shareholder by Li Hongzhang. He did not consider investors the leaders of the enterprises, but regarded them as "friends" who helped the Qing government establish these companies. As such, he referred to them as "friends of investment," not shareholders. In the 3rd Year of the Guangxu Reign (1887), he stated in "Regulations on Mohe Gold Mining" that "all the friends of investment could hold power in the factory." He agreed that "those who invested more than 10,000 taels gold could enter the factory themselves or assign people to enter to monitor finances. If there were suitable positions in the factory, they would be appointed and paid based on the quality of their work. If they knew nothing about operations or no positions were available, they would only be supplied with food. They could check the financial statements to ensure there was no embezzlement in the factory, but were not permitted to deal with other business affairs. If an accountant made mistakes, they could only inform the general

[46] Zhongguo Jindaishi Congshu Bianxiezu. (1973). *Yangwu Yundong, Juanliu* (Westernization Movement, Vol. 6, 洋务运动, 卷6), Shanghai: Shanghai Renmin Chubanshe, p. 44.

[47] Zheng, G. (1988). *Zheng Guanying Ji, Shengshi Weiyan Houbian, Juanshi Xiace* (Zheng Guanying works, Warnings in the Flourishing Age, Vol. 10, 郑观应集·盛世危言后编, 卷10, 下册). Shanghai: Shanghai Renmin Chubanshe, pp. 804–808.

[48] Ding, W. (1900). *Zhongguo Chunqiu* (A Cycle of Cathay, 中国春秋). As sited in Zhang, G. (1979). *Yangwu Yundong yu Zhongguo Jindai Qiye* (洋务运动与中国近代企业). Beijing: China Social Sciences Press, p. 323.

manager, who would then check and deal with it."[49] The shareholder had no access to the business other than supervising the accountant. Dealing with any issues depended on the general manager assigned by the government, who the shareholder had no hand in recommending. Obviously, this situation was not conducive to the development of the enterprise and resulted in increasing general shareholders' concern about this risky practice.

Reform of the government-supervised and merchant-managed enterprises was conducted based on two ideas. Major Westernization governors reformed government-supervised and merchant-managed enterprises following the approach of the traditional administrative reorganization of the traditional era. They strongly wanted to improve these enterprises, not only because it was their duty to do so and to defend their country as major officials, but also because the fate of their faction was closely linked with the Westernization cause. Therefore, they were ready to do their best to solve the problem of inefficiency. A large volume of memorials, electrical drafts, letters, and other materials in their corpus outline the following as their reform approaches:

1. To improve the leadership team: The leadership of government-supervised and merchant-managed enterprises rested with major Westernization governors. They wanted to adapt the leadership group to improve operating efficiency. For example, the personnel of China Merchants Steamship Company were adjusted several times from 1872, when Li Hongzhang assigned Zhu Qi-ang and Zhu Qizhao to manage the affairs of the company, to the early 1890s. The most impactful adjustment was in 1873 when Tang Tingshu, Xu Run, Sheng Xuanhuai, and others replaced Zhu Qi-ang and Zhu Qizhao to take charge of the company. In the mid-1880s, Sheng Xuanhuai and Ma Jianzhong took over the company from Tang Tingshu and Xu Run, and in the early 1890s, Yan Gan, Tang Dexi, Chen You, and others were assigned to handle business affairs. In general, the efficiency of the enterprise improved after the reform. However, two problems proved difficult to solve. The first was the low motivation to develop. The second was the uncertainty related

[49] Li, H. *Li Wenzhonggong Quanshu, Mohe Jinkuang Zhangcheng Zhe, Juanliushiyi* (Complete Works of Li Wenzhong, Vol. 61, 李文忠公全书·漠河金矿章程折, 卷61).

to ensuring a newly elected enterprise leader was better than the former one. For example, it was proposed to establish Shanghai Machine Weaving Company in 1876, but this enterprise only went into production with complete investment in 1893. During that period, major enterprise leaders were replaced six or seven times.

2. Propose tougher punishments for enterprise leaders who commit corrupt acts: Key figures of the Qing government who supervised the Self-Strengthening movement including Li Hongzhang, Zuo Zongtang, and Zhang Zhidong proposed tough punishments for enterprise leaders who committed corrupt acts. For example, when Xu Run was in charge of China Merchants Steamship Navigation Company, he was removed from the company for his unlawful embezzlement and asked to return his illegal gains, finally "losing all his family property and never rising again."[50] Similarly, after embezzling funds from Shanghai Mechanical Textile Bureau, Zheng Guanying suffered the same fate. Even Zheng's daily expenses were covered by his friends. Sheng Xuanhuai's help to Zheng during this time was the main cause of their relationship. Regarding other mistakes, when Sheng Xuanhuai took over the coal mine in Guangji and Daye in Hubei Province, because of the failure of the business, he was asked by Li Hongzhang to advance 16,000 *chuan* to the government as payment. The case was closed in 1884. The interest-bearing government funds of nearly 143,000 *chuan*, which belonged to the budget surplus of the coal mine, was deposited early into Hu Guangyong's account, but was later in deficit because of Hu's bankruptcy in the financial crisis. Furthermore, the Qing Ministry of Revenue ordered him to turn over the copper money he made to pay compensation of 150,000 taels. Sheng Xuanhuai expressed his resentment of Li Hongzhang to the then Grand Councilor of State Yan Jingming: "It has been nearly 14 years since I was transferred by Li Hongzhang to the job. It is known to all that I have almost sold all my family properties to pay the compensation. I may not be able to live hand-to-mouth in this worsening situation. My father is more than 70 years old and there is no home to which I can return.

[50] Xu, R. *Xu Yuzhai Zishu Nianpu* (The Chronicle of Xu Yuzhai, 徐愚斋自叙年谱).

I have become an unworthy descendent who owes a great debt to the government."[51]

According to the work of Li Hongzhang, he voiced his discontent by scolding the enterprise leaders who had performed poorly, which was also a punishment. For example, when the former alternate official of Sichuan Province Peng Rucong managed the China Merchants Steamship Company, he was lambasted by Li Hongzhang for his poor management and eventually removed from his position. Critical comments included: "You are ridiculous. Your behavior is hypocritical, deceptive, and impractical. You harbor no good intentions and lack character."[52] Li Hongzhang also criticized Ma Jianzhong's charge of Shanghai Mechanical Textile Bureau for his poor performance: "You are far from being practical when handling affairs. While fundraising in Tianjin, I realized no one has confidence in you."[53] Ma had no choice but to leave office. Sheng Xuanhuai, who substituted for Li Hongzhang in running the affairs of the Self-Sin addition strengthening movement, was once trusted by Li, but also reprimanded by him after the failure of the coal mine in Hubei Province: "Your handling of affairs is ridiculous." Later, a letter written by Sheng defending himself was sent to Li, to no avail. Li responded, "Your endless argument makes you hardly live up to expectations."

3. Pressure enterprises to perform better with shareholders' concern: It would take time to salvage the past tattered reputation of government-run industry and commerce. People were not eager to buy shares in government-supervised and merchant-managed enterprises until the 1880s. In 1877, to acquire Shanghai Steam Navigation Company, China Merchants Steamship Navigation Company was expected to raise funds of 1.5 million taels from society in various ways: By convincing the former to purchase the latter's shares with its original capital stock of 0.2 million taels, which belonged to overseas Chinese capital; selling 7000 shares to the salt

[51] Sheng, X. (1884). *Shengdang: Shang Li Fuxiang Lunchuan Zhangcheng, Xuyan* (Archives for Sheng Xuanhuai: Sheng Yihuai Report to Yan Jingming, 盛档: 禀阎敬铭).

[52] Zheng, G. *Shengshi Weiyan Houbian, Juanqi* (Warnings in the Flourishing Age, Vol. 7, 盛世危言后编, 卷7).

[53] Li, H. *Li Wenzhonggong Quanshu, Diangao, Juanshisan* (Works of Li Hongzhang, Vol. 13, 李文忠公全书·电稿, 卷13).

merchants of Huai River area to raise funds of 0.79 million taels; and selling the latter's shares to treaty port merchants. The huge fundraising effort was, however, boycotted by various merchants and only 45,000 taels was finally raised. Li Hongzhang was irritated by the result: "To make a mark and encourage rapid trade, and to maintain justice and stability, rich merchants from wherever should come and make some effort."[54] Leaders of the latter, at the will of Li Hongzhang, had to improve the performance of the company to attract more merchants, including punctual dividend distribution. In the second year of China Merchants Steamship Navigation Company, 10% of the dividends were distributed as per the regulations. Furthermore, in every year of the 1870s, interest was duly paid regardless of the enterprise's gain or loss. In 1875, dividend distribution was increased from 10 to 15%. According to the statistics, 70 taels could be earned after 7 years by buying every share of China Merchants Steamship Navigation Company with 100 taels when it was newly established. Even though the company was said to be constantly challenged by foreign competitors, it had a healthy balance sheet that yielded a budget surplus.

From the above, it is clear that the Self-Strengthening movement officials were ambitious in terms of improving the management of government-supervised and merchant-managed enterprises, and did resolve to tackle the corruption in these companies. Furthermore, their deficits were caused by erroneous decisions. The core problem, however, was not their ambition to develop the enterprises, but their ability to do so. In a traditional agricultural society, a local public finance deficit caused by mismanagement could be covered by the relevant officials. While the method of enhancing the cost of making mistakes to increase operation efficiency had proven feasible in the past, it was no longer relevant in modern enterprise management. Even though people were often kicked out or reprimanded, their businesses were still not on the right track. In reality, the third method mentioned above on enterprise reform conformed to the principle of the market economy and would play a pivotal role in advancing businesses. However, the problem was rooted in

[54] Li, H. *Li Wenzhonggong Quanshu, Pengliao Hangao, Juanshier* (Works of Li Hongzhang, Letters from/to Friends and Colleagues, Vol. 12, 李文忠公全书·朋僚函稿, 卷12), p. 36.

their internal operational inadaptability to external market competition, leading to low efficiency. Here, incentive and restraint mechanisms were vital to enterprise development.

Based on business operation principles, ideologues of the Self-Strengthening movement reformed government-supervised and merchant-managed enterprises by transferring the power held by officials to merchants.

In the mid-1880s, Zhong Tianwen, in his essay *How to Avoid Two Incidents in the Steamship and Telegraph Industries to Achieve Sustainability*, contended that the executive office that acted on the government's behalf was too powerful, and its interests were not closely related to those of enterprises. Merchants, in contrast, had offered all they had to the enterprises and regarded them a matter of life and death. Thus, the redistribution and devolution of the concentrated power of executive office should be initiated to truly benefit the enterprises. Zhong said, "It is critical that we are now following the examples of Western enterprises. However, the main problem causing business failure in government-supervised and merchant-managed enterprises is the over-concentrated power of their executive offices." Zhong further proposed following every "Western practice" in every aspect: "Western enterprises were established on consensus among its assembly. A 12-person board of directors will be elected by the shareholders, among which 1 chairman and 1 deputy chairman will be decided by the board. The members, chairman, and deputy chairman of the board are required to hold their own shares. Any decision should be made by the majority of the board, and any expenditure should be approved by the board meeting, which means no dictatorial management is allowed. If requested by the majority of the board, a larger meeting could be held to audit the accounts at liberty. The chairman of the board is subject to the will and control of the majority and every director of the board, and directors of the board are subject to the will and control of every shareholder." He suggested that meetings could be held to check everything only if there were more than five people on the board: "The chairman of the board and every executive should pay close attention when there is any suspicion of something, thus guaranteeing the proper distribution of power and impartial enforcement of law."[55]

[55] Zhong, T. *Yuezu Ji, Waipian* (Outer Chapter of Zhong's Righteous Words, 刖足集·外篇).

Evidently, Zhong was in favor of an enterprise managed by those closely related to it (shareholders) and who were the most capable of management. Only in this way could the operational efficiency of an enterprise be enhanced. I believe that the efficiency of government-supervised and merchant-managed enterprises would have been bolstered had Zhong's recommendations been implemented.

Zheng Guanying and Zhong Tianwei had similar ideas. Regarding the shareholding system, he stressed that "the British practice is so good we need to follow it," which meant that Chinese enterprises should be managed as per the Western shareholding system. Regarding the relationship between officials and merchants in government-supervised and merchant-managed enterprises, Zheng stressed that "merchants are there for their own benefits. This is why we need to protect their interests and follow their suggestions. We cannot depend on the management and control of the government for everything."[56] Here, Zheng's remarks revolved around what Li Hongzhang had insisted on earlier: "Report whatever occurs to the executive office and do not act on your own."[57] This reflects the policy of the government's tightening control over enterprises.

Compared to Zhong Tianwei and Zheng Guanying, who still had confidence in the sound and fast development of government-supervised and merchant-managed enterprises, Tang Shouqian, in contrast, had already lost faith in them and proposed a different type of merchant-managed enterprise. He contended, "Financial management in most Westerners' views is not based on the combination of merchants and government officials. However, our enterprises are now based on this combination, in which officials are very powerful and merchants are not. It is often seen that initial capital is raised by the merchants, while the profits it yields are shared by officials, which seems like a trick to fool people." The reform plan he proposed was that "government officials should act as the enterprise initially advocates. When merchants later take

[56] Zheng, G. (1982). *Zheng Guanying Ji, Shangzhanshang, Shangce* (Zheng Guanying works • Commercial War I, Vol. 1, 郑观应集·商战上, 上册). Shanghai: Shanghai Renmin Chubanshe, p. 593.

[57] Gu, J. & Nie, B. (1983). *Zhongguo Jindai Hangyunshi Ziliao, Diyiji* (Materials for Chinese Navigation History, Series 1, 中国近代航运史资料). Shanghai: Shanghai Renmin Chubanshe, p. 873.

over the business, officials should not intervene."[58] This meant that while the officials advocated and established the business in the early stages, they should leave the management to merchants without meddling in such affairs. This would stop officials from micromanaging the enterprises, which would instead be managed by the merchants. Later, according to an essay on how to build the railway system, Tang Shouqian proposed that the government "engage in fundraising and in inviting bids. Railway ownership will be given to the person doing construction and part of the profits to the government."[59] In the essay, Tang Shouqian clarified that the ownership of the railway system belonged to those who invested in its construction. In his view, the government was limited to promoting investment, but would benefit from the railway's tax revenue.

This recommendation by Zhong Tianwei, Zheng Guanying, and Tang Shouqian was constructive, but the question was how to strengthen the merchants' power and transform the enterprises from government-supervised and merchant-managed to completely merchant-managed.

To answer this question, some of the Self-Strengthening movement proposed that enterprises be independent of government funds, or repay them in a timely way to break away from "government supervision." In 1882, when investors were actively raising funds for the Telegraph Office, shareholding merchants like Zheng Guanying, Jing Yuanshan, and Xie Jiafu were eager to repay the government funds in the future to become independent of its supervision and transform the company into a merchant-managed enterprise. This proved impossible at the time. Since the government considered government-supervised and merchant-managed enterprises the pioneers in the military industry and modernization, it would certainly not shift its attention from them. According to the regulations written by Sheng Xuanhuai on attracting investment for the Telegraph Office, "the outstanding government funds of 0.1 million taels will be in the office account forever and no repayment is needed, but will start bearing interest together with the merchant funds in 10 years." This made it impossible for the Telegraph Office to break away from government control. Furthermore, according to the regulations, government-owned shares of the Telegraph Office would benefit

58 Tang, S. *Tangshi Weiyan, Kaikuang* (Warnings from Tang, Mining Industry, 汤氏危言·开矿).

59 Tang, S. *Tangshi Weiyan, Tielu* (Warnings from Tang, Railway, 汤氏危言·铁路).

from the budget surplus and someday account for the overwhelming majority. This would make it possible for the Beiyang Bureaucratic Group to take possession of the Telegraph Office.

Other figures in the Self-Strengthening movement like Tang Shouqian insisted that the government's investment in enterprises be treated like government-owned shares. This meant the government should suffer from any deficit the same way merchants did if a loss was recorded. In Tang's view, this would strengthen merchants' power and reduce that of the government (the government knew nothing about conducting business and had no choice but to rely on merchants) so that the enterprise could be managed as per business principles.

Zheng Guanying, who had much experience in governmental management, suggested that enterprises not be able to easily seek protection from the government, since "even when enterprises only seek government protection but gain no extra advantage, they will still be extorted by local officials. If they gain an extra advantage, they will be far more likely to be extorted." The reason was that "in autocratic China today, there are still no rules or laws in force for commerce, making it impossible for shareholders to seek legal protection when needed. Overseas Chinese merchants have more confidence in Western merchants than in government-supervised and merchant-managed ones."[60] Clearly, he had already foreseen that government-supervised and merchant-managed enterprises would eventually be taken over and privatized by the government.

In short, officials and merchants in government-supervised and merchant-managed enterprises were scrambling for control in the early 1880s, during which time the merchants wanted to manage as per business principles but the officials were determined to hold power considering their priority of developing the military industry. The power struggle culminated in the merchants' defeat, not only because of officials' greater power, but also because of a shortage of capital caused by the suspension of attracting investment. When requesting loans from Western banks, enterprises had to rely on the government's guarantee, which led to the concentration of officials' power and violation of merchants' rights.

Low efficiency, however, would still bring the downfall of the powerful officials, meaning that a reform was the only solution to improving

[60] Zheng, G. *Shengshi Weiyan Houbian, Juanshier* (Warnings in the Flourishing Age, Vol. 12, 盛世危言后编, 卷12), p. 4.

efficiency. They had been forced to implement reform in small and medium-sized enterprises since the mid-1880s and started to shift their attention to large enterprises in the 1890s.

During the crisis in the early 1880s, government-supervised and merchant-managed small and medium-sized mine bureaus, which were controlled by private capital, were undergoing a production halt. Faced with a large demand for copper and iron, the Qing government could not afford to start a business on its own or obtain loans from foreign banks like large enterprises could do. Thus, it had no choice but to rely on the products of the government-supervised small-sized financially supported by private capital. Examples included the gold factory in Yisimenqing area, Datong County, Xining, Gansu Province in 1884; lead mine in Shi Zhushan, Fuzhou in 1885; and silver mine in Chengde, Rehe Province in 1883. Under these circumstances, the operation and finance of the enterprises fell on merchants' shoulders, and government intervention was limited: "Mining bureaus will keep their nose out of everything" and only "provide protection and focus on product inspection and procurement." A certain percentage of the products was procured by the government and the rest could be handled as per "their own sales policies." Obviously, the government's decreasing intervention in enterprises was more beneficial than its direct control over production, personnel, and finance. However, some product buyers purposefully caused difficulties for the enterprises.

It had been difficult since the 1890s for some large government-supervised and merchant-managed enterprises to continue operations in the traditional way, which meant they had to do business according to business principles. After Shanghai Mechanical Textile Bureau burned down in 1893, the newly appointed superintendent Sheng Xuanhuai privatized the new textile bureau to revive the textile industry in China. Li Hongzhang agreed with him that "management should follow common regulations and business principles in case of any government attempt to control the enterprise on its own." Li responded that the textile bureau should be made the central factory and managed under business principles.[61] The newly built enterprise was renamed Huasheng Textile Central Factory. The relationship between officials and merchants was the same as that in post-reformation small and medium-sized government-supervised and merchant-managed enterprises. According to the regulations of the

[61] Li, H. *Li Wenzhonggong Quanshu, Diangao, Juanshiwu* (Works of Li Hongzhang, Telegraph, Vol. 15, 李文忠公全书·电稿, 卷15).

new enterprise, 1 tael should be donated on every bag of yarn to compensate for the government's loss with the Shanghai Mechanical Textile Bureau. As such, a dedicated department was established to guarantee the government's interest. Clearly, some of Huasheng Textile Central Factory had been transformed into private property, and other large government-supervised and merchant-managed enterprises would undergo the same transformation. Since the Xuantong Reign, China Merchants Steamship Navigation Company, one of the earliest government-supervised and merchant-managed enterprises, had been completely merchant-managed. In 1900, Kaiping Mining Bureau was transformed into a British capital enterprise that was merchant-managed.

Enterprises' transformation from government-supervised and merchant-managed to completely merchant-managed came at a huge expense for shareholders, which was well exemplified by the great damage incurred to Shanghai Mechanical Textile Bureau and its ending. The enterprise had undergone a few reorganizations during which the government had more control over it while private capital had less. In 1887, when the Gong brothers (Gong Shoutu and Gong Yitu) were "doing some cleaning" at the Mechanical Textile Bureau, they knocked 30% off the initial merchants' shares, intensifying the conflict between officials and merchants. Shen Bao(Shanghai newspaper) disclosed that "shareholders were being treated unjustly" in the textile bureau and asked that "wrong scores be settled."[62] When the textile bureau burned down in 1893, its leaders decided that the merchants' shares were to be regarded as the remnants of the fire disaster and were greatly reduced in price. Shareholders whose initial investment was 100 taels and an additional investment of 30 taels were only refunded about 10 taels. Bureaucrats of the Self-Strengthening movement ultimately transformed the enterprise and pocketed the money, which at the time, was a typical practice reflecting the development path of government-supervised and merchant-managed enterprises. Witnessing major government-supervised and merchant-managed enterprises being reduced to the private properties of bureaucrats of the Self-Strengthening movement in the 1890s, Zheng Guanying noted, "Both China Merchants Steamship Navigation Company and Kaiping Mine were initially established by merchants. Officials began to seize the power as soon as the enterprises performed well.

[62] (1888, Jul 13). *Shen Bao* (the Chinese newspaper Shenpao, 申报).

Officials, initially under the false pretense of protecting the merchants, were in fact exploiting them. The mode of government supervision and merchant management was fiercer than that of a tiger."

10.5 Views on Government-Supervised and Merchant-Managed Enterprises

The establishment of government-supervised and merchant-managed enterprises was the most popular during the time of the Self-Strengthening movement. These were based on a shareholding system and capitalized on the advantages of the government and merchants. Although the government had absolute control over natural resources, its lack of funds made it impossible to establish large profit-making enterprises on its own. It was difficult to find non-governmental capital investment for modern industry because of the government's prohibition on the private ownership of the industrial and mineral industries, and because the conservative faction believed that modern technology would bring "fierce floods and dreadful monsters" and "hinder people's livelihoods," which would "destabilize the society" and "destroy Feng Shui." The establishment of government-supervised and merchant-managed enterprises finally broke through the deadlock, making it possible to invest in modern industry with private capital and to raise funds under the shareholding system for key navigation, textile, telegraph, and mining enterprises. This facilitated the development of the capitalist modern industry in traditional China and accelerated the country's transformation from a traditional to modern society.

In addition to officials raising capital by floating shares to establish government-supervised and merchant-managed enterprises, to seek government protection, merchants initially transformed their enterprises into that mode of operation as well. In the late 1870s and early 1880s, there was great fervor in establishing mining enterprises and applying Western methods to the mining of coal, copper, gold, and other kinds of metal. Developers of the mining industry were mostly local officials and ordinary merchants not backed by political power trying their utmost to garner the support of key officials of the Self-Strengthening movement. Although most small and medium-sized mining enterprises were established by private capital, they were labeled as "government-supervised and merchant-managed enterprises" to ensure protection. Enterprises like Chizhou Coal Mine in Anhui Province, Yixian Coal Mine in Shandong Province, and Liguoyi Coal Mine in Jiangsu Province were typical cases related to key officials of the Self-Strengthening movement and comparatively independently managed by private capital. However, inadequate incentives meant that most government-supervised and merchant-managed enterprises performed poorly. During the financial crisis in the mid-1880s, nearly all small and medium-sized government-supervised and merchant-managed enterprises suspended their production, and large enterprises just made ends meet with government support and loans. Considering this a dangerous road that sparked wide criticism, merchants from then on shifted their attention from government-supervised and merchant-managed enterprises to private factories. Despite the objection that academic circles still have to the concepts of government-supervised and merchant-managed enterprises, I believe their influence should be fairly and objectively evaluated.

Considering that investing in new industry was not popular at that time, that "common people are impoverished, and the government has financial difficulties," and that "fundraising from common people is very difficult,"[63] developing a company system in China depended on government assistance. The development of world economic history showed that whether a nation's capitalist enterprises could develop rapidly during the transformation from a traditional to modern society largely depended on how much the nation would support them in an environment in which mercantilism reflected state intervention. Developing countries required more national support when catching up with developed countries. Even already strong Western capitalist enterprises require national support at times.

Using the construction of railways in western countries as example, Ma Jianzhong pointed out the important role of cooperation between the government and merchants in the development of enterprises. He explained that Western railway joint-stock companies were established with investment from different sources: "Some are established by merchants or officials, and others are based on the cooperation between the government and merchants." If railway companies could not benefit from trade, they could be "solely managed by the government, or first

[63] Ma, J. (1960). *Shikezhai Jiyan, Jie Waizhai yi Kaitiedao Shuo* (Shikezhai Words, View on Building Railway by Loan, 适可斋记言·借外债以开铁道说). Beijing: Zhonghua Book Company, p. 21.

established by the government and then transferred to merchants, or first established by merchants and then transferred to the government." If a railway company "proved to be unprofitable and could not afford the manufacturing and management costs, it could be run based on the cooperation between the government and merchants." Common cooperation patterns were as follows: "One case is that the government leases land to merchants for free, decides the lease term according to the interest, and finally nationalizes the property. Another example is that merchants manage the company, and the government only offers subsidies, or the government supports merchants by paying the interest for them, or the government vouches for merchants who have difficulties raising funds."[64] These were cases of successful joint-stock companies in the modern industry of developed Western countries. Unfortunately, influenced by the traditional notion of the government being more powerful than ordinary people, the Qing government did not play as efficient a role as foreign governments. As such, its bureaucrats did not contribute much to the development of modern industry. The widely approved mechanism of establishment through raising funds from merchants was a step in the right direction, but not perfect. Ma Jianzhong mentioned that most British or American companies "established through funds raised by merchants" without government intervention eventually sought government support when facing bankruptcy caused by "competition, low prices, and huge losses."[65] In addition, China's national capitalistic industry and commerce at that time was vulnerable to the competition of international capitalism. Under the circumstances of an unpopular joint-stock system and non-existent investment market, how could modern industry, especially large-scale industry and commerce, survive and thrive amid international competition? For these reasons, most advocates of the Self-Strengthening movement wanted government support for enterprise development. The ideologues, who not only disapproved of the weakness of government-supervised and merchant-managed enterprises but also advocated fundraising and management by merchants, emphasized the significance of government support in enterprise development. For example, Zheng Guanying, an advocate for commercial war, stressed the

[64] Ma, J. (1960). *Shikezhai Jiyan, Jie Waizhai yi Kaitiedao Shuo* (Shikezhai Words, View on Railway, 适可斋记言·铁道论). Beijing: Zhonghua Book Company, p. 11.

[65] Ma, J. (1960). *Shikezhai Jiyan, Jie Waizhai yi Kaitiedao* Shuo (Shikezhai Words, View on Railway, 适可斋记言·铁道论). Beijing: Zhonghua Book Company, p. 11.

importance of the new type industry and commerce, which were based on cooperation between the government and merchants: "Not only should government support be garnered, but government power should also be relied on to develop industry and commerce." Simply put, "government support should reach where merchants have difficulties."[66]

However, officials and ideologues of the Self-Strengthening movement had a different understanding of national support. Officials interpreted it as government intervention in enterprise management, which to them meant that the "government decides the development route of enterprises and examines their advantages and disadvantages." However, the ideologues held that government support be concentrated in fields beyond the reach of ordinary people to protect and investigate them, but not to replace them as the enterprise manager. They also believed it was the merchants' responsibility to manage the enterprises. Enterprises had to pay taxes and the government was in charge of tax collection.

In the author's opinion, during the early stage of a nation's modernization, flawed enterprises managed by or associated with government were not well off. Government-supervised and merchant-managed enterprises had a role in the following two aspects of China's modernization:

> First, medium and large-scale enterprises with modern meaning were established. Without government support, large private enterprises such as China Merchants Steamship Navigation Company and Kaiping Mining Bureau would not have been founded.
> Second, more civil industry had come into being and acted as a pioneer in further development. At that time, private industry thrived in large cities where government-supervised and merchant-managed enterprises were located, whereas it was fairly underdeveloped where no such enterprises were located. Therefore, the emergence of government-supervised and merchant-managed enterprises not only promoted the spread of technology and managerial know-how, but also aroused people's interest in investing in modern industry.

[66] Zheng, G. (1982). *Zheng Guanying Ji, Shangzhanshang Shangce* (Zheng Guanying works • Commercial War I, Vol. 1, 郑观应集·商战上, 上册). Shanghai: Shanghai Renmin Chubanshe, p. 590.

Since the 1880s, with the development of the new capitalist economy in China, an increasing number of people had begun to take an interest in investing in the new economy. As such, the government's policy on comprehensive intervention in the economy had to shift its focus from micro-management to macro-control, which Adam Smith also advocated in his theory of economic liberalism. At the time, adhering to the abovementioned policy would have the following results.

1. It would greatly hinder the development of private enterprises: Considering that the competition with domestic industry counterparts would impede the development of the military industry, officials of the Self-Strengthening movement relied on patent rights and a monopoly to support government-supervised and merchant-managed enterprises, which while important during the early stage of economic development, was becoming an obstacle to the development of private industry. About the industry monopoly, people wondered "how one man alone can resist the enemy when binding the hands and feet of the rest."[67] A review of China Merchants Steamship Navigation Company by a British columnist noted that "its managers are very satisfied with their participation in trade and peaceful co-existence with foreign competitors, and government's intervention in private enterprises has greatly hindered their development. Two steamships purchased by the governor of Taiwan for its trade development were forbidden by the protectors of China Merchants Steamship Company from conducting trade in northern China, as they believed the ships would invade their market."[68] Those who longed for the development of the enterprise system disapproved of the policies that would hinder economic growth,

[67] Duan, Z. *Fangzhi Sanyao, Huangchao Jingshi Wen Sanbian, Juan Liushiyi* (Three Key Points of Textile, Government Administration Affairs Three Series, Vol. 61, 纺织三要, 皇朝经世文三编, 卷61), p. 6.

[68] Zhongguo Jindaishi Congshu Bianxiezu. (1973). *Yangwu Yundong, Juanba* (Westernization Movement, Vol. 8, 洋务运动, 卷8), Shanghai: Shanghai Renmin Chubanshe, p. 441, p. 442.

denouncing the monopoly as "shortsighted" and "detrimental to China but beneficial to foreign countries."[69]

2. It would impede enterprise development: A capitalist economy survives and thrives in competition. Free competition among enterprises acts as the driving force in improving enterprise management, technology, and market innovation, and thus enhances production efficiency. People such as Li Hongzhang were in favor of a monopoly without domestic competition. However, this type of monopoly did not stimulate the improvement of enterprise management, technology, and market innovation, resulting in the stagnation of businesses. Li Hongzhang's concept of industry monopoly negatively impacted the protection of an advanced productive relationship, and impeded social development and economic growth. However, it played a positive role in protecting everything backward and curbing the development of government enterprises in the Self-Strengthening movement.

[69] As cited in Ruan, F., Zuo, B. & Zhang, M. (1985). *Yangwu Yundong Shi Lunwen Xuan* (Selected Works of Westernization Movement, 洋务运动史论文选). Beijing: People's Publishing House, p. 495.

PART III

National Economy

Traditional Chinese society was based on agriculture; thus, maintaining agricultural dominance was the prerequisite for the development of other types of production. Modern society, however, is based on industry, around which everything revolves. The Self-Strengthening movement aimed to transform Chinese society from traditional to modern, and from an agricultural to industrial standard, thus becoming involved in restructuring China's traditional national economy.

Based on the understanding of the relationship between different dimensions of the national economy, Westernization underwent a development process. Before the Sino-Japanese War, the Westernization Group contended that industry and commerce constituted the backbone of a country, and recommended building a national economy system based on commerce. After the War, following the further development of China's modern economy, the Westernization Group proposed positioning the modern machinery industry at the center to establish a national economy system.

CHAPTER 11

Views on Development of Modern Agriculture

In traditional Chinese society, agriculture is the most important economic sector. The role of agriculture is to first address people's food and clothing requirements. Second, it is an important source of fiscal revenue. Third, it provides the material basis for war. To ensure the development of agriculture, thinkers paid a great deal of attention to this sector of the economy. After the First Opium War, China opened its borders and thus, its economy to the international market. Furthermore, as commerce and industry boosted the country's economy, they reduced the importance of agriculture therein. While agriculture was the most important industry, now, industry, commerce, and mining were on par. Second, the people valued agriculture and adhered to the old regulations. People's taxes were reduced, pension and relief were provided, and irrigation and canal treatment prevented the risk of flooding. Today, agriculture includes methods introduced from the West: Department of Agriculture, Institute of Agriculture, and Agronomic Fair were established, and machine production as well as modern agricultural science and technology were employed to transform traditional agriculture, catapulting it from a state of self-sufficiency to the world market.

J. Zhou, *Westernization Movement and Early Thought of Modernization in China*, Palgrave Studies in Economic History,
https://doi.org/10.1007/978-3-030-86985-4_11

11.1 Role and Status of Agriculture in the National Economy

Chinese agricultural products became part of the international agricultural market after the Opium War, especially after the Second Opium War. Chinese agricultural products were affected by the demand in the international grain market, which required the Westernization Group to handle arising issues from the viewpoint of foreign agricultural trade. As Chinese and foreign exchange products were mainly agricultural, the Westernization Group recommended developing the sector to resist foreign economic aggression.

Feng Guifen strongly considered "bread the soul of life," suggesting that "it is better to promote the paddy field when you want to be become wealthy."[1] He had two ideas: One was that to promote the development of a country, tea and mulberry trees must be planted, and mining exploited,[2] a view including agriculture. Second, he considered what agriculture could offer in terms of exporting products for foreign trade. For him, tea and mulberry trees were the main sources for China's development. For example, the foreign trade in Shanghai would collect 45 million taels, of which silk and tea would account for a larger proportion than opium and other foreign goods, which accounted for less of the income and was paid for in silver. If the West holds a large volume of opium, and China had no silk and tea, the country would perform poorly.[3] In other words, today's agriculture is not only food and clothing to meet people's needs in a traditional agricultural system. It must also increase the country's foreign trade and boost its wealth.

In 1888, *Save Industrial and Commercial Livelihood Economic Rights in China* by Zhong Tianwei proposed a comprehensive program of import substitution, which included many projects related to agriculture. He stated, "In response to plants such as grapes, vintage, and carrots, we

[1] Feng, G. (1998). *XiaoBinlu Kangyi, Xing Shuili Yi* (Reform Proposals Written in Xiaobin Cabin, Irrigations, 校邠庐抗议·兴水利议). Zhengzhou: Zhongzhou Ancient Books Publishing House, p. 112.

[2] Feng, G. (1998). *XiaoBinlu Kangyi, Chou Guoyong Yi* (Reform Proposals written in Xiaobin Cabin, Raise the country with justice, 校邠庐抗议·筹国用议). Zhengzhou: Zhongzhou Ancient Books Publishing House, p. 148.

[3] Feng, G. (1998). *XiaoBinlu Kangyi, Chou Guoyong Yi* (Reform Proposals Written in Xiaobin Cabin, Raise the Country with Justice, 校邠庐抗议·筹国用议). Zhengzhou: Zhongzhou Ancient Books Publishing House, p. 148.

also produce refined sugar, cigars, cigarettes, and etc. Furthermore, alongside good animal husbandry and cattle, milk cakes, lobster, and yellow grasshopper could also be sold to foreigners as foodstuff."[4]

By "trade war," Zheng Guanying was referring to developing agriculture in view of foreign trade. In his book first published in 1880, he stated that "local officials should be commended to persuade farmers to plant and manage mulberry trees and tea in the mountains. Improved methods to harvest and prepare the tea should be deliberately sought, and someone who made it better must be rewarded. We must use the land rationally and ensure appropriate crops. This will increase the output and lower the price, sales will increase, and people will benefit from a sound economy."[5] In *Warnings in the Blooming Age*, he listed products suitable for the trade war with foreigners, such as silk, tea, opium, cloth, woolen cloth, cigarettes, sugar, wine, cotton, and flowers. These products were directly or indirectly related to agriculture. He reiterated that China would not win the battle if it did not develop its agriculture.[6]

After the 1894–1895 Sino-Japanese War, Chapter One of *The Policy for Enriching the Country Sequel* by Chen Chi details how to develop a commercial agricultural system including issues pertaining to water conservancy, afforestation, development of fruit, mulberry, wine, paper, camphor, wood, rubber, tea, cotton, sugar, tobacco, coffee, grain, livestock, fisheries, and other projects. Therein, Chen Chi's views reflect the impact of Westernization thinking after the 1894–1895 Sino-Japanese War on how to develop market-oriented agriculture.

In summary, the Westernization thinkers' understanding of modern agriculture had two characteristics. The first was developing commercial agriculture. They believed that in an era of multinational traffic, agriculture was not important in terms of personal consumption but for sales in the international market, and for the Western powers to expand the

[4] Zhong, T. *Yuezu Ji, Wanhui Zhongguo Gongshang Shengji Liquan Lun Er* (Zhong's Righteous Words, Save the China Industrial and Commercial Livelihood Economic Rights Theory II, 刖足集·挽回中国工商生计利权论二).

[5] Zheng, G. (1982). *Zheng Guanying Ji, Lun Shangwu Shangce* (Zheng Guanying Works, Business Affairs, Vol. 1, 郑观应集·论商务, 上册). Shanghai: Shanghai Renmin Chubanshe, p. 74.

[6] Zheng, G. (1982). *Zheng Guanying Ji, Shangzhanshang Shangce* (Zheng Guanying Works, Commercial War I, Vol. 1, 郑观应集·商战上, 上册). Shanghai: Shanghai Renmin Chubanshe, p. 589.

war. The second was to develop a holistic agricultural system, which not only plants subsistence crops, but also grows cash crops including trees, tea, mulberry and fruit, cooperated with developing other complementary industries like fisheries, animal husbandry, and so on. Zhang Zhidong explained, "Outside Setagaya, fruits and trees are planted, and livestock and fish farming are all part of agriculture. While the various products are expensive, whole grain alone does not offer enough economic benefit to survive."[7]

During this period, the Westernization thinkers also studied the relationship between agriculture and other industries in the new environment. Chen Chi noted the relationship between agriculture and industry and commerce as follows: "Agriculture is the foundation of business. All things will prosper once agriculture flourishes."[8] As such, agriculture was to provide raw materials and products for industry and commerce, and only when it flourished, would commerce and industry advance. In this sense, agriculture was considered the foundation of the national economy. However, this transcended the view of traditional agriculture, and the shift now was to value agriculture in terms of its ability to develop business and an agricultural economy to meet market needs.

In 1898, in *Exhortation to Learning*, Zhang Zhidong analyzed the relationship among agriculture, industry, and commerce, stating, "These three factors express themselves and each other. When agriculture is weak, industry will decline. When industry is hindered, commerce will decline, and if both industry and commerce decline, agriculture will perform poorly."[9] After three years, he emphasized that a country must focus on agriculture to accumulate wealth. Without agriculture, the development of industry and commerce is limited.[10] Certainly, Zhang demonstrated a profound awareness of the importance of agriculture.

[7] Zhang, Z. (1998). *Quanxuepian, Nonggongshang Xue Dijiu* (Exhortation to Learning, Agriculture, Industry and Commercial IX, 劝学篇·农工商学第九). Zhengzhou: Zhongzhou Ancient Books Publishing House, p. 143.

[8] Chen, C. (1997). *Chen Chi Ji, Chuangli Shangdu Shuo* (Chen Chi Works, On Commerce Ministry Establishment, 陈炽集·创立商都说). Beijing: Zhonghua Book Company, p. 232.

[9] Zhang, Z. (1998). *Quanxuepian, Nonggongshang Xue Dijiu* (Exhortation to Learning, Agriculture, Industry and Commercial IX, 劝学篇·农工商学第九). Zhengzhou: Zhongzhou Ancient Books Publishing House, p. 146.

[10] Zhang, Z. *Zhang Wenxianggong Quanji, Zunzhi Chouyi Bianfa Jinni Caiyong Xifa Shiyitiao Zhe, Juan Wushisi* (Collected Works of Zhang Wenxiang, Respect the West

In view of the importance of agriculture in the modern economy, Zhang criticized the backward nature thereof: "Silk, cotton, tea, and flax are now the property of mass production. The profit is now being plundered because we can offer the products but they do not sell well, or we sell the products to our own people. This is a silly act."[11] To change this situation, he personally invested in improved varieties from the United States, established a Sericulture Bureau, and became involved in the processing of corn. Furthermore, he communicated with the Chinese Minister to Russia on approaches to price and technology to reform the old and open up the environment.[12]

Despite that Westernization emphasized the development of commerce, agriculture was still needed to support the people. China's high population meant it would be difficult to address issues pertaining to food in the country. In his book *Reduce Private Rent Theory*, Zhong Tianwei argued that rent was so high that peasants living in squalor may cause civil disturbances: "The tenant farmers who do not have land realize that there is insufficient production for making a living. Some live as thieves or break the laws. This cannot be attributed to limited resource or primitive customs do. Since private rent is too high, people live in terrible environments. The officers do not ask about their livelihoods of no-count, but also take the risk."[13] Chen Chi added that "the country stands in support of its people, and hunger breeds discontentment. The people play a significant role if a country wants to become wealthy, and water conversancy is also necessary for the people."[14] This was included in *Implementation of Policies to Enrich Countries*: *Water Conservancy*. He again stressed the importance of agriculture in *The Policy for Enriching*

Methods in eleven Items, Vol. 54, 张文襄公全集·遵旨筹议变法谨拟采用西法十一条折, 卷54).

[11] Zhang, Z. (1998). *Quanxuepian, Nonggongshang Xue Dijiu* (Exhortation to Learning, Agriculture, Industry and Commercial IX, 劝学篇·农工商学第九). Zhengzhou: Zhongzhou Ancient Books Publishing House, p. 143.

[12] Zhang, Z. *Zhang Wenxianggong Quanji, Diandu Ershijiu, Juan Yibaiwu* (Collected Works of Zhang Wenxiang, Vol. 150, Electric slips 29, 张文襄公全集, 卷150, 电牍29).

[13] Zhong, T. *Yuezu Ji, Nei Pian* (Zhong's Righteous Words, Domestic Affairs, 刖足集·内篇).

[14] Chen, C. (1997). *Chen Chi Ji, Shuili Fuguo Shuo* (Chen Chi Works, The Water Conservancy to a Country, 陈炽集·水利富国说). Beijing: Zhonghua Book Company, p. 153.

the Country Sequel on Agricultural Theory, emphasizing that people would go hungry if not for it.[15]

11.2 Developing Modern Agriculture Using Western Methods

In a traditional agricultural society, people pay attention to the use value of agricultural products and pay less attention to their quality, cost, and price. However, in the era of international trade, agricultural products entered the international commodities market, wherein product quality, price, and cost, which are related to the increase in agricultural productivity, must be considered. As an understanding of Western approaches increased, the Westernization Group moved toward transforming the traditional agricultural system using these Western methods.

At the end of the Xianfeng Reign, Feng Guifen acknowledged the high efficiency of Western agricultural machinery, stating, "Organizations with tools require hundreds of hands. As more machines are used, people will be more successful because while less labor will be required, productivity will increase."[16]

In 1888, in *Save Industrial and Commercial Livelihoods in China: Economic Rights Theory II*, Zhong Tianwei wrote that only through machine production could we "sell large volumes of silk and tea to make money, without which there is no competitiveness to compare with the West." He pointed out that Chinese silk and tea would not be competitive in the foreign market unless machine-produced to lower the cost. At that time, Chinese tea and silk was not machine-produced but handcrafted. In addition, "the quality of the silk and tea is better and a bright color" when machine produced. Thus, Chinese products were not considered competitive in the international market.

In 1891, in *Study on Western Countries Leading Livelihoods and Wealth,* Xue Fucheng outlined the efficiency of agricultural production. He believed that the land in European countries was less fertile than that in China, but that despite that, the Chinese people had low earnings,

[15] Chen, C. (1997). *Chen Chi Ji, Jiangqiu Nongxue Shuo* (Chen Chi Works, Creation of the Ministry, 陈炽集·讲求农学说). Beijing: Zhonghua Book Company, p. 173.

[16] Feng, G. (1998). *XiaoBinlu Kangyi, Cai Xixue Yi* (Reform Proposals written in Jiaoban Cabin, Study from the West, 校邠庐抗议·采西学议). Zhengzhou: Zhongzhou Ancient Books Publishing House, p. 210.

while the British and French were wealthy. He wondered why this was so. The reason was their developed agricultural production technology, which he considered "the source of their wealth." He explained, "Westerners know the art of planting and animal husbandry, and the benefits of irrigation and water conservancy, which is more important than fertile soil."[17] Accordingly, he believed that through machine production, China could become one of the wealthiest countries worldwide.

How could Western methods be taken advantage of to develop a modern agricultural system in China? Zheng Guanying emphasized the introduction of the latest research results of the Agronomy Institute in various Western countries. He appreciated the importance Western countries attached to the development of agricultural science and technology. He suggested that China "set up a meeting, recruit talent from those in the field, and conduct research to ensure a profit." The research results should be "made public to all countries to provide knowledge and to use." Zheng Guanying further believed that although some took advantage of methods in sericulture in China, most "only know what it is and not why they should apply it. They still follow the old method, with zero increase in annual output. Moreover, some wild silkworms are not managed." In response to this situation, Zheng Guanying advocated that "we Chinese adopt the methods in books to prevent a disaster and make a profit. The result will increase income. Those who want to develop commerce should have this knowledge."[18]

Chen Chi focused on popularizing agricultural science and technology, and advocated the development of agriculture through educating farmers. He recommended that the government acquire books on farming from in and outside China, and presented the content thereof in detail. The books could cover farming in ancient and modern times both in China and the West, and include the Southern and Northern areas. "We do not intend to use valuable editions or ancient language. Rather, we can express the content through lyrics and poems, which we can disseminate

[17] Xue, F. (1987). *Xue Fucheng Xuanji, Xiyang Zhuhou Dao Minshengcai Shuo* (Selected Works of Xue Fucheng, On Financial Issues in Western Countries, 薛福成选集·西洋诸国导民生财说). Shanghai: Shanghai Renmin Chubanshe, p. 367.

[18] Zheng, G. (1982). *Zheng Guanying Ji, Shangwuwu Shangce* (Zheng Guanying Works, Business Affairs V, Vol. 1, 郑观应集·商务五, 上册). Shanghai: Shanghai Renmin Chubanshe, pp. 628–629.

to the counties and use to teach children." He believed that a new environment could be developed if using this method: "Agricultural policy will enrich the people and strengthen our country."[19] Zhang Zhidong shared Chen Chi's views. Zhang attributed the low traditional agricultural productivity to the fact that "farmers do not like to study and farm using traditional methods without any innovation. The poor results are concerning, especially in terms of industry and commerce alongside no progress in the agricultural sector."[20] To reverse this situation, Zhang advocated promoting scientific agricultural principles to farmers focusing on the "cultivation of fertile soil, identification of grains seeds, fertilizer storage, water conservancy, use of sunshine, and chemistry." Furthermore, he proposed that the government teach farmers to effectively use farming tools and efficient irrigation, and on the use of pesticides, cultivation, and grinding mills, some of which use wind or water power. Doing so will increase output."[21]

Zhang further recommended establishing an Agricultural School where "people who would like to study agriculture can study, conduct research on animal husbandry methods, and learn the science of cultivation." He believed this would "encourage the local officials and wealthy to boost agriculture, after which the people would likely follow suit." Zhong Tianwei agreed Zhang's views. Contributing two chapters to *Methods of Silkworm Rearing*, he suggested establishing an Agricultural Policy Academy in the area of Jiangsu and Zhejiang Provinces, as well as a silkworm school, where talented people should be selected to study. They would be taught by experts from the West. After three years of study, the school should send them to Italy and France to conduct research. Zhang also suggested setting up another Tax Department through which the funds collected would enable 10 students who could speak Italian and French to travel for leisure. "Do research on the methods of seed selection, incubation, silkworm rearing, disease, cocoon picking, and silk production to teach new students at the school." He believed that only

[19] Chen, C. (1997). *Chen Chi Ji, Nong Zheng* (Chen Chi Works, Agriculture Policy, 陈炽集·农政). Beijing: Zhonghua Book Company, p. 27.

[20] Zhang, Z. *Zhang Wenxianggong Quanji, Juan Wushisi*, (Collected Works of Zhang Wenxiang, Vol. 54, Chapter 54, 张文襄公全集, 卷54, 奏议54).

[21] Zhang, Z. (1998). *Quanxuepian, Nonggongshang Xue Dijiu* (Exhortation to Learning, Agriculture, Industry and Commercial IX, 劝学篇·农工商学第九). Zhengzhou: Zhongzhou Ancient Books Publishing House, p. 143.

through these two methods could China become the "most prosperous country in the world."[22]

Some in the Westernization Group also supported the "Agronomy Department" in promoting the development of modern agricultural production. In *Warning in the Blooming Age - Agricultural Works*, Zheng Guanying stated, "In Western agricultural policy, an Agriculture Department handles the framework and control." Each province was to launch an Agronomic Fair to obtain property and investigate land productivity. Different types of grain would be planted according to the soil properties. After the harvest, the Fair was to reward people based on the quality of their production. Furthermore, "talented people will be recommended to the authority and asked to teach their effective methods to other. Each county will follow the most effective methods, and the officials will support the people. However, the officials will also ensure that no laws are broken."[23] Zheng Guanying explained why it was necessary to promote the role of the state apparatus: "The masses are satisfied with their own harvest, but cannot help in rapidly developing our country. The authority's help is needed to progress."[24] Zhang believed that the application of modern agricultural science and technology would be at a considerable cost that ordinary people would not be able to afford.[25] The goal could only be achieved through the support of the country.

Chen Chi also researched the mode of operation of modern agriculture. He compared the land systems of Britain and France, and envisaged two modes of farm management. One was the large-scale farm operations of Britain. The large scale made it possible to "focus on new methods of agronomy, cultivation, culture obstructions, and harvesting to achieve the goal that one person could complete the work of 50 men, and the harvest of 1 *mu* could receive the harvest of 50." Otherwise, it could run the

[22] Zhong, T. *Yuezu Ji, Wai Pian* (Outer Chapters of Zhong's Righteous Works, 刖足集·外篇).

[23] Zheng, G. (1982). *Zheng Guanying Ji, Nong Gong, Shangce* (Zheng Guanying Works, Agriculture Policy, Vol. 1, 郑观应集·农功, 上册). Shanghai: Shanghai Renmin Chubanshe, p. 735.

[24] Zheng, G. (1982). *Zheng Guanying Ji, Nong Gong,* Shangce (Zheng Guanying Works, Agriculture Policy, Vol. 1, 郑观应集·农功, 上册). Shanghai: Shanghai Renmin Chubanshe, p. 735.

[25] Zhang, Z. (1998). *Quanxuepian, Nonggongshang Xue Dijiu* (Exhortation to Learning, Agriculture, Industry and Commercial IX, 劝学篇·农工商学第九). Zhengzhou: Zhongzhou Ancient Books Publishing House, p. 143.

business for mulberry, cotton, grape, coffee, tobacco, and so on. Furthermore, "Farmers will benefit from matching agriculture with industry and commerce, as well as from using high-quality farming tools." The second mode was to invest in the methods used in France for the management of small and medium-scale operations. France applied the traditional method of dividing land equally between the nobles. Thus, people could own land of up to hundreds of *mu* or as little as just a few mu. Unable to purchase machinery, they applied an intensive management approach to the urban needs of crop production, such as trees, grapes, vineyards, and so on. Chen Chi argued that China should "choose the best way to develop itself." He also persuaded provinces in the northern and southern areas to operate as per the mode used in British farming operations, namely to "harvest based on new methods, purchase new machinery, and gain the biggest profit with less investment." In contrast, farmers who own only 10 *mu* of land will fare better by "adapting the methods from France to local conditions. This will not only boost the number of trees or livestock, but also enable developing a water conservancy system. This will enable the poor to become wealthy."[26]

11.3 Paying Attention to Water Conservancy

Water is the lifeblood of agriculture. Since ancient times, China has been prone to flooding, so the development of a water conservancy system bore big responsibilities. Chen Chi had highlighted the importance of water resources on numerous occasions. He noted that in South China, the economy had developed quickly, while North China remained economically backward: "There is a clear difference between Jiangsu and Zhejiang provinces. Canals have been integrated in Hangjiahu plain in Zhejiang and Susonchangtai in Jiangsu, and the harvest from 1 *mu* is worth 10 *zhong*." This was the reason for the rapid economic development in South China. However, in the provinces of North China, "In the flood season, the water resources are too much for the land, while in the dry season, it is not adequate. People living around the Yellow and Yongding Rivers must constantly move because of the annual flooding, and the officials

[26] Chen, C. (1997). *Chen Chi Ji, Jiangqiu Nongxue* Shuo (Chen Chi Works, Creation of the Ministry, 陈炽集·讲求农学说). Beijing: Zhonghua Book Company, pp. 173–174.

require high tax, which adds even more pressure to the people."[27] How could the development of modern agriculture be promoted through the development of water conservancy? The Westernization Group suggested opening the canals to plant trees to promote the development of water resources in modern agriculture.

According to Zheng Guanying, flooding was a big problem in ancient China. As such, all the dynasties paid great attention to protection against flooding. Despite the great cost, these mechanisms had no effect because they "merely addressed the surface of the problem." How could a resolution be decided? Zheng stated, "*Zhou Li* suggests opening the canals to plant trees, but the methods of open canals will decrease the officials' benefits and cause other problems. Thus, how can we build and collect money?" Why should the canals be opened and trees planted? In Zheng Guanying's opinion, "After we plant trees, we can have large high-quality trees and use those of poorer quality as fertilizer. The trees' roots can absorb the soil's nutrients and decomposing soil, and change the fertileness of the soil. The tree's body will release oxygen and moisten the root, ensuring arid areas can be watered. Besides, as the roots can change the properties of the sand and rock to soil, the wall can be rooted deeper."[28]

Chen Chi pointed out that "100 years ago, the western countries were the same as China. However, since Voltaire, the Frenchman who first proposed planting trees and developing water conservancy projects, France opened up more than 700 waterways within 3 years. Other countries in the West followed the example of France in opening canals. Britain, with its 3 islands, also dredged up to 1800 rivers."[29] He thought that officers took over mountains and rivers in ancient China. After the Qin and Han dynasties, the management of mountains and rivers were lax, and the canals clogged up and streams flowed into rivers. Since the relaxation of the prohibition of cutting down trees in mountains, hardly any of these trees were left, a situation worse in the five provinces in the

[27] Chen, C. (1997). *Chen Chi Ji, Shuili Fuguo Shuo* (Chen Chi Works, The Water Conservancy to a Country, 陈炽集·水利富国说). Beijing: Zhonghua Book Company, p. 151.

[28] Zheng, G. (1982). *Zheng Guanying Ji, Zao Liao, Shangce* (Zheng Guanying Works, Flooding, Vol. 1, 郑观应集·旱潦, 上册). Shanghai: Shanghai Renmin Chubanshe, p. 744.

[29] Chen, C. (1997). *Chen Chi Ji, Shuili Fuguo Shuo* (Chen Chi Works, The Water Conservancy to a Country, 陈炽集·水利富国说). Beijing: Zhonghua Book Company, p. 152.

Northwest. He argued that "the leader had better readjust the northern civil governors and military governors and order them to determine how many canals were abandoned and on how many mountains trees were felled, clogging the rivers. The officers should then repair the deserted channels and open up the clogged rivers, prohibit the cutting of trees, and plant more trees in the mountains. The government should grant resources and help where needed. If someone does not do as ordered, he must be punished by law. Considering the difficulty in raising funds, the governors can use all the relief funds. Considering the difficulty in controlling petty servants, the governors can hire capable gentries. We will first put up posters, set a prize for them, and inquire about their work. Officials who treat people poorly should be punished, as should those who perform their work carelessly. The governors should praise exceptional people and punish transgressors. Those who make mistakes should be urged to perform better."[30]

Zheng Guanying and Chen Chi stressed the importance of planting trees because the Western doctrines had been introduced to China. Before Western academia was introduced in China, trees were planted only for silk production. Thereafter, the Chinese learned that trees were also helpful in water conservancy and irrigation. At the time, Faber, a German missionary, wrote *Rule Imperatives*, in which he recommended that the government plant tress as a first step to implementing Westernization.

[30] Chen, C. (1997). *Chen Chi Ji, Qu Shu* (Chen Chi Works, Open Canals and Plant Trees, 陈炽集·渠树). Beijing: Zhonghua Book Company, p. 23.

CHAPTER 12

The Thought to Develop Modern Industry

The Qing Dynasty of the modern industry was under foreign military power. The bureaucrats, influenced in part by the powerful West and under the guidance of the new apparatus, started modernizing the military industry and extended their efforts to the civilian industry. Chapter 4, Part 1 discusses the development of the military industry. This chapter focuses on the development of views regarding the Westernization of civilian industries.

12.1 The Thought on Modern Mining and Metallurgical Industry

In the late Qing Dynasty, the modern mining and metallurgy industry including machinery mining (coal, iron ore, copper, and tin were mined underground) and two machine metal manufacturing sectors for the construction of the military industry had high technical requirements and needed large-scale capital investment. It was also the second-most intense technical sector after the military industry. Westernization officers Li Hongzhang, Zhang Zhidong, and others paid great attention to this sector, and Westernization thinkers including Zheng Guanying and Xue Fucheng were also interested in the developments here.

Why should the modern mining and metallurgical industry be developed? The Westernization thinkers noted the following in this regard:

J. Zhou, *Westernization Movement and Early Thought of Modernization in China*, Palgrave Studies in Economic History,
https://doi.org/10.1007/978-3-030-86985-4_12

1. To solve the issue of energy and raw materials needed for military industrial production: According to Li, "Iron and coal are the materials needed to manufacture ships and cannons."[1] However, local production output in China was too low and of a poor quality. Thus, Li, who is responsible for front-line defense, petitioned to set up the Kaiping Mining Bureau. He noted the purpose of the mine as follows: "The bureau can offer coal to the Chinese soldiers, and we do not need to buy outside China. If facing a war, we can fight with our own weapons." In his view, "this is the most important in ensuring the prosperity of our country."[2] In 1889, Zhang petitioned to build a steel plant in Guangdong, writing in his memorial: "I humbly believe that the beginning of strengthening ourselves involves developing new materials and preventing external consumption. Not only the weapons we use, but also our people's everyday use of trains and electricity is closely related with iron."[3] Later, when he was civil governor and military governor of Hunan and Hubei, he built the largest steel plant in Asia, namely the Hanyang Iron Factory.
2. To end the aggression of foreign powers: For example, the development of Mohe Gold Mine was to prevent the aggression of Russia. Ma Jianzhong explained, "The gold mine in Mohe had large-scale production, and because it is located close to the Russian border, foreigners wanted to own it. We should build it ourselves quickly."[4] He Qi and Hu Liyuan also pointed out that China had sufficient minerals without having to open up, and thus "can prevent foreigners from taking over. There are many pirates, and now that

[1] Li, H. *Li Wenzhonggong Quanshu, Zougao, Juanjiu* (Complete Works of Li Wenzhong, Memorials, Vol. 9, 李文忠公全书·奏稿, 卷9), p. 50.

[2] Li, H. *Li Wenzhonggong Quanshu, Zougao, Juansishi* (Complete Works of Li Wenzhong, Memorials, Vol. 40, 李文忠公全书·奏稿, 卷40), p. 26.

[3] Zhang, Z. *Zhang Wenxianggong Quanji, Choushe Liantiechang Zhe, Juanershiqi* (Collected Works of Zhang Wenxiang, To Set Up Ironworks, Vol. 27, 张文襄公全集·筹设炼铁厂折, 卷27).

[4] Ma, J. (1960). *Shikezhai Jiyan* (Political Proposals Written in Shike Study, 适可斋记言). Beijing: Zhonghua Book Company, p. 84.

China is renowned for its treasure, if we do not exploit it, the foreigners will come to steal it."[5]

3. To solve the problem of a lack of coins: Chen Chi believed that China was facing "the scourge of today's non-food shortage and insufficient goods." This situation could be attributed to three reasons: First, the volume of commodity trading had expanded: "In the old days of millet cloth trading, people had no contact with neighbors and no money. Someone with 100 Qian was admired by his/her neighbors. However, now, benefit comes first, and the government does not seek benefits for their people. Thus, prices on the street have increased." The second reason was the foreign trade deficit: "Since Westerners started trade, they have earned much profit. Moreover, neighbors also care about benefits, and the negative effects thereof are emerging now." Third, "the world trade currency is gold, and China mostly uses silver, leading to a big disadvantage in foreign trade. Three materials are equal to money: gold is much more expensive than silver, and silver is much more expensive than copper. Chinese were used to use the copper coins, as there are fewer silver mines than copper and gold mines." At that time, gold in China was not expensive and silver was not necessarily cheap. The US and Mexico opened their silver mines widely, shipping it to China in exchange for gold. The Chinese considered silver more precious than copper, and while there were many gold mines in China, gold was not valued. In contrast, foreign countries took gold as the standard. Thus, "if the Chinese want to buy foreign goods, they must pay with gold." He believed that "if we maintain the status quo for a decade, foreigners' goods will become more expensive, while ours will become cheaper. To change the situation, we must open mines to make coins."[6]
4. To solve the problem of refugees and to increase employment: Xue Fucheng believed that mining was like farming. Not only could you make money, but you could also create employment. According to

[5] He, J. & Hu, L. (1994). *Xinzheng Zhenquan, Xinzheng Lunyi* (The Real Interpretation of the New Policy · Discussion on New Policies, 新政真诠·新政论议). Shenyang: Liaoning People's Publishing House, p. 153.

[6] Chen, C. (1997). *Chen Chi Ji, Weichi Kuangzheng Shuo* (Chen Chi Works·On Maintain the Mining Administration, 陈炽集·维持矿政说). Beijing: Zhonghua Book Company, pp. 178–179.

him, "The fertile land will not yield grains if it is not cultivated, and the mine will not yield gold if it is not mined. When a man opens a mine, 10,000 people can be employed. If we employee tens of thousands of people, the land must take 100,000 *mu*, and if we employ 1000 people, the land must take 1000 *mu*. The land is limited and the people are poor. We must open mines to meet current needs."[7] He added, "To open mines, we must manufacture ships and carriages, and have technical works."[8]

5. To ensure the country's prosperity: For Wang Tao, "The benefits of the coal and iron are shown. There is no shortage of machinery and ships, and there is no shortage of supplies. Each year, coal is transported from foreign countries to the trade port to supply demand. The amount of gold is more than a thousand or hundreds of millions and the iron is as much as 3–4 million. The mine is prosperous, as is its benefits."[9] Zheng Guanying continued, "Since historic times, western countries have become wealthy by benefiting from their mines."[10]

In various mineral projects, the Westernization Group focused on the mining of coal and iron. Ma Jianzhong valued gold mining most. He pointed out that China has "diverse minerals, but the most important are coal and iron. Coal and iron can help the country become wealthy, not because they are intrinsically valuable metals. Gold and silver mines are prosperous. Chinese gold and silver mines are situated countrywide, and three provinces in the area of Shandong have rich mineral resources. If we can raise the capital to investigate and estimate the progress, we can thereafter open it ourselves. I believe we can accumulate wealth over

[7] Xue, F. (1987). *Xue Fucheng Xuanji, Shuzhou Guankuang Renhou* (Selected Works of Xue Fucheng · Articles Written to the Heirs of the Iron Industry Officials, 薛福成选集·书周官矿人后). Shanghai: Shanghai Renmin Chubanshe, p. 430.

[8] Xue, F. (1987). *Xue Fucheng Xuanji, Chouyang Chuyi* (Selected Works of Xue Fucheng · My Humble Opinions About the Westernization Movement, 薛福成选集·筹洋刍议). Shanghai: Shanghai Renmin Chubanshe, pp. 546–547.

[9] Wang, T. (1998). *Taoyuan Wenlu Waibian, Daishang Guangzhoufu Fengtaishou Shu* (Tao Yuan's Works of Foreign Affairs, A Letter to Prefecture Chief Feng, 弢园文录外编·代上广州府冯太守书). Zhengzhou: Zhongzhou Ancient Books Publishing House, p. 75.

[10] Zheng, G. (1982). *Zheng Guanying Ji, Kaikuang Shang, Shangce* (Zheng Guanying Works, Mining I, Vol. 1, 郑观应集·开矿上, 上册). Shanghai: Shanghai Renmin Chubanshe, p. 702.

several years. When the US and Australia opened up, they developed a train between these two countries. Furthermore, other grains are also sufficient, and most of those places are rich in gold. Thus, if we do not use Western methods, we can develop it ourselves. But once we decide to adopt their methods, we must open the gold mines."[11]

Zhang valued coal mining most: "According to the resources, the Bratain's development hinged on coal, and the Western countries opened coal mines to benefit their people. The value of coal is higher than that of the other five types of natural resources." Chen Chi also attached great importance to coal mining, saying, "The Westerners who traveled in China found the coal resources here the richest in the world. The amount of coal in Hunan and Shanxi provinces equals the wealth of Britain. Britain is rich in coal and iron, and the country can earn 300 million in gold each year. However, in China, the amount of coal is just a portion of the whole country."[12]

How could China's mineral resources be developed? The Westernization Group addressed this question as follows:

1. Acquire the technologies: Zheng Guanying believed that "even though China is rich in mines, the problem is how to mine and acknowledge them. People should learn geography to pinpoint the location according to depth, and learn chemistry to classify the mine based on various mineral resources."[13] He advocated learning more about machine mining from the West, and believed that "while Chinese mining uses much manpower and huge effort, it is not effective. However, the West uses machine mining with good results." Zheng Guanying replied that it depends on the circumstances: "Workers in western countries are expensive, but labor in China is cheap. Therefore, the Chinese work is based on human labor, and only when humans cannot complete the work, will we use machinery." He thought Belgium manufactured the best mining

[11] Ma, J. (1960). *Shikezhai Jiyan, Fumin Shuo* (Political Proposals Written in Shike Study, Wealthiness, 适可斋记言·富民说). Beijing: Zhonghua Book Company, pp. 7–8.

[12] Chen, C. (1997). *Chen Chi Ji, Fenge Caimei Shuo* (Chen Chi Works, Mining, 陈炽集·分塥采煤说). Beijing: Zhonghua Book Company, p. 184.

[13] Zheng, G. (1982). *Zheng Guanying Ji, Kaikuang Xia, Shangce* (Zheng Guanying Works, Mining II, Vol. 1, 郑观应集·开矿下, 上册). Shanghai: Shanghai Renmin Chubanshe, p. 711.

machinery, and suggested purchasing it from that country.[14] Chen Chi hoped that China could learn about managing the coal mines from the British, stating that among the countries worldwide, "the company policy of the British is perfect, including how to prevent fire, disease, pressure, closure, conflict, and waterproofing. Other countries should learn from it."[15]

2. Emphasize government support: At that time, the social environment was conservative and Feng Shui was strongly valued, seriously affecting the opening of mines. Furthermore, the mines were usually located in remote mountainous areas where government authority was deeply ingrained. Therefore, the Westernization Group advocated that officials play a state power role to stop any issues. Once "more than 1000 people have gathered, the troops will come to dispel them and mine workers will be trained to prevent arising issues."[16] For tax collection, Chen Chi thought, "because of varying circumstances, mining tax is not fixed. We may imitate Western countries and collect it in a ratio of 20:1. We can change the rules and enact laws according to the situation."[17] Zheng Guanying also advocated that they "not fix the tax amount. Tax should be related to the mine's resources, which is a reasonable approach." He thought that if the mining tax were too high, it would increase the cost of mineral resources and weaken market competition.[18]
3. Highlight the importance of balanced relations with local residents to reduce objections to exploiting the mines: According to Zheng Guanying, "In China, when a mine was about to be exploited, the local residents usually disagreed. The reason was that the exploiters were so aggressive they did not care about residents' needs. To

[14] Zheng, G. (1982). *Zheng Guanying Ji, Kaikuang Shang, Shangce* (Zheng Guanying Works, Mining I, Vol. 1, 郑观应集·开矿上, 上册). Shanghai: Shanghai Renmin Chubanshe, pp. 703–704.

[15] Chen, C. (1997). *Chen Chi Ji, Fenge Caimei Shuo* (Chen Chi Works, Mining, 陈炽集·分塥采煤说). Beijing: Zhonghua Book Company, p. 85.

[16] Chen, C. (1997). *Chen Chi Ji, Qishi Ren* (Chen Chi Works, Seventy People, 陈炽集·七十人). Beijing: Zhonghua Book Company, p. 85.

[17] Chen, C. (1997). *Chen Chi Ji, Qishi Ren* (Chen Chi Works, Seventy People, 陈炽集·七十人). Beijing: Zhonghua Book Company, p. 86.

[18] Zheng, G. (1982). *Zheng Guanying Ji, Kaikuang Shang, Shangce* (Zheng Guanying Works, Mining, Vol. 1, 郑观应集·开矿上, 上册). Shanghai: Shanghai Renmin Chubanshe, pp. 704–705.

change this situation, we should calculate the proportion clearly and fairly, and be just when buying the land from local farmers so that they do not lose their job, causing disputes. For those not willing to sell their land, we can assess it as capital stock and pay them the dividend yearly. If we can do as above, the people who have land with a mine will prefer giving out their land to resist mining activity."[19]

4. Pay attention to the combination of the mining and military industries and adopt a Mine Storing Measure: Xue Fucheng stated, "Besides the Green Army, there are troops in each province that consume a large amount of payments and provisions by doing nothing outstanding. If we disarm these troops, the enemies in the neighborhood will not be daunted. For example, the Yu Army in Xinjiang and Huai Army in the capital open up wasteland and grow food grain to subsidize their consumption. The army can also help with the flood-prevention work done on rivers, and construction of water conservancy projects, batteries, and city walls. It is an important way to cut down expenses and balance income and expenses. I heard there were many kinds of mines in Yunnan, Guizhou, Hubei, Guangdong, Shaanxi, and Sichuan provinces. The army in the area at first sent one or two battalions to try exploiting the mine, and then more to do the job to achieve a 60% profit. I also heard that when employing workers to exploit the mine, the profit will match expenses and more profit will be made from mines with a higher grade. If the soldiers are hired to do the job, the payment they get may not be as much as their expenses: they can get 50–60% of the expenses. Then, half the soldier's pay and provisions will be saved. When more troops adopt this method, more payments will be saved, which is the first advantage. If the soldiers are idle, they will form a habit of idleness and cause social unrest. When the army exploits the mine in the mountains after training in their spare time, it will help them remain courageous, which is the second advantage. Since the mines are usually located in poor and remote places, when there is an army, the barbarians and bandits will be restrained, which is the third advantage. When the government decides to exploit a mine, it is difficult to raise capital especially for the workers' salaries. As for

[19] Zheng, G. (1982). *Zheng Guanying Ji, Kaikuang Shang, Shangce* (Zheng Guanying Works, Mining, Vol. 1, 郑观应集·开矿上, 上册). Shanghai: Shanghai Renmin Chubanshe, p. 704.

> the soldiers, they have their payments, so initially, the government only needs the capital for purchasing machinery and hiring those experienced in mining. Since the costs are reduced, the mining work will be more productive. This is the fourth advantage. When mining starts, ships and carriages are needed to transport the resources, and craftsmen are needed to smelt them, which can provide many jobs for the people. This is the fifth advantage. With the development of exploitation, the production of gold, silver, copper, iron, and other metals in China will increase, which will help reduce imports from abroad. The influence thereof will accumulate over the years. This is the sixth advantage. Having these six advantages, Army Mining is better than state-operated commerce."[20]

In the process of preparing the Mohe Golden Mine, Ma Jianzhong proposed a similar Mine Storing measures to Xue Fucheng. He advocated selecting brave soldiers from the backlands to exploit the gold mine. However, their opinions differed in some regards. Ma Jianzhong had noticed the importance of arousing the soldiers' enthusiasm. He disagreed with "the government supervising the people for the exploitation of the mines" or establishing the mine by "setting up a company by selling shares." He suggested the private activity of exploiting under the management of the government: "The gold they exploited can be sold on the market. If the government must buy it, the price cannot be intentionally reduced." Ma Jianzhong thought the advantage of his suggestion was that "no labor or capital will be wasted, national defense will be reinforced, and our enemies will be anticipated to ensure peace in and outside the country."[21] Moreover, the more the gold was explored, the lower the price ratio of gold and silver would be. This also meant that loans would not be influenced, and domestic and foreign trade would not be impacted by the declining price of silver. In this way, "access to loans" would not be affected by the "loss of the pound," and the "trade of Chinese merchants" would not be affected by the decreasing silver price in both domestic and foreign trade.

[20] Xue, F. (1987). *Xue Fucheng Xuanji, Kuang Zheng* (Selected Works of Xue Fucheng, on Mine, 薛福成选集·矿政). Shanghai: Shanghai Renmin Chubanshe, pp. 546–547.

[21] Ma, J. (1960). *Shikezhai Jiyan* (Political Proposals Written in Shike Study, 适可斋记言). Beijing: Zhonghua Book Company, p. 88.

Since Chao Cuo suggested relocating people to the boundaries, various plans to reclaim and cultivate wasteland were proposed over the preceding 2000 years. These focused on relocating the people from the inland to the boundaries, and using the capital from businessmen to fund this practice. The soldiers stationed for border defense would farm the land, and local people would be hired to assist the farming endeavors. Their suggestions abstracted the advantage of former policies and combined job supply and economic development with the features of the time.

Regarding the organization of the mine company, some Westernizationists from the Westernization Group stressed that the government must cooperate with the businessmen; that is, exploiting the mine under the authority of the government and the people's desire driven by the interests of this exploitation. Some also thought it would be better if "private businessmen could make the decisions on their own."

Chen Chi proposed that the government and private businessmen cooperate. In his opinion, nothing is more powerful than the government, but the government has its defects in running the business of a company. The reason was that "when the government invests in a program, it cannot afford to lose money. In that case, the program will likely be suspended, and the businessmen will insist on operating and making money. Thus, it would be better if the businessmen run the business." Meanwhile, the government is needed to maintain economic order, since the businessmen, driven by their interests, may cheat on their partners or consumers, and gathering workers may quarrel and cause trouble. He said: "The profiteer in Shanghai raised funds that were then wasted in the name of mine exploitation. After they lost their credit, it was difficult for them to recollect the money. Even if the money could be recollected, the gathering workers may cause trouble and there would be so much hatred toward the profiteers that only officers from the government can stop the fight. Thus, when private businessmen run the business, the government should supervise the process."[22] Zheng Guanying also mentioned, "When the government is in charge of the whole program, the funds will be difficult to raise. If private businessmen can participate, the funds will be collected quickly. When private businessmen are in charge, malfeasants may try to extort them or thwart their efforts. Thus, it is necessary that

[22] Chen, C. (1997). *Chen Chi Ji, Weichi Kuangzheng Shuo* (Chen Chi Works, On Maintain the Mining Administration, 陈炽集·维持矿政说). Beijing: Zhonghua Book Company, p. 178.

the government be in charge of supervision to ensure the businessmen can assume their responsibility. The businessmen will make their efforts to sell their shares to collect money for the business and the government will properly inspect and tax them. As such, the combination of the two sides can remedy the defects of each side."[23] Clearly, Chen and Zhang's opinions differ from those of Li Hongzhang. The former thinks that government-supervised and merchant-managed companies should be managed by businessmen and follow business principals. In this case, the government needs only to maintain order and support the company, which is what the master of economic liberalism Adam Smith purported, namely that the government only play its role in a particular field.

He Qi and Hu Liyuan did not agree that mining companies be government-supervised and merchant-managed. Because it cannot be ignored that the power of the government often restrained people's rights, they insisted that except for mines that concerned the national economy and people's livelihood, all other mine exploitation should be carried out by the people. According to them, the government should "choose the best source area of gold, silver, and copper to exploit, and the metals can be used to manufacture coins to meet the country's needs." Regarding other kinds of mines, they suggested the government "encourage private businessmen to exploit and charge a small amount of money as the price of the land or charge no money at all, but give them a license to permanently exploit that mine. The purpose was to drive businessmen to accelerate their exploitation to gain revenues. This is also a way of making money." Why should this be done? He Qi and Hu Liyuan explained: "Material that is not developed is the same as material that never existed. The same is true for land without people on it. For those people who want to exploit the mine, if the government provided them with the land they need, they could gain more revenue. The government should tax these exploiters less and help them with transportation. When the businessmen have exploited enough mines, the government could build railways to their mines to help them save transportation costs

[23] Zheng, G. (1982). *Zheng Guanying Ji, Kaikuang Shang, Shangce* (Zheng Guanying Works, Mining, Vol. 1, 郑观应集·开矿上, 上册). Shanghai: Shanghai Renmin Chubanshe, p. 704.

and charge them for the railway. Both sides will then be able to keep their profit."[24]

Although the Westernizationists established many mining companies, only a few made any revenue, and most suffered a loss. Only the Kaiping Mining Administration and Mohe Gold Mine were well managed. How did this situation come about? The Westernizations attribute the situation to two reasons:

1. Inadequate exploration technology: According to Zhen Guanying, "The Chinese did not truly understand the technology. When they started to exploit, they did not select the right place, so all the work was for nothing. Sometimes, they did exploit the mine, but did not know how to smelt it properly. The only way was to hire foreign technicians. However, before doing so, the technicians hired by the company knew nothing about mining at all. Furthermore, the best foreign technicians often had jobs in their own countries, and were not keen to cross the ocean to help us." He advocated, "The bureau should send envoys to inspect the experienced technicians and employ them at a high wage so that they want come to China."[25] Zhang Zhidong also said that in the past 20 to 30 years, there was no outstanding profit from mining because the Chinese did not learn Western technology before starting to mine. He stated, "Provinces with mines should set up an institution of mining and raise funds for selected learners to study mine exploitation abroad. When they finish their studies and return, mining can start. First inspect the character of the mine and then purchase the machinery needed."[26]
2. Obstruction from officers: Zheng Guanying highlighted that officers hindered the development of mining in China, as they were

[24] He, J. & Hu, L. (1994). *Xinzheng Zhenquan, Xinzheng Lunyi* (The Real Interpretation of the New Policy, Discussion on New Policies, 新政真诠·新政论议). Shenyang: Liaoning People's Publishing House, p. 155.

[25] Zheng, G. (1982). *Zheng Guanying Ji, Kaikuang Xia, Shangce* (Zheng Guanying Works, Mining II, Vol. 1, 郑观应集·开矿下, 上册). Shanghai: Shanghai Renmin Chubanshe, pp. 711–712.

[26] Zhang, Z. (1998). *Quanxuepian, Kuangxue Dishiyi* (Exhortation to Learning, Mining Science XI, 劝学篇·矿学第十一). Zhengzhou: Zhongzhou Ancient Books Publishing House, p. 155.

> overcautious and greedy. When the exploitation of mines began, gathering workers would cause trouble, which is the situation the officers were afraid of. When mining operations ran smoothly, the officers would try to benefit through illegal methods, which would collapse the industry.[27] Chen Chi explained, "Officers from high levels often support the mining while the officers from lower levels do not. Even if supervision is carried out, the officers from lower levels reported that no mines were found, about which the higher-level officers could do nothing. In addition, some officers still send their followers to blackmail the exploiting company." How could this situation be dealt with? Chen Chi recommended four actions.

First, unify public opinion. Chen Chi said that in the past, the government closed the mine in each province. When they were opened today, people would not believe it: "When the orders have been issued, the officers and people will hesitate and worry that it may disturb the people, not be maintained for long, and bring no benefit. Then nothing can be accomplished. Or, some ignorant people who know nothing about the country's policy may be instigated to thwart the process." As such, he proposed that "the government broadcast the policy and analyze the pros and cons to make sure the people form the proper opinion."

Second, he suggested putting the shoe on the right foot and arousing the enthusiasm of the local officers. Chen Chi said that the local officers were not willing to exploit the mine because "they are afraid that there is less advantage of exploitation than the disadvantage thereof, namely that they might lose their original profit because of the mining. Thus, if they do not exploit the mine, there will be no loss at all." How could their confusion be addressed? Chen Chi proposed, "We should learn from suppressing salt smuggling that the officers in whose region the mines are exploited will be promoted. The more mining that takes place, the higher he will be ranked. Officers who intend to not exploit the mine will be stripped of their posts, and those with excuses will be warned. This will drive all the officers to actively exploit the mines."

Third, he recommended reducing the tax to ensure a profit from mining. Chen Chi noted, "In Western countries, the tax rate for mines is

[27] Zheng, G. (1982). ***Zheng Guanying Ji, Kaikuang Xia, Shangce*** (Zheng Guanying Works, Mining II, Vol. 1, 郑观应集·开矿下, 上册). Shanghai: Shanghai Renmin Chubanshe, p. 712.

5%, but in China, we taxed as much as 20%. The government uses this as an excuse to close the mine. Today, we have decided to exploit the mines again, so we should also tax 5% of the revenue, and gold, silver, and copper should be handed in to the government. The government should buy these metals as per the market price and use this material to manufacture coins. This is also the policy in Western countries."

Fourth, he proposed setting up special agencies to maintain social and market stability. Chen Chi explained, "To make mining effective, we need to set up special agencies like the salt industry. In the beginning, we must select a province with the best mines like Yunnan, Sichuan, Hunan, Shanxi, and the three northeastern provinces of China, and send authorities to supervise and use the money from the country to prepare for the exploitation. The government assists businessmen in doing the work. They will be treated fairly, and given the credit, profit, and rights they need. This will lead to increased profits."[28]

12.2 Development of Manufacturing

The development of manufacturing in modern times was stimulated by the huge profit made in China by foreign businessmen. On how to develop manufacturing in China, the Westernizationists had the following thoughts:

1. Importance of using machinery to develop manufacturing.

The Westernizationists advocated using machinery as much as possible in the agricultural, textile, and mining industries. For example, Feng Guifen insisted that machinery be used to farm the land with less labor in the 1860s: "Using machinery such as farming and textile tools will increase productivity and save on labor." Wang Tao added, "The textile industry should take advantage of machinery to make more profit. It will enable us to do half the work and obtain double the results."[29]

[28] Chen, C. (1997). *Chen Chi Ji, Weichi Kuangzheng Shuo* (Chen Chi Works, On Maintain the Mining Administration, 陈炽集·维持矿政说). Beijing: Zhonghua Book Company, pp. 179–180.

[29] Wang, T. (1998). *Taoyuan Wenlu Waibian, Xing Li* (Tao Yuan's Works Collection, Making Profit, 弢园文录外编·兴利). Zhengzhou: Zhongzhou Ancient Books Publishing House, p. 97.

Why use machinery to develop production? The Westernizationists believed that only machine-manufactured products could compete with foreign goods. Xue Fucheng explained that foreign goods were of superior quality and priced competitively, highlighting that "it is natural that people prefer foreign goods. This situation cannot be stopped by law, and the people cannot be convinced by virtue or guided by the government's advice."[30] Why were machine-manufactured products of better quality at a lower price? The reason was that the machinery could manufacture products that could not be made by hand. Furthermore, the machinery could be operated by only 1 worker, not the 100 required to make products by hand. Thus, workers could make more products than before. As such, manufacturing the same amount of product required less labor, which reduced the cost thereof. When the cost of the product is 10% of what it cost in the past, or even 2–3% thereof, people will rush to purchase it. Xue roughly calculated the cost, but still concluded that manual operations could not compete with machine operations. He also mentioned that foreign everyday necessities were better and cheaper than Chinese goods. "When Chinese people do not buy foreign goods, if the government tries to convince them, foreign businessmen will not be grateful. When the Chinese people buy foreign goods, if the government tries to stop them, foreign businessmen will not be concerned."[31] Xue objectively analyzed the problem through the market rule without prejudice toward Chinese or foreign goods. In general, Xue thought that China's only choice in this situation was to adopt machine production. "In machine production, the profits go to Chinese businessmen. If not, it will go to foreign businessmen. If Chinese businessmen profit, these earnings can be partly used to help the poor people in the country. However, if the foreign businessmen get the profit, the country will lose its foundation for development, which will negatively influence China."[32]

[30] Xue, F. (1987). *Xue Fucheng Xuanji, Yong Jiqi Zhicai Yangmin Shuo* (Selected Works of Xue Fucheng, Making Money Through Machines to Support the People, 薛福成选集·用机器殖财养民说). Shanghai: Shanghai Renmin Chubanshe, p. 420.

[31] Xue, F. (1987). *Xue Fucheng Xuanji, Haiguan Churu Huojia Xulue* (Selected Works of Xue Fucheng, Discussion on the Prices of the Goods in and Out of the Customs, 薛福成选集·海关出入货价叙略). Shanghai: Shanghai Renmin Chubanshe, p. 489.

[32] Xue, F. (1987). *Xue Fucheng Xuanji, Yong Jiqi Zhicai Yangmin Shuo* (Selected Works of Xue Fucheng, Making Money Through Machines to Support the People, 薛福成选集·用机器殖财养民说). Shanghai: Shanghai Renmin Chubanshe, pp. 420–421.

2. How to develop manufacturing: The Westernizationists suggested the following actions to develop manufacturing:

   First, focusing on skills education. Zheng Guanying wrote in his book *Warning in the Blooming Age - Skills* that China should establish schools to educate students to develop their skills. He said, "The Western countries are wealthy and powerful because they have art as their foundation. China should hire well known teachers to teach students who have learned a foreign language as well as math and art. The students can then learn reading and skills so that they can contribute to industry, business, or even the country."[33] He appealed that the country raises money to open schools to educate talent and teach them about natural phenomena to acquire knowledge and practice manufacturing. "When the products become increasingly delicate and plentiful, they can be exported abroad to make a profit. When the products are used for the weapons in the army, more weapons will be made in China, strengthening the national defense, which will help build a wealthy and powerful country."[34]

   Second, establishing a patent system. Chen Chi believed that a patent system stimulated the development of technology in Western countries. As such, if China wanted to develop industry, the government should encourage people to do the job, meaning the country should establish a patent system like in other countries. He explained, "Several hundred years ago, the Western countries were the same as China. Since the French King Charlemagne built the patent system, the people in France who invented a new method, theory, or machine that were helpful to the nation, would be invited by the King to testify to his invention in the court. If his invention could be testified, the King would give him a certificate and gold medal, and make sure his patent would be effective for many years and that others could not imitate his innovation." Suddenly,

[33] Zheng, G. (1982). *Zheng Guanying Ji, Jiyi, Shangce* (Zheng Guanying Works, Skills, Vol. 1, 郑观应集·技艺, 上册). Shanghai: Shanghai Renmin Chubanshe, pp. 719–720.

[34] Zheng, G. (1982). *Zheng Guanying Ji, Jiyi, Shangce* (Zheng Guanying Works, Skills, Vol. 1, 郑观应集·技艺, 上册). Shanghai: Shanghai Renmin Chubanshe, p. 723.

many people started to "do research day and night, hoping to become rich and famous by owning their own patent. At that time, much talent rapidly emerged," and the technology in Europe developed quickly. In Chen Chi's opinion, the function of the patent system was that "generous rewards roused one to heroism. The countries trading with China all have this system. Each year, 3000–4000 people come to own their patent with splendid inventions." Thus, if China wants to be wealthy and powerful, it should also "build its own patent system like other countries."[35]

Third, establishing a rewards system. Zheng Guanying thought that the transition from a traditional to modern society was a process of transforming social traditions. To encourage people to use machinery for production, the country should take advantage of their desire for fame and fortune and establish a rewards system. He stated, "Chinese people always desire fame and fortune, a tradition that is stubborn and unchangeable. If the country established a rewards system like in Western countries, the talent would try their best to research manufacturing."[36] He thought little learning from the West took place in the past because the talent who had succeeded in studying the West were not put in important positions: "They were not put in important positions because they were Chinese, so they were then hired by foreigners."[37] He advocated that in each province, the agricultural and manufacturing products should be reported. Furthermore, the local officers and workers in provinces with plenty of products should be rewarded. Provinces that do not report will be punished.[38]

[35] Chen, C. (1997). *Chen Chi Ji, Quangong Qiangguo Shuo* (Chen Chi Works, on Powering the Country Through Industry Development, 陈炽集·劝工强国说). Beijing: Zhonghua Book Company, pp. 200–201.

[36] Zheng, G. (1982). *Zheng Guanying Ji, Jiyi, Shangce* (Zheng Guanying Works, Skills, Vol. 1, 郑观应集·技艺, 上册). Shanghai: Shanghai Renmin Chubanshe, p. 726.

[37] Zheng, G. (1982). *Zheng Guanying Ji, Jiyi, Shangce* (Zheng Guanying Works, Skills, Vol. 1, 郑观应集·技艺, 上册). Shanghai: Shanghai Renmin Chubanshe, p. 720.

[38] Zheng, G. (1982). *Zheng Guanying Ji, Jiyi, Shangce* (Zheng Guanying Works, Skills, Vol. 1, 郑观应集·技艺, 上册). Shanghai: Shanghai Renmin Chubanshe, p. 729.

Furthermore, Zheng Guanying suggested the government use expositions to raise their enthusiasm for the work: "The Western countries have three factors to promote the business. The exposition is used to initially start the development of business, the company is used to maintain the management of the business, and tax is used to ultimately supervise and balance the business. China did not do the right thing at the right time or think of its essence. Thus, business in China did not develop well."[39] As a result, he asked, "In China, there should be expositions in the capital city or town in each province, where the goods and machinery should be displayed so that the people can see and compare them. They will then be able to learn about the advantages and disadvantages, which will help the workers inspire each other. The technology will develop quickly after this."[40] Zhang Zhidong added, "We should set up expositions at communications centers and ports so that people can come and see the products, and learn about their advantages and disadvantages. The best products will be sold out and those with defects will expose their disadvantages. This is also a way to inspire people to develop technology."[41]

In this period, some Westernizationists proposed developing a machine building industry. They pointed out, "All the products are made by machines, but only China cannot build these machines. All the production materials need to be imported from abroad."[42] How could Chinese goods compete with foreign goods? Thus, they suggested that China develop the machine building industry. Zheng Guanying noted, "When I read foreign books, I find that manufacturing is the basic foundation of business, and machine building is the essence of manufacturing. However, our country only knows how to buy and use machinery. Here, knowing how to build machinery can help us use it to its fullest potential. Thus,

[39] Zheng, G. (1982). *Zheng Guanying Ji, Jiyi, Shangce* (Zheng Guanying Works, Skills, Vol. 1, 郑观应集·技艺, 上册). Shanghai: Shanghai Renmin Chubanshe, p. 730.

[40] Zheng, G. (1982). *Zheng Guanying Ji, Jiyi, Shangce* (Zheng Guanying Works, Skills, Vol. 1, 郑观应集·技艺, 上册). Shanghai: Shanghai Renmin Chubanshe, p. 729.

[41] Zhang, Z. (1998). *Quanxuepian, Nonggongshang Xue Dijiu* (Exhortation to Learning, Agriculture, Industry and Commercial IX, 劝学篇·农工商学第九). Zhengzhou: Zhongzhou Ancient Books Publishing House, p. 145.

[42] Chen, C. (1997). *Chen Chi Ji, Zhiji zhi Gong Shuo* (Chen Chi Works, Theory on Machine Making, 陈炽集·制机之工说). Beijing: Zhonghua Book Company, p. 224.

we should establish factories to make machines."[43] Furthermore, Chen Chi mentioned, "Foreign goods are made by machinery so that they can make a profit from us. When we produce these goods, we should also use machinery so that we can keep the profit. All the products are manufactured by machinery, but only China cannot build this machinery. The key to making a profit then is held in the hands of foreign businessmen. If China cannot make machinery on our own, industry and business in the country will not advance."[44] Zheng Guanying also considered it important to cultivate Chinese talent that could make machinery to develop the machine building industry. He advocated "establishing schools to teach machine building, technology, and the nature of things to cultivate talent for the country."[45]

The Westernizationists emphasized three negative effects in the national industry should China not develop its own machine building industry:

First, it will be inconvenient to buy machinery from abroad, which will affect business. When all the machines used in government-controlled or private factories are from abroad, if we find new business and need to buy new machinery, "we need to send letters abroad and order the machinery. It will then take at least half a year or year to transport the machinery to China. This will put the profits of half a year completely in the hands of others. Furthermore, the business situation changes with time, and if the machinery is delayed for a long time, they may no longer make a profit when they eventually arrive. We will then need to find another way out."[46]

Second, we often buy low-quality machines at a high price. Zheng Guanying noted, "The foreign businessmen know that we cannot make

[43] Zheng, G. (1982). *Zheng Guanying Ji Shangwuwu Shangce* (Zheng Guanying Works, Business Affairs V, Vol. 1, 郑观应集·商务五, 上册). Shanghai: Shanghai Renmin Chubanshe, p. 627.

[44] Chen, C. (1997). *Chen Chi Ji, Zhiji zhi Gong Shuo* (Chen Chi Works, Theory on Machine Making, 陈炽集·制机之工说). Beijing: Zhonghua Book Company, p. 224.

[45] Zheng, G. (1982). *Zheng Guanying Ji, Shangwuwu Shangce* (Zheng Guanying Works, Business Affairs V, Vol. 1, 郑观应集·商务五, 上册). Shanghai: Shanghai Renmin Chubanshe, p. 626.

[46] Chen, C. (1997). *Chen Chi Ji, Zhiji zhi Gong Shuo* (Chen Chi Works, Theory on Machine Making, 陈炽集·制机之工说). Beijing: Zhonghua Book Company, p. 224.

our own machinery, so they deliberately raise the price and sell us second-hand machinery, which ultimately leads to losses."[47]

Third, the cost of repairs is high. Since China cannot make its own machinery, we do not "know the principals of these machines, and when broken, we must hire foreigners to repair them. If they are not willing to do the repairs, the broken machines are useless. This means our business is completely externally controlled."[48]

The Westernizationists were confident in the prospect of the machine building industry. According to Chen Chi, "The Shanghai Manufacturing Bureau can make silk spinning machines, and iron factories like Xiangsheng and Fachang can manufacture ships, wheels, machinery, and small machinery for embossing, sewing, papermaking, and printing. Some Chinese businessmen also hire foreigners to build machinery to make screws, copper sheets, and iron sheets. Once this gains impetus, more people will follow."[49] They contended that government support of this would accelerate the development of industry in China.

[47] Zheng, G. (1982). *Zheng Guanying Ji, Shangwuwu Shangce* (Zheng Guanying Works, Business Affairs V, Vol. 1, 郑观应集·商务五, 上册). Shanghai: Shanghai Renmin Chubanshe, p. 627.

[48] Zheng, G. (1982). *Zheng Guanying Ji, Shangwuwu Shangce* (Zheng Guanying Works, Business Affairs V, Vol. 1, 郑观应集·商务五, 上册). Shanghai: Shanghai Renmin Chubanshe, p. 627.

[49] Chen, C. (1997). *Chen Chi Ji, Zhiji Zhigong Shuo* (Chen Chi Works, Theory on Machine Making, 陈炽集·制机之工说). Beijing: Zhonghua Book Company, p. 225.

CHAPTER 13

Ideology of Developing Modern Business

To transform China from a traditional to modern society, it is also necessary to reform traditional into modern business.

13.1 Ideology of Trade Relations with Foreign Countries

Before the Opium War, foreign trade formed only a small part of the national economy. Traditional rulers considered trade the "bounty" paid to foreign countries. After the two Opium Wars, the progressing Chinese acknowledged the trend of foreign trade. In 1864, Wang Tao noted, "The great powers worldwide invaded China, which is a new situation our country has not faced before." China had no choice but to adjust to the situation. He contented, "A good ruler will worry about the management of the country, not the great powers outside. The invasion of those great powers will not weaken China, but harden exceptional figures and make China a more powerful country."[1]

Why did China need to trade with foreign countries? Xue Fucheng explained that "isolated China has become an opened country." That is, for China to link with the world market, trade with foreign countries

[1] Wang, T. *Taoyuan Chidu, Daishang Sufu Ligongbao Shu, Juanqi* (Tao Yuan's letters, the letters to Li Gongbao, Vol. 7, 弢园尺牍·代上苏抚李宫保书, 卷7).

J. Zhou, *Westernization Movement and Early Thought of Modernization in China*, Palgrave Studies in Economic History,
https://doi.org/10.1007/978-3-030-86985-4_13

was the only choice. He further highlighted that after opening five ports, China's negative attitude toward foreign trade had caused the foreign traders earned at least 30 million taels each year and 0.3 billion taels over 10 years. This was "because there is only import but no export, so China is becoming poorer, and the country is in great danger." As a result, "to develop the country, we cannot stop foreign trade, but must efficiently manage our business."[2]

The Westernizationists also considered foreign trade a benefit for China, not merely a trend. They suggested the country expand its opening up and increase the number of trading ports. Guo Songtao thought that foreign businessmen should establish trading ports in China: "Chinese businessmen were involved in transportation and ensured supply in the market."[3] This benefited both China's government and its people. From a commodity circulation and national tax fund perspective, he thought that one more trading port "will be good for the country and the people." Li Hongzhang had a similar view: "We are always afraid that more people will come and live in China, and cause problems"; however, "there is no big difference or harm between ten people or one or two. The Western countries allow people from other countries to live in theirs, and they remain wealthy and powerful. Thus, the real problem is that we lack self-improvement, not the foreign people who come to China."[4] Of course, while Li Hongzhang used these words to defend his diplomatic policy, he believed that the real problem in China was not foreign trade, but a lack of self-improvement, which was why western countries, which engaged in foreign trade, were wealthier than China, which did not.

Following the discussion above, the ideology of modern business derived from the development of foreign trade differs from the old business ideology to focus on trade inside the country. Since the main factor driving the development of the modern economy was foreign trade, the

[2] Xue, F. (1987). *Xue Fucheng Xuanji, Chouyang Chuyi* (Selected Works of Xue Fucheng, My Humble Opinions about the Westernization Movement, 薛福成选集·筹洋刍议). Shanghai: Shanghai Renmin Chubanshe, p. 541.

[3] Guo, S. *Yangzhi Shuwu Yiji, Yin Fashitiao Chenshizhengshu, Juanshier* (Works of Yangzhi Study, Discussion on Law Works and Politics, Vol. 12, 养知书屋遗集·因法事条陈时政疏, 卷12).

[4] Li, H. *Li Wenzhonggong Quanshu, Pengliao Hangao, Juan Shiliu* (Complete Works of Li Wenzhong·Letter with Friends, Vol. 16, 李文忠公全书·朋僚函稿, 卷16).

Westernizationists purported mercantilism, which positioned business as a critical part of the national economy.

According to Wang Tao, "Business supports the national economy and the people's livelihood in Britain. All its profit comes from sailing.[5] There are three advantages to foreign trade: Craftsmen with fine skills can earn their living; wanderers can find a dwelling; and when the businessmen are wealthy, so is the country. They can supply money when the country needs it. This is why western countries take business as their foundation."[6]

In 1890, Xue Fucheng, who had been sent to Britain, France, Italy, and Belgium on a diplomatic mission, proposed the ideology that business support the development of education, agriculture, and manufacturing. He believed that "when there is business, scholars will study harder because their knowledge can be practiced, farmers will grow better crops because they can be sold and make a profit, and craftsmen will work even harder because their products can make money. In the process, business is the ultimate supporter."[7] He advocated the development of foreign trade: "When China makes more products, foreign businessmen will make less profit, and the Chinese will be able to earn more money for living. Then, the country could take the profit from foreign businessmen to assist our people. There is no better way. The government and businessmen in China would both benefit and share the profit. We need to expand the profit we own, and we must take that monopolized by foreign businessmen. If we do these things, China will be wealthy."[8]

The same year, Ma Jianzhong wrote *Wealthiness*, in which he discussed how to make a country wealthy through foreign trade. He explained how

[5] Wang, T. (1998). *Taoyuan Wenlu Waibian, Ying Zhong Tongshang* (Tao Yuan's Works of Foreign Affairs· Britain Attach Importance to Foreign Trade, 弢园文录外编·英重通商). Zhengzhou: Zhongzhou Ancient Books Publishing House, p. 179.

[6] Wang, T. (1998). *Taoyuan Wenlu Waibian, Daishang Guangzhoufu Fengtaishou Shu* (Tao Yuan's Works of Foreign Affairs, A Letter to Prefecture Chief Feng, 弢园文录外编·代上广州府冯太守书). Zhengzhou: Zhongzhou Ancient Books Publishing House, p. 368.

[7] Xue, F. (1987). *Xue Fucheng Xuanji, Yingjili Liyong Shangwu Pi Huangdi Shuo* (Selected Works of Xue Fucheng, discussion on England Using Business to Open Up Wasteland, 薛福成选集·英吉利利用商务辟荒地说). Shanghai: Shanghai Renmin Chubanshe, p. 297.

[8] Xue, F. (1987). *Xue Fucheng Xuanji, Chouyang Chuyi* (Selected Works of Xue Fucheng, My Humble Opinions about the Westernization Movement, 薛福成选集·筹洋刍议). Shanghai: Shanghai Renmin Chubanshe, p. 543.

the Western countries became rich through gaps between imports and exports, and pointed out that the UK, the US, France, Russia, Germany, and so on all "became wealthy through foreign trade. A country whose exports exceed, or equal imports makes a profit. A country whose imports exceed exports makes no profit. To make China wealthy, we need to export more and import less. When we export more, the money we lost could be regained. When the country imports less, more money will be saved."[9]

As the Westernizationists realized the importance of foreign trade, some referred to the competition with foreign countries as a "trade war" to differentiate it from a "military war." In 1888, Zhong Tianwei proposed in *Zhong's Righteous Words · Save the Industrial and Commercial Livelihood Economic Rights of China Theory* that when trading with foreign countries, the Western countries "could take up a thousand miles of land without sacrificing one soldier or wasting one dollar. As such, it is evident that foreign trade is the clue to how to destroy a country."[10] Here, Zhong Tianwei did not use the phrase "trade war," but expressed the meaning thereof. Thereafter, Zheng Guanying wrote *Trade War I* and *Trade War II*, in which he proposed the term "trade war." He thought that military war would cause obvious damage, and trade war would cause massive damage. Military war would be a temporary solution, while a trade war would strengthen the foundation of the country. He called for "ensuring victory through a trade war."

After the 1894–1895 Sino-Japanese War, because of the need to develop the capitalist industry and commerce in China, some Westernizationists like Zhang Zhidong gradually formulated the ideology of a modern industry structure centering on the development of the modern mechanical industry. Zhang Zhidong disagreed with the idea of "founding the country on the basis of business," emphasizing that "industry is the belt connecting agriculture and business. Promoting agriculture inside the country and developing business with foreign countries

[9] Ma, J. (1960). *Shikezhai Jiyan, Fumin Shuo* (Political Proposals Written in Shike Study, Wealthiness, 适可斋记言·富民说). Beijing: Zhonghua Book Company, p. 2.

[10] Zhong, T. *Yuezu Ji, Wanhui Zhongguo Gongshang Shengji Liquan Lun Er* (Zhong's Righteous Words, Save the China Industrial and Commercial Livelihood Economic Rights Theory II, 刖足集·挽回中国工商生计利权论二).

is because of the development of industry."[11] Even so, he still considered the position of business in the national economy important. He acknowledged the active dynamic role of commercial distribution in reacting to industrial production, and thought that "the transportation of goods" could facilitate and stimulate the expansion of the scale and output of industrial production. "When the goods are transported quickly, and the transportation business is prosperous, more people will join the industry and more sophisticated goods will be produced. Thus, when business and industry are prosperous, but there is no transportation or market for the goods, industry will not develop well." He concluded, "The government cannot persuade people to develop industry, but business can."[12] This recognizes the active role of the commodity economy, and indicates modernity in his economic ideology.

Furthermore, for Zhang Zhidong, the second reaction was that collecting and exchanging market information in the circulation domain and feeding it back to industrial enterprises would help them improve the sales and competitiveness of their goods. "People who are good at doing business can start the business first, and then develop the industry. First, they need to know what goods are useful, marketable, and original; what method can reduce the cost; what country needs what goods; and what technology can compete with that of other countries. Then, we could hire engineers to innovate new crafts and new machinery for the business." Zhang Zhidong further proposed that production should follow the market, as "business generates the demand of manufactory."[13]

Zhang Zhidong understood the relation between production and transportation, knowing it was characterized as an "industry body for business usage." He also knew that "business is the core and industry the complement," and as such, "both sides bring out the best in each other

[11] Zhang, Z. (1998). *Quanxuepian, Nonggongshang Xue Dijiu* (Exhortation to Learning, Agriculture, Industry and Commercial IX, 劝学篇·农工商学第九). Zhengzhou: Zhongzhou Ancient Books Publishing House, p. 145.

[12] Zhang, Z. Zhang Wenxianggong Quanji, Juanereryi, Shuzhaba, Fu Shangbu (Collected Works of Zhang Wenxiang, Vol. 211, part 8, 张文襄公全集, 卷221, 书札8, 复商部).

[13] Zhang, Z. (1998). *Quanxuepian, Nonggongshang Xue Dijiu* (Exhortation to Learning, Agriculture, Industry and Commercial IX, 劝学篇·农工商学第九). Zhengzhou: Zhongzhou Ancient Books Publishing House, p. 145.

like a ring without an end."[14] Thus, when he prioritized the development of the machine building industry, he also paid attention to promoting the development of business to ensure mutual benefit and the simultaneous development of industry and business. He suggested that the newly established Ministry of Commerce "teach business, map out the business law, open the Chamber of Commerce, and examine the business situation."[15] Furthermore, when Zhang Zhidong was Governor of Hu-guang, he put into practice what he had advocated, and ran a business newspaper; established business schools, business associations, and the Chamber of Commerce; and took measures to develop business. This was all to "persuade the businessmen in Hubei province on one hand and reward them on the other. Doing this is to help businessmen break old traditions and cultivate their worldview and ability to win the trade war. In this way, the benefit and rights the country has lost can be redeemed, and the local economy can be prosperous again."[16] Under his efforts, business in Hubei developed quickly. In the 34th Year of the Guangxu Reign (1908), "the annual volume of trade in Hankou totaled 0.13 billion taels, exceeding that of Tianjing and nearing that of Guangdong. It was still the second trade port of the Qing Dynasty, and may catch up with Shanghai in the future. Some observers call it Chicago in Asia."[17]

13.2 Methods to Develop Modern Business

To promote the development of modern commerce, the Westernizationists made numerous claims and summarized its main points. Their main ideas were as follows.

[14] Zhang, Z. (1998). *Quanxuepian, Nonggongshang Xue Dijiu* (Exhortation to Learning, Agriculture, Industry and Commercial IX, 劝学篇·农工商学第九). Zhengzhou: Zhongzhou Ancient Books Publishing House, p. 145.

[15] Zhang, Z. *Zhang Wenxianggong Quanji, Juanereryi, Shuzhaba, Fu Shangbu* (Collected Works of Zhang Wenxiang, Vol. 211, part 8, 张文襄公全集, 卷221, 书札8, 复商部).

[16] Zhang, W. Zhang Wenxianggong Zhieji (Zhang Zhidong's Governance in Hubei Province, 张文襄公治鄂记), p. 33.

[17] Mizuno, Y. *Han Kou* (Hankou, 汉口). Qouted from Feng, T. (1985). Zhang Zhidong Pingzhuan (Critical Biograph of Zhang Zhidong, 张之洞评传). Kaifeng: Henan Education Press, p. 311.

1. They requested that the Qing government implement policies to protect merchants. In 1864, Wang Tao proposed that officials coordinate to help businessmen: "When dealing with Western businessmen, the officials should help to protect them to ensure high profits. I heard about merchants handling their affairs on their own who met with problems. Today, we act in a different way to ensure the economic rights belong to us so that our country can be prosperous in the future."[18] Wang asked the Qing government to change the policy blocking the development of businessmen to one that would ensure obeying the business law while protecting merchants and promoting business development.[19]

The Westernizationists had many ideas on how to improve the social status of businessmen, such as establishing the House, to which businessmen who conducted themselves well could be elected as a member. Furthermore, they recommended establishing a ministry to manage business, protect the interests of merchants, and give businessmen full freedom to invest. For those who established a company to develop business productivity, "the State will provide it with a praise card." For those whose businesses failed, as long as they reported their poor performance, "the government will promise tolerance."[20]

2. To develop foreign trade, they suggested tariff autonomy. According to Chen Chi, "Tax regulations are the basis of business. Our tax is too high and that of others too low. Our cost must be higher than that of others. This will lead to our failure to benefit compared to others who will benefit highly when the price is the same. The result is that we will not be able to sell our goods." He stressed that tariff autonomy must be recovered first to revitalize business, and that to develop a business, "if you do not first change the tax return, such

[18] Wang, T. *Taoyuan Chidu, Daishang Sufu Ligongbao Shu, Juanqi* (Tao Yuan's Letters, the Letters to Li Gongbao, Vol. 7, 弢园尺牍·代上苏抚李宫保书, 卷7).

[19] Zheng, G. (1982). *Zheng Guanying Ji, Shangwu Er Shangce* (Zheng Guanying Works, Business Affairs, Vol. 1, 郑观应集·商务二, 上册). Shanghai: Shanghai Renmin Chubanshe, p. 612.

[20] Zheng, G. (1982). *Zheng Guanying Ji, Shangwu Er Shangce* (Zheng Guanying Works, Business Affairs, Vol. 1, 郑观应集·商务二, 上册). Shanghai: Shanghai Renmin Chubanshe, p. 563.

> as providing help to save those going under, people will not want to open a company." Zhong Tianwei also pointed out three major mistakes since China engaged in foreign trade. The first was that the "Jinling Treaty (Nanjing Treaty), named the Tariff Charter, was set at 5%. From as silkworm entangled but not self off carry."[21]

However, if weak, how would China take food from the tiger's mouth to recover tariff autonomy? The Westernization thinkers emphasized the use of international law to improve the foreign trade situation in China. Zheng Guanying mentioned that the third chapter of *International Law* focused on the nation's fellowship and the hospitality of the people in foreign cases. In the second section, it is mentioned that "all the articles of association are set by the sovereignty of all countries."[22] China had lost its tariff autonomy because the foreigners were not familiar with *International Law*. Thus, the country absolutely had the right to request to change the tariff. However, when should the tariff requirements be put forward? The Westernization movement generally advocated that China revise the treaty. Ma Jianzhong stated that when revising the treaty with foreign countries, "according to the Western countries' tariff laws, change China's tax increase charter amendments."[23] Zheng Guanying added, "Considering that the West is not allowed, please replace the treaty in advance. If it is not conducive to the people of our country or there are obstacles to the autonomy of the people, allowance must be made to change the treaty on their own at any time."[24]

How should the tax regulations have been revised? The Westernization thinkers proposed levying import taxes to protect the national industry, and lightening export taxes to develop it. However, regarding how much

[21] Zhong, T. *Yuezu Ji, Wanhui Zhongguo Gongshang Shengji Liquan Lun Er* (Zhong's Righteous Words, Save the China Industrial and Commercial Livelihood Economic Rights Theory I, 刖足集·挽回中国工商生计利权论二).

[22] Zheng, G. (1982). *Zheng Guanying Ji, Shui Ze, Shangce* (Zheng Guanying Works, Tax, Vol. 1, 郑观应集·税则, 上册). Shanghai: Shanghai Renmin Chubanshe, p. 544.

[23] Ma, J. (1960). *Shikezhai Jiyan, Fu Li Boxiang Zhayizhong Waijiaoguan Jiaoshe Yishi Yanghuo Ru Neidi Mian Li Bing* (Political Proposals Written in Shike Study, Reply to Li Boxiang About Negotiation Between the Foreign Officials and the Chinese Officials, 适可斋记言·复李伯相札议中外交官交涉仪式洋货入内地免厘禀). Beijing: Zhonghua Book Company, p. 75.

[24] Zheng, G. (1982). *Zheng Guanying Ji, Shui Ze, Shangce* (Zheng Guanying Works, Tax, Vol. 1, 郑观应集·税则, 上册). Shanghai: Shanghai Renmin Chubanshe, p. 544.

import tax to charge, which products to tax heavily, and which products to tax lightly, the Westernizationists did not have much to say, except Ma Jianzhong. Ma Jianzhong highly recommended revising the tax regulations. In 1879, British Minister Thomas Wade negotiated with the Chinese government on numerous issues including that foreign product imported into the mainland be exempted from taxation. Ma Jianzhong advised Li Hongzhang on the matter, stating, "It is better to stick with the plan. Changes to China's tax increases are used to cover likin(lijin) tax." He argued that exports would not be taxed to increase the competitive power thereof in the international environment. Even if it would be taxed, the tax rate will not be too high, and only exclusive products in the overseas market that were not controlled by others would be re-taxed for exportation.

Tax should be applied differently to imported goods. In this regard, four types of tax could be charged. The first was for natural resources from mining, which would be taxed at 5% of the actual value. The second was for manmade calico manufactured in China, which would be taxed at 15% of the actual value. The third was for products not made in China that only the wealthy could afford, such as watches, glasses, and umbrellas, which would be taxed at 25%, and wine, cigars, sugar, and vegetables, which would be taxed at 30%. The fourth type was for opium, which is harmful like poison, and as such, the tax would become increasingly higher to control it." Other types of groceries were taxable under the actual value of 15%.[25]

The Westernizationists also believed that achieving tariff autonomy should involve the jurisdiction of customs. Zheng Guanying urged the Qing government to exonerate Hird and appointed a group of foreigners to deal with customs duties in China. He pointed out, "At the beginning of the tax treaty, the price of Chinese commodities is not equal to the foreign price." As for the argument that the Chinese were unfamiliar with customs affairs and unsuitable to do this job compared to Western people, Zheng responded, "Foreign trade has taken place for

[25] Ma, J. (1960). *Shikezhai Jiyan, Fu Li Boxiang Zhayizhong Waijiaoguan Jiaoshe Yishi Yanghuo Ru Neidi Mian Li Bing* (Political Proposals Written in Shike Study, Reply to Li Boxiang about Negotiation Between the Foreign Officials and the Chinese Officials, 适可斋记言·复李伯相札议中外交官交涉仪式洋货入内地免厘禀). Beijing: Zhonghua Book Company, pp. 77–78.

decades. The Chinese are also proficient in tax and familiar with tax regulations, but rather than helping others to protect other nations, this is what Chinese people did." He hoped that "the specific articles should be selective, and suggested selecting three p'in officials familiar with the situation to work with the inspector general. The tax department and deputy were gradually controlled by the Chinese to do things according to the rules and regulations and manage large sums of money on their own without the involvement of Westerners. The special tax administration should be of great advantage to China."[26]

They also strongly criticized other treaties that hindered the business development of China, such as the consular jurisdiction, inland waterway transport, and establishing the right circles, and called for their abolition. In addition, the Westernizationists hoped to abolish the likin(lijin) tax to ensure commercial prosperity.

3. To enhance the market competitiveness of Chinese businessmen, the Westernizationists proposed that organizations advance the advantages of capital management. Ma Jianzhong noted that if Chinese tea and silk were produced by multiple operators, conflict would arise and the villagers would raise the price thereof, which would increase the cost. Then, at an auction, foreign merchants would seize the opportunity to keep the prices down, inevitably losing money. For example, "by combining many small businesses into several large companies, it is easy to consult on prices without a high risk. Since the capital is high and the interest payments low, light cargo to various ports does not need to rush to attract buyers from foreign suppliers. Without Yangcheng, losses would not be as frequent."[27] In addition, large companies have the advantage of being able to guarantee product quality and establish the credibility of the company, unlike small companies, which with no long-term business plan, cannot guarantee product quality and even produce counterfeit and low-quality products. As such, they damage the reputation of Chinese products, resulting in the loss of foreign markets. Chen Chi's view was similar to that of Ma Jianzhong, but differed for

[26] Zheng, G. (1982). *Zheng Guanying Ji, Shui Ze, Shangce* (Zheng Guanying Works, Tax, Vol. 1, 郑观应集·税则, 上册). Shanghai: Shanghai Renmin Chubanshe, pp. 546–547.

[27] Ma, J. (1960). *Shikezhai Jiyan, Fumin Shuo* (Political Proposals Written in Shike Study, Wealthiness, 适可斋记言·富民说). Beijing: Zhonghua Book Company, p. 3.

mainland and export companies. He said that because the capital of mainland companies is abundant, the size of business benefits could be maintained. As this makes it easier to make a profit, they need not act like "smuggling" vendors. This meant the government could "reduce the steps in the process and the number of personnel, and save on fiscal expenditure in the public or private sectors. To drum up a large number of capital operations, export companies should not be run by small businesses vulnerable to foreign traders to manipulate the market price; thus, it is better for Chinese people to enjoy the dividends and expand trade."[28]

4. Zhang Zhidong recommended establishing a "special economic zone." In 1901, when Russia attempted to monopolize the three provinces in Northeast China, Zhang made an exchange for the support of other capitalist countries to force Russia to return the three provinces, and suggested that the Qing government take measures to implement an "open trade" policy. He would rather totally open the three provinces in the Northeast than Russia occupied the area, so that "countries in the world can trade there. All mining, and industry and commerce based on interests. People from different countries can conduct their business affairs, while our country's duty is to collect the tax." He added, "The three provinces in Northeast China have a vast territory and rich products. The mining industry and commerce are very favorable, and if we do not attract foreigners by opening it up, China's capital will be difficult to raise. So difficult it is, that if we discard the advantages of the geographic location, how can we become prosperous and strong?" In this case, Zhang Zhidong thought: "China's life relies on these four words: implement an 'open door to trade' policy. From then on, Russia's pocketing of the Manchuria plan is bound to fail."[29] This was the first time a special economic zone was proposed in modern China. However, at that time, it was not likely his vision would be realized: "The total of their profits with other countries, but self-jurisdiction of trade. All my income off interest will come

[28] Chen, C. (1997). *Chen Chi Ji, Jiuji Gongsi Shuo* (Chen Chi Works · On Company, 陈炽集·纠集公司说). Beijing: Zhonghua Book Company, p. 235.

[29] Zhang, Z. *Zhang Wenxianggong Quanji, Zhi Xian Xingzai Junjichu, Juan Bashier* (Collected Works of Zhang Wenxiang, To the Military Aircraft Office in Xi'an, Vol. 82, 张文襄公全集·致西安行在军机处, 卷82).

from tax, and I will install the officials. With the rights of the landlord, no losses will be made." The late Qing government rejected this proposal.

CHAPTER 14

The Thought of Developing Transportation and Communication

The rapid growth of material and information transmission is a prominent feature of modern society. The rise of public transportation and communication has led to the modern social industrial structure, and is an important symbol distinguishing modern from medieval society. Shipping, communication, railways, and the postal service represent the "weapons" of modern transportation. The development of modern transportation and communication is closely related to the military and conducive to becoming a modern economy. Therefore, the emergence thereof cannot be stopped. In their discussion on modern transportation and communication, the Westernizationists focused on the significance of economic development, and how to plan and manage related aspects.

14.1 Developing Land Transportation

Overland transportation includes railways and roads, and railways are considered most important. This book mainly analyzes the ideological Westernization railway development in terms of overland transport.

1. Significance of developing railway transportation.

First, it eases the deployment of soldiers. In 1876, Ding Richang served as the Governor of Fujian Province. He recommended building the

J. Zhou, *Westernization Movement and Early Thought of Modernization in China*, Palgrave Studies in Economic History,
https://doi.org/10.1007/978-3-030-86985-4_14

Taiwan Railway to prevent breaches of external security. Li Hongzhang supported Ding's idea, claiming, "The journey to Taiwan is long. There are ports, but without a railway, we will be able to attract the world's attention." Zhang Zhidong also believed that "the soldiers' railway would enable 300,000 troops to keep fighting."[1]

Second, the quantity of modern transportation infrastructure is a sign of whether a country is wealthy or poor. On his way to make emergency repairs to the railway, Chen Chi noted, "When we talk about the world's poverty or wealth, the amount of railways is a criterion. The UK and the US have the highest quantity of railways, so they have strong commercial strength. Following the UK and the US are Germany, France, Russia, and Austria. China has the least railways worldwide, and its national welfare and the people's livelihood are the poorest."[2] Therefore, to achieve the purpose of creating a relevant China, the railway had to be repaired. In *Exhortation to Learning*, Zhang reviewed foreign nations' haste to build the railway, pointing out, "An overview of all things foreign over the last 30 years is without exception the construction of the railway. Dense like a spider web, big railways spread hundreds of thousands of *li*, and even small ones cover 20,000–30,000 *li*."[3] He hoped China would be able to catch up later.

Third, railway transportation contributes to improving national fiscal revenue. Ma Jianzhong wrote two articles ("On the Rail" and "Borrowing to Open the Railway") to promote the benefits of constructing the railway, which include facilitating the military industry, transportation, relief, and business, and contributing to prosperity and wealth: "Before constructing the railways, wealth was counted in units of thousands, but after, it was tallied in units of billions. With the fast speed of rail transportation, greater distances can be traveled. Ten years is not long to

[1] Zhang, Z. (1998). *Quanxuepian, Tielu Di Shier* (Exhortation to Learning, Railway XII, 劝学篇· 铁路第十二). Zhengzhou: Zhongzhou Ancient Books Publishing House, p. 157.

[2] Chen, C. (1997). *Chen Chi Ji, Jixiu Tielu Shuo* (Chen Chi Works, Railway Theory, 陈炽集·急修铁路说). Beijing: Zhonghua Book Company, p. 237.

[3] Zhang, Z. (1998). *Quanxuepian, Tielu Di Shier* (Exhortation to Learning, Railway XII, 劝学篇· 铁路第十二). Zhengzhou: Zhongzhou Ancient Books Publishing House, pp. 157–158.

operate, and now money must be collected. It is therefore necessary to construct a strong and prosperous base."[4]

Fourth, it reduces transportation costs and as such, facilitates business development. Xue Fucheng highlighted the advantages of the railways as follows: "Free people can work, and to avoid traffic inconveniences, people can catch the train, which saves money and enables scattered groups to gather together."[5] The relationship between traffic conditions and economic development in North and South China showcased the importance of the development of transport and communications: "Today, most of north Jianghuai is connected through a land route, the southern provinces have many water routes, and although the land there is not rich, the people are wealthy thanks to the flow of goods through the waterway. In the Northern provinces, both the land and the people are poor because the road is blocked and goods cannot be transported. If the NorthWestern provinces can build a railway like they do canals in the south, these poor conditions can be improved. In the southeastern provinces, the construction of the railway can supplement the weaknesses of the waterway, which will improve people's wealth and increase the tax."[6]

Chen Chi explained that "the most important way to develop business is through transportation. Railway transportation will save costs on freight by alleviating blockages. A free and flowing route is key to business success."[7] Zhang added that China's roads had long been neglected. In urban areas, roadblocks and traffic congestion made people afraid to go out. However, if there was a railway in China, "farmers could farm along the railways and the land would not be abandoned. If there is a railway, will have time. Work will be improved because through the railway, machinery can be transported to the mines to exploit for minerals

[4] Ma, J. (1960). *Shikezhai Jiyan, Tiedao Lun* (Political Proposals Written in Shike Study, Railway Theory, 适可斋记言·铁道论). Beijing: Zhonghua Book Company, pp. 10–11.

[5] Xue, F. (1987). *Xue Fucheng Xuanji, Chuangkai Zhongguo Tielu Yi* (Selected Works of Xue Fucheng, Create the China Railway, 薛福成选集·创开中国铁路议). Shanghai: Shanghai Renmin Chubanshe, p. 108.

[6] Xue, F. (1987). *Xue Fucheng Xuanji, Chuangkai Zhongguo Tielu Yi* (Selected Works of Xue Fucheng, Create the China Railway, 薛福成选集·创开中国铁路议). Shanghai: Shanghai Renmin Chubanshe, p. 108.

[7] Chen, C. (1997). *Chen Chi Ji, Jixiu Tielu Shuo* (Chen Chi Works Railway Theory, 陈炽集·急修铁路说). Beijing: Zhonghua Book Company, p. 238.

and coal." In short, the railway provides "provincial power. A day can govern ten days, the government will be competent, and the people do not lose."[8]

Fifth, it is conducive to improving society. Zheng Guanying believed, "China is governed by the Qing government, and it is difficult to change the situation. The railway will open the door toward changing customs, and perhaps change the minds of some of the literati and officialdom who hate Western culture."[9] According to Zhang Zhidong, the railway "will change previous idleness and pedantic statements will disappear. Thus, officials will no longer oppress the people. Mail will be transported, the tax burden will be reasonable, and natural disasters will not cause too much concern, forming a virtuous circle." Essentially, he considered the railway the "veins and arteries" of the national economy, and that with it, "the whole world is like a family, every place is like the arm, and land of 700,000 square *li* is the same as land elsewhere. All people are citizens."[10]

Although Zhang Zhidong's view was idealized, his wish was aligned with the views of modern social production, exchange and consumption, and distribution, which are dependent on the railway link to coordinate development. For this reason, he persevered through many hardships until his death to build the Lu-Han and Yue-Han Railways.

While the construction of the railway had many benefits, ordinary people in society, shackled by their traditional perceptions, objected to it. Xue Fucheng analyzed their concerns.

First, regarding the military, people were concerned the railway would lead the enemy into China. Using the Franco-Prussian war as an example, Xue Fucheng stated, "In the war against France, the Prussians destroyed the French railway. French forces were slow to react, leading to their downfall. The enemy used the construction of the railway to their advantage. Thus, troops must be stationed to guard the camp. If we suffered

[8] Zhang, Z. (1998). *Quanxuepian, Tielu Di Shier* (Exhortation to Learning, Railway XII, *劝学篇· 铁路第十二*). Zhengzhou: Zhongzhou Ancient Books Publishing House, p. 157.

[9] Zheng, G. (1982). *Zheng Guanying Ji, Tielu Shang, Shangce* (Zheng Guanying Works, Railway I, Vol. 1, *郑观应集· 铁路上, 上册*). Shanghai: Shanghai Renmin Chubanshe, p. 652.

[10] Zhang, Z. (1998). *Quanxuepian, Tielu Di Shier* (Exhortation to Learning, Railway XII, *劝学篇· 铁路第十二*). Zhengzhou: Zhongzhou Ancient Books Publishing House, p. 157.

an attack, all will be paralyzed. Therefore, the railway will not be used by our enemies."

Second, regarding employment, the people were concerned about the livelihoods of ordinary people. According to Xue Fucheng, "If the railway company is operating, the road industry can also increase its trade. Many jobs will be created such as mechanics, drivers, inspectors, and those delivering the carriages. The official salary per month will be enough to sustain a family of eight. Hotels can be opened on route, which will create more jobs. The fear of unemployment is misdirected."

Third, regarding society, "people are afraid that building a railway may cover their families' graves and that the crops will be destroyed." Xue Fucheng clarified, "The Chinese government must comply with the wishes of the people. If a burial mound blocks the road, it should be diverted to avoid it. However, only a few feet are needed on both sides of an open space; thus, how will there be challenges?" He further pointed out that as the economy developed, so too would customs and habits. As such, he proposed, "To develop a prosperous place, build several railways and call for people to submit their criticisms and suggestions. Over time, their objections will change into support. Once their mindsets change, investments will be made, officials will hold the decree, and tax will be charged. People's wishes will gradually dissipate. Without the approval of the people, it will be impossible to revive the economy."[11]

To dispel the concerns of the people living along the railway and to avoid their disruption of the construction, Xue Fucheng suggested, "If you decide where to construct the railways, you should recruit local rail shares, and if not, you can find other businesses to replace them. Hold local recruitment drives for road workers, supervisors, officers, and staff, and if that is not enough, supplement the staff shortage from elsewhere. Contributing toward the people's livelihood will make it easier for them to support the construction."[12]

Ma Jianzhong believed that the time for railway construction was good: "I think the railway is feasible for China. Immediate construction

[11] Xue, F. (1987). *Xue Fucheng Xuanji, Chuangkai Zhongguo Tielu Yi* (Selected Works of Xue Fucheng, Create the China Railway, 薛福成选集·创开中国铁路议). Shanghai: Shanghai Renmin Chubanshe, pp. 110–111.

[12] Xue, F. (1987). *Xue Fucheng Xuanji, Chuangkai Zhongguo Tielu Yi* (Selected Works of Xue Fucheng, Create the China Railway, 薛福成选集·创开中国铁路议). Shanghai: Shanghai Renmin Chubanshe, pp. 112–113.

is good for the country. Why? Dating back to the creation of the water-wheel, after several modifications, it became increasingly perfect. China has a wide Plain, and the North and South can be opened to traffic. Even if there are mountains and rivers, we can pass them. The terrain is feasible for this. China is abundant in iron steel material and has an abundant labor force."[13] In other words, China could catch up with other countries in terms of railway construction.

2. Railway layout and construction methods

How could railway transportation be organized?

First, acknowledge the value of its military significance. Li Hongzhang, Liu Mingchuan, and other Westernization officers considered the situation from the perspective of strengthening defense. Early in 1880, Li Hongzhang inspired Liu Mingchuan to recommend Chen Baochen on behalf of *the chip manufacturing railway self-improvement fold*. For Chen, "The truth of self-improvement lies in military training, and manufacturing equipment is important too. The key is to build railroads quickly. First construct the Beijing-QingJiangpu railway to connect North and South." In 1887, Li Hongzhang supported the construction of the Jin-Tong railway to strengthen defense.

In terms of the location of the railway, Zheng Guanying focused on protecting the sovereignty of the border: "Britain, France, and Russia have seized the opportunity to construct a railway to connect to Chinese roads. This means China is surrounded on three sides. If they connect the sea to other places, China will be surrounded by four enemies." If China's railway could extend to the border, then those on the mainland could travel to the border to conduct business affairs, which would render the barren land fertile and prosperous. In this case, the invasion of the powers of the land would not succeed. As such, he concluded, "The enemy has no railway. If all the countries in the world have railways and there is no railway in our country, our country has failed."[14]

[13] Ma, J. (1960). *Shikezhai Jiyan, Tiedao Lun* (Political Proposals Written in Shike Study, Railway Theory, 适可斋记言·铁道论). Beijing: Zhonghua Book Company, p. 15.

[14] Zheng, G. (1982). *Zheng Guanying Ji, Tielu Shang, Shangce* (Zheng Guanying Works, Railway I, Vol. 1, *郑观应集· 铁路上, 上册*). Shanghai: Shanghai Renmin Chubanshe, p. 652.

Second, acknowledge the value of its economic significance. Xue Fucheng suggested that China's railway deployment "start with capital and then employ the sickles for the roads in Taiyuan, South Road in Bianliang (Kaifeng), and East Road in Qingjiang PU. From Taiyuan to the West, it can be connected to Xi'an, Lanzhou, Sichuan, Yunnan, and Guizhou. From Bianliang to the south, it can be connected to Hankou, Changsha, and Guilin. From Qingjiangpu to the south can be connected to Jiangxi, Jiangsu and Anhui, Zhejiang, Fujian, and Guangzhou. It should be connected with the four sides not far from the border."[15] The reason was that the construction of the railway could play a role in promoting the development of local businesses.

Zhang explained, "For the construction of the railways, the tangible benefit is for commercial gain and the intangible benefit is for our country. The limited interest is for businesses along the road, and the infinite interest is for the people. Freight and inn rentals are limited benefits. Conscription, transfer rates, trade, mineral resources, tax increases, provincial division of labor, wide knowledge and an open environment, and the speed of a decree are virtually unlimited interests.[16] The convenience of the railway will expedite the exchange of goods and make people rich." To ensure maximum support for his proposal, Zhang Zhidong recommended a selection standard, namely that the "railway must be constructed so far as to serve neighboring cities. The two ends of the city must be bustling areas that include a department of transport, assembly business, tax increases, and all types of interest must come from the railway. If both ends of the track have poor communication with railway construction in the middle, then businesses will not know which way to go and department stores will not flourish. Christians will have constructed and increased the cost of the railways but with no income."[17]

[15] Xue, F. (1987) *Xue Fucheng Xuanji, Chuangkai Zhongguo Tielu Yi* (Selected Works of Xue Fucheng, Create the China Railway, *薛福成选集·创开中国铁路议*). Shanghai: Shanghai Renmin Chubanshe, p. 108.

[16] Zhang, Z. *Zhang Wenxianggong Quanji, Juan Sishisi, Zouyi Sishisi, Luhan Tielu Shangban Nancheng Lingchou Banfa Zhe* (Collected Works of Zhang Wenxiang, Another Way to Solve the Difficulties in Merchant-Operated Luhan Railway, Vol. 44, Memorial 44, *张文襄公全集, 卷44, 奏折44, 卢汉铁路商办难成另筹办法折*).

[17] Zhang, Z. *Zhang Wenxianggong Quanji, Juan Sanshiqi, Zouyi Sanshiqi, Huizou Jiangnan Heyun Nanfu Tielu Liji Wuduo Zhe* (Collected Works of Zhang Wenxiang, Jiangnan River Transportation Is Difficult and Railway Benefit Is Not much, Vol. 37, Memorial 37, *张文襄公全集, 卷37, 奏折37, 会奏江南河运难复铁路利济无多折*).

According to this standard, Zhang Zhidong argued that Lugou Bridge should first be constructed to the hinterland on the Hankou route. In the communication, Zhang further demonstrated the significance of building the road: "Luhan railway is China's entire road network. In the future, this will reach south Guangdong and north of Jilin from the base here. The momentum overall will benefit places especially at the end of the line. Locally, we can connect the provinces of the country, and further away, we can reach the European countries without the risk of delays stemming from travelling by road."[18]

Both Li Hongzhang and Zhang Zhidong were commanders of border provinces; thus, why did their views differ? I think this may be related to the different regions they governed and their different responsibilities. Li Hongzhang started his career in the military. His jurisdiction was the coastal front, where the military defense mission was prominent. Therefore, most of his views on economic modernization centered on military industrialization. Zhang Zhidong started his career in literature. His jurisdiction included the inland provinces, where the military defense mission was not as prominent as in Li's area. When Zhang Zhidong was involved in the Westernization Movement, Westernization officers who prioritized the development of the military industrial route were criticized in society, shifting Westernization attempts to the civil industrial field. Therefore, his views of industrialization emphasized civil industry.

How would the railway be constructed?

Zheng Guanying proposed constructing the railway through businesses: "Western railways are constructed by sharing stock, or limiting it to ten years and then selling it to the public. This stock can be used by the military or for relief affairs. Merchants would own the railways, so they should bear the transportation defense and maintenance costs. Official business is better. Only China owns a vast expanse of land. If we do not recruit contractors, this may not be good. Recently, I heard that Chinese and Western businessmen wanted to be involved in a joint venture. Running the railways through the national fund will be a waste of resources. If it is owned by the Chinese without the help of Westerners, I am concerned it would be difficult to raise large amounts of capital. Thus, a Chinese-Western joint venture to construct the railway is more

[18] Zhang, Z. *Zhang Wenxianggong Quanji, Juan Qishijiu, Dianzou Qi, Zhi Zongshu* (Collected Works of Zhang Wenxiang, To General Administration of Customs, Vol. 79, Cable Memorial 7, 张文襄公全集, 卷79, 电奏7, 至总署).

desirable." He also believed that to construct the railway in China, the country should learn from countries that constructed theirs at a low cost and most efficiently."[19]

Chen Chi agreed that the railway distributor roads were best run by officials, and that in that case, the country would not be harmed if the money was insufficient or borrowed from foreign contractors. He stated, "If the money is insufficient or borrowed from foreign contractors, this will not harm the country. We must handle the railway distributor roads. Troop movements and transport machinery are changeable. To avoid a subsequent repurchase, the government should take charge."[20]

In addition to railways, the Westernizationists also considered highway construction important. According to Zhang Zhidong, "The road is essential to the people of the party. It must enable quick flow, the flexible transfer of information, and circulation of people and goods. The market is growing, contributing to people's livelihoods and making them rich."[21] In the construction of Shanxi, Hebei, and the channel, the governor of Guangdong and Guangxi will open the road to development as a pioneer project in Hainan Island. Governor is particularly committed to the construction of the municipal road. Zheng Guanying's views on highway construction are reflected in his works *Road Construction*. He believed, "This should be ordered to provinces worldwide. The current roads should be expanded, narrow ones widened, and rugged areas filled and flattened." He also highlighted two points regarding repairs. One pertained to when to imitate the Western countries: "stone road, dirt roads, gravel roads, tarred roads, and railroads are all constructed China has a sand road to worlds apart." The other was that the central government should surrender and open up. "This should not be at great cost. The provinces, states, and counties should handle the procurement of the land and material. The governor should also be involved, which would

[19] Zheng, G. (1982). *Zheng Guanying Ji, Tielu Xia, Shangce* (Zheng Guanying Works, Railway II, Vol. 1, *郑观应集·铁路下, 上册*). Shanghai: Shanghai Renmin Chubanshe, pp. 656–658.

[20] Chen, C. (1997). *Chen Chi Ji, Jixiu Tielu Shuo* (Chen Chi Works, Railway Theory, 陈炽集·急修铁路说). Beijing: Zhonghua Book Company, p. 239.

[21] Zhang, Z. *Zhang Wenxianggong Quanji, Juan Sishiyi, Zouyi Sishiyi, Jinling Sheli Dunchuan Xiuzao Malu Pian* (Collected Works of Zhang Wenxiang, Nanjing Built a Port to Build Roads, Vol. 41, Memorial 41, 张文襄公全集·金陵设立趸船修造马路篇, 卷41, 奏议41).

ensure the appropriate use of funds." He further highlighted how public funds should not be used: "The city should award squires who made large sums of money." Regarding the management of the constructed highway, he advocated," It must select a member, cooperated with local squires to handle engineering issues, repairs, garbage removal, and to ensure there are no pollution violations. The provinces and world travel will take on new life, which will benefit the country."[22]

14.2 Significance of Developing Waterway Transportation

Beyond the development of land transport, the Westernizationists also considered the development of waterway transportation important, which includes sea and inland waterway transport. In 1872, the establishments of shipping merchants were a major step in the development of maritime transport. Since the second Opium War, foreign vessels increasingly sailed along the coast to the Yangtze River, and the transport of passengers and freight generated great profit. Some domestic businessmen wanted to establish their own shipping office to regain profits. In 1872, Sheng Xuanhuai noted, "Since the ships have come to China, they have been welcomed by businessmen who bring goods to the country for use. However, we should conduct our own affairs, and not be controlled by the Westerners."[23]

Chen Chi advocated the development of maritime transport, and focused on the role of shipping in reducing transport costs: "In the business world, transporting by vessels and by human-power, which will gain a profit? Most cases are transporting by vessels. Knowing that a vehicle is better than human power, and that transporting by ship or rail is faster than on foot, we should put ship and rail in the priority and these are much faster than traditional transport vehicles." He further pointed out that due to the backward technology in China, its products were of a

[22] Zheng, G. (1982). *Zheng Guanying Ji, Xiu Lu, Shangce* (Zheng Guanying Works, Road Works, Vol. 1, *郑观应集·修路, 上册*). Shanghai: Shanghai Renmin Chubanshe, pp. 661–663.

[23] Sheng, X. (1873). *Shengdang: Shang Li Fuxiang Lunchuan Zhangcheng, Xuyan* (Archives for Sheng Xuanhuai: Letters to Li about Articles of Association, Preamble, *盛档: 上李傅相轮船章程·序言*). As cited in Xia, D. (1998). *Sheng Xuanhuai Zhuan* (The Biography of Sheng Xuanhuai, *盛宣怀传*). Tianjin: Nankai University Press, p. 11.

lower quality than those manufactured abroad. He added that if transport costs were high, there would be no profit opportunity: "When goods are bulky and heavy, they should be shipped by water or rail, as road transport would be dangerous, even though arrive at a port finally and freight is expensive."[24]

How could maritime transport be developed? The Westernizationists recommended first expanding the domestic trading port, and then the overseas market to open up routes to Singapore, San Francisco in the US, and other places. Zheng Guanying thought China should build sturdy ships for sailing to treaty ports and Chinese residential areas such as the South Pacific Islands, northern Vladivostok, Korea, and Japan to "transport our best-selling goods from country to country."[25] Xue Fucheng stressed, "Since the rise of the steamship, Westerners' profits are up to 40%, but our country has managed to recover at least three-fifths of the profits. Several officers who take charge over the 27 ports have limited energy." He advocated "supporting people with a lot of wealth and power to make up for the lack of official power, or appointing bureau merchants, calling on capable people who were distributed to operate the port according to their ability. Regardless of profit and loss, the public could not intervene. In addition, merchants had the ability to rent several, or a dozen, or more, all to hear him sign up for an official. If you are worried about the trade conflict, appoint inspectors to the unified program. If you are worried that businesses will not make up for the shortage, then use national discretion to get taxed rice to fill a vacancy. I hope merchants in China promote the ports to the South East of the island, and extend this to the Western countries."[26]

Westernizationists also considered the development of inland river shipping important. In 1885, Sheng Xuanhuai, an official in Shandong Denglaiqing Dao, proposed that Li Hongzhang, the minister of the north, develop the inland waterways. He said, "The years of foreign

[24] Chen, C. (1997). *Chen Chi Ji, Bianshi Lunchuan Shuo* (Chen Chi Works Ship, *陈炽集·遍驶轮船说*). Beijing: Zhonghua Book Company, p. 241.

[25] Zheng, G. (1982). *Zheng Guanying Ji, Xiu Lu, Shangce* (Zheng Guanying Works, Road Works, Vol. 1, *郑观应集·修路, 上册*). Shanghai: Shanghai Renmin Chubanshe, pp. 661–663.

[26] Xue, F. (1987). *Xue Fucheng Xuanji, Shangzheng* (Selected Works of Xue Fucheng, Commercial Policy, *薛福成选集·商政*). Shanghai: Shanghai Renmin Chubanshe, pp. 541–542.

wealth and prosperity started with business. The port traders and I together made mainland trade independent. Therefore, it is necessary to make China wealthy and powerful to wield the fire wheel, set up a mainland shipping company, and establish a merchant bureau to take advantage of its own business in the country."[27] In his view, the military advantage of developing inland waterways "was sufficient enough to make a military brigade and prepare to master the waters." Regarding business:

1. Tax increases: Sheng Xuanhuai contended that the situation in the port of Shandong province differed from that in Tianjin and Shanghai. "Yantai serves as a trade port, while the goods entering and leaving must be transported by land. The mountain roads are rugged and the freight is heavy. If you can open inland river shipping, it will be a case of the higher the quantity of goods, the better. The circulation of goods has been accelerated, and the tax revenue has increased naturally. This is a good thing for the benefit of the people."
2. A Good Samaritan. Sheng Xuanhuai noted that in the Shandong Peninsula region, "in half of the mountain, the people are very poor, making straw hats as a means of livelihood. Over land by road to Yantai, for every 100 jin, 3 or 4 strings are needed. In the event of a storm, the tide will change, the boat will be in danger, and the businessmen will long suffer. These flaws could be overcome through inland water transportation."
3. Fight against the outside world: Sheng Xuanhuai also pointed out that "the export of land goods is one point, and silver is another. Furthermore, we can seize foreign markets. Recently, the Japanese have come to know the value of straw crops, which can be easily borrowed. Our establishments can be modeled on this and new patterns made. The country's rulers will be particular about quality and availability of cargo. If they produce more, we sell less." He

[27] Sheng, X. (1886). Shengdang: Neidi She Lunchuan Gongsi Yi (Archives for Sheng Xuanhuai: Inland Shipping Company, *盛档: 内地设轮船公司议)*. As cited in Xia, D. (1998). *Sheng Xuanhuai Zhuan* (The Biography of Sheng Xuanhuai, 盛宣怀传). Tianjin: Nankai University Press, p. 124.

believed that only by speeding up the transportation process and improving products would China harm the enemy.[28]

With the support of Li Hongzhang and others, the inland waterways gradually developed in Shandong, Guangdong, and Taiwan.

14.3 Significance of Developing Telecommunication

In modern China, the communication industry mainly referred to the telegraph and postal service. The ideas of the Westernization Group regarding the development of communication are reflected below.

On the meaning of developing the communication industry:

1. It is conducive to the development of military affairs: In 1879, Li Hongzhang thought that "all countries, and even Shanghai, should set up a telegraph system, which would enable them to talk to each other instantaneously. Chinese documents are still delivered by hand, although this causes delays. As such, the telegram provides a necessary boost to defense. Therefore, the Haikou telegraph should offer a direct link between the battery and Tianjin Dagu North Pond, which will enable a call to arms for each camp." Zheng Guanying also clarified the telegram's significance in the military: "The environment is changing, and the times are different. Once the territory is occupied, the people will report to the temple, and the temple will be given away for a long time. And he will lead the way with electric wires, such as the drum, and as soon as possible, it will be decided."[29]
2. Facilitate information communication: According to Chen Chi: "The most important thing in business is communication. If prices can be compared, the person who knows it will win, and the

[28] Sheng, X. (1887). *Shengdang: Bing Li Hongzhang* (Archives for Sheng Xuanhuai: To Li Hongzhang, 盛档: 禀李鸿章). As cited in Xia, D. (1998). *Sheng Xuanhuai Zhuan* (The Biography of Sheng Xuanhuai, 盛宣怀传). Tianjin: Nankai University Press, p. 128.

[29] Zheng, G. (1982). *Zheng Guanying Ji, Dianbao, Shangce* (Zheng Guanying Works, Telegraph, Vol. 1, 郑观应集·电报, 上册). Shanghai: Shanghai Renmin Chubanshe, p. 665.

person who knows nothing will fail."[30] He further emphasized the significance of transportation and communication for business development: "For China and the ports worldwide, we know nothing before the ships enter the harbor, but others already know all the information, for example, about a shortage in cargo, price fluctuations in the gold and silver market, and transportation costs. People in China are not only ignorant, but also unable to know. They believe that the profit and loss of trade is due to the fate of the arrangement, so that all trade is loss. There is no hope of reviving technology, commerce, and prosperity without following these rules."[31]

3. Economic benefits: Zheng explained, "This will be very profitable and efficient for the postal service. It is an easy thing to do without consuming many resources. You can get there quickly enough without worrying about the information. This is beneficial to people of different classes, and no one is hurt."[32] He also cited Japan as an example of the economic benefits of the postal service. According to him, "since 1877, the post office of Japan has collected more than 813,800 silver dollars, of which the cost was 768,000 silver dollars and the profit more than 45,000 silver dollars. Within a few years, they had collected more than 1,424,000 *yuan*. The total wages of all the officials were 10,800 silver dollars, and more than 1,347,000 silver dollars were spent on the wages of other staff and foreigners. This benefits the country's shipping companies, business firms, and donors, yielding a surplus of more than 76,000 silver dollars. This will improve our self-sufficiency."[33]

[30] Chen, C. (1997). *Chen Chi Ji, Guangtong Youdian Shuo* (Chen Chi Works, Widespread Electricity Postal Services, 陈炽集·广通邮电说). Beijing: Zhonghua Book Company, p. 242.

[31] Chen, C. (1997). *Chen Chi Ji, Guangtong Youdian Shuo* (Chen Chi Works, Widespread Electricity Postal Services, 陈炽集·广通邮电说). Beijing: Zhonghua Book Company, p. 243.

[32] Zheng, G. (1982). *Zheng Guanying Ji, Youzheng Shang, Shangce* (Zheng Guanying Works, Postal I, Vol. 1, 郑观应集·邮政上, 上册). Shanghai: Shanghai Renmin Chubanshe, p. 669.

[33] Zheng, G. (1982). *Zheng Guanying Ji, Youzheng Shang, Shangce* (Zheng Guanying Works, Postal I, Vol. 1, 郑观应集·邮政上, 上册). Shanghai: Shanghai Renmin Chubanshe, p. 670.

Regarding the construction and deployment of communications, the Westernization Movement advocated military and commercial considerations for telegraphy. While working at the General Administration of the Telegraph, Sheng Xuanhuai arranged to install electric wires to facilitate military use in coastal defense, river defense, and the border areas, and emphasized the importance of also installing them in prosperous commercial areas. To collect fees, Sheng Xuanhuai proposed that in addition to the Grand Council and Minister Judgment Hall, the national and provincial governors and ministers of Westernization, telecommunication, and military affairs charge returning officers and that provincial government telecommunications take a cash payment before transmitting the message. He explained, "There is too much government intervention in the provinces. If there are exceptions, there will be no money. This is in accordance with the regulations of the steamship bureau."[34] On the question of cable charges, Chen Chi objected to the accusation that the telegraph department charged too much, which would affect the development of the country's business. He stated, "Although China has electricity, the fee is expensive, although it is slightly cheaper than in other countries. However, the price is ten times more than that in foreign countries."[35]

Regarding the construction and deployment of postal services, the Westernization Movement emphasized commercial interests. Zheng Guanying advocated imitating the experience of Europe: "In the area of the town, town of the town, and town of the country, correspondence regarding the establishment of the letter hall, general manager, dispatcher-manager, official documents, and private letters are all delivered."[36] For postal charges, Zheng Guanying advocated a higher price: "At the beginning of the establishment, prices must not be lowered because there is not much capital in China today. However, there is some depreciation,

[34] Sheng, X. (1881). *Shengdang: Dianbaoju Zhaoshang Zhangcheng* (Archives for Sheng Xuanhuai: The Telegraph Office Investment Regulations, *盛档: 电报局招商章程*). As cited in Xia, D. (1998). *Sheng Xuanhuai Zhuan* (The Biography of Sheng Xuanhuai, 盛宣怀传). Tianjin: Nankai University Press, p. 78.

[35] Chen, C. (1997). *Chen Chi Ji, Guangtong Youdian Shuo* (Chen Chi Works, Widespread Electricity Postal Services, *陈炽集·广通邮电说*). Beijing: Zhonghua Book Company, p. 243.

[36] Zheng, G. (1982). *Zheng Guanying Ji, Youzheng Shang, Shangce* (Zheng Guanying Works, Postal I, Vol. 1, ***郑观应集·邮政上，上册***). Shanghai: Shanghai Renmin Chubanshe, p. 669.

and people will not support it. Therefore, the price should be based on the distance."[37]

On how to develop the communication industry, the Westernization Group recommended that it be government-supervised and merchant-managed. In his opinion on the creation of the telegraph office, Sheng Xuanhuai said, "It is not easy to start, and it is harder to create. If the officer is not maintained, it will not be initiated. If it is not for business, it will not last. Businessmen are greedy for profit and officials are greedy for power. This is a truth that cannot be overturned."[38] In terms of creating a postal service, Zheng Guanying mentioned, "Every time a foreigner wants to do something, he will be prepared to have a lot of money, attract a lot of talent, and obtain a subsidy from the state. While it is initially really expensive, it will generate a lot of money." However, Chen Chi did not agree having the postal service, telegraph business, and official office government-supervised and merchant-managed. He said: "All the foreign countries know that the telegraph business and postal service secure the future and prosperity of the country. However, businessmen are selfish and want short-term benefits regardless of future harm. When initially established, there are official and private telegrams, but in the end, they will be nationalized."[39]

[37] Zheng, G. (1982). *Zheng Guanying Ji, Youzheng Xia, Shangce* (Zheng Guanying Works· Postal I, Vol. 1, *郑观应集·邮政下, 上册*). Shanghai: Shanghai Renmin Chubanshe, pp. 671–672.

[38] Sheng, X. (1881). *Shengdang: Xiangding Dalue Zhangcheng Ershitiao* (Archives for Sheng Xuanhuai: Stipulation of Twenty Articles of General Regulations, *盛档: 详定大略章程二十条*). As cited in Xia, D. (1998). *Sheng Xuanhuai Zhuan* (The Biography of Sheng Xuanhuai, 盛宣怀传). Tianjin: Nankai University Press, p. 75.

[39] Chen, C. (1997). *Chen Chi Ji, Guangtong Youdian Shuo* (Chen Chi Works, Widespread Electricity Postal Services, 陈炽集·广通邮电说). Beijing: Zhonghua Book Company, p. 242.

CHAPTER 15

The Thought to Develop Modern Financial

One major feature of the industrial society is the large amount of commodity trading and high-speed currency circulation, which calls for a systematic reform of a monetary system that has existed since the Middle Ages. Since Chinese industrialization started late, we can use the successful examples of monetary system reform in other countries for reference to avoid problems.

15.1 Views Regarding the Making of Coins

Given the historical background of the severe impact of machine production on manual production, the Chinese traditional monetary system has suffered grave setbacks. On the one hand, China's domestic currency had been affected by the world currency market after the country entered the world market. At that time, all major capitalist countries adopted the gold standard system, and the cancellation of silver coins led to an increasingly lower silver price. However, in China and India, which used silver coins, "the gold price was increasingly expensive, and the silver price increasingly cheaper."[1] This so-called "pound-loss," which refers to the loss caused by the rise of the pound exchange rate when China adopted silver or silver

[1] Chen, C. (1997). *Chen Chi Ji, Tongyong Jinbang Shuo* (Chen Chi Works, Common Gold, *陈炽集·通用金镑说*). Beijing: Zhonghua Book Company, p. 265.

J. Zhou, *Westernization Movement and Early Thought of Modernization in China*, Palgrave Studies in Economic History,
https://doi.org/10.1007/978-3-030-86985-4_15

dollars for its foreign payments, emerged in international trade. The Westernization Group called for China to "urgently employ gold coins" to "avoid the disadvantage of an unstable weight of silver coins" in international trade.[2] On the other hand, the disordered monetary system had not been suited to the demand of developing trade at home and abroad. At that time, the Chinese government applied the system of taking silver ingots as its currency without a unified measuring standard. Moreover, the measuring standard of the government (i.e., the "official standard") and that of the people (i.e., the "unofficial standard") existed side by side. There were also three types of official standard, namely the "national treasury standard" (the measuring standard of income and expenses in the national treasury), "water transportation standard" (the measuring standard of taxes in the water transportation of grain), and "customs standard" (the measuring standard of customs collection). The above situation strongly impacted the development of business, even in terms of fiscal payment. Furthermore, the Chinese government suffered the loss of "Pingshe and Huohao." Pingshe refers to the additional silver for the Ministry of Revenue in traditional China when local governments were handing over taxes to the central government in the Qing Dynasty. Huohao refers to the loss of silver when pieces of silver were recast to form a larger one to hand over to the central government in the Ming (1368–1644) and Qing (1644–1912) Dynasties. The Westernization power therefore submitted a proposal of a unified casting of silver currency to the central government so that "the weight of coins was unified" and "people were pleased to use it." In other words, the Chinese government mainly used silver coins domestically and gold coins for foreign trade.

Views on coin-making were closely related to the introduction of the Western monetary system in China. Since the middle Ming Dynasty, Western silver dollars (mainly Mexican silver dollars which the Chinese people called eagle dollars on account of their eagle pattern) began coming into China with the increasing domestic and foreign trade. Foreign silver dollars had gradually become popular circulation currencies because of their uniform shape and beautiful patterns, as well as

[2] Ma, J. (1960). *Shikezhai Jiyan, Shang Lixiangbo Fuyi Hexueshi Ruzhang Zoushe Shuishi Shu* (Political Proposals Written in Shike Study, Submission to Li Hongzhang to Reconsider the Proposal of Establishing Navy of He Ruzhang, *适可斋记言·上李相伯复议何学士如璋奏设水师书*). Beijing: Zhonghua Book Company, p. 70.

the lack of any need to weigh them, which inspired Chinese people to have their own silver dollars. Senior officials in the Qing Dynasty, such as Tao Shu, Lin Zexu, Wei Yuan, Gong Zizhen, and others had thought of making silver coins before the self-strengthening movement. The Self-Strengthening movement was a period of institutional reforms initiated in China during the late Qing Dynasty following a series of military defeats and concessions to foreign powers. In this movement, more Chinese people advocated making coins by themselves, including silver and gold coins, to enhance their connection with the world.

During this period, some officials of the Westernization Movement, such as Sheng Xuanhuai and Zhang Zhidong, adopted the practice separately in their own administrations. Sheng Xuanhuai, the official of Denglai qing Dao in Shandong Province, manufactured silver coins with machines in Yantai in 1886. When he presented the coins to Li Hongzhang, Li said, "The pattern of this silver coin is wonderful. However, coin-making is so important that we cannot support it without the cooperation of the Ministry of Commerce. It is especially hard to employ professional staff. So, do not hurry to make the steel mold."[3] Since coin-making involved the national monetary system, it could be considered "of great importance." Sheng, Li, and the other officials had to give up on the idea, as they were not able to take on this responsibility as middle-class officials. In 1889, Zhang Zhidong, the provincial governor of Guangdong, madeand Guangxi Provinces at that time, made silver coins by himself in Guangzhou City. mamade silver coins that he divided into five grades, among which the big silver coin weighed 26.94 g, 0.37 g heavier than the eagle dollar. Zhang hoped this practice could compete with and crowd out the eagle dollar; however, his practice had violated Gresham's Law. Realizing this, he later decreased the weight of silver coins to 26.57 g, the same as that of the eagle dollar. Zhang's silver coins were commonly known as "dragon dollars" because of the curled-up dragon pattern on the face. From then, other provinces followed this practice and finally established the "dragon dollars" series.

In 1896, Sheng Xuanhuai submitted a written statement to the imperial court, of which the most important parts pertain to building banks and making silver coins. Sheng emphasized the boycott of foreign currency. According to him, it was difficult to resist foreign coins since the

[3] Li, H. *Li Wenzhonggong Quanshu, Ji Yantai Shengdao, Juan Shiyi* (Complete Works of Li Wenzhong, Persuasion to Yantai Officer, Vol. 11, 李文忠公全书·寄烟台盛道), p. 8.

weight of the silver coins cast in various provinces in China was the same as that of foreign coins. He advocated casting silver coins of one tael, as "national coin-making has been an established system from ancient times till now. There is not one country in the world that follows the system of others."[4] He added, "Only domestic currency can be employed in one country to strictly protect their right to decide."[5] Sheng pointed out that the monetary system of one country should be "an act-by-itself system"; however, he proposed the idea in China of changing the weight of a silver coin to 1 tael, which fueled a dispute about the monetary system, namely whether the silver coin should adopt Chinese tael or foreign yuan as its unit.

Zheng Guanying believed that the specific operation of coin-making should not learn from the West where it was handled by private companies. According to Zheng, "the quality of Western coins can be guaranteed because Western people want to make money and they keep faith. Moreover, their coin-making procedure is supervised by government supervisory personnel. In contrast, corrupt practices consequently occur during the coin-making procedure in China because most Chinese people are addicted to profit and dishonest, and besides, they have no supervisory personnel."[6] Zheng further suggested that China's coin-making be carried out by the Chinese government. "There must be a strictly regulated law and a general bureau established by the Ministry of Revenue for checking purposes, and a number of high-ranking and honest officials who are good at accounting and selected by their civil governor and military governors to take charge of casting silver coins."[7] Having been cast in accord with a certain standard, these silver coins had to be checked by the civil governor and military governors personally first, then thousands or hundreds of coins would be tested by the general bureau in the Ministry of Revenue. Sheng agreed with Zheng's proposition that silver coins be made by the government, but thought it should be operated following

[4] Sheng, X. *Yuzhai Cungao, Juanyi* (Memorials of Sheng Xuanhuai, Vol. 1, *愚斋存稿, 卷1*), p. 7.

[5] Sheng, X. *Yuzhai Cungao, Jinni Chouxiang Shiyi, Juansan* (Plan of Collecting Military Expenses, Memorials of Sheng Xuanhuai, Vol. 3, 愚斋存稿·谨拟筹饷事宜, 卷3), p. 53.

[6] Zheng, G. *Zheng Guanying Ji, Zhuyin, Shangce* (Zheng Guanying Works, Silver Casting, Vol. 1, 郑观应集·铸银), p. 693.

[7] Zheng, G. *Zheng Guanying Ji, Zhuyin, Shangce* (Zheng Guanying Works·Silver Casting, Vol. 1, 郑观应集·铸银), p. 694.

business principles. According to Sheng, "China's silver coin-making is a national monetary system without too much cost but with a large amount of profit; so, it is proper for the government instead of the enterprise to deal with it. However, we should also be acquainted with business affairs and not confined by the government to avoid losses."[8]

Chen Chi suggested stipulating the exchange rate of different coins by law, in which 1 gold coin was equal to 10 silver coins or 10,000 copper coins.[9] He also designed the size, shape, weight, and color of these three types of coins.[10] Karl Marx noted that it was difficult to maintain the long-term stability of the exchange rate of two kinds of currencies in the history of currency,[11] let alone three kinds of currencies. Thus, it was impossible to maintain a fixed exchange rate over the long term. Nevertheless, various kinds of currencies would have a certain legal exchange rate in a given period. Essentially, as a figure living in a transitional era, Chen Chi knew the function of the market, and reserved the traditional practice of the government's intervening in the economy.

15.2 Views Regarding the Issuing of Paper Money

The issuance of paper money such as the "Jiaozi," a paper money issued in the Northern Song Dynasty in China, was an inevitable result when the commodity economy had developed into a certain stage. In the Self-Strengthening movement, the increase of commodity trade volume required more paper money. The Westernizationists paid much attention to the issuance and control of paper money, taking it as a necessary object of modern society. They also adopted both metallic coins and paper money because "paper money can replenish the lack of gold, silver, and

[8] Sheng, X. (1895). *Shengdang: Zhu Yinbi Yijian* (Documents of Sheng Xuanhuai: Proposal of Silver Casting, *盛档: 铸银币意见*).

[9] Chen, C. (1997). *Chen Chi ji, Tongyong Jinbang Shuo* (Chen Chi Works, Common Gold, *陈炽集·通用金镑说*). Beijing: Zhonghua Book Company, p. 267.

[10] Chen, C. (1997). *Chen Chi ji, Kaikuang Jintong Shuo* (Chen Chi Works, Opening the Mine to Prohibit Copper, *陈炽集·开矿禁铜说*). Beijing: Zhonghua Book Company, p. 191.

[11] Marx, K. (1953). *Zibenlun, Diyijuan* (Das Kapital, Vol. 1, *资本论, 第1卷*). Beijing: People's Publishing House, p. 84.

copper"[12] and was convenient to take along.[13] Their views regarding the paper money issued during the past dynasties in China were relatively objective. They knew the advantage that "when paper money was prosperous, both the imperial court and common people trusted its use and it had been adopted more than the metallic coin." They also realized its disadvantages, namely that over time, "as more counterfeit paper money appeared, its value decreased and it lost its original function."[14] With the introduction of modern monetary theories from the West, Chinese people began to recognize that the circulation of paper money was part of the modern financial system and its key point for circulation was to provide sufficient reserves. Therefore, they highlighted that "(issuing paper money) it was feasible only when there was enough reserve funds."[15]

In *Monograph on Food and Currency* of *Annals of Japan*, Huang Zunxian stressed that "paper money was adopted for the convenience of the people, not for profit. The paper money represents metallic coins. It was practical to replace gold and silver with paper money, but not practical to regard paper money as gold and silver. For the convenience of the people, the metallic coin and paper money should be adopted together. In contrast, it would be a failure that the paper money was made without any limitation and adopted alone without metallic coins." Based on this, Huang proposed that the amount of paper money issued should be equal to that of metallic coins: "If a country made hundreds of millions of metallic coins, it should also make hundreds of millions of metallic coins and promise its people not to poorly and hastily manufacture money. Banks were established to circulate the money for the permanent benefit of both the government and people."

In 1889, in his discussion on building the railways, Zhong Tianwei proposed printing and issuing paper money. He was opposed to the idea of fiat money, as "Western countries adopted paper money for the

[12] Chen, C. (1997). *Chen Chi Ji, Jiaochao* (Chen Chi Works, Paper Money, 陈炽集·交钞). Beijing: Zhonghua Book Company, p. 87.

[13] Chen, C. (1997). *Chen Chi Ji, Chuangban Yinhang Shuo* (Chen Chi Works, Banks Establishing, 陈炽集·创办银行说). Beijing: Zhonghua Book Company, p. 263.

[14] Chen, C. (1997). *Chen Chi Ji, Chuangban Yinhang Shuo* (Chen Chi Works, Banks Establishing, 陈炽集·创办银行说). Beijing: Zhonghua Book Company, p. 263.

[15] Chen, C. (1997). *Chen Chi Ji, Chuangban Yinhang Shuo* (Chen Chi Works, Banks Establishing, 陈炽集·创办银行说). Beijing: Zhonghua Book Company, p. 263.

convenience of the people. They issued paper money only when they had the same amount of silver coins." Furthermore, "in foreign countries, all silver coins were kept in the banks as receipts, and paper money was issued as security to avoid exchanges, so it was beneficial to the country." He also suggested "the opening of dozens of exchange shops by Shanxi merchants. In each province, a bank was established by the government and permitted to make paper money and cast silver coins. Merchants were in charge of all regulations, and the national government tried its best to support them." The advantage of issuing paper money was that "millions of silver brought about millions of paper money, so half the financial resources were saved for us to build the railway."[16]

Before the 1894–1895 Sino-Japanese War, Chen Chi presented in *Yongshu·Jiaochao* that a paper money policy could be used to compensate for the deficiency of gold, silver, and copper. "The paper money policy was feasible only when people believed it. Moreover, it was feasible only when there was enough reserved money." The purpose of issuing paper money was for the convenience of both the government and common people. From a national economy viewpoint, "Each year, when there was an income of 10 million silver coins, the government made the same amount of paper money. Both silver coins and paper money were adopted at the same time, so there was 20 million in available money every year." In addition, paper money could help to avoid forwarding expenses. Regarding people's livelihood, "The metallic coin was not convenient for daily business transactions. It may have been stolen by robbers or lost in a fire or flood when travelling. This cannot be compared with paper money."

Chen Chi considered the issuance of paper money an important measure "to support merchants and common people, maintain enough food and military forces, promote business affairs, and sustain the national economy and people's livelihood." In Chen's *Continuation of the Tactics of Enriching the Country· Theory of Building Banks*, he emphasized the issuance of paper money as one of the businesses of banks, stressing that "the paper money in the bank had its own reserved silver money saved for people to get at any time. This method was honest and highly regarded. People all adopted paper money instead of silver coins and saved paper

[16] Zhong, T. *Yuezu Ji, Zhongguo Tielu Ruhe Qudao Weibian Lun* (Zhong's Righteous Words, How Chinese Railway Makes Its Way, *刖足集·中国铁路如何取道为便论*).

money instead of silver coins, by which 10 million silver coins could be used as 20 million in paper money."

In 1901, Qian Xun, the supervisor for Hubei students studying in Japan, introduced *Fourteen Reserve Methods of Issuing Bank Notes* by W. S. Jevons. The 14 methods included a reserve method of the gross amount, reserve method of the partial amount (when there was no cash reserve for a certain amount of paper money and there should be some cash reserve for its excess), reserve method for the minimum amount (the minimum reserve amount was regulated), flexible issuing method (taxes should be paid on the part that exceeded the highest issuing amount), reserve method of security, reserve method of real estate, foreign exchange method (the issuing amount depended on the fluctuation of foreign exchange), free issuing method, price parity method (paper money was the same price as that of the metallic coin), taxes-paying method (people should pay taxes for fiat money), exchange-delaying method (appointment would be promised a few years later), and non-exchange method (fiat money). All these methods had made great strides compared to only the reserve method of the gross amount before.

15.3 Views Regarding the Building of Banks

Banks are the central nervous system of the development of modern industry and commerce. Since society should provide funds to promote great progress of modern industry and commerce, and only banks can collect the distributed funds of society—excepting some joint-stock companies could also collect money in local regions—people should strive to build banks and modern financial systems.

Chinese financing institutions at that time included pawnshops, money shops, banking houses, banking shops, account offices, and exchange shops. Money shops and banking houses were the same, although referred to by two different names, and from the perspective of business field, they were equal to foreign banks. Regardless, they failed to develop into a more up-to-date form of bank. After the Second Opium War (1856), Western banking systems were introduced into China, among which the Hong Kong & Shanghai Banking Corporation (HSBC), founded in 1864, controlled the country's financial and economic lifeline. As the industrialization of the self-strengthening movement developed, thinkers of the Westernization movement gained deeper insight into banking.

Consequently, the Commercial Bank of China, the first Chinese bank, was founded in the late 1890s.

Why should a banking system be established in modern society?

According to Zheng Guanying, "Business affairs are the core of the self-strengthening movement, and banks are the basis of business. Western countries established banks to develop their business affairs, support their various industries, earn good finances, and maintain their overall situation." Zheng highlighted the following 10 advantages for the nation and people of establishing a banking system: (1) To gather the wealth of the whole nation for the benefit of the whole nation; (2) to prepare funds for various national projects; (3) to satisfy the urgent needs of the nation at any time; (4) to lend low-interest loans to the nation; (5) to enable the nation to borrow money without using customs revenue as collateral; (6) to enable well-off banking houses and money shops to borrow money to extend their business and maintain market conditions in the case of insufficient funds to meet their needs; (7) to enable the deposit of the public funds of all provinces in banks to avoid plots of theft; (8) to ensure the income of the government and people could be saved in banks to earn interest; (9) to enable Chinese merchants to exchange funds when abroad; and (10) to enable that when there was a lack of silver in the market, bills of exchange could be used to balance resources.[17] These banking benefits were important for the people's livelihood and for the national economy. He furthermore emphasized the urgency of establishing the banking system: "Since there are 20,000 to 30,000 money-dealers' shops with hundreds of thousands of loans, it will be of great matter even in the case of only a small failure. This is a case of giving the sword to others for the sake of hurting themselves. Therefore, the most urgent task currently is to raise a vast sum of money to establish banks to save businesses."[18]

Chen Chi also highlighted the function of circulating the necessary funds of banks. Because "not all merchants have that much money, and the wealthy are good at business," there should be a place for them to circulate their money. Since the convenient exchanges in Shanxi exchange shops were confined within China, banks needed a broader view, so

[17] Zheng, G. *Zheng Guanying Ji, Yinhang Shang, Shangce* (Zheng Guanying Works, Banks I, Vol. 1, *郑观应集·银行上, 上册*), pp. 679–680.

[18] Zheng, G. *Zheng Guanying Ji, Yinhang Shang, Shangce* (Zheng Guanying Works, Banks I, Vol. 1, *郑观应集·银行上, 上册*), pp. 679–680.

"Western people established many banks at each treaty port." The businesses of banks could be divided into paper money, bill of exchange, stocks, deposit money, mortgage, and loans. Chen Chi believed there were big differences between having banks or not; however, there were no banks in China and the government was in no hurry to establish them. This made it difficult for the government to raise funds to cover military expenses and for common people to do business. Banks were likened to the blood of the Chinese economy: "Other people are healthy because they have traversing blood vessels, so it is easy for them to climb the mountain or face challenges. In contrast, Chinese people are unhealthy because our bodies have ulcers in some places with too much blood, and paralyses in other places on account of the lack of blood. How should these unhealthy people fight the strong?" This stressed the need to build banks to boost commerce.[19]

In September 1896, Sheng Xuanhuai stated, "The Western people are gathering their wealth to support their economy and industry through the ties of banks. It is time for China to follow and adopt their practice."[20] The Commercial Bank of China was founded in 1897, the first bank founded by the Chinese people.

How was a bank to be established? According to Zheng Guanying, there were two types of Western banks: official and commercial banks. Zheng recommended that these two types of banks also be founded in China. Official banks could be founded in the capital city and supervised and managed by officers in the Ministry of Revenue. Moreover, the government could allocate 40% of taxes as an investment cost to found the banks. Meanwhile, the stockholding system could be adopted in commercial banks where both officers and common people could become shareholders. However, because of the bad reputation of the joint-stock companies at that time, "all people who hear this news are uncertain about that. First, they think the companies will fail, and second, they do not believe in their stability. Third, they do not think these companies will last for long." Under the circumstances, Zhang advised the government to support the establishment of banks, or "it will ultimately be a

[19] Chen, C. (1997). *Chen Chi Ji, Chuangban Yinhang Shuo* (Chen Chi Works, Banks Establishing, *陈炽集·创办银行说*). Beijing: Zhonghua Book Company, p. 264.

[20] Sheng, X. *Yuzhai Cungao, Juanyi* (Memorials of Sheng Xuanhuai, Vol. 1, *愚斋存稿, 卷1*).

failure."[21] Therefore, he suggested that the government and merchants jointly operate the banks in China. Specifically, "the national government should serve a fundamental role and then, merchants' shares should be collected. Regarding the principle of raising money, the government's interests should be protected first. Each year, the paper money will be issued by the government, and everyone will come to depend on and believe in this currency, making it easy for merchants to make money."[22]

The Commercial Bank of China, the first bank in China, was established according to this official-merchant joint management principle. Sheng Xuanhuai opposed that the government run the banks because of the risk of possible corruption, and he disapproved of completely civilian-run banks for two reasons: First, for the Chinese Commercial Bank, "it is hard to deal with foreign bills of exchange as it has to depend on the official bills of exchange in various provinces." Therefore, "merchants have no ability to call upon the bills of exchange if they do not hold official shares." Second, "since the conduct of casting silver coins and issuing paper money means superpowers and high profits, it is certain that disputes will occur. It is better for the government and merchants to operate jointly to avoid losing the confidence of the common people." Sheng proposed sending ministers to select fair and wealthy merchants as directors and to collect 5 million silver coins. They planned to found the Bank of China in Beijing and Shanghai and gradually establish branches in other provincial capital cities and various ports. Sheng thought that only in this way could they "gather the financial resources to found the banks around China. If Chinese banks can earn one share of profit, they can take back one share of rights from foreign banks."[23]

Banks earned profits by charging the margin between savings and loans. If investment mistakes occurred or the borrowers ran off with money, the banks would be certain to suffer tremendous losses. To reduce the possible risks in the operation of the banks, Zheng Guanying advised that they "follow the practice of Western countries." He also recommended that "when trade occurs between foreign banks and the common

[21] Zheng, G. *Zheng Guanying Ji, Yinhang Xia, Shangce* (Zheng Guanying Works, Banks II, Vol. 1, 郑观应集·银行下, 上册), p. 683.

[22] Zheng, G. *Zheng Guanying Ji, Yinhang Xia, Shangce* (Zheng Guanying Works, Banks II, Vol. 1, 郑观应集·银行下, 上册), pp. 686–687.

[23] Sheng, X. *Yuzhai Cungao, Juanyi* (Memorials of Sheng Xuanhuai, Vol. 1, 愚斋存稿, 卷1).

people, there must be some bonded money in it. As for the principle of bonding, people evaluate the value as a standard. If the goods are valued at 100%, the bonded money should be valued at 60–70%, and not more than 80%. Both sides keep one copy of the contract with a clear date printed on it. If one party fails to return the money within the deadline, his bonded goods will be sold to compensate another party, and if the auction price was not enough to compensate the bonded money, another party could ask for money for its counterpart."[24]

Solid legislation should be carried out by the right person. Considering the transaction disputes in companies in the past, Zheng proposed that China establish the Ministry of Commerce to protect the interests of merchants. According to him, "The envoys abroad should translate detailed regulations of various nations and then choose and follow the proper one according to their actual conditions. The government protected the merchants, the merchants assisted the government, and both sides cooperated to use this regulation to achieve success."[25]

[24] Zheng, G. *Zheng Guanying Ji, Yinhang Xia, Shangce* (Zheng Guanying Works, Banks II, Vol. 1, *郑观应集·银行下, 上册*), pp. 684–685.

[25] Zheng, G. *Zheng Guanying Ji, Yinhang Xia, Shangce* (Zheng Guanying Works, Banks II, Vol. 1, *郑观应集·银行下, 上册*), p. 685.

CHAPTER 16

Thinking on Transferring the Surplus Workforce in an Agricultural Society

In the history of the world economy, the emergence of a new industry has always led to the elimination of old industries. During this period, the key problem was how to transfer the workforce. In general, if the industrial structure of a society develops naturally, the cost of structural transformation will be lower because people have a comparatively long period to adapt. In contrast, if the structural transformation of a society is oppressed by its external forces instead of its internal development, it will be difficult for people to reach consensus quickly because they lack sufficient time to adapt. This will lengthen the process of economic structure transformation and increase the cost thereof. Unfortunately, the transformation of the economic structure in China's self-strengthening movement took the form of the latter. The Westernization Movement paid too much to garner society's support for their reform proposals.

16.1 Machine Production Was the Solution to Transferring the Surplus Workforce

After the Second Opium War (1856), alongside the advancement of machine production in China emerged a mass of unemployed people in society, from which sprung the idea that "machines deprive the people of their livelihood" in various societal strata. Noteworthy was that the Westernization Movement could implement a capitalist mode of production in

J. Zhou, *Westernization Movement and Early Thought of Modernization in China*, Palgrave Studies in Economic History,
https://doi.org/10.1007/978-3-030-86985-4_16

China amid this social reality. They believed this social reality—machinery increasing the unemployment rate—was temporary, and the employment of Chinese people depended on the advancement and promotion of this production mode in China in the long term.

In the 1870s, Xue Fucheng contended that the railway would not take the bread out of people's mouths, but in contrast, would improve people's livelihood: "There are only one or two thousand kilometers of railway, but more than several hundreds of thousands of people who can live off the railway. Moreover, mines such as for coal or iron are exploited to support an uncountable number of poor people. All these methods are used to support people's livelihoods."[1]

After Xue Fucheng's mission to Europe, Xue had a clearer understanding that the surplus workforce in the agriculture industry was transferred to the department of industrial and mineral industry. In 1891, he noted that "having inspected the European countries, I concluded that the population of those countries was many times that of China. There were 94 persons per 10 square *li* in the European countries and 48 in China."[2] As such, Europe's population density was twice that of China's, and its land was not as fertile. However, its people were well off because Europe "can circulate its financial resources." Moreover, their machine production was a major contributor to the continent's success. Therefore, Xue advocated the theory that machines support people. He added, "The Chinese population is 10 times that of western countries. Someone says that the application of the machines will lead to unemployment. However, the western countries have been good at cultivating people through machines. Chinese goods cannot only be sold in foreign countries, but also locally. Chinese people cannot earn their own living and believe it is not useful to do that. Furthermore, Chinese people are not able to produce goods to compete with those in the West. In contrast, they fight to buy foreign goods they can enjoy, which is of great benefit to those in the West. Therefore, it is natural that commerce falls into

[1] Xue, F. (1987). *Xue Fucheng Xuanji, Dai Li Boxiang Yiqing Shiban Tielu Shu* (Selected Works of Xue Fucheng, Li Hongzhang's Proposal of Building Railway, *薛福成选集·代李伯相议请试办铁路疏*). Shanghai: Shanghai Renmin Chubanshe, p. 138.

[2] Xue, F. (1987). *Xue Fucheng Xuanji, Xiyang Zhuguo Daomin Shengcai Shuo* (Selected Works of Xue Fucheng, People's Making Money in the Western Countries, *薛福成选集·西洋诸国导民生财说*). Shanghai: Shanghai Renmin Chubanshe, p. 367.

decay. This makes the people's lives difficult and leads to the stagnation of the country's development. Thus, the statement that machines are detrimental to employment is wrong."[3]

Zhong Tianwei considered the issue of the surplus workforce in agriculture from the broader view of developing a capitalist mode of production. According to him, the more China opened to the outside world, the more its national economy would thrive, and the more job opportunities would be available to the Chinese people. In the early 1880s, while traveling in Europe, Zhong wrote *Building the Railway & Placing the Electric Wire*, in which he states: "As the number of ports increase, the more workers are needed. For example, a port has been extended as five ports for commerce in Guangdong province, increasing the number of employed people to millions. When ports have opened in Shanghai, the same phenomenon will occur. These examples are clear evidence for the waterway ports and land routes. If dozens of ports are opened in the interior land quickly, it is certain that several tens of thousands of people would get jobs. This is the same for various countries in the West."[4]

Based on the fact that the Western countries had shifted attitudes toward machine production from fierce opposition to active support, Chen Chi noted that machine production promoted the employment of the workforce. He said, "When machines first appeared in Western countries, the craftsmen there thought their craft would not be able to compete with machines, and they went to work in factories. The initial wage was very small, but after a period of time, their income increased. The factory provided more people with jobs."[5] Simply put, "The appearance and use of machines enabled workers to work in a different way, rather than deprive them of their jobs."[6] Therefore, he contested that

[3] Xue, F. (1987). *Xue Fucheng Xuanji, Yong Jiqi Zhicai Yangmin Shuo* (Selected Works of Xue Fucheng, Making Money Through Machines to Support the People, *薛福成选集·用机器殖财养民说*). Shanghai: Shanghai Renmin Chubanshe, pp. 420–421.

[4] Zhong, T. *Yuezu Ji, Nei Pian* (Zhong's Righteous Words, Domestic Affairs, *刖足集·内篇*).

[5] Chen, C. (1997). *Chen Chi Ji, Gongyi Yangmin Shuo* (Chen Chi Works, Saying of Feeding People by Technology, *陈炽集·工艺养民说*). Beijing: Zhonghua Book Company, pp. 228–229.

[6] Chen, C. (1997). *Chen Chi Ji, Bianchi Lunzhou Shuo* (Chen Chi Works, Saying of Ship, *陈炽集·遍驰轮舟说*). Beijing: Zhonghua Book Company, p. 240.

machine production deprived people of their livelihoods, arguing instead that it could support the people: "There was a large number of and the easiest jobs in the machine factory for the poor to make a living.[7] If various factories in the provinces of China have been established, millions of poor people can immediately have ample food and clothing and families. The manual workers in the past can also enjoy life."[8] In Chen's eyes, the machine mode of production was most favorable in terms of improving the livelihoods of the poor, because "as the rising of the machines takes place, one worker's work can support ten people's food. The rich invested in founding factories where thousands of poor people work. The rich only get 1–2% of the benefit, and the salaries of the workers have been increased by several times. Therefore, the rise of the machine is especially convenient for the poor."[9]

It is believed that it was correct for the Westernization Movement to develop the capitalist economy as one way to promote employment in China. However, there were many difficulties from the view of the actual conditions in the country at that time. First, the industrial mode of production was too undeveloped to absorb a surplus population. Second, even if new industries could offer many jobs, it still needed a certain period to balance the demand and supply of the workforce. As such, how could these surplus populations find employment as soon as possible? How could they be provided with basic living security when they had not found employment? How could the pains of the social transition be shortened and alleviated? The Westernization Movement proposed the following methods:

1. Work on agricultural production: According to Zheng Guanying, "there are hundreds of millions *qing* of uncultivated lands in China such as Jilin Province and Heilongjiang Province in the Northeast,

[7] Chen, C. (1997). *Chen Chi Ji, Gongyi Yangmin Shuo* (Chen Chi Works, Saying of Feeding People by Technology, 陈炽集·工艺养民说). Beijing: Zhonghua Book Company, p. 230.

[8] Chen, C. (1997). *Chen Chi Ji, Gongyi Yangmin Shuo* (Chen Chi Works, Saying of Feeding People by Technology, 陈炽集·工艺养民说). Beijing: Zhonghua Book Company, p. 230.

[9] Chen, C. (1997). *Chen Chi Ji, Yang Min* (Chen Chi Works, Feeding People, 陈炽集·养民). Beijing: Zhonghua Book Company, pp. 135–136.

Rehe Province and Hetao Region in the North, Hovd in the North-West, and Lop Nor in Xinjiang Province. The local people are not aware of the benefits of cultivation in this boundless land and consequently give up. Moreover, on the borders of Sichuang, Yunnan, Guizhou, and Guangxi Provinces in the SouthWest, Qiongzhou of Guangdong, and the hills of Taiwan, the lands are barren, and interests largely ignored. Because the local officials do not care about these lands, the foreign people invade them." Furthermore, there were many unemployed poor in China's inland; thus, "these unemployed people should be recruited to leave for the uncultivated lands with their families." Zheng listed five advantages of this method: "First, the inland poor would be free from hunger and cold. Second, the border areas and the important places would be cultivated. Third, people who live in the border areas will against invaders hardly to protect themselves. Fourth, the soldiers conscripted from the local people, the soldiers' pay and provisions from the local land taxes. Fifth, the poor people who living along the coast can now move to Taiwan and Qiongzhou with better living conditions."[10]

2. Living abroad, that is, using immigration to a foreign country to solve the problem of overpopulation: According to Xue Fucheng, China was renowned for housing the largest population worldwide. However, its lands were not correspondingly as large. Furthermore, the machine cultivation led to the farmers have nothing to do. These factors impoverished the people and made living hard. In contrast, the labor force of other countries such as the United States, Brazil, and Mexico could not meet their economic development. As such, they were hiring workers from underdeveloped countries. Therefore, Xue advocated that "rather than extensively developing resources to benefit our people, it would be better to permit them to work in foreign countries."[11] Which countries were better to immigrate to? Xue encouraged people to immigrate to Brazil and Mexico: "Few Chinese people are willing to immigrate to Africa on account of its uncivilized society and unhealthy environment." In the United

[10] Zheng, G. *Zheng Guanying Ji, Ken Huang Shangce* (Zheng Guanying Works, Wasteland Cultivation, Vol. 1, 郑观应集·垦荒, 上册), pp. 740–741.

[11] Xue, F. (1987). *Xue Fucheng Xuanji, Lun Baxi Zhaogong Shiyi Shu* (Selected Works of Xue Fucheng, Discussion about Recruitment of Brazil, 薛福成选集·论巴西招工事宜书). Shanghai: Shanghai Renmin Chubanshe, p. 472.

> States, Peru, Australia, the Netherlands, and Spain, Chinese people were deported or maltreated, and "only the newly developed Americas, the vast territory with a sparse population, spare no efforts to appeal to the common people who live far from it. Moreover, its policy treats these common people well." Therefore, Brazil and Mexico were considered the most suitable places to which to immigrate. Thus, when envoys from these two countries visited China to discuss the hiring of Chinese workers, Xue Fucheng suggested that the Court reach an agreement with Brazil and Mexico regarding their employment: "Chinese people can be servants, do commerce, or deal with plants or open mines in foreign countries. Moreover, we can also establish consulates there to protect and control them. Besides, we should also sign agreements with these countries that they give preferential treatment to Chinese workers from the onset and will not deport them like the US." Xue believed this practice would "develop Chinese regions abroad in which Chinese people can live. This is an important practice to rescue China."[12]

There was probably some truth in Xue's ideas. During the integration of the world economy, it was normal and frequent that production factors flew freely in the international market, which reflected China entering the world market. It was also implied that Xue had broken through the limits of the traditional view of small-scale farming by individual owners and started to consider issues from a world and international market perspective.

However, it was difficult to export the labor force to foreign countries. The imperial court had to know the different political and legal institutions of various countries as well as different national cultures and traditions. To maximize national interests, the labor force exporting country had to apply the related principles of International Law to protect itself. Because China had weak national power and low international standing, so that other countries such as the United States demanded a large number of Chinese laborers during its economic development. However, once its domestic economy changed, they deported the immigrated workers. To reduce the risks in the process of exporting the labor

[12] Xue, F. (1987). *Xue Fucheng Xuanji, Xu Baxi Moxige Liyue Zhaogong Shuo* (Selected Works of Xue Fucheng, Discussion about Recruitment in Brazil and Mexico, *薛福成选集·许巴西墨西哥立约招工说*). Shanghai: Shanghai Renmin Chubanshe, p. 366.

force, Xue Fucheng, who served as the envoy to the United Kingdom, France, Spain, and Belgium negotiating the agreement with Brazil and Mexico, he emphasized that "Chinese laborers are free to work in foreign countries, but it is inappropriate for other countries to come to China to hire workers." This would ensure that "every worker has the right to make the decision." "As for the foreign people who bring large sums of money or drive huge ships, they recruit hundreds or thousands of Chinese people to their countries and sell them. Regulations and laws must strictly forbid their conduct."[13]

These "relief" measures were considered by the Westernization Movement at that time. They believed they would provide unemployed or impoverished people with basic life guarantees through a series of methods including social relief to avoid social disruption. Jing Yuanshan was known for his strong support of relief measures. He recommended that expenditures be slashed to help disaster areas through difficult times. He also asked local governments to save money to be used as a relief fund. However, others thought this was not a sufficient method to deal with the severe situation and to contribute money toward disaster relief. Jing Yuanshan explained, "Suppose that there are 18 provinces in China. A severe disaster occurred in 2, but there are still 12 untouched provinces. If there are 60 prefectures and counties in each province, there are 100,000 people in each county. If each were to save 1 penny a day, 72,000,000 pennies could be saved per day, and 25,920,000,000 pennies each year. Except for the paper money issued by the government, the donations of wealthy merchants and grains of neighboring countries can all be made a public possession. In this way, why can our country not be saved?"[14] Regarding the implementation of non-governmental relief, he supported the principle of it "being donated by and run by the people."[15]

[13] Xue, F. (1987). *Xue Fucheng Xuanji, Lun Baxi Zhaogong Shiyi Shu* (Selected Works of Xue Fucheng, Discussion about Recruitment of Brazil, 薛福成选集·论巴西招工事宜书). Shanghai: Shanghai Renmin Chubanshe, pp. 472–473.

[14] Jing, Y. *Juyi Chu Ji, Jiquan Sisheng Zhenjuan Qi* (Original Works of Juyi, A Persuasion for Four Provinces to Donate, 居易初集·急劝四省赈捐启), pp. 1–2.

[15] Jing, Y. *Juyi Chu Ji, Jiquan Sisheng Zhenjuan Qi* (Original Works of Juyi, A Persuasion for Four Provinces to Donate, 居易初集·急劝四省赈捐启), pp. 1–2.

16.2 Transfer of the Surplus Population in Non-Production Departments in an Agricultural Society

In the previous section, the author discussed the transfer of the surplus population in production departments in the traditional or agricultural society. As the capitalist mode of production continued to develop in the field of domestic economy, it was requested that economic or non-economic management departments that countered this progress be dissolved. Which administrative departments were to be dissolved and how?

According to the Westernization Movement, the dissolving standard should be based on economic principles, namely to acquire the greatest economic benefits at the lowest cost. Based on this view, they recommended that the following departments be dissolved:

1. The Department of Water Transport: All officials, soldiers, and other staff who work for the transportation of grains under the management of the minister of water transport should be dismissed. The Department of Water Transport was originally established by the Court to transport grains from the south; however, the South-to-North grain transfer had changed from river to sea transport on account of the rise of new types of Western steamships. Under the circumstances, the existence of the Department of Water Transport had become worthless.
2. The Department of River Affairs: All officials and soldiers under the management of the minister of river affairs should be dismissed. Floods were common in China. To prevent the damages caused by the floods and to unblock the Grand Canal, the Qing Dynasty invested millions of silver each year, but "it is not effective enough for that." Furthermore, as the function of canals decreased, it was advised that this department "be incorporated into the local governments."[16]
3. The Department of Supervision: All departments involved in the supervision of weaving should be dissolved because "the business

[16] Zheng, G. *Zheng Guanying Ji, Tai Rong, Shangce* (Zheng Guanying Works, Redundancy, Vol. 1, 郑观应集·汰冗, 上册), p. 458.

of weaving has been simple enough to be assigned to local governments. Since the supervision taxes of various ports are very low, it is better to dismiss the related officials and assign local officers to deal with it. Moreover, the affairs of various customhouses are also easy and simple, so they can also be canceled. The government can assign someone who knows both Chinese and foreign languages well and is good at calculations to serve as the customs commissioner, which is convenient and economic."[17]

4. The Department of Salt Affairs should be dissolved appropriately: Zheng Guanying advised dissolving the Department of Salt Affairs appropriately because "the official positions of salt and iron have a long history, so it is not proper to abolish them directly, but as for the minister of salt affairs and other involved officials, it is of no great importance to keep these positions."[18]
5. Administrative departments in the government: The modern industry required both a suitable political system and a higher standard of the quality of officials. It was obvious that the official circles during the Late Qing Dynasty faced a great challenge in terms of adjustment according to the abovementioned requirements. Zheng Guanying considered the biggest disadvantage of official circles at that time the redundant personnel and expenses, in which the redundant expenses were caused by the redundant personnel. He said, "In terms of the officials in the capital city, excepting the official Council of State and the Censorate, the others are all idle. As for various departments, except the main chargers, the others are wasting the Court's expenses in vain. Therefore, all extra officials can be dismissed."[19] It was better for the local officials at different levels to be dismissed properly. He also pointed out that "the Governor in the same city as its Governor-general can also be dismissed. In this way, the salaries, military expenses, and servants' spending can also be saved each year." He also recommended dismissing the Provincial Surveillance Commissions who take charge of criminal law in

[17] Zheng, G. *Zheng Guanying Ji, Tai Rong, Shangce* (Zheng Guanying Works, Redundancy, Vol. 1, 郑观应集·汰冗, 上册), p. 458.

[18] Zheng, G. *Zheng Guanying Ji, Tai Rong, Shangce* (Zheng Guanying Works, Redundancy, Vol. 1, 郑观应集·汰冗, 上册), p. 458.

[19] Zheng, G. *Zheng Guanying Ji, Tai Rong, Shangce* (Zheng Guanying Works, Redundancy, Vol. 1, 郑观应集·汰冗, 上册), pp. 460–461.

various provinces because "their work is just in name and not practical."[20] Similarly, local governments should also dismiss their own redundant personnel so that Chinese official institutions could be more capable, efficient, and adaptable to the demands of modern industrial and commercial societies.

6. The Department of Armed Forces: The Manchurian soldiers and Green Standards should be dissolved because if the modernization of the armed forces was pursued, they had to reduce the number of forces and the military officers correspondingly. "Regardless of the scale of the forces, all should be cut down by half." Chen Chi noted that "more than 600,000 soldiers in the Green Standards cost more than 20 million taels each year, which takes up half the national finances and taxes. However, once a revolt occurs, they are defeated and dispersed quickly." Thus, the existing soldiers were not useful but harmful, and should be dismissed. He further proposed a timeline of 10 years to dissolve all the Manchurian soldiers and Green Standards, which would enable saving money to equip modernized troops.[21]
7. As for the issue of the "Eight Banners," the reformers advocated changing the existing system of national support to finding their own means of livelihood, because "almost 80–90% of national finances and taxes were used for them each year."[22]
8. Regarding the post houses, the reformers advocated changing these into postal services. Chen Chi contended that China should establish the postal services by learning from the Western countries, taking the existing post houses as a foundation, and cooperating with the telegraph offices so that the people could save the charges of post houses and the government could earn a high postal service income. [23]Zheng Guanying added, "The Western people once stated that Chinese people should have known and earned two major kinds of

[20] Zheng, G. *Zheng Guanying Ji, Tai Rong, Shangce* (Zheng Guanying Works, Redundancy, Vol. 1, *郑观应集·汰冗, 上册*), p. 459.

[21] Chen, C. (1997). *Chen Chi Ji, E Bin* (Chen Chi Works, Soldiers, *陈炽集·额兵*). Beijing: Zhonghua Book Company, pp. 41–42.

[22] Chen, C. (1997). *Chen Chi Ji, E Bin* (Chen Chi Works, Soldiers, *陈炽集·额兵*). Beijing: Zhonghua Book Company, p. 63.

[23] Chen, C. (1997). *Chen Chi Ji, Yi Zhuan* (Chen Chi Works, Post System, *陈炽集·驿传*). Beijing: Zhonghua Book Company, pp. 114–115.

incomes: first, the expenses of each post in various provinces each year could be saved, which cost 10% of national grains. Second, post bureaus should be established to collect taxes. If the post bureaus were operated in China now, postal expenses can be reduced or saved."[24]

9. The reformers also suggested dissolving all Wei Tun, two types of administrative organizations established in the early Ming Dynasty. Wei Tun was originally established in the early Ming Dynasty to defend against Japanese pirates. "In the wide and dilapidated land, the army builds granaries and fortresses, which can be cultivated and guarded, and cultivated in the absence of war."[25] The institutions in the Qing Dynasty had been slightly adjusted from the existing function of defending against Japanese pirates to the assisting function of "transporting grain by water to the capital." After the Opium War, sea transportation increased, while water transportation decreased. Thus, it was obvious that "using Wei Tun to assist transportation" had not been suitable to the new situation and reform was imperative. As such, the Westernization thinkers recommended dissolving the Wei Tun. The government repealed the function of the garrisons of "assisting water transport," and all its people became common citizens managed by the nation. This would enable the Court to save a lot of money and collect "2.5 million taels in taxes each year."[26]

Discussing the reemployment of the staff of the dissolved departments mentioned above, the opinions of the Westernization thinkers could be divided into the following aspects:

1. To encourage the staff to work in new industries: Alongside the rise of new industries in China, many new occupations also emerged, which would enable these staff to get a new job. Regarding the issue of the Eight Banners, Zheng Guanying believed that excepting some who inherited official salaries between generations, all other Eight

[24] Zheng, G. *Zheng Guanying Ji, Yizhan, Shangce* (Zheng Guanying Works, Post, Vol. 1, 郑观应集·驿站, 上册), pp. 676–677.

[25] Zheng, G. *Zheng Guanying Ji, Wei Tun, Shangce* (Zheng Guanying Works, Wei Tun, Vol. 1, 郑观应集·卫屯, 上册), p. 905.

[26] Zheng, G. *Zheng Guanying Ji, Wei Tun, Shangce* (Zheng Guanying Works, Wei Tun, Vol. 1, 郑观应集·卫屯, 上册), p. 906.

Banners should "make a living on their own. They can do something in agriculture, commerce, and so on."[27] As for the children of soldiers who garrison outside the capital city, "children aged 10–20 years who are smart can be selected to study in the Schools of Foreign Language, Sports Pavilions, Navy Colleges, or Technology Schools. Their children were free to read or do business at their own will."[28] He also expected that the staff of some traditional industries such as water transport and the post houses could work in the new industries after the railway, postal services, and shipping industries had been established. At that time, many soldiers were transferred to engage in civilian work.

2. To work in agricultural production: Zheng Guanying believed that the young generations of the Eight Banners should be "sent to farm in Zhili Province and other places nearby." Regarding departments that had used agriculture to generate their financial resources, for example, the Wei Tun, he advised "converting the armed forces to civilian production" locally by relying on the original lands and farm tools. These civilians could become "residents" who bear tax for the country.
3. The imperial court would provide certain financial support. Also, regarding the Eight Banners, Chen Chi said, "The people in the Eight Banners who are willing to give up their special rights can be lent 10 years' pay. They will be offered lands if they want to farm, they will be financed if they want to do business, and they can also do something about technology."[29] Zheng Guanying proposed that the Eight Banners who were willing to do farm work in Tianjin could get five years of grains in advance by the Court, and the Court could adjust this payment in accordance with the price of certain commodities as their farming capital. As for the Banners who

[27] Zheng, G. *Zheng Guanying Ji, Qi Ji, Shangce* (Zheng Guanying Works, Eight Banners, Vol. 1, *郑观应集·旗籍, 上册*), pp. 474–475.

[28] Zheng, G. *Zheng Guanying Ji, Qi Ji, Shangce* (Zheng Guanying Works, Eight Banners, Vol. 1, *郑观应集·旗籍, 上册*), p. 476.

[29] Chen, C. (1997). *Chen Chi Ji, Ba Qi* (Chen Chi Works, Eight Banners, *陈炽集·八旗*). Beijing: Zhonghua Book Company, p. 64.

> were willing to do farm work in Rehe and Chaoyang, they could get 10 years of grain money and be free from 10 years of taxes.[30]

When considering the adjustment of the economic structure, it was far-sighted for the Westernization thinkers to talk about the reemployment of people who "live off government money." Unlike the general unemployed people, these staff enjoyed higher social positions and influenced government policies; thus, their reemployment would directly impact the course of Chinese modernization. However, the author does not think the Westernizationists' opinion on this issue was well considered. Excepting many discussions on the reemployment of the Eight Banners, they seldom considered the reemployment of other departments, which was not helpful to the development of early Chinese modernization. When the people of other departments were pushed into society involuntarily, a series of social problems would be certain to occur, which not only impacted social stability, but also complicated any reform efforts. Let us take water transport as an example. Everyone knew this system was unreasonable and those with insight submitted numerous reform proposals. However, until 1900, the Qing government ordered that silver be collected, but maintained 1 million *shi* of grains transported to the capital by water. This problem was finally solved with the death of the regime after the Revolution of 1911. This reform was not connected to the basic interests of a dynasty, so why could it not be implemented? This was because the Qing government did not know how to arrange troops for large-scale water transport. Since there were many robbers in the Green Woods, failing to solve this problem would lead to severe social problems, which was what the Qing government was trying to avoid at all costs. For the "stability" of the reform, this problem was shelved. "Only the current political rulers consider it, while the personnel and workers involved in water transport have no jobs to live on. Thus, it is inevitable that they cause trouble."[31] This illustrates Zheng Guanying's contradictory attitude toward the government.

[30] Zheng, G. *Zheng Guanying Ji, Qi Ji, Shangce* (Zheng Guanying Works, Eight Banners, Vol. 1, *郑观应集·旗籍, 上册*), p. 475.

[31] Zheng, G. *Zheng Guanying Ji, Ting Cao, Shangce* (Zheng Guanying Works, Water Transport of Grain, Vol. 1, *郑观应集·停漕, 上册*), p. 277.

PART IV

Aftermath

This section highlights problems to consider before concluding the book.

In the previous three parts, the author analyzed the inquiries and discussions of the Westernization Group regarding the new mode of production of enterprise management; development of the departments of the national economy; and political, cultural, and educational reform to ensure China's transition from a traditional to modern society. This part analyzes the origin and views of the Westernization thinkers on modernization as well as the relationship between the Qing government and Westernization.

CHAPTER 17

The Origins of Westernization Thought

The author believes there were three sources of Westernization: the influence of the ideological trend of Confucian statecraft, influence of traditional economic thought, and influence of Western culture.

17.1 Influence of the Ideological Trends of Confucian Statecraft on Westernization Thought

The rise of the ideological trend of Confucian statecraft, which is based on the confluence of studying Confucian classics in Li calligraphy and Neo Confucianism, was reactionary to the period of emperors Qianlong and Jiaqing ideology. This was characterized by academic criticism and was an ideological emancipation movement that greatly influenced thinking in the late Qing Dynasty.

Studying Confucian classics in Li calligraphy emphasized reading the sage's literal meaning to ensure knowing the implied meaning. Thus, it was better than studying classics in majuscule seal script, which was characterized by a detailed philological exegesis of Chinese classics, to respond to real challenges. In the later Qing Dynasty, Gong Zizhen and Wei Yuan, masters of Confucian classics in Li calligraphy, planned and mapped important aspects related to national interests, satirized the current politics, and slandered the autarchy, achieving almost celebrity status. Liang

J. Zhou, *Westernization Movement and Early Thought of Modernization in China*, Palgrave Studies in Economic History,
https://doi.org/10.1007/978-3-030-86985-4_17

Qichao once said, "If you wanted to know the secret to changing ideological trends, the most important is to pay attention to the emerging Changzhou School (the school of Confucian classics in Li calligraphy). Representing this spirit were Gong Zizhen and Wei Yuan, whose works and comments greatly influenced the circle of thought in early Guangxu (the 11th emperor of the Qing Dynasty) period."[1]

Compared with the unrestricted words and enlightening remarks of the school of Confucian classics in Li calligraphy regarding Gong Yang's "Three Eras" (the simple evolutionary view of Chinese ancients) and "Three Unifications" (the three kinds of calendars of the Xia, Shang, and Zhou Dynasties) to narrate social changes, the merits of Neo Confucianism did not apparently lie in freely discussing the reform of the era. However, Neo Confucianism made "maintaining cardinal guides and constant virtues, passing on the sages' knowledge, correctly positioning the heaven and earth, and giving birth to everything" the root, and highlighted "implementing humanization, making custom pure and honest, and striving for peace" as the pursuit of ideal life. However, practically, this seemed idealistic, deep, suggestive, and broad, and represented the spiritual strength able to unite Chinese society. When textual research spread widely from its birthplace—Jiangsu and Anhui provinces—Hunan province was least affected. Thus, Hunan and Jiangxi provinces became the base camp of Neo Confucianism after the Jia-Dao period (the period of emperors Jiaqing and Daoguang). Many Neo Confucianism masters had a profound impact on histories, such as Tang Jian, Zeng Guofan, Luo Zenan, Guo Songtao, and Liu Rong. They further developed the environment for the generation of scholar-bureaucrats who administered affairs.

To solve real social problems, the two main schools (Han School and Song School), with long-held conflicting views in Chinese academic history, shifted toward an intersection and transcended their respective academic limits at this time. They emphasized the importance of cultivating morality and personality, and the role of scholar-bureaucrats with social leadership responsibility in changing the general mood of society and motivating people. Because "the will of the people was the foundation of common customs, and common customs were the foundation of

[1] Liang, Q. *Qingdai Xueshu Gaikuo, Yinbingshi Heji, Heji Di Ba Ce* (The Album of the Academic Introduction of Qing Dynasty, the Collected Works of Liang Qichao, Vol. 8, *清代学术概论, 饮冰室合集, 合集第8册*.).

governors' destiny, if the governors lost the will of people, social order would descend into chaos. Once social order had descended into chaos, the old dynasty would be replaced with a new one."[2] They also emphasized theory and practice, as well as the causes and contributions, and highlighted that this knowledge would be applied to government affairs and the kingcraft would save and help the common people.

Based on the unity of "respecting virtues and stressing learning," the statecraft ideological trend in the late Qing Dynasty was supported by the supreme governor who was eager to reduce difficulties and consolidate his regime. This would enable dominating the circle of thought after the Qian-Jia period. For example, Emperor Daoguang repeatedly stressed, "If the scholar-bureaucrat did not master the classics, his knowledge would be insufficient to be used. Learning classics did not entail selecting passages and choosing phrases, but learning the useful knowledge therein."[3] In 1835, when talking with a member of the Imperial Academy, he warned, "At home, you should read books about statecraft and try to think what good the prose and verse could bring for the country. However, members of the Imperial Academy had to do this."[4] The regime of the successive Emperor Xianfeng was slightly shorter, because he was involved in suppressing the Revolutionary War of the Taiping Heavenly Kingdom (1851–64). However, while it was difficult for him to make a difference, he still abided by his father's opinion and emphasized to his liegemen that "reading more useful books, whether you can or cannot write articles is of little importance, but performing real deeds is."[5] Under their advocacy, many capital officials and high officers of the frontier made administering affairs their own responsibility and sent official dispatches to comment on current politics and advocate reform, fueling the statecraft ideology.

The statecraft ideological trend had two notable features.

[2] Gong, Z. (1975). *Gong Zizhen Quanji, Pingjun Pian* (The Complete Works of Gong Zizhen, the Peroration about Average, 龚自珍全集·平均篇). Shanghai: Shanghai Renmin Chubanshe, p. 78.

[3] Zhonghua Book Company. (1986). *Qing Xuanzong Shilu, Juan Sanbai Wushiyi* (The Memoir of Qing Xuanzong, Vol. 351, *清宣宗实录, 卷*351). Beijing: Author, p. 343.

[4] Zhang, J. (1981.) *Dao Xian Huan Hai Jianwenlu* (The Informative Record of Officialdom in Dao Guang and Xian Feng Period, 道咸宦海见闻录). Beijing: Zhonghua Book Company, pp. 20-21.

[5] Guo, S. (1981). *Guo Songtao Riji, Juanyi* (The Dairy of Guo Songtao, Vol. 1, *郭嵩焘日记, 卷*1). Changsha: Hunan People's Publishing House, p. 203.

The first was that it was concerned with the national economy and people's livelihood, and had a strong sense of crisis. Confucianism emphasized that "an educated gentleman cannot but be resolute and broad-minded, for he has taken up a heavy responsibility and a long course," and advocated that the "rise and fall of a nation rests with every one of its citizens" who should "die for a just cause." This enabled the scholar-bureaucrats advocating statecraft to face the reality and have the courage to expose social ills. In academic thought, they criticized the Han school of classical philology, which was unrealistic and specialized in trivial textual exegesis, and the Song school of classical philology, which was also unrealistic and mostly empty talk about the meaning or opinions of words or articles. In politics, they criticized the corruption of the traditional bureaucracy and pointed out that traditional bureaucratic organizations were "dispirited and lifeless." In culture, they denounced the imperial examination system, arguing that it restricted talent. "A great number of writings in the imperial examination hall in this age followed each other, each imitating the words of the original writer. Thus, the printed editions displayed on street stalls were as many as the mountains and seas. Selecting talent based on 'four-legged essays' had taken place for 500 years, and tens of thousands of those considered talent were selected in this way. Therefore, the imperial examination system had reached its extreme."[6] In diplomacy, they criticized the closed-door policy of the Qing government and expressed their unhappiness and discontent that "the Chinese officials did not entirely know foreign government affairs, but did not explore and study to search for solutions." They also pointed out that the closed-door policy led to the Qing government had no measures for defense or in handling foreign affairs.

However, as the men of letters trained by the traditional culture, the sense of crisis of the scholar-bureaucrats advocating statecraft was closely linked with loyalty to the emperor. Taking Lin Zexu's proposal of forbidding opium as an example, he first considered that the abuse of opium would mean "China would almost have no army to fight, and no soldier's pay and provisions to support the army" several decades later. Here, Lin Zexu was considering the long-term interest of the traditional dynasty. He was later exiled to the frontier to defend Xinjiang, and bearing in mind the indefinite royal graciousness, recited parts of the poem that "the

[6] Gong, Z. (1975). *Gong Zizhen Quanji* (The Complete Works of Gong Zizhen, 龚自珍全集). Shanghai: Shanghai Renmin Chubanshe, p. 344.

royal graciousness was unforgettable in every meal." On his deathbed, he dedicated his dying words, sent through an official dispatch: "Without devoting to even a little work like shooting an arrow, it was really a regret even after death," and wished to repay the "grace" from the other life.[7]

The second point was that the statecraft ideological trend was devoted to solving various realistic problems in society under the basic tenets of Confucianism. The scholar-bureaucrats advocating statecraft usually promoted each other as "seeking truth from facts," and opposed emptiness, superficiality, impracticality, and stubbornness. They also devoted themselves to the study of practical affairs. The basic premise of the internal trend of the Confucians was mastering the classics and positioning them as tenets. The extreme case here was rendering the classic words as the standard of rightness and wrongness, which countered the spirit of emphasizing reality. The scholar-bureaucrats were strongly critical of judgment based on the classics. They contended that theory must be combined with the actual situation and opposed quoting and associations with the classics. According to Wei Yuan, "The doctor who only studied the medical books of the Yellow Emperor and Shennong mechanically was called the barber-surgeon. The Confucian scholar who only studied the writings of the Duke of Zhou and Confucius mechanically, but was unable to govern the country, was called a commonplace Confucian scholar. This had negative short-term effects and decreased people's belief in the Tao of the sage."[8]

The scholar-bureaucrats advocating statecraft emphasized solving social problems through reform. According to the traditional outlook on variability, they considered that "since ancient times, all systems without exception would be made to change, all situations without exception would change, people's views on things without exception would change, and the social environment without exception would change."[9] The strong reform carried out by the ruled class was not as good as the self-reform carried out by the ruling class. Regarding reform, the scholar-bureaucrats advocating statecraft thought that while the basic

[7] Lin, Z. (1965). *Lin Zexu Ji, Zougao* (The Corpus of Lin Zexu·the Drafts of Official Dispatch, 林则徐集·奏稿). Beijing: Zhonghua Book Company, p. 1182.

[8] Wei, Y. (1976). *Wei Yuan Ji, Shangce* (The Corpus of Wei Yuan, Vol. 1, 魏源集, 上册). Beijing: Zhonghua Book Company, p. 49.

[9] Gong, Z. (1975). *Gong Zizhen Quanji* (The Complete Works of Gong Zizhen, 龚自珍全集). Shanghai: Shanghai Renmin Chubanshe, p. 319.

social system was good, problems emerged in certain links. Therefore, they emphasized restoring the normal social order through eliminating malpractices. Wei Yuan explained, "There was no way to set up a cause of interest; however, the cause of interest would prosper if various malpractices were eliminated."[10] How could these malpractices be eliminated? The scholar-bureaucrats believed this could be accomplished through careful reform that paid attention to the means and methods and did not act with undue haste. They thought the opposition would be stirred by aiming for speed in finding a cure for disease, painting one's enemy in a negative light, and removing the disadvantages beyond the limit. Therefore, they stressed that "the gentleman should be cautious to act as per the views of political reform, but should only remove the disadvantages beyond the law. The law will still recover its original appearance if the disadvantages are removed."[11]

The reform of the scholar-bureaucrats advocating statecraft was carried out mainly around five political affairs including the style and performance of local officials, water transport of grain to the capital, river engineering project, law about salt, and soldier's pay and provisions.

The content of the reform differed before and after the Opium War. Before the Opium War, the reform program proposed by the scholar-bureaucrats advocating statecraft was mainly methods to rectify the style and performance of local officials, broaden sources of income and reduce expenditure, have better troops and simpler administration, and implement the policy of station troops to open up wasteland. However, the implementation of these previous effective reform programs could not continue in China before and after the Opium War. For example, at that time, all government officials and the people knew the Eight Banners (military-administrative organizations of the Man nationality in the Qing Dynasty) soldiers and Green Standards had already become corrupt. Imperial edicts of the court to eliminate these age-old malpractices had been promulgated but had little effect, because there was no way out for the army in addition to dissolution and reconstruction. However, this would be risky because the dissolution of the old army would immediately increase social unrest. As such, the governor had misgivings.

[10] Wei, Y. (1976). *Wei Yuan Ji, Shangce* (The Corpus of Wei Yuan, Vol. 1, 魏源集, 上册). Beijing: Zhonghua Book Company, p. 438.

[11] Wei, Y. (1976). *Wei Yuan Ji, Shangce* (The Corpus of Wei Yuan, Vol. 1, 魏源集, 上册). Beijing: Zhonghua Book Company, pp. 45-46.

Furthermore, according to the military system of the Qing Dynasty, local high-ranking officials had their own soldiers. For example, the Governor-general commanded an army named Du Biao, and Governors commanded an army named Fu Biao. In addition, both the Director-general of Grain Transport and the Director-general of the Grand Canal commanded their soldiers. Money was collected from all these areas. Therefore, some informed people were determined to reform, but the construction of these armies had become hopeless.

Why could the previous effective reform program not be continued in the era of Dao-xian (the Daoguang and Xianfeng Reigns)? The author believes this can mainly be attributed to the change of era. Because of the development of the commodity economy in the Ming and Qing Dynasties, commodity exchange relations had penetrated various aspects of society, meaning the drawbacks of the traditional society were also changing. Only a reform program adaptive to the commodity economy could eliminate social malpractices; however, these contents were not found in the esteemed Confucian classics piously worshiped by the scholar-bureaucrats advocating statecraft. Classical Confucianism emerged in the Spring and Autumn and Warring States Period when commodity economy relations were undeveloped, and the great masters of Confucianism were unable to reflect in their own writings the problems that would emerge in society 2,000 years later. However, some traditional scholar-bureaucrats concerned for the fate of the nation, in the name of statecraft and governing the advantages and disadvantages of the counties and states throughout China, they discussed various issues such as administration, the judiciary, government finance, customs, trade, traffic, water conservancy, and agricultural and manual production. However, these discussions were related to the agriculture-oriented traditional economic policy. The fundamental task put by history before the Chinese people in the nineteenth century was realizing the transition from a natural to commodity economy. Obviously, asking them to deal with social problems from a commodity economy perspective was beyond the boundaries of the inherent framework of the scholar-bureaucrats advocating statecraft at the time.

After the Opium War, Western culture permeated China, opening the eyes of the scholar-bureaucrats advocating statecraft to how Western countries developed a commodity economy as their object of reference when designing the plan to eliminate malpractices. Thus, their programs were modern. Among them, Wei Yuan was exceptional. His knowledge on studies of Chinese ancient civilization (including philosophy, history, archeology, and literature) enabled him to express his understanding of Western learning (a late Qing Dynasty term for the natural and social sciences in the West) in authentic Confucianism form, which contributed to reducing social opposition. His in-depth knowledge of social ills enabled him to design a program to eliminate malpractices with considerable operability based on lessons learned from Western learning. The characteristic of his reform program was "learning the foreigners' advanced techniques to deal with them." Outward, it was "learning the foreigners' advanced techniques to deal with them" to get ahead in the race with the Western powers. Domestically, it was "learning the foreigners' advanced techniques" to abolish maladministration in China. About the former, the literature includes many studies; thus, the author does not elaborate here. Regarding the latter, the extant research is not sufficient; thus, the author says a few more words in this regard. In Wei Yuan's view, the traditional ways had been unable to overcome the malpractices of China, and these chronic diseases could only be overcome using Western methods. Specifically, he advocated substituting administrative with economic means when abolishing the malpractices of government in managing the economy, which would break through the resistance of forces with vested interests and avoid the ending of "when a man in power dies, all political measures he instituted will cease." To ensure the stability of society, the Chinese tradition devoted particular care to "only people who had a certain ownership income had a certain moral concept and behavior criteria," and advocated, "enriching the people." However, this was difficult to do in the Qing Dynasty when there were more people and less land. Thus, Wei Yuan proposed learning from the Western countries and encouraging people to engage in industry and commerce to become wealthy. When it came to developing industry and commerce, considering the various drawbacks of China's government-run handicraft industry, he proposed adopting the Western method to strictly limit the officials' involvement in economic affairs and implementing the policy of civil use and private operation. Regarding the reform of the imperial examination system, while criticized, but no solutions to substitute selecting talent through the system were proposed. Wei Yuan proposed a partial reform of the imperial examination system, starting with the most urgent navy personnel and selecting talent who could manufacture utensils, and build and drive the ships based on an examination.

In short, after the Opium War, faced with a serious national and social crisis, the statecraft ideological trend developed in the direction of learning Western methods to reform maladministration. This went beyond the set pattern of reform in the traditional era. The scholar-bureaucrats advocating statecraft were the ideological predecessors of the Westernization group, and Westernization was the concrete practice of their theories. In fact, some among the Westernization Group had a teacher-student relationship with the scholar-bureaucrats advocating statecraft. For example, Shen Baozhen was Lin Zexu's son-in-law and Feng Guifen was Lin Zexu's student. With the changing times and circumstances, many scholar-bureaucrats turned from theoretical writings to Westernization practices, becoming supporters of the movement.

The author believes the statecraft ideological trend had the following positive influences on the development of Westernization:

First, it created the social atmosphere of encouraging research on realistic problems and seeking solutions positively, which was conducive to the continuous development and progress of Westernization. In the concrete practice of learning from Western countries, the problem of how advanced Western technology could be combined with traditional Chinese culture arose. The Westernization Group explored in depth how to solve these problems. For example, they had come up with many ways in which to deal with the problem of how to improve enterprises. The dispute of government-run versus merchant-managed enterprises also arose internally within the Westernization group. This resulted in advocating for merchant-managed enterprises. All these discussions advanced the spread of Western learning in China and the continuous, in-depth development of Westernization.

Second, it encouraged the Westernization Group to act with courage and determination to advance their careers. Li Hongzhang, a high-ranking official in the Westernization group, was politically criticized by scholars, mostly for emphasizing only the benefits. In 1888, Yu Lianyuan, the censor, impeached Li Hongzhang, stating, "Therefore, the foreigners lured Li Hongzhang, and he jeopardized national interests because of his interests."[12] Before this, scholar-bureaucrats advocating statecraft, who were respected by the members of the Westernization Group including Lin Zexu, faced similar accusations. For example, Ding Yan, an old

[12] *Yangwu Yundong, Juanliu* (The Westernization Movement, Vol. 6, 洋务运动, 卷6). Shanghai: Shanghai Renmin Chubanshe, p. 207.

school personage, attacked the scholar-bureaucrats, contending, "Their surprising and satisfying theories must be proposed if old rules and regulations were slandered and changed. Initially, only a few scholars spoke about the benefits, but this practice has long spread and expanded among the commanding officers. High-ranking officials who had developed a new habit of material gain and concealed their far-reaching plan of statecraft lost their faith and implemented their ideas by force. They were sure to break with the old laws and regulations and destroyed them, which became an unmanageable trend."[13]

Again, the statecraft ideological trend constructed the development mode of the Westernization movement. After the Opium War, to save the nation from subjugation and ensure its survival, the scholar-bureaucrats proposed saving the nation through "self-reform" and "learning the foreigners' advanced techniques." This reflected the Westernization group's views of "Confucianism as the root and Western learning as specific measures." Thus, the views of the scholar-bureaucrats advocating statecraft led to perspectives on Westernization.

Of course, the statecraft ideological trend had weaknesses as well. It functioned within the allowable range of Confucianism and could not completely break free of the boundaries of its most basic principles. When the scholar-bureaucrats explored how to use Western learning to abolish traditional maladministration, they could not have forecast that introducing Western learning would impact the traditional mode of production as well as traditional ethics and morals. However, this problem emerged with the spread of Westernization. The intensifying conflicts between Western learning and the traditional mode of production meant the scarfskin of Confucianism could not already hold the content of Western learning. At the time, the issue was not how to eliminate malpractices, but how to innovate. However, with Confucianism at the root and specific measures derived from Western learning, the Westernization Group was unable to accomplish this task. For instance, Li Hongzhang could not explain how Westernization enterprises such as railway construction, mining, and the development of transportation and communications were related to Confucianism. He could only persuade others based on gains and losses, and stated it was how China must move forward. The results were caused by the current situation. Discussing the

[13] Sheng, K. *Huangchao Jingshiwen, Xubian, Juan Shier* (The Sequel of Writings about Administrating Affairs of Dynasties, volume 12, 皇朝经世文续编, 卷12), p. 44.

situation and not the reason was a major characteristic of the Westernization Movement and why it increasingly lost the force to unite the will of the nation. Discussing the hardships of handling foreign affairs with Xue Fucheng, Li Hongzhang noted, "Handling foreign affairs was like wading through stormy waves and finishing a task if you had already suffered. Foreign affairs increased each day, and the hardships thereof were exposed day by day."[14] Why did foreign affairs increase and why were the hardships thereof exposed day by day? It was because the conflicts between Confucianism and Western learning became increasingly intense with the gradual spread of Westernization. Therefore, a shift from transformation through Confucianism as the root and Western learning as specific measures to reform views was needed.

The scholar-bureaucrats advocating statecraft strived for practicality and utility, which was to their advantage. However, unavoidably, their actions were mired by seeking quick successes and instant benefits, and their discussions lacked systematic theoretical thinking. The Westernization Group also had a tendency of utility in learning from the Western countries, based on which they only emphasized lessons learned from the Western experience and systems of developing the economy, not studying the economic theory behind these systems and experience; thus, the group achieved only half the results with double the effort. However, in Japan in the same period, the learning of Western methods was comprehensive. The Japanese considered Western learning important at the material level, as well as studying the culture and academy underlying the material. As such, they achieved twice the results with half the effort. According to Wang Kangnian, "China had once sent envoys to travel in European countries in the Xian-tong period (during the Xianfeng and Tongzhi Reigns), when Japan also sent its own envoys to learn from them. Our envoys learned only about steam engines, ships, and artillery, but ignored other aspects. Otto von Bismarck, the then Germany premier, heard about it and said, "Japan will prosper because they know the origin of everything." This was the criticism leveled at the Westernization group's tendency to seek quick successes and instant benefits.

[14] Xue, F. (1987). *Xue Fucheng Xuanji, Dai Li Boxiang Fu Shen Pinlian Guancha Shu* (Selected Works of Xue Fucheng, the Observation Letters of Replying Shen Pinlian on Behalf of Li Boxiang, *薛福成选集·代李伯相复沈品莲观察书*). Shanghai: Shanghai Renmin Chubanshe, p. 84.

17.2 Traditional Economic Thought and Conflicts Between Government-run and Merchant-managed Enterprises

Focusing on how to manage the country's national economy, Chinese traditional economic thought comprised two views: One was represented by the theory of valuableness and cheapness, and focused on strengthening the control of and intervention in the national economy. This was the typical theoretical form of national economic intervention. The second view was to limit this control and intervention so that the national economy itself could operate more naturally, which is the typical form of economic laissez-faire. In essence, the conflict regarding the development of Chinese enterprises as government-run or merchant-managed was actually the reappearance of the dispute between the two modes of traditional national economic management theory in a new historical context.

From the government's viewpoint, the theory of valuableness and cheapness advocated that the governor should not use only administrative and legal means, but also economic means. They thought, "If the governor does not understand the theory of valuableness and cheapness, he cannot organize the economy to control the people. If the governor cannot adjust the people's interests, he cannot strive to control the economy to realize national stability."[15] Here, the theory of valuableness and cheapness referred to the use of economic means. They proposed that the government control the economy to ensure that the people's production and livelihood depended on the government and that all people without exception were connected to the monarch. In this way, state power would be consolidated. They also believed that "if people were too rich, the wealth and position would not send them on errands, and if people were too poor, any punishment would not repress them."[16] Thus, the governor must apply the theory of valuableness and cheapness to regulate the people's economic interests. This would ensure that "the bestowal or deprivation and people's affluence or poverty were all decided

[15] Guan, Z. (1993). *Guan Zi, Guo Xu* (Guan Zi, the Food Reserve of the State, 管子·国蓄). Changsha: Yuelu Press, p. 613.

[16] Guan, Z. (1993). *Guan Zi, Guo Xu* (Guan Zi, the Food Reserve of the State, 管子·国蓄). Changsha: Yuelu Press, p. 613.

by the monarch."[17] In this way, two results could be achieved: One was that "the governor can use the financial resources of the people furthest," meaning people's enthusiasm for labor will come into full play. The other was that "people supported their monarch as a leader like a sun and a moon, and were also as close to their monarch as their parents."[18] This would strengthen the centripetal force of the regime.

How did the government apply the theory of valuableness and cheapness? They stressed that the government should monopolize industries that significantly impacted the national economy and people's livelihood, and not grant the wealth of the resources to the people. They also believed that "people were happy if the governor bestowed wealth to them and angry if he deprived them of their wealth."[19] Through the monopoly on various natural resources, such as through managing them and the benefits of mountains, forests, rivers, and lakes, "when bestowing interests to the people, the governor was required to have a distinct form and to not reveal privileged information when depriving them of these interests."

The monopoly of China's successive dynasties on various natural resources such as mountains and rivers, and the establishment of the government-run handicraft industry were the concrete application of the theory of valuableness and cheapness. In traditional society, these products were closely related to people's livelihood and had low demand elasticity. If the government wanted to increase revenue, it needed to increase the prices of the products, but not through increasing tax revenue. Having figured this out, it is not difficult to understand why China's successive dynasties monopolized the salt industry, which had lower demand elasticity.

In general, when a dynasty had financial difficulty but retained a degree of dominance over social resources, it tended to implement a state intervention doctrine. Modern government-run enterprises including those that were government-supervised and merchant-managed were established under these conditions.

[17] Guan, Z. (1993). *Guan Zi, Guo Xu* (Guan Zi, the Food Reserve of the State, 管子·国蓄). Changsha: Yuelu Press, p. 613.

[18] Guan, Z. (1993). *Guan Zi, Guo Xu* (Guan Zi, the Food Reserve of the State, 管子·国蓄). Changsha: Yuelu Press, p. 613.

[19] Guan, Z. (1993). *Guan Zi, Qing Zhong Yi* (Guan Zi, the Valuableness and Cheapness B, 管子·轻重乙). Changsha: Yuelu Press, p. 645.

After the rise of the Westernization Movement, Reverential Prince absorbed the wisdom of how to govern a country from Zuo Qiuming's annotation for the *Chunqiu Dynasty Annals:* "The way to govern a country lies in the fact that managing state affairs could win the will of the people, and the safety and danger of the nation depended on the success and failure of the government's administration. If the liegemen were stronger than the monarch, and the political power of the nation was transferred downward to the liegemen, the governor wanted the government decree performed, and how could this be possible? The country took the people as the root, and what would the country have if it had no people? The country became poor day by day, and the royal families became better, the monarch wanted not to lose the will of the people, and this was impossible."[20] Obviously, Reverential Prince wanted to enhance the national power to enrich the country and make its military force efficient. He also wanted to maintain the rule of the people. In this regard, the high-ranking officials among the Westernization Group were deeply influenced by traditional views. (At the beginning of the Westernization movement, their understanding of Western countries was confined only to the practical and utilitarian levels, such as having knowledge of ships and artillery.) As such, they could only implement the policy of the state intervention doctrine and industry monopoly policy of managing natural resources and the benefits of mountains, forests, rivers, and lakes according to the theory of valuableness and cheapness. The government-supervised and merchant-managed joint-stock companies they established contributed toward making the country wealthy and met people's desire to invest in the new industry and commerce. This represented the economic intervention doctrine in the form of the enterprises established and the revised version of Shang Yang's "economic rights and interests mastered by the nation alone" (the means by which the common people realized the goal of making the family rich was unified with the means by which the nation realized the goal of making the country rich) in the new era. It was also the crystallization of the fusion of Chinese and Western culture because the notion of joint-stock

[20] Aisin Gioro, Y. *Ledaotang Wehchao, Nv Shu Qi Zhi Li Lun, Juansan* (The Selected Works of Yue Daotang, Nv Shuqi's Opinion of Knowing Etiquette, Vol. 3, *乐道堂文钞·女叔齐知礼论, 卷3*), p. 30.

companies originated in Western countries, while that of government-supervised and merchant-managed enterprises was influenced by Chinese culture.

In the traditional Chinese economic management view, the theory that the best economic policy was to conform to the natural development of folk production and trade activities is contrary to the theory of valuableness and cheapness. It considered economic development a private matter and held that people motivated by the pursuit of interests would spontaneously propel society forward. Furthermore, it held that the differentiation between the rich and poor was the result of natural competition. Therefore, the essence of national economic management thought for the state was "acclimatization," namely conforming to people's pursuit of wealth but not aiming to regulate the rich and poor. They proposed a standard of evaluating national economic management, namely that the best economic policy was to conform to the natural development of folk production and trade activities. The second-best economic policy was that through material interests, the state used economic levers to guide society and the economy to benefit both the nation and people. The third-best economic policy was that by means of education, the state encouraged people to engage in certain economic activities and discouraged them from inappropriate economic behavior. The fourth-best economic policy was that through coercive measures such as the law, the state-regulated people's economic activities. The worst economic policy was that the state directly engaged in economic activities and competed with people for profits.[21] This economic management view took "making the family rich" as the source and core. In their opinion, good economic management should make both the country and family rich because "making the family rich" was the foundation of "making the country rich."

The theory that the best economic policy was to conform to the natural development of folk production and trade activities opposed that the state directly manages the industry and commerce to profit. First, in their opinion, engaging in profitable production and trade was a private matter. If the regime and its officials engaged in this kind of activity, it took the interests originally belonging to the private and competed with the people for profit, which was the worst economic policy. Second, commerce would undoubtedly be combined with power and create a

[21] Sima, Q. (1994). *Shi Ji, Huozhi Liezhuan* (Shi Ji: Biographies of Merchants, 史记·货殖列传). Nanjing: Nanjing University Press, p. 1597.

monopoly if the state was engaged in business, which would increase the price of second-rate products and cause popular discontent.

Since they emerged in the Western Han Dynasty (206 BC–AD 24), the theory of valuableness and cheapness and the theory that the best economic policy was to conform to the natural development of folk production and trade activities became the basic models of traditional economic management thought in China. Hereafter, various economic management perspectives in ancient China could not eliminate the scope of these two models. In general, national economic management thought that advocated state control and intervention in the economy dealt with the inheritance, development, and revision of the theory of valuableness and cheapness. In addition, economic management thought that opposed state intervention in the economy and required the state to adopt a laissez-faire approach to private economic activities was more influenced by the theory that the best economic policy was to conform to the natural development of folk production and trade activities, representing the inheritance, development, and revision thereof. In these two basic modes, the local government preferred interventionism because it conformed to the governor's need to maintain and strengthen the rule. However, after intervening for a period and especially under the emergence of corrupt practices (the inefficiency of government-run industry and commerce, and people had nothing to depend on for their livelihoods), people often criticized the interventionism under the laissez-faire banner.

These two theories strongly influenced the conflict between the "official" and "commercial" Westernization of modern enterprises in China. Other influences included Western culture, the opposition of the Westernization Group to official industrial policy, and the economic development of the West. However, without an in-depth understanding of Western culture in modern China, when discussing the Western experience, which was often based on perceptual rather than rational knowledge, they opposed the official policy and applied the theory of the best economic policy was to conform to the natural development of folk production and trade activities as their theoretical basis.

Guo Song-Tao strongly opposed government-run industrial policy in the article *On the Imitated West Act with Friends* in the 1860s: "People can benefit from natural resources by themselves and do not need the government's intervention. If the resources are all explored by the government, it may hurt people's livelihoods and interrupt many things.

People will not obey the government, and the officials will get less profit too, which will cause a great waste of resources."[22] Reflected here are two important points on state intervention in the best economic policy theory: One is the inefficiency of government-run enterprises, where more losses than gains are made. The other is that officers should not compete with the public for profit. The conservatives interpreted this in the opposite way to the Westernization thinkers, believing that "official merchants running businesses deprive people from their livelihood."[23] However, their starting point also differed from that of the Westernization thinkers.

17.3 The Westerners in China and the Formation of Modernization Thought

If the Westernization Movement's views regarding the rise and development of power stemmed from the spirit of Confucianism, which viewed the world's development as its own, and the conflict between "official/government-run" or "commercial" enterprises was based on traditional economic thought, thus the content of the Westernization Movement's views on modernization depends on the spread of Western culture.

The knowledge diplomatic envoys and overseas students took back influenced people's perceptions. According to statistics, more than 800,000 Chinese had engaged in foreign visits, studies, business, and working abroad in the late 1870s. However, Western people in China played a more important role in promoting the formation of the Westernization Movement and development, and were the largest source of information in this regard.

Reportedly, during the Westernization Movement, a large number of Westerners lived and worked in China. Some were diplomats; some were specialists that accepted government employment in terms of taxation, in the military, industrial construction, and other aspects; More of them as the role of missionaries to participate in the field of culture and education or engaged in translating and publishing activities. They did much work in terms of introducing Western science and technology achievements,

[22] Guo, S. (1984). *Guo Songtao Shiwen Ji, Juan Shisan* (Guo Songtao Anthology, vol. 13, *郭嵩焘诗文集, 卷13*).

[23] Fang, J. *Erzhixuan Wencun, Jiqi Lun, Juan Yi* (Machine, *二知轩文存·机器论, 卷1*).

impacting the political, economic, and cultural dimensions, as well as current events coverage, opening the gate to increase the Westernization thinkers' knowledge of Western culture.

Western Diplomats in China and the Formation of Modern Thought

During the Westernization Movement, Western people in China provided the Qing Government with recommendations and advice. The first books proposing recommendations for reforms in China's internal and Foreign Affairs, which had considerable influence on the merging of the formation of modern thought, were Hart's—a Brit working in the taxation department—*Outside Sitting on the Sidelines* and the acting Foreign Minister of the United Kingdom Thomas F. Wade's *The New Discussion*. Their main points are summarized below.

First, the nominal standards of whitewashing and endemic corruption had put China into a dangerous situation.

Hart and Wade criticized the Chinese bureaucracy's corruption, highlighting that province officials "pay less attention to duty and more to private business," while capital officials "have so many areas to manage they have no time to perform their own duties. Some officials ask for money and decide whether to agree or disagree based on the bribe they get from people, leading to the criticism of even fair and just local officials." They also lambasted the army's lack of fighting capacity: "Soldiers lack real practice on using the bow and lifting stone, and only feed the birds to enjoy themselves." In addition, they emphasized that the traditional education system provided knowledge that could not be put into practice: "They are good at writing articles and poetry, but do not know how to respond to and deal with things they should know if they become officials."

Furthermore, they believed that "many wrong things caused the tamest people in China turmoil."[24] If the situation was not changed, China would be divided. "When China suffers and faces interventions from other countries, will it rule itself or be divided, becoming the property of other countries? Of course, the latter is the answer."

Second, China did not appropriately deal with Foreign Affairs.

[24] Hart, R. *Juwai Pangguan Lun, Chouban Yiwu Shimo, Tongzhi Chao, Juan Sishi* (History of Diplomatic Affairs in Late Qing Dynasty [Tongzhi], *局外旁观论, 筹办夷务始末, 同治朝, 卷40*), pp. 14-18.

Hart and Wade noted that after decades of interacting with foreigners in China, the Qing government was not able to appropriately deal with foreigners and foreign equities, leading to many disputes and losses. "Officials treated foreigners like dogs, because these officials lacked wisdom and strength."[25]

Third, China must reform.

They insisted that China must reform, stating that if the old laws did not change, "within a few years, China will be ruled by many nations." At that time, if foreigners implemented political reform, "foreigners were employed and paid money while they leave China aside. Was that independence?"[26]

Fourth, if China wants to safeguard national independence, it must learn from Western reform to ensure Self-Strengthening and to live in harmony with foreign countries.

They contended that "China's independence lies in the following things: First, implementing reform to thrive while avoiding disadvantages. Second, try to establish peaceful relationships with other countries. Even if China cannot send ambassadors to another country, they should enter into agreements and enact rules to reduce their doubts."[27] They also thought that peaceful relationships with Western countries hinged on "acting as per the agreement."

Hart and Wade's suggestion profoundly impacted the Qing reforms. The Premier Government permitted central and local officials to discuss their suggestions, which had a great influence. However, the spread of these views made those worried about their motherland concerned about learning from the Western countries. In 1874, *The Globe Magazine* published the two recommendations again, making its impact greater. We know that China is pushed to the world political and economic stage without proper preparation. Facing new requirements of the times, the

[25] Hart, R. *Juwai Pangguan Lun, Chouban Yiwu Shimo, Tongzhi Chao, Juan Sishi* (History of Diplomatic Affairs in Late Qing Dynasty [Tongzhi], *局外旁观论, 筹办夷务始末, 同治朝, 卷40*), pp. 15-16.

[26] Wade, T. F. *Xomzheng Lunlue, Chouban Yiwu Shimo, Tongzhi Chao, Juan Sishi* (History of Diplomatic Affairs in Late Qing Dynasty [Tongzhi], *新政论略, 筹办夷务始末, 同治朝, 卷40*), p. 22.

[27] Wade, T. F. *Xomzheng Lunlue, Chouban Yiwu Shimo, Tongzhi Chao, Juan Sishi* (History of Diplomatic Affairs in Late Qing Dynasty [Tongzhi], *新政论略, 筹办夷务始末, 同治朝, 卷40*), p. 35.

Qing government and its management started planning for Westernization. The Premier Government did not have the ability to implement the programmed action programs. At that time, only the domestic scholars Feng Guifen and Guo Songtao proposed a relatively realistic reform program, and Guo's recommendations were buried in the archives of the Premier Government. Feng's "*Xiaobinlu kangyi*" (Essays of Protest) is the only version that was disseminated. Its "Learn from Other Countries" and "Harmony as One Country" echoes the Hart and Wade recommendations. Since after the Second Opium War, the Western powers in China improved their status, the Hart and Wade's recommendations drew the attention of Chinese officials. Certainly, their recommendations played a positive role in the rise of the Westernization of modern ideology; thus, these are two important documents in the beginning of Westernization thought.

Missionaries in China and the Development of the Westernization Thinkers' Views on Modernization

Missionaries from many countries lived across China during the Westernization Movement.

As with any human population, some Western missionaries in China were good and others were not. However, under the historical condition in which China knew little about the outside world, people seldom understood foreign languages cultured Western missionaries did much work to facilitate communication between the Chinese and Western cultures. Until the twentieth century, as more intellectuals with knowledge of Western languages and culture as well as the sciences appeared, their roles as a "bridge" and "window" gradually disappeared.

They established a number of schools to teach people Western knowledge, marking the beginning of modern education in China. According to statistics, in 1875, there were nearly 800 such schools with approximately 20,000 students. By 1899, the number of schools had increased to 2,000 with around 40,000 students. These students provided favorable conditions for the modernization of Westernization. Later, some became successful luminaries in some fields, such as Rong Hong (Yung Wing), Ma Jianzhong, and Wu Tingfang.

They established the foundation of current news and the press. Until 1890, 60% "of the 76 newspapers are Church Newspapers.[28] Among them, most are propaganda newspapers with less or no cultural value. There are also magazines such as *Chinese Industrial and Scientific Magazine* mainly aimed at introducing science and technology knowledge. However, most disseminate religious propaganda, and cover articles on science and technology and politics. *Multinational Communiqué* is an example." In addition to editing newspapers, the Western missionaries also wrote books, and according to incomplete statistics in 1878, they "love to write all kinds of books such as on astronomy, geography, science, medicine, and arithmetic."[29] According to the *Anthology of East and Western Countries* written by Xu Weize in 1899, 571 books introduced Western science in the nineteenth century, of which 462 (81%) were Western people's translations (most in cooperation with the Chinese). As such, before the 1890s, the main role of the Western people in China was introducing China to the West.

According to the missionaries' activities, the following aspects were involved in the modernization of Westernization:

First, we must fully and seriously learn from Western countries to become prosperous and strong.

The prosperous and strong the Westernization Movement pursued referred to the state of the Western capitalist countries. Thus, Western people established subjects such as "wealth strategies" and so on in new types of schools. They considered learning from the West as the only way to realize country prosperity. "Those who think Western learning is not suitable in the current situation are wrong."[30] This was the general perception of both the Chinese and Western people in China at the time. They only differed in terms of what and how to learn from the West.

It was known that the Westernization Movement could go in the wrong direction. In 1875, Lin Lezhi(Young John Allen) pointed out: "If we wrongly think by recruiting many soldiers, and widely purchase ships and guns, this will be like a donkey in the skin of a lion, and sooner or

[28] (1891, Sep). *The Review of the Times*, Vol. 32, p. 11.

[29] Muirhead, W. (1878, Nov 16). *Lun Zhonghua Jinyou Zhishi, Juan Wuyisi, Wanguo (论中华今有之事). The Globe Magazine*, Vol. 514, p. 197.

[30] Author (1881, Nov 19). *Xi Xixue Buyi Zhuanxi Xixue Shuo (习西学不宜专习西文说,). The Globe Magazine*, Vol. 665, p. 128.

later, we will be eaten by the lion."[31] At that time, only Guo Songtao, Wang Tao, and a few Chinese citizens were aware of the problem.

Their views focused on prosperity as the basis of strength. To become prosperous, we must engage in mining, fix the roads, establish factories, and develop trade. Thus, we need talent, and we must learn Western science and technology. Therefore, it is urgent to translate books and establish new kinds of schools. To realize these aspects, the political reform is needed, and we must improve the work between the central and local governments, solve problems pertaining to the barriers between the monarch and people and their lack of trust in the government, and deal with officials who follow the old rules and do not want our country to become prosperous and strong by changing extant laws. In criticism, they noted that the Qing government "thinks new knowledge alone can help them become strong. However, states set up weapons based on laws developed by scholars, which often change and become more subtle. If China merely follows the pattern of Western law without establishing new schools, I am concerned the dream of strong soldiers cannot be realized. Thus, knowledge is not only good for the military, but also for a peaceful and prosperous society."[32] However, these recommendations were not accepted.

Second, oppose the government-run route and advocate developing private capitalism.

Westerners in China opposed the military-oriented course of modernization Westernization, maintaining that government-run businesses were prone to corruption. Thus, they proposed changing course and establishing commercial-run ventures.

First, they considered developing trade and market mechanisms as key to developing the economy. Lin Lezhi (Young John Allen) wrote in 1876: "The planting and manufacturing technologies are advanced, while the goods are not easy to be sold, and consumers are not easy to get. This is because the trade does not obey the rules! The demand of trade must be recognized before planting and manufacturing. Trade between provinces and the world is good. If you want to know a country is strong or not and whether the people benefit or not, you should first observe their

[31] Allen, Y. J. (1875, Dec 25). *Zhongxi Guanxi Luelun, Zongjie Qianlun (中西关系略论·总结前论)*. *The Globe Magazine*, Vol. 368, p. 245.

[32] Matter, C. W. (1881, Sep 3). *Zhenxin Xuexiao Lun, Cuowu (振兴学校论·错误)*. *The Globe Magazine*, Vol. 654, p. 30.

trade law."[33] Key to economically transitioning a medieval to modern society is pushing all of society's products to the commodity economy through exchange. Many Westernization bureaucrats did not have much knowledge on the modern capitalist economy, for example, they only knew about modern Western technology, namely that "new technology and skills" were better than the traditional government-run handicraft industry in China but did not know that different operating mechanisms are applied.

Then, they repeatedly advocated supporting the development of the private economy. They used examples from Europe and the United States to demonstrate that commerce should be relied on to develop the economy: "As to things that people can do by themselves such as make ships or construct railways, the Court should not forbid them, but help them with money if they lack capital."[34] Regarding the challenges of the lack of funds and unsustainability of the military industry, they compared China and the West, pointing out that the difficulty stemmed from the Qing government's different approach to economic development. According to Mu Weilian (Wiliam Murihead), "The Chinese and foreigners have different methods. As to big events and benefits, China depends on the government, which is difficult to perform. Western countries depend on people. For example, when constructing the railway, those with the land run it. People pay tax to the government while increasing their own wealth as well." Thus, the way to solve the problem of capital is to approach businessmen in China. "If China needs capital, why loan it from other countries? China has many rich businessmen. They hide because they are afraid of barriers." It is important to remove their doubt and make them believe "there are no barriers to running a business. In this way, they will feel at ease and help out."[35]

For the same reason, they sharply criticized the Westernization officials' suppression of civil capital development. "To open new work such as mining, the railways, trains, or manufacturing, they must first report to the Registrar for approval. If they do it privately, they may be punished, so people dare not do that. If China suppresses people's thoughts and

[33] Allen, Y. J. (1876, Dec 16). *Zhongxi Qiangguo Limin Lun (强国利民论). The Globe Magazine*, Vol. 418, p. 234.

[34] (1875, Jun 26) *Limin Zhi Zheng (利民之政). The Globe Magazine*, Vol. 342, p. 580.

[35] Muirhead, W. (1878, Aug 3). *Gong Bao Mou Yan (公报牟言). The Globe Magazine*, Vol. 500, p. 687.

blocks everything that helps them thrive, how can it become wealthy?"[36] It must be pointed out that the phrase "do after approval" is not the so-called industrial and commercial registration according to the law that Western countries use now, but the officials randomly tackling things they do not like. Before and after the 1894–1895 Sino-Japanese War, they noted that "things such as railways, ships, manufacturing, and mining can all be done by the people. The government only needs to enact regulations and afford a credit card. When talking about the current situation, all the world is the so-called railway wheels manufacturing mining companies. If the company was not forewarned, the government has no need to examine it. There is no such thing as China's officials causing trouble or being corrupt. There is also nothing regarding setting up a special department to purchase merchant ships and appoint a general official."[37] The corruption of government officials as well as the monopolies and interventions in enterprises were the actions the Qing government took for granted in daily life.

Third, introduce modern economic knowledge, and advocate determining and improving economic efficiency.

The running of any social or economic system depends on appropriate guidance. Advanced Chinese intellectuals in the nineteenth century considered Western capitalism as a model of prosperity, but they had limited knowledge of the system. The Western people in China helped fill this gap.

They focused on Adam Smith's theory of economic freedoms, and introduced the division of labor, capital, wages, rent, profit, interest, and the economic cycle as capitalistic economic concepts, hoping that China would focus on economic liberalism toward modernization. British missionary Joseph Edkins wrote: "In the British, *The Wealth of Nations written by* Adam Smith illustrated clearly about the economic principles, which is the reason why the United Kingdom flourished. His books make people aware of the benefits of not banning trade and having no fixed limits on work. This book had been published for more than a century.

[36] Muirhead, W. (1878, Nov 23). *Lun Zhonghua Jinyou Zhishi (论中华今有之事). The Globe Magazine*, Vol. 515, p. 198.

[37] Allen, Y. J. (1894, Jul). *Yingguo Tielu Kao (英国铁路考). The Review of the Times*, Vol. 66, p. 4.

What a pity that so many people do not admire his law and oppose his thoughts!"[38]

For the practical aspects of economic life, they introduced practical knowledge including the regulation of banks and companies, currency unification and distribution, establishing a budget and final accounts for the modern financial system, and a financial and accounting system compatible with capitalism. They also introduced a labor dispute and conflict resolution mechanism and cooperation between the economy and other fields of knowledge to prevent intensified social conflicts.

Their main concerns were the economic benefits of investment. When some enterprises successfully organized a public offering plan in the early 1880s, they reminded the government to prevent misuse while boosting the benefits. "If China uses improper officials, more disadvantages will appear and the benefits will decrease or disappear. Investors will be dissatisfied and may invest in other fields, and there will be no way to like today's situation."[39] They also highlighted investigating the market, calculating the current product market and future sales, and locating a factory as close as possible to the source of raw materials before operating a business. In 1878, when Zuo Zongtang's machine-woven bureau was prepared to establish in Lanzhou, they stressed, "This is useless and may be harmful." The first reason was that government-run enterprises had many disadvantages, and in countries such as Germany, weaving bureaus were set up by private capital. Another reason was that "as the bureau is set up in Gansu Province, it can only benefit one province. If it is set up and sells goods to other provinces, it will cost a lot in transportation. Thus, the bureau will lose money and be blamed for wasting the country's tax. If so, this will be a heavy burden for China."[40] However, Zuo Zongtang ignored their recommendations and went his own way. When the factory was operating in 1880, more than half the machines remained unused, and as water and raw material could not be guaranteed, the business deteriorated. The bureau had to shut down in 1883, with a loss of 1,390,000 silver dollars.

[38] Edkins, J. (1892, Aug). *Fuguo Yangmin Ce (富国养民策). The Review of the Times*, Vol. 43, p. 10.

[39] (1882, Dec 16). *Kuangwu Yi Yongren Wei Zuiyao Lun (矿务以用人为最要论). The Globe Magazine*, Vol. 719, p. 164.

[40] (1878, Sep 14). *Zhongguo Nikai Zhini Ju (中国拟开织呢局). The Globe Magazine*, Vol. 505, p. 58.

Fourth, they advocated self-reliance while actively using foreign capital and technology.

The Western missionaries suggested that China should follow the international practice and extend the use of foreign funds. With the railways as example, "States on the West of Thailand constructed the railways to benefit merchants. Where local production is not essential, many have set up companies in other countries to do so. Countries who can afford capital repay it through the benefits of the railway, and those with railways paid trade taxes, meaning equal interests for both."[41]

In the 1870s, upon the Japanese invasion, the question of how to develop and defend Taiwan emerged. Some Westerners in China recommended establishing special economic zones: "Taiwan is a lonely island overseas with a different situation. It has abundant prosperity, but fewer goods to ship. I want to ask the local government to release tax rates to attract prosperous trade. This will attract many merchants. You could also develop planting, divide the land among the people, and change the platform within three years."[42] For China with its lower funds, this program would help develop the border areas.

While promoting foreign investment in China's opening, they insisted that the country become self-reliant and noted that a country causes "its own strengths or weaknesses,"[43] "The government reduces the strength of China's influence."[44]

Furthermore, to pursue profits, they called on China to actively develop mining and transportation companies and to trade at home and abroad. For example, they thought China should engage in mining: "If you import iron from England, it only benefits the people of that country. If China does its own mining, it will save the money of many bureaus and enable selling the iron to Western countries, thus benefiting from them." In another example, China is rich in gold, silver, and copper mining. "If China can explore these markets and meet the demands of tax, and cast

[41] (1974, Dec 5). *Kai Moxige Tielu Xingli (开墨西哥铁路兴利)*. *The Globe Magazine*, Vol. 314, p. 192.

[42] (1878, Sep 7). *Minsheng Chuanzheng Bingni Fangzhao Geguo Zhuanshang Yishu Shuo (闽省船政并拟仿照各国专尚艺术说)*. *The Globe Magazine*, Vol. 504, p. 48.

[43] Beijing Yizhizi. (1880, Dec 4). *Lun Xianjin Zhongguo Zhishi (论中国现今之势)*. *The Globe Magazine*, Vol. 617, p. 145.

[44] Muirhead, W. (1878, Jul 13). *Guanai Zhonghua Disan Shu (关爱中华第三书)*. *The Globe Magazine*, Vol. 497, p. 645.

gold, silver, and copper coins for the market and benefit of the people, it will not all depend on the silver dollars of Western countries." Besides, "Western people mainly sell goods to China. If we manufacture our own, the goods will be cheaper and the costs will be lower. Furthermore, there is no need for shipping. The price will be cheaper than in Western countries, so how would they enjoy all the benefits?" In addition, we should "encourage people to set up companies on their own and buy ships to transport goods and visitors via the river. The bigger ships can also sail to other oceans and ship goods to European countries. Gradually, China will gain many benefits."[45]

Although none of the Western people in China was an economist, but as the heterogeneous culture nurtured maturing intellectuals, they gained more understanding of the new system that China implemented in the nineteenth century. Compared with the route the Westernization officers implemented, their views were superior and responded to the perspectives of the Westernization thinkers. Obviously, their recommendations were not perfect. For example, their limitations included investment and a quick profit for the light industry, but neglected the textile industry. They criticized Foreign Affairs bureaucrats' focus on military equipment, but also over-emphasized projects needing a lot of capital such as the railways, coal, and iron.

Fifth, they suggested advancing political reform.

As pioneers actively learning from the West, when discussing eliminating China's weaknesses, the Westerners in China advocated reform to decrease the corruption rampant in the bureaucratic authoritarian regime.

When Westernization officers were purchasing ships and cannons, and they believed this would boost their power, missionaries from the West since the 1870s revealed that bureaucratic stupidity and corruption enshrouded the new military in danger. "If nobody uses useful things, these useful things are useless."[46] The situation in the navy was that "those in charge of the ship are chosen from among those with relationships with officials, and they go to the ship only once a day and even once a month. They know almost nothing about the affairs of the ship.

[45] (1878, Oct 12). *Zhongguo Weili Sou Lun (中国为利薮论). The Globe Magazine*, Vol. 509, p. 114.

[46] (1875, Jul 3). *Zhongguo Yanpin Li Jiangjun (中国延聘李将军). The Globe Magazine*, Vol. 343, p. 594.

If they must go to war, maybe they will know what to do."[47] This was about 14–20 years before the 1894–5 Sino-Japanese War.

The corruption at all levels was even more serious. "Once seduced by benefits, they lose their principles and stop at nothing to get what they want."[48] "At this time, a lot of revenue is charged when people have disputes. When jailed, the jail keeper insults them first and then charges them money. After giving him money, the people can come freely in and out. This happens frequently."[49] The relationship between officials and the people was sharply so that many businesses closed down.

At that time, the officials were paid a very low salary, and corruption was a public secret. However, diplomats who earned good salaries were also corrupt. There were numerous inept officials in various departments. A newspaper in London criticized China's British Embassy in the UK: "Chinese business in the UK is exclusive. The Chinese embassy does not have that much to do, although the number of those working there is more than all the people from the Russian, French, German, American and Italian embassies combined. This not only costs a lot of money, but may also lead to trouble."[50]

They pointed out the relationship between the monarch, officials, and people were in a state of obstruction, which was causing corruption. Lin Lezhi (Young John Allen) noted, "A country may be in danger if the monarch is alienated from the people. If the monarch lives in his palace and the people in the countryside, but they do not connect with each other, the country will be poor and the people will be weak. Only the officials will benefit. If so, the country is in trouble. Thus, the monarch should deal with the relationship between the people and officials."[51] To address this problem, they made recommendations for political reform, mainly regarding the democratic system. According to Lin Lezhi (Young

[47] (1881, Jan 22). *Lun Shuishi Dangqiu Jiashi Zhanjianyuan Mou (论水师当求驾驶战舰员牟)*. *The Globe Magazine*, Vol. 624, p. 208.

[48] Muirhead, W. (1878, Nov 16). *Shoulun Zhonghua Qianxing Zhishi (首论中华前行之事)*. *The Globe Magazine*, Vol. 514, p. 184.

[49] Muirhead, W. (1878, Nov 23). *Shoulun Zhonghua Qianxing Zhishi (首论中华前行之事)*. *The Globe Magazine*, Vol. 515, p. 198.

[50] (1890, Jan). *Yihua Rong Yuan (议华冗员)*. *The Review of the Times*, Vol. 12, p. 24.

[51] Allen, Y. J. (1875, Oct 9). *Zhongxi Guanxi Lun Lue (中西关系论略)*. *The Globe Magazine*, Vol. 357, p. 78.

John Allen), democracy is "employed in many countries West of Thailand, and I do not know if China can use it."[52] The recommendation was an important symbol, but superficial in terms of people's knowledge of demanding that China instills a democratic system.

Initially, the Western people in China spread Western knowledge and skills to improve their own nations' business to better develop the market. After all, only through China's reform could the country become a member of the world market system of Western capitalism. Therefore, many proposed meeting the requirements of Westernization modern development. Their work to introduce Western knowledge and skills greatly contributed to inspiring Chinese thought and promoting modern Westernization. This was possible because they were intellectuals belonging to and influenced by another civilization. As they stood in the giant of the capitalist world, they could make useful recommendations for the modernization of the Westernization Movement. According to Hart, "The dwarves on a long man's shoulder can see farther than the long man. Obviously, this benefits the development of the modernization of Westernization." Whether Westernization officers or Westernization thinkers at that time, all gained knowledge and were inspired by them, and the thinkers were particularly enlightened. In Zheng Guanying's book, *Spirit of prophecy*, he appendixes many works of Westerners in China, providing sound evidence of their impact on him. Second, Westernization factions used as the basis for their arguments the fact that society worshiped all things foreign. This enabled them to gain the support of public opinion and help advance the cause of Westernization modernization.

[52] Allen, Y. J. (1875, Oct 9). *Zhongxi Guanxi Lun Lue (中西关系论略)*. *The Globe Magazine*, Vol. 357, p. 78.

CHAPTER 18

Ideological Evaluation of the Westernization Movement

The rise of the Westernization Movement in the late Qing Dynasty is the outcome of the knock-on effects of "eternal transformation" in modern times that reflect the transition of an agricultural to industrial society. However, based on the perspective of the history of economic ideology, how should the Westernization Movement be evaluated? Why should it be replaced by the views of the Reformists? This chapter will analyze these issues.

18.1 Acknowledging the Modern Economy

In the views of the sources of wealth in the industrial and commercial modern society, the Westernizationists implemented changes from circulation to production; in other words, changes from "mercantilism" to "industrialism."

As is known, in the history of economics, the first discussion of a capitalist economy is mercantilism. According to Marx, mercantilism was "the first theoretical discussion on modern production methods."[1] It conforms to the point that the only form of wealth is currency, and analyzing the growth of wealth from circulation, considers foreign trade the only source

[1] Marx, K. (1953). *Ziben Lun, Di San Juan* (Das Kapital, Vol 3, 资本论, 第3卷). Beijing: People's Publishing House, p. 376.

J. Zhou, *Westernization Movement and Early Thought of Modernization in China*, Palgrave Studies in Economic History,
https://doi.org/10.1007/978-3-030-86985-4_18

of wealth. To increase the wealth of a country, a surplus in foreign trade must be maintained to ensure the increased domestic inflow of gold and silver.

In the process of national transformation from an agricultural to industrial society, what would the theoretical form of mercantilism apply to? Here, developed commercial capital is a must to bridge an agricultural and industrial economy. Commercial capital has the force to break up an agricultural economy through the combination of a means of production based on labor and land, thus creating the conditions for the capitalist mode of production. Marx said: "The process of creating capital relations can only be the process that separating the laborers and its conditions. On one hand, this process transforms social subsistence and production into capital, and on the other, transforms direct producers into employed workers."[2] Unlike the mercantilism in Western Europe, that in China did not develop from a commodity economy but was generated in the process of foreign trade. Owing to the severe long-term foreign trade deficit, the people who concerned about China's destiny and prosperity, especially considering the economic problems stemming from foreign trade circulation. To solve this deficit problem, they believed that learning from the Western means of machine production should be linked. This led the Westernizationists to combine the revitalization of commerce to the detriment of art, and emphasize the commercial economy. Mercantilism included industrial and commercial capitalism, laying the foundation of the sources of growth in national wealth, which transitioned from circulation to production.

Xue Fucheng proposed on one hand that "businessmen grip the key of four classes," because they can "enable officials to put their knowledge into practice and obtain more knowledge. Farmers can transport the crops via businessmen and obtain a better harvest, and workers can sell their artifacts and in that way, increase production." On the other hand, he proposed "utilizing business based on industry," stating, "Western societies are always based on industry and commerce. They serve industry as their national rules and commerce as operational methods. Thus, industry

[2] Marx, K. & Engels, F. (1972). *Makesi Engesi Xuanji, Juaner* (Selected Works of Karl Marx and Frederick Engels, Vol.2, 马克思恩格斯选集, 卷2). Beijing: People's Publishing House, p. 220.

has priority over commerce."[3] Furthermore, Zheng Guanying advanced a "Commercial War," a popular notion in the late 19th and early twentieth centuries. He argued, "If we do not revitalize our business, the greedy invasions of the West will not stop. Thus, I contend it is better to learn from the commerce than from military."[4] Meanwhile, he also proposed the concept of the "self-made machine," explaining, "People only know to buy the machine, not that the machine can be produced by their own hands and be continuously used. It is better to establish a factory specializing in machines, select machines that have been used before, and to purchase other types of machines that have not been used before when imitating their ways."[5] According to Marx, "Large-scale industry must master its unique means of production, that is, the machine itself, using machines to create machines. In that way, large-scale industry is able to build the foundation of skills adapted to itself."Zheng Guanying's "self-made machine" has great significance in the history of China's modernization thought, indicating that the Chinese people, who were advancing toward a source of growth of national wealth, had been transitioning from circulation to production, and from mercantilism to industrialism.

After the Sino-Japanese War, capitalism in China ushered in its first golden period. The advancing Chinese people gained a better understanding of the new economic relationship in internal departments, and began to realize that the social source of wealth lies not in circulation, but in production. This led to the claim of the importance of developing a large-scale machine industry. At that time, Kang Youwei, Liang Qichao, Yan Fu, as well as Westernization representatives Zhang Zhidong, Li Hongzhang, and Zheng Guanying advocated the development of large-scale industrial machines. Kang Youwei and other reformers claimed that China should develop a large-scale machine industry. After comparing

[3] Xue, F. (1987). *Xue Fucheng Xuanji, Yingjili Liyong Shangwu Pi Huangdi Shuo* (Selected Works of Xue Fucheng, Discussion on England Using Business to Open up Wasteland, 薛福成选集·英吉利利用商务辟荒地说). Shanghai: Shanghai Renmin Chubanshe, p. 297.

[4] Zheng, G. (1982). *Zheng Guanying Ji,Shangzhan Shang, Shangce* (Zheng Guanying Works, Commercial War, Vol. 1, 郑观应集·商战上, 上册). Shanghai: Shanghai Renmin Chubanshe, p. 586.

[5] Zheng, G. (1982). *Zheng Guanying Ji Shangwuwu Shangce* (Zheng Guanying Works, Business Affairs V, Vol. 1, 郑观应集·商务五, 上册). Shanghai: Shanghai Renmin Chubanshe, p. 586.

China with Western countries and understanding the development trend of the times, they contended that this would position China as an industrial economy. Zhang Zhidong, Li Hongzhang, and Zheng Guanying, who engaged in businesses through practice and in fieldwork pertaining to foreign economic development, believed that the large-scale machine industry would lead the development of the national economy. Both political sides argued that large-scale industry would transform China, clearly reflecting the social transformation from an agricultural to industrial society in China's period of modernization. During the large-scale practice of modern industry and commerce, Zhang Zhidong produced a more systematic ideology of industrialism. According to him, "People said that the Western countries were rich in business but did not know that they are rich in the industry. Traders transported finished goods, while workers made unfinished goods. They refined crude goods to make them exquisite, changed the cheap into the expensive, and rendered waste useful. There are enough crafted goods to ensure businessmen have goods to sell."[6] Thus, for him, "chemical exploration should be prioritized, and mechanization dealt with last."[7]

After the First Sino-Japanese War, Li Hongzhang seldom directly engaged in economic activity. However, his views were changed by visiting Europe and the United States, as he realized that a modern economy needs coordinated development in agriculture, industry, and commerce. He vividly likened agriculture, industry, and commerce to three women, saying, "In the peaceful world, there are three beautiful women. That is agriculture, industry, and commerce. They struggled with each other, meaning a peaceful world can weigh a lot." On this basis, he believed China's economic development lagged behind that of the Western powers because it lacked the coordinated development of agriculture, industry, and commerce. Thus, "Although Chinese civilization had a great impact on the world, it cannot advance."[8] This indicates that the

[6] Zhang, Z. *Zhang Wenxianggong Quanji, Zunzhi Chouyi Bianfa Jinni Caiyong Xifa Shiyitiao Zhe, Juan Wushisi* (Collected Works of Zhang Wenxiang, Respect the West Methods in Eleven Items, Vol. 54, *张文襄公全集·遵旨筹拟变法谨拟采用西法十一条折, 卷*54).

[7] Zhang, Z. *Zhang Wenxianggong Quanji, Zouyi, Juanershiqi* (Collected Works of Zhang Wenxiang, Memorials, Vol.27, *张文襄公全集·奏议, 卷*27).

[8] Cai, R. *Li Hongzhang Liping Oumei Ji (李鸿章历聘欧美记)*. Changsha: Yuelu Press, p. 141.

future direction of China's economic development should be revitalized to the extent of that in the West.

A prolific thinker, Zheng Guanying's views continued developing after the Sino-Japanese war. In 1900, he published eight volumes of the "*Golden Age Prophecy*," in which he pointed out that "the reason the Western world is rich is that it relies on industry, not commerce. Businessmen transport finished goods, while workers create unfinished goods. They refined crude goods to make them exquisite, changed the cheap into the expensive, and rendered waste useful. Craftsmen make the goods, which are sold by merchants."[9] The words of Zheng Guanying and Zhang Zhidong are similar, highlighting the development of the large-scale machine industry, the notion of which had become more accepted among intellectuals.

In *Das Kapital*, Marx states, "The real economic science starts from the theoretical study when it transforms from the circulation toward production."[10] The transformation from mercantilism to industrialism in modernization ideology conforms to the rules of modern economic theory and indicates the transition of farming-centered thought to modern thought in China's economic thought.

The long-term change of the modern economy from mercantilism to industrialism revolved around the management of the country's economy and the role of government in the process of modern economic development. The Westernizationists also transitioned from a state-controlled economy to economic liberalism; that is, from "official control" to "listening to the people running the market."

The major features of mercantilism include that it requires national intervention in the economy, makes the protectionism policy external, and enables franchises and tax reductions to support internal private enterprises in developing their competitiveness. With the increase in the number of industrial enterprises and improvement of status in the national economy, the emerging bourgeoisie required fair internal competition and opposed various monopolies that restricted competition. Externally,

[9] Zheng, G. (1982). *Zheng Guanying Ji, Shangzhanshang Shangce* (Zheng Guanying Works, Skills, Vol. 1, *郑观应集·技艺, 上册*). Shanghai: Shanghai Renmin Chubanshe, p. 729.

[10] Marx, K. (1953). *Zibenlun, Disanjuan* (Das Kapital, Vol 3, *资本论, 第3卷*). Beijing: People's Publishing House, p. 376.

it required free trade to obtain the cheap raw materials industrial production required and opened up product selling markets. Adam Smith, the renowned scholar of economic liberalism, was their spokesperson. Smith believed that the invisible hands of the market would automatically lead the people to the pursuit of wealth, which would increase the welfare of the whole society. Furthermore, he posited that the state does not need to intervene in the economy, as it rather has to play the "watchman" and maintain market order. Smith's book, *The Wealth of Nations*, marked the ideological and theoretical maturation of the era.

At the beginning of Westernization in China, "Government Commerce Enterprises" was established that reflected the comprehensive national intervention in the economy and were generally welcomed by the community. Since the Qing government's economic policies did not permit people to setting up of mining and industry, traditional customs positioned modern technology as a "scourge" that would "impede the ordinary people's livelihood," "shake the earth," and "sabotage geomancy." This allowed the businessmen, bureaucrats, and landlords who had accumulated considerable wealth to invest in modern civil industry. This situation changed direction through the emergence of "government-supervised and merchant-managed" enterprises, which met their needs to gain high profits under official protection. According to Zheng Guanying, "business prospects with industry" and "officials control taxation." This indicated the significant role of private capital. However, with the increase of private desire and disappointment in the inefficiency of government enterprises, an increasing number of private capitalists began establishing factories in the early 1880s. To open the way for their own development, these private entrepreneurs criticized the monopoly policy of government-run enterprises, requiring that mining, shipping, and spinning be controlled by citizens to ensure "listening to the people" and opening without restrictions. Those businessmen who invested in government-supervised and merchant-managed enterprises first asked the government to appropriately delegate, and then that it eliminate businesses in micro-management areas. Instead, the government should create favorable conditions for the development of enterprises in macro-management areas such as drafting quotient laws, developing education, raising tariffs, improving transportation and communication facilities, and so on, which are in fact, the requirements of economic-liberal policies. Representatives of these notions include Zheng Guanying, Ma Jianzhong, Xue Fucheng, and Guo Songtao.

In the mid-1880s, some small and medium government-supervised and merchant-managed enterprises were a step ahead in the privatization path. In these companies, the merchants had mastered factory property rights, control and residual claims, the right to restrict officials' ability to maintain order, and suppressed workers' revolt, and asked the factory to sell a certain number of products at less than the market price. As such, these are the characteristics of private capitalist enterprises. After the Sino-Japanese War, the Qing government encouraged private businessmen and Chinese people abroad to take over the military industry, which was suffering losses. This meant many taboos affecting the development of private capital were no longer relevant, and the principles of economic liberalism had been implemented in wider and deeper practice. Government-run military and civilian enterprises, as well as government-supervised and merchant-managed companies, represented the growing trend of privatization. These were rented, sold, or contracted to merchants to operate, or parts of army factories were converted into civilian enterprises. In short, they sought to operate companies according to a modern enterprise business approach.

18.2 The Inevitability that Reformist Views Would Replace Westernization Thought

The Westernization Movement started from the study of the Western military and technology. However, it was accepted based on the current general social values and emotions because the value of social ethics at this level was low, disrupted, and impacted the core values of society, and was weak in terms of staving off resistance.

The Westernizationists could adhere to their beliefs and protect the inner structure of the cultural system without interference from Chinese traditional ethics. They were stubborn in fending off a resurgence of the old system, arguing, "We are talented people who oppose the dross of Tang, Yu, Shang, and Zhou for their bad habits."[11] However, with the constant introduction of Western knowledge, the conflict between new and traditional production methods increased. The Westernization modern view of "protecting the old with the new" could not resolve

[11] Zeng, J. (1984). *Zeng Jize Yiji, Lundun Zhi Ding Yusheng (曾纪泽遗集·伦敦致丁雨生)*. Changsha: Yuelu Press, p. 171.

this conflict, and it is impossible to expect "Chinese culture in Western use" to catapult China into industrialism. In this case, history shows the adoption of reforms to "clear the cobwebs and develop new things" to break the Westernization of the long-term uncoordinated state between China's structure and the knowledge of the West. It was advocated that China's traditional culture be guided by that from the West, which is aligned with the views of China's modernization development. Using Western knowledge to save China had become the mainstream approach. The Westernizationists had to follow the times, or they would be abandoned in history. After the Boxer Rebellion, they broke boundaries in terms of the "Western methods based on China's structure," advocating that China transform with Western rules. China's modernization entered a new chapter with the publication of the "new policy."

Constant reforms were contained in profound historical insights derived from the Westernization Movement. Marx and Engels, who co-conceptualized scientific socialism, explained the theory from different perspectives. Once the industry is stimulated, the consequences for all other departments will be positive as they grow based on that.[12] People change their mode of production by gaining new modes of production. As production changes, so too do the social relations among people.[13] However, the originators of manufacturing did not expect such impacts, and "certainly did not know and expect this innovation to lead to social consequences. There was no awareness that this 'minor' innovation would lead to the reconfiguration of social forces."[14] The direct purpose of their activity was to fend off foreign aggression. Thus, they were "often very thankful of state power," although they could not predict the profound social changes that occurred.

Westernization thinkers and officials were sincere when proposing "Western methods based on China's structure." They believed that

[12] Marx, K. & Engels, F. (1956). *Makesi Engesi Quanji, Di Yi Juan* (Collected Works of Karl Marx and Friedrich Engels, Vol. 1, *马克思恩格斯全集, 第1卷*). Beijing: People's Publishing House, p. 671.

[13] Marx, K. & Engels, F. (1956). *Makesi Engesi Quanji, Di Yi Juan* (Collected Works of Karl Marx and Friedrich Engels, Vol. 1, *马克思恩格斯全集, 第1卷*). Beijing: People's Publishing House, p. 108.

[14] Stalin, J. V. (1964). *Lun Bianzheng Weiwu Zhuyi He Lishi Weiwu Zhuyi* (On Dialectical and Historical Materialism, *论辩证唯物主义和历史唯物主义*). Beijing: People's Publishing House, p. 656.

"China can transform humble things with innovation, and surpass the West after a century."[15] They further thought that "rich customs and positive people would strengthen soldiers and the army, and the West would automatically be exploited by our hands."[16] However, any cultural system has integrity: "In a cultural conflict, once a minimum gap in social defense has been opened, one event will relentlessly continue to trigger another event."[17] Westernization led by the West "is a catalyst to compensating for the collapse of China's traditional society." Kang Youwei and other Westernizationists could stand on the shoulders of the Westernization Movement and claim dissatisfaction, which was caused by the opportunities of constant innovation and opening up.

Regarding introducing changes based on Western social ideas, Liang Qichao of the *Wuxu Reform* stated the following: "The country was deeply harmed in the early Tongzhi period. Zeng Guofan learned about the advantages of Western thought from their army. Officials were shamed regarding Westernization and did not agree with those discussing, as Westernization was considered the seed of evil." Into the 1870s, "Officials learning more about Westernization could no longer refuse it completely, and they became more willing to be open to it." By the 1890s, more views of Westernization emerged nationwide, including that the "Chinese have to restore the Old Country with new views." Even the Imperial champion realized, "From now on, the title is unreliable. People always need some Western knowledge to manage business to be able to amount to anything."[18] This reflected the growing momentum of Westernization on one hand, and on the other, showed that "Western thought based on China's structure" had lost the power that united society. Even the orthodox Confucian, Weng Tongsu and Sun Jianai, began to favor Westernization and reforms, and noted the increasing tendency of radical political issues. This indicates that the Westernization Movement had completed its historic mission and had to give way to social forces that

[15] Wang, T. *Gezhi Shuyuan Keyi (格致书院课艺)*.

[16] Wang, T. (1998). *Taoyuan Wenlu Waibian, Yangwu Xia* (Tao Yuan's Works of Foreign Affairs· Westernization II, 弢园文录外编·洋务下). Zhengzhou: Zhongzhou Ancient Books Publishing House, p. 83.

[17] Yoynbee, A. J. (1988). *Wenming Jingshou Zhe Kaoyan* (Civilization on Trial, 文化经受着考验). Hangzhou: Zhejiang People's Publishing House, p. 280.

[18] Zeng, P. *Nie Hai Hua (孽海花)*. As cited in Zhou, J. (1996). *Zuichu de Jiyuan* (The Beginning of the Era, 最初的纪元). Beijing: Higher Education Press, p. 154.

could lead China toward modernization. At the time, these new social forces could only be the Reformists of Kang and Liang. Although this power was a weak party composed of a group of scholars, which lacked the recognition and experience of other political and social forces, it represented China's future and hope. Since the Reformists of Kang and Liang left China's political arena, the country had been transformed, and they had become representative of mainstream thinking of Chinese intellectuals and unified the people. As a result, the ideology of "Chinese-style Westernization" became a historical term, dropping out of the stage of historical events.

CHAPTER 19

The Far-Reaching Impact of Westernization Movement

As the earliest modernization movement to learn from Western countries in modern China, the Westernization Movement had a far-reaching impact. Inspired by the reviewers, four topics will be discussed here. First, the development of economic thought, manufacturing, and entrepreneurship was ignited by the Westernization Movement. In specific, the Westernization Movement re-established the traditional Silk Road, which had been designed to promote trade between Asia and Europe, and meanwhile advanced the great development of the commodity economy since the Southern Song Dynasty. Second, the connection between the 1860 Westernization Movement and the 1978 Reforms and Opening-up. Third, the restrictions on the further development of China's economic thought. Fourthly, the rise of the Chinese merchant class and the transformation of ideology accompanied by the Westernization Movement.

19.1 The Westernization Movement and the Progress of China's Economic Thought

The trade between China and Europe has been developing since the Song and Yuan Dynasties, and it reached a peak during the Ming and Qing Dynasties. However, the living environment, business philosophy, and methods of the enterprises are pretty different after 1860.

J. Zhou, *Westernization Movement and Early Thought of Modernization in China*, Palgrave Studies in Economic History,
https://doi.org/10.1007/978-3-030-86985-4_19

First, the industrial revolution in Europe had not yet been completed during this period; both China and Europe were in the stage of manual production. The considerable population led to low labor costs and strong product competitiveness in China's commodities. Therefore, in the trade with Europe, China was on the surplus side while Europe was on the deficit side for a long time. Chinese products with good quality and low prices were popular among most countries globally. The Chinese tea, silk, porcelain, homespun, and so on became the bulk export commodities. A large amount of silver flowed into China, which made China abandon its paper money from Song Dynasty after the Middle Ming Dynasty. Silver became the basic monetary unit in China.

Second, China was in a closed state during this period. Although there was a large amount of trade between China and the rest of the world, mainly with Europe, the government did not allow foreign enterprises to trade in hinterland China. Instead, the trade could only be conducted with Chinese firms at prescribed trade ports; furthermore, the trade policy became tighter and tighter. During the reign of Emperor Kangxi, four trade ports were opened in coastal areas: Guangdong Customs (Guangzhou), Fujian Customs (Xiamen), Zhejiang Customs (Ningbo), and Jiang Customs (Shanghai). In Emperor Qianlong's reign, only one trade port of Guangdong Customs (Guangzhou) remained. This did not meet the needs of the era of increasingly developed social productivity and commodity economy, and it is also why the conflicts were inevitable between the European countries and China.

Third, affected by the closed-door policy, the domestic market competition in China was not fierce, the enterprise bankruptcy rate was not high, and the management methods were mainly unlimited liability. Suppose the workers and the upstream and downstream partners do not make significant mistakes. In that case, the long-term contracts should be entered, and enterprises will not dismiss employees or change partners easily. In terms of staff training, the apprenticeship of the master and the apprentice is adopted. The advantage of an apprenticeship is that it is easy to build relationships rather than a cold financial relationship. Moreover, the weakness is that this system is hard to standardize and inefficient in the age of mass production.

Fourth, credit lending is generally carried out in the financial sector instead of mortgage lending; The self-owned funds or partner funds are generally loaned out, and deposits are absorbed with a small scale; Reducing financial risks through blood relationships, laws, primarily through multiple religious beliefs of Confucianism, Buddhism, and Taoism. The ban on foreign companies that are not allowing trade in the hinterland of China guarantees the safety of domestic companies so that the bankruptcy rate is relatively low and credit lending can be maintained.

China's commodity economy was relatively developed during this period. Therefore, the Ten Great Merchant Guilds represented by Shanxi merchants and Huizhou merchants who carried out long-distance trade sprang up. They have carried out many innovations in logistics and capital flow, but because of limited vision, the innovations were restricted to the scope of one region. The recognition of globalization had not been formed, and the business model cannot be applied to a larger scope.

After 1860, the enterprise's living environment and management philosophy and methods had significant development. First, the Industrial Revolution in Europe had been completed at that time, and the competitive transition from manual production to machine production was extraordinarily strong. Thus, European countries have started to substitute imports from China for products made in Europe. Silk, tea, ceramics, cotton cloth, etc., which were imported from China in the past, can now be produced in large quantities and with lower cost and can be exported to China. This has dramatically impacted China's traditional economy and forced China from an exporter of finished products to an exporter of raw materials and a market for product sales.

Second, The Industrial Revolution forced China to move from a closed state to a complete opening state to Western countries; China opened up more trade ports and allowed foreign companies to invest, purchase, and sell in hinterland China.

Third, under the intense competition and stimulation of Western companies, Chinese companies have to learn from Europe to develop machine production. The Westernization Movement is to learn from the West and carry out the reform movement of machine production and factory production by Western methods. The corporate management mode transformed from unlimited liability to limited liability, shortening the contract period with employees and upstream and downstream partners and managing according to the contract. This is inseparable from the social reality of fierce global competition and a high corporate failure rate. At the same time, staff with professional skills will be cultivated to improve the enterprise's competitive advantage throughout modern education.

Fourth, it has generally moved from credit loans to mortgage loans in the financial sector. On the one hand, the higher risk of credit lending caused by the fierce competition among enterprises and the increased failure rate. On the other hand, a new financial format came from Europe, Bank, implementing the shareholding cooperation to expand its scale and released the mortgage lending to reduce the financial risks and improving its competitiveness. Under such circumstances, the traditional finance of China has begun to transform to modern finance, partnership system to shareholding system, implementing mortgage loans and extensive deposit absorption, etc.

In this period, China's commodity economy began to integrate with the world commodity economy and was affected by the trend of the world commodity economy. Although it suffered lots of failures in the initial period, it was stimulated by high profits brought by advanced science and technology and driven by the unwillingness of backwardness. The vision of entrepreneurs became wider; more entrepreneurs had a global perspective. They carried out machine production according to Western technologies, and their socialization was not high. In some areas, the student surpasses the master. Thus, the transformation from traditional merchants to modern merchants had started, and promoting the development of China's modernization.

19.2 The Connection Between the Westernization Movement in 1860 and the 1978 Reforms and Opening-up

After 1978, China ended its confrontation with the West and reopened to the West countries. China absorbed several technologies, capital, and management methods from the West and exported many commodities to the Western markets. This was another large-scale movement to learn from the West after 1860. The differences between the 1860 Westernization Movement and the in 1978 Reforms and Opening up are:

> First, during the 1860's opening up, China, were passive activities. China did not have the right of autonomy on tariffs. Therefore, China could not set appropriate tariffs based on the development level of social productivity and be unable to better promote the progress of the national industry. This is why China was called a dish of scattered sand before 1949 and why Chinese people launched

revolutions against imperialism. The 1978 Reforms and Opening-up were proactive. China already had autonomy on tariffs at that time. So that China can set up appropriate customs based on the development of national industries, it is important for China's rapid economic development since the 1978 Reforms and Opening up.
Second, when the Westernization Movement was launched in 1860, the rulers did not have enough understanding of the history of the development of the Western commodity economy since the Industrial Revolution. They mainly learned the technical and material aspects. They believed the Chinese traditional institution system and culture were good for the institutional side, and there was no need to learn from the West. This is Zhang Zhidong's theory of "Chinese learning as the body, Western learning for use," which seriously reduced the effect of the Westernization Movement. Thus, the Sino-Japanese War of 1894 was defeated by the small country, Japan. During the 1978 Reforms and Opening-up, the leaders of China were highly internationalized. The state leaders such as Deng Xiaoping and Chen Yun all had the experience of studying in France and the Soviet Union. They understood the gap between China and the West at that time, and they advocated learning from the West in all aspects of technology, economy, institution, and culture. The Reforms and Opening-up are centered on economic reforms; the reforms at the political and cultural levels have allowed reforms to proceed orderly. This is another crucial reason for the tremendous achievements of the 1978 Reforms and Opening-up.

With China's accession to the WTO in 2002, opening to the West has become more vigorous, and China has been able to develop rapidly and narrow the gap with the West. China is beginning to emphasize independent innovation, but the foundation of independent innovation is still based on actively learning European and American commercial civilization.

19.3 The Restrictions on the Further Development of China's Economic Thought

On learning from the West in modern China, what to learn and the extent it learned were firstly affected by the development of social productivity in a certain period. For example, during the Westernization Movement, China's industrial development policy took the military industry as the major industry. The main methods used were government-run or government-supervised and merchant-managed. Therefore, China has learned more about ships, ordnance, railways, telegraphs, steel production, etc., from the West. The objects of study were mainly European countries represented by Britain, Germany, and France, which are the first to industrialized. With the further deepening of China's industrialization, China's industrial form began to move from heavy industry to light industry, the operation form moved from government-run to private-run, and the content of learning naturally shifted to the field of light industrial production textiles and flour. Modern management knowledge such as the shareholding system and Taylorism entered China at this time. The objects of study have also been more diversified. There are not only European countries that are the first to achieve industrialization, but also countries such as the United States and Japan that have achieved industrialization lately.

On the other hand, the development of China's economic thought is also influenced by its deep-rooted cultural traditions. Unlike the cultural traditions of beyond-blood in Western society, the Confucian cultural traditions of blood ties prevailed in Chinese culture. Therefore, there will be a problem of localization of foreign economic management thoughts. In other words, the capital, technology, the equipment can be absorbed from abroad, and the raw material purchases and product sales can also deal with foreign countries. However, for the economic management system that combines human capital, financial and material resources, must also adopt a factory system compatible with machine production. To this end, it is necessary to study the West vigorously, but it must have a certain degree of localization, that is, to a certain extent, accept the local cultural traditions that emphasize blood and geography. This is the relationship between internationalization and localization. For example, when Zhang Zhidong established the Textile Bureau in Hubei, he considered the Chinese tradition of body contact as not allowed in handing over and taking over between men and women. He had to break the principle of mixing men and women in the workshop, which is popular and efficient in the West, putting the employees of the same gender in the same workshop. For another example, whether during the Westernization Movement or the 1978 Reforms and Opening up, the employees of some factories were generally recruited by the workshop supervisors using the cultural traditions of blood and geography, which means the employees of a certain workshop were all Cantonese, and the employees in the other workshop are all Hunanese. This is the reason why the term "Chinese-style Management" became famous.

With the deepening of China's globalization, its economic management system has become more international, but it still retains some native features. For example, the tradition of blood ties led to a solid emotional connection among Chinese people. The advantage of blood ties is called "A gentleman is ready to die for his bosom friends in ancient Chinese," which is conducive to improving work efficiency; the weakness is that the emotional connection is too strong to weaken the rationality, so the phenomenon of making institutional mistakes occur frequently, especially in the financial field. To solve this problem, we need to strengthen the system construction and assessment and establish the avoidance system to correspond with the particularity of Chinese culture, just like what China currently does. What to learn from the West, and how is the extent of learning affected by the specific stage of social and economic development, but also by the deep-rooted cultural traditions of the Chinese people.

19.4 The Rise of Chinese Merchant Class and the Transformation of Ideology Accompanied by the Westernization Movement

The Westernization Movement was a new trend in China due to the adoption of machine production and economic development by Western methods. Only the experienced businessman who adopted the new thoughts were willing to practice the Western methods. This mainly refers to comprador business people, overseas Chinese business people, and staff of Westernization officers who engaged in economic work, such as Sheng Xuanhuai and Li Jinyong. The modernization improved the status of these merchants and promoted them from the traditional merchants who worked on manual production to the modern merchants who worked on machine production, which also promoted the development of Chinese economic thoughts.

In traditional China, business people mainly improve their social status through donations. The donation system is a system in which the government exchanges official titles and honors for private wealth to solve financial problems. The donation system is fiscal and political. It is not only can improve government revenue but also can reserve talents in some particular regions for the government. Therefore, the donation system had gotten support from society and the public. It was the way for the civilians to improve their social status and a system for the government to mobilize the wealthy and wealthy to serve society and incorporate it into the scope of state management. It has "received support from the society, especially the general public."

In the Qing Dynasty, with the development of the commodity currency economy, the demand of industrialists and commercialists to improve their status became stronger. More people started to seek status and reputation improvement using the informal approach of donations instead of the formal imperial examinations. From the nation's point of view, only the donations from the public, especially the industrialists and commercialists who obtained a higher standard of living, can provide political and economic support, not the formal imperial examinations. Especially in the period of significant changes in modern Chinese society, the donation has also made significant contributions to attracting wealthy people into the ranks of gentlemen to expand the nation's reserve of human capital and improve the level of modern industrial and commercial management. This is because the development of social productivity and commodity currency economy not only request the government to expand investment in public goods such as transportation, communications, water conservancy, and disaster relief but also put forward the requirements for the scholars to apply their knowledge to the real world in the aspect of human resources. At that time, most intellectuals who were educated in the imperial examinations resisted social reforms; they thought China should stick to its old path. Thus, some geniuses who used informal donations to gain social status played an essential role in the Westernization Movement, such as Wei Yuan, Xue Fucheng, Ding Richang, Chen Chi, Huang Zunxian, Liu Jintang, Zhang Yinhuan, etc.

Li Hongzhang, the leader of the Westernization Movement, deeply regretted that the imperial examinations could not be used for the training of Westernization talents. He once advocated that to modify the imperial examinations to adopt the Westernization Movement. The donation system just made up for the imperial examination and collected many money and talents for the social reforms. Sheng Xuanhuai, Tang Tingshu, Xu Run, Zheng Guanying, Li Jinyong, Yan Xinhou, etc., who "set up the School for Training Translators, the Machine Manufacturing Bureau, and the China Merchants Steamship Navigation Company; opened up Coal and Iron Mines in Cizhou, Kaiping, Gold Mine in Mohe; constructed railways, electric wires, textile bureaus, and medical schools; purchase of warships; constructed dockyard terraces in Dagu, Lushun, and Weihai; sending officers to Germany to learn the military technologies; trading with Japan and Britain. Everything built is unprecedented." Many of the people who entered the ranks of bureaucracy through donations were merchants or local gentlemen; they had rich management experience and resource deployment capabilities. Therefore, the provincial governors who were devoted to the Westernization Movement at that time "donate with military service," which improved the donation system to a higher level at the end of the Qing Dynasty. Take China Merchants Steamship Navigation Company as an example; the donation rate was 83% among the senior managers from 1872 to 1890. In the Hubei Coal and Iron Bureau, founded in 1876, the number of people entering the management level through donations was similarly significant. In the first three years of its establishment, there was one alternate Tao-tai, three alternate prefects, 32 alternate Tong-Zhi, and one alternate deputy governor.

The late Qing Dynasty had a different approach to property rights protection from Western countries. The Western countries promoted the protection of property rights through franchise rights and constitutional democracy in the pre-industrial and industrial periods. In the late Qing Dynasty, modern industry and commerce promoted the protection of property rights by donating officials to improve their social status. The donation system has become a meaningful way to stimulate officials and gentlemen to participate in social-economic activities and promote modern industry and commerce development. According to Hao Yanping: "In the 40 famous compradors in Shanghai around 1900, at least 15 of them donated official titles, it is about 30% of the total number, and many people donated very high official titles." In this way, the merchants of the late Qing Dynasty communicated their political demands after becoming one of the bureaucratic systems. They played an essential role in Boycotted American Goods Activity in 1905, Reclaim Profits and Rights Movements, promotion of the constitutional reforms, the practice of local autonomy, and development of education and business, etc.

CHAPTER 20

The Qing Government and Westernization

The history of world economic development highlights the quality of government work and control of social resources in the transformation process. A high quality of government work provides the correct future direction, while strong government control means the ability to lead the national realization of development based on appropriate objectives. In short, only those with a strong modern orientation and strong government social control will be successful. A government with only one regime is unable to meet the conditions for success. Unfortunately, the late Qing government was neither modern-oriented nor characterized by a strong internal control regime. Thus, it was expected that the outcome of Westernization would be unsatisfactory.

20.1 Support from the Qing Government

Marx emphasized in *Communist Manifesto*, "The bourgeoisie, by the rapid improvement of all instruments of production and immensely facilitated communication, drew all nations, even the most barbarian, into civilization. Its low-price commodities could destroy all of the Great Wall and enable foreigners to conquer the barbarians' intensely obstinate hearts. It compels all nations to adopt the bourgeois mode of production in order that they not perish. This forces them to introduce what it

J. Zhou, *Westernization Movement and Early Thought of Modernization in China*, Palgrave Studies in Economic History,
https://doi.org/10.1007/978-3-030-86985-4_20

calls civilization in their own system, that is, to become bourgeois themselves."[1] Westernization is the "self-reliance" campaign with which the Qing government struggled. The government only supported Westernization to ensure death did not ensue from the needs of self-existence. Based on the deepening of foreign aggression, the Qing government's support of the Westernization Movement constantly grew.

As the final ruler of the late Qing Dynasty, the Empress Dowager Cixi was a shrewd and scheming ruler who understood the power behind the policy, not the policy itself. She was able to react quickly based on experience and relied on feeling rather than theories of domination to develop and adjust the rule policy. Certainly, she supported the rise of the Westernization Movement in the 1860s. Thus, while the Westernization Movement was attacked and hindered by multiple parties, its activities went uninterrupted, and it remained well known. Realizing Cixi's intention, Li Hongzhang stated a letter to Li Zongxi in January 1875, "The Empress Dowager summoned six times at 22, 23, and 26, respectively, showing ambitious ideals in this urgent situation." In the 11th Year of the Guangxu Reign (1885), in a letter to Zeng Guoquan, he revealed: "The Empress Dowager summoned five times over a two-day stay in Beijing. Tsz San Di has the intention to reform, but officials lack the capacity for revitalization." Both Li Zongxi and Zeng Guoquan were close to Li Hongzhang, who was in return sincere in his dealings with them. Noteworthy is how the Empress Dowager dealt with two potentially concerning situations. The first was when Wo Ren objected to regarding the West as teachers, believing there was no reason for concern in terms of lacking talent and no need to learn from other nations. The Empress Dowager let the Ministry of Foreign Affairs test the candidates and then ordered Wo Ren to have several teachers proficient in science and choose a good place to establish a school for teaching to compete with others. Once extravagant Wo Ren got real order, there was nothing he could do. He admitted. "Your humble servant does not know anyone good at astronomy and arithmetic." Regarding the second situation, in the Sino-French War, a Qing general criticized the military and diplomatic issues pertaining to the Westernization officers. To deal with this, the Empress Dowager sent the leader of Zhang Peilun in the Qing government to the

[1] Marx, K. & Engels, F. (1972). *Makesi Engesi Xuanji, Di Yi Juan* (Selected Works of Karl Marx and Frederick Engels, Vol. 1, 马克思恩格斯选集, 第1卷). Beijing, People's Publishing House, p. 255.

front line, and appointed him as the minister of Fujian Haijiang, although likening his integrity to that of a canoe: "Piety and faith are intangibles, and cannons tangible. Using the intangible to attack the tangible and thinking it would be effective in the battlefield too, is that possible?"[2] The outcome for Zhang Peilun was not good. The Empress Dowager was impressed that this was like attacking your shield with your spear.

Note that although the Empress Dowager used the Qing Congress to control Westernization, this was a generally trusted initiative. A letter written by Li Hongzhang to Yi Xuan commented as below: "If it is not supported by the Empress Dowager and your (Prince Yi Xuan), I (Li Hongzhang) could not proceed the movement with the opposition of others."[3]

The support of the Qing government for the Westernization Movement was also reflected in the growth of their assistance to enterprises. On the one hand, paying government funds and cutting down taxes were strategies often used to improve the external competitiveness of government-run enterprises. For example, in China's first business-run enterprise, the Steamship Navigation Company, at the beginning of its preparation, Li Hongzhang petitioned the Ministry of Revenue to borrow a 200,000-string pad system to be "donated as a setup supply, which will demonstrate the government's integrity to the public." Subsequently, Li borrowed more than 190 million taels of silver from official funds. In 1877, while the Steamship Navigation Company was competing with Swire Group and Jardine Matheson, he asked the Ministry of Foreign Affairs to delay accepting interest for three years to make a turnover.[4] To enhance the company's competitiveness, Li also gained the privilege to transport grain. This certainly stagnated the development of the Steamship Navigation Company. On the other hand, supporting enterprises helped them overcome the obstruction of traditional domestic forces and promoted the growth of government-run enterprises. The

[2] Gu, H. (1985). *Zhang Wenxianggong Mufu Jiwen, Gu Hongming Wenji* (张文襄公幕府记闻·载辜鸿铭文集). Changsha: Yuelu Press.

[3] Li, H. *Li Wenzhong Gong Quanshu, Haijun Hangao, Juansan* (Complete Works of Li Wenzhong·Letters of Navy, Vol. 3, 李文忠公全书·海军函稿, 卷3), p. 6.

[4] Sheng, X. (1881). *Shengdang: Xiangding Dalue Zhangcheng Ershi Tiao* (Archives for Sheng Xuanhuai: Stipulation of Twenty Articles of General Regulations, 盛档: 详定大略章程二十条). As cited in Xia, D. (1998). *Sheng Xuanhuai Zhuan* (The Biography of Sheng Xuanhuai, 盛宣怀传). Tianjin: Nankai University Press.

businessman Sheng Xuanhuai, who ran the Shanghai Telegraph Office, emphasized that Chinese enterprises "not officially maintained would not be able to begin operations" because the companies initially founded faced much resistance from the government and people. Even if the general population believed it was "destroying Feng Shui," the "livelihoods of others would be affected" as long as stubborn bureaucrats opposed machine production. In this case, if an official is not careful to provide protection, "the waste could be worth tens of thousands, and the Chamber would be laughed at by foreigners if they failed to explain to the people that officials commanded the superintendent. If the local governors collectively cared about protection, things would be more secure."[5]

20.2 The Inability of the Qing Dynasty to Complete Its Historical Mission

First, the Qing government's support for Westernization was half-hearted. Unlike the monarchy and bourgeoisie, who jointly dealt with the traditional aristocracy in British capitalism and the development process, the Chinese Westernization Movement combined the government and growing bourgeoisie to jointly deal with the Western powers. For the Qing government, the traditional bureaucracy and ruling gentry were the foundations of the Qing Dynasty, and the growing bourgeoisie was a source of available power. To free the Qing Dynasty from Western powers, it had to develop a capitalist foundation, which would affect the traditional methods of production and attract strong opposition from traditional conservative forces. Therefore, the Qing government policy of modern development was like walking a tightrope: it did not pay attention to the Westernization Movement or severity of external influences. Facing serious foreign aggression, they more actively engaged in Westernization, but once the threat was removed, they returned to business as usual.

The compromise on the traditional forces rendered it impossible to obtain greater funds for Westernization through traditional agriculture.

[5] Sheng, X. (1882). *Shengdang: Bing Li Hongzhang* (Archives for Sheng Xuanhuai: To Li Hongzhang, 盛档: 禀李鸿章). As cited in Xia, D. (1998). *Sheng Xuanhuai Zhuan* (The Biography of Sheng Xuanhuai, 盛宣怀传). Tianjin: Nankai University Press, p. 128.

This is the most essential capital collection channel for a country transformed from a traditional to modern society. According to the research, after the Japanese Meiji Restoration, the reform of the traditional agricultural land tax system and the establishment of a modern agricultural tax system laid a solid foundation for Japan's economic expansion. In the Japanese land tax reform basic scheme, the various taxes collected by the Shogun and Phan regime routinely changed to unify charges under the direct control of the new central government. This currency was fixed at the same rate of 3% of the premium and defined land 8.5 times as the average annual output; thus, its tax burden was equivalent to 25–30% of annual food prices. Initially, the new land tax provided 94% of government fiscal levy, almost more than 50% that the nineteenth century. Land tax reform played a vital role in the Meiji Restoration in Japan. According to the American expert Norman, "The land tax reform was not a hasty temporary measure but a reform. Over a very long period, it occupied the government's most important goal—They might build a modern budget system as the result of a fixed source of revenue."[6] When a nation has no agriculture and lacks tax, it is natural that the massive cost of the military and factory farm model relies on land tax, which as such, should not fluctuate. This indicates the best possible use of effective financial resources in the Meiji government and illustrates the important role of agricultural taxation in backward countries.

Based on the Qing government's half-hearted focus on the Westernization Movement, Li Hongzhang said with indignation, "One matter cannot be resolved without another."[7]

Second, the impact of domestic revolt and attack by Western powers greatly weakened the social control of the Qing government, making it unable to dominate powerful social resources and reducing its capacity to promote China's modernization drive. Since the fight against the Taiping Rebellion, the power of the central government weakened, making it impossible to mobilize the power of the nation to promote the development of the Westernization Movement. Based on the strike of the Taiping War, the Qing government formed an administrative system of "relatives,

[6] Feuerwerker, A. (1990). *Zhongguo Zaoqi Gongyehua* (China's Early Industrialization, 中国早期工业化). Beijing: China Social Sciences Press.

[7] Li, H. *Li Wenzhonggong Quanshu, Pengliao Shougao, Juan Shijiu* (Complete Works of Li Wenzhong·Letter with Friends, Vol.19, 李文忠公全书·朋僚函稿, 卷19), p. 43.

officials, and the prime minister to control the country's main Excellencies, with power directed down toward the people."[8] This included military and political affairs, in which people provided their collective wisdom and engaged in extensive consultation, and delivered orders to governors. Thus, the opinions of these governors heavily influenced the decisions of the Qing government. Therefore, Zuo Zongtang wrote a letter to establish the Board of Admiralty: "I oversaw the Governor bonds and participated in official matters. I humbly watched internal and external political affairs. The power of the internal minister was controlled by the external minister, whose influence made it difficult to integrate."[9] The situation is out of control. While providing opportunities for other high officials in local companies, it appears to be spontaneous development at the beginning of the modern deployment organization. "Discussing how to raise rates, how to train, how to open the Ordnance Department, how to open a bank, and how to construct iron coins, they are not listening to the people or obeying the rules."[10] Li Hongzhang and other Westernization officials had long been aware of the weakness of industrialization in the late Qing Dynasty, and tried to resolve the issue. In October in the 13th Year of the Tongzhi Reign (1874), a former Huai Army general, when governor of Fujian, proposed the use of national financial resources to make ends meet, developing a comprehensive plan, and establishing an army. He said, "In military forces in the past, the naval defense system shall follow uniform financial terms, and the coastal defense system, especially the army, should be based on the amount of human and financial resources. I thought that initially, this foundation would be sufficient for the overall funding plan and the province could deal with the funds for any preparatory items. I was then forced to train the army, simplify the military, and to build ships."[11]

[8] Wang, Z. (1985). *Mengjiaoting Zhaji, Jindai Baihai, Diyiji* (The Collection of Modern China Vol. 1, 梦蕉亭札记, 近代稗海, 第1辑). Chengdu: Sichuan People's Publishing House, p. 363.

[9] Zuo, Z. *Zuo Wenxianggong Wenji, Zougao* (Corpus of Zuo Wenxiang, Memorials, 左文襄公文集·奏稿).

[10] Kang, Y. *Kangnan Haiguan Zhiyi, Juanliu* (The Political Thoughts of Kang Youwei, Vol. 6, 康南海官制议, 卷6). Taiwan: Wen Hai Press Company.

[11] Zhou, J. (1996). *Zuichu De Jiyuan* (*The Beginning of the Era*, 最初的纪元). Beijing: Higher Education Press, p. 142.

Li Hongzhang and Wang Kaitai approached the issue of "social mobilization" during modernization. In this social mobilization, the government redeploys the limited resources of a country and utilizes them in the most crucial department. One reason Japan developed rapidly in the early course of modernization is that the Japanese government carried out effective social mobilization. The late Qing government could not collect the capital of the whole society and develop an overall plan for its modernization process; therefore, it delayed modernization progress. Furthermore, the shortage of finance in the late Qing era was a hindering factor in the development of the Westernization Movement. A large amount of money is needed to establish new enterprises, "If you do not have a huge amount of money, you cannot start a business, and if you do not have an unlimited source of money, the business cannot last long."[12] However, since the beginning of the Opium War, "The guards of the sea increased suddenly, taxation of the provisions for the soldiers occurred frequently, and the army's expenditure was great. The cost of the Battle of Recovering Xinjiang, Sino-French War, and Sino-Japanese War, the military expenditure, reparations, and debts totaled 7.37 billion taels. During the 1st year to 21st year of the Guangxu Reign, payment related to the three wars was 36–37 million taels or so annually, accounting for nearly half the fiscal revenue. Once there is a place that can make money, it is certain the government will rob it, which will lead to the predicament of businessmen and impoverishment of the people. This is a dangerous situation."[13] The shortage of finances restricted the Qing Dynasty's capacity to invest in industrial and mining enterprises, which can be compared to the development of early modernization in Japan. According to related records, by 1885, the Meiji government had invested 0.21 billion *yen* to establish official enterprises, while during the whole period of the Westernization Movement, the late Qing government invested 50 million taels in the military industries, and 40 million taels in mining and transportation and telecommunication enterprises. Exchanging the currency into silver dollars, the investment value of the Meiji government was about

[12] *Yangwu Yundong Juanyi* (Westernization Movement, Vol. 1, 洋务运动, 卷1). Shanghai: Shanghai Renmin Chubanshe, p. 29.

[13] Li, H. *Li Wenzhonggong Quanshu, Fanyi Shu Hangao, Juan San* (Complete Works of Li Wenzhong, Letter of Translation Department, Vol. 3, 李文忠公全书·翻译属函稿, 卷3), p. 18.

0.25 billion yuan, while the investment value of the late Qing government was around 0.12 billion yuan, half that of the investment value of the Meiji government.[14] The investment of China, a country with a vast territory and large population, in modern industrial enterprises, was inferior to that of a small island nation, highlighting the development prospects of modern industrial enterprises in the two countries.

20.3 The Qing government's Inability to Contribute to the Establishment of a Modern Enterprise System

Enterprises are the micro productive bases of modern society. Only when the micro productive bases are well-founded can we say the capitalist mode of production has been established. Like a seed needs the appropriate light, temperature, and humidity to sprout, a suitable external environment and government support, especially in terms of constructing social ethics and a solid legal system, is needed to establish a well-structured enterprise system.

First, the intervention of enterprise management led the modern enterprise system to a premature end. Modern enterprises demand clarity regarding property rights and unity in ownership, control rights, use rights, and residual claims. In the capitalist-run and officer-supervised enterprises of the Qing government, the government had no investment in the enterprises (the government's funding support for enterprises appeared as the name of the creditor's rights) but owned the right of control and use rights for enterprise capital and residual claims. As such, while the capitalists owned the capital, they did not own the control rights, use rights, and residual claims. This would inevitably lead to poor business conditions.

Second, the legal environment that influences the establishment of an enterprise system was inappropriate. The modern market economy is a law economy, which has explicit market rules. These are aspects enterprises cannot do or cannot do well. Thus, the government must intervene in the economy according to the rules of modern society. To this end,

[14] Zhou, J. (1996). *Zuichu De* Jiyuan (The Beginning of the Era, 最初的纪元). Beijing: Higher Education Press, p. 142.

the government enacts regulations related to the ongoing business, especially insolvency laws, anti-unfair competition laws, securities laws, and so on. Not realizing the significance of the relevant laws, the late Qing government did not enact them.

Third, ethics adapted to capitalist development had not been established; thus, mutual trust relationships could not be forged, which is disadvantageous in the formation of a modern enterprise system. While the great productivity brought about by the Industrial Revolution could shorten the period of transition between the two modes of production, the Qing government did not focus on modernization; thus, this advantage was not harnessed, prolonging the period of transformation. The situation significantly influenced social ethics. On the one hand, the traditional notion of ethics was shattered, and the pursuit of profit and fortune became a societal trend. On the other, businessmen did not become the main body; thus, ethics that met the development of capitalist industry were not established. Instead, ethics different from those of previous times (pursuit of money) also differed from the new ethics (pursuit of fortune) that appeared in society, reflecting the stillbirth of the capitalist mode of production in China.

The operations of modern enterprises were large-scale and required a different type of management than that of small-scale family workshops. In an enterprise, the relationship between workers is a multilevel principal-agent relationship. This includes the principal-agent relationship between the director and management staff, the principal-agent relationship between management staff and ordinary employees, and the principal-agent relationship between all levels of management staff. Only when mutual trust has been established in this multilevel relationship, namely when the principal rewards agents who have accomplished their tasks as arranged, without making an excuse to reduce wages, and agents fulfill their tasks according to the principal's requirements without receiving kickbacks and damaging the company's interests of the company, will the operating efficiency of a company improve. From this viewpoint, Confucianism, which emphasizes social order, will contribute to establishing the modern enterprise system in eastern countries.

During the transformation from a traditional to modern society, if one country wants to establish a modern enterprise system in a short time successfully, it must play its role as the only legitimate aggressor. On one hand, it needs to play the role of enlightenment to reform the traditional culture to meet the requirements of modern society and transfer people's loyalty to the king to the enterprise. On the other, it needs to strengthen the legal system and establish a law system appropriate for modern society. Its roles can be crystallized as improving the operation efficiency of enterprises by increasing the expected cost of employees' mistakes. Unfortunately, the Qing government was unwilling and incapable of doing so. Therefore, in the Westernization Movement, neither official nor business enterprises could transition from destruction to construction, creating internal friction and low operational efficiency.

It is said that immoral activities erupted in the official Westernization enterprises because of Li Hongzhang's greed. Those below follows the example of those above, as per the old Chinese saying: "Fish begins to rot from the head." Disputes abound in the literature on whether Li Hongzhang was corrupt; thus, I do not comment on that here. However, Zuo Zongtang and Zhang Zhidong were honest officials acknowledged in the literature. While they demonstrated good conduct, they were unfamiliar with the laws of socialization production and lacked managerial knowledge. As such, they were unable to manage the officials in affiliated enterprises, which led to large-scale corruption. Thus, it is evident that to manage a modern enterprise well, it must be managed according to the law of modernization mass production and must learn from the West—Europe and the United States—the pioneers of modernization.

Postscript

After years of hard work, my doctoral dissertation is going to be published. I extend my thanks to my supervisor Shi Shiqi, Mr. Zhao Jing, Zheng Xueyi, Chen Weimin, my doctoral dissertation advisor Zhu Jiazhen of the Chinese Academy of Social Sciences, and Mr. Yu Zuyao of Renmin University of China.

I majored in history as a student at Shandong University, and obtained my bachelor's degree in 1986 and Master's in History at Peking University in 1991. I then decided to shift my studies from history to economics, a move largely attributed to my master's supervisor Cheng Hanchang, the late history professor at Peking University.

Prof. Cheng, former deputy director of the History Department, and director of the Teaching and Research Office of Modern History at Peking University was dedicated to the study of the modern land system and land reform. He was a middle-aged scholar with great academic achievement. His works include *Land System and Land Reform of China* and *The Culture of Contemporary Farmers*.

He believed that history scholars who studied the land system through mastery of several economic theories would make academic breakthroughs and great achievements. At that time, the lecturers in the Teaching and Research Office of Modern History at Peking University were studying political and cultural history, not economic history. Therefore, when he was informed that I wanted to pursue a Doctorate degree, he made great efforts to persuade me to study economics. However, the

J. Zhou, *Westernization Movement and Early Thought of Modernization in China*, Palgrave Studies in Economic History,
https://doi.org/10.1007/978-3-030-86985-4

greatest obstacle for me in preparing for the doctoral qualifying examination for economics was higher mathematics. Since entering university, I had never studied mathematics. Thus, unsurprisingly, Economics was like hieroglyphics to me. Encouraged by Mr. Cheng, I started with junior middle school mathematics, spent a month and a half reviewing high school mathematics, and then joined the undergraduate physics students to start learning calculus, linear algebra, and so on. Economics is easier to learn once one has a certain level of mathematical knowledge. To master my knowledge of Economics, I attended numerous courses given by professors of economics. For microeconomics, I completed *Primary Microeconomics* for undergraduates and *Intermediate Microeconomics* for graduates taught by Prof. Liu Wenxin. After a period of hard work, I, a layman in economics, was admitted to the doctoral program of the Economics School of Peking University in 1995. My younger brother Zhou Jiantao was also admitted to the same doctoral program the same year, and supervised by Professor Sun Shangqing. Unfortunately, just a week before my Doctorate entrance examination, Mr. Cheng, my tutor, passed away aged only 49 years. Informed that I had been admitted to the PhD program, Mr. Cheng Hanchang's wife told me in tears: "If my husband could hear the news that you two brothers were admitted to the PhD in Economics, he would be so gratified!" As students of Mr. Cheng, my brother and I could do nothing but study hard as a sign of thanks for his instruction.

In the four years I pursued my Doctorate, I received strict education in economics and improved my capability therein. In terms of professional course study, I enrolled in *The History of Chinese Economic Thought* taught by professor Shi Shiqi and Zhao Jing for three semesters, *History of Western Economic Thought* taught by Yan Zhijie, *Economic Thought* taught by Zheng Xueyi, and *Management Thought of Japanese Enterprises* taught by Chen Weimin. As such, I acquired a basic understanding of the differences in the economics and history of economic thought between China and Western countries. Regarding my study of economic theories, at that time, the economic research center of Peking University had just been established, and a group of young scholars who studied overseas had just returned to the university to teach, including Lin Yifu, Zhang Weiying, Zhou Qiren, Song Guoqing, Yi Gang, and Hai Wen. In this way, I was influenced by the latest in Western economic thought. During that period, I selected *Advanced Microeconomics: The Theory of the Firm* taught by professor Zhang Weiying, *Advanced Macroeconomics* taught by professor Song Guoqing, *China's Economic Reforms* taught by professor Lin Yifu, and *Historical Perspectives of Economic Systems and Organizations* taught by professor Zhou Qiren to acquire a solid foundation for the mastery of Economics theories. In addition, I seized various opportunities to participate in social investigations during my doctoral studies, and went to more than a dozen provinces throughout the country and more than 60 enterprises to conduct my research. The enterprises I visited included Haier, Hisense, and Double Star in Qingdao, Jiangsu Landy Foods Co. Inc., VV Group, Sanmao Group, and Jiangsu Sunshine Group, after which I published nine articles on economics. My article, "Economic thought of changing the management system of collectively owned orchards of Baitengkou Village," was awarded first prize at a "Hundred Doctors into Hundred Villages" activity organized by the Ministry of Agriculture in 1996, and I was honored to meet the state leaders Jiang Chunyun and Lei Jieqiong.

I selected modernization thought as the topic of my doctoral dissertation based on the encouragement of Prof. Lin Yifu. When Prof. Lin taught *China's Economic Reforms*, he assigned homework on system innovation, and I wrote an article on the transformation just an hour before his class. To my surprise, he was satisfied with it. He also praised my other assignments on economic reform. In fact, the article that won the first prize at a "Hundred Doctors into Hundred Villages" activity organized by the Ministry of Agriculture was originally conceived as an assignment for Prof. Lin's class. He thought the Westernization Movement enterprises were of great enlightening significance to the current reform of state-owned enterprises, and encouraged me to make it the topic of my doctoral dissertation. However, I was little interested in the topic at the time, considering it too difficult. There were three reasons: First, I considered the span of time too long. Second, many people and events were involved; thus, I would have needed to read a vast volume of books. Third, the literature includes considerable research on this topic, rendering innovation difficult. Thus, I initially did not want to choose this topic for my doctoral dissertation, instead considering as my subject the land system reform of the 1930s. My master's degree supervisor was studying this field, and I dabbled in it when doing my degree. As such, I was confident I could handle it with ease.

However, after listening to my report, Prof. Shi rejected my proposal, and asked me to instead adopt the study of the thoughts of the Westernization Movement as the theme of my doctoral dissertation. He assumed this was of great academic and practical significance, which is in keeping with the principle that the selected topic of a Doctoral dissertation demonstrates innovation. As for difficulties, Prof. Shi assured me these were normal, or a doctoral degree would be too easy to pursue.

I spent two years writing my dissertation, which I attribute to four reasons. First, I had mastered some knowledge of history, so I know how to find historical materials skillfully. As Prof. Shi said, many previously unused historical materials were employed in this dissertation, especially in the research of enterprise management. This can be considered an innovation in terms of historical aspects. Second, I am well educated in economic theory. To understand the transformation of the Westernization Movement, I read numerous books related to the transition from mercantilism to economic liberalism, especially the masterpieces *The Economics before Adam Smith* and *Classic Economics* by Prof. Yan Zhijie, Dean of the Economics School of Peking University.

Furthermore, to determine the essence of enterprise theory, I listened to the course taught by Prof. Zhang Weiying twice, and without his theoretical guidance, I would not have been able to write Chapter 6 of Part II of this dissertation. Prof. Zhang was concerned about the writing of this study, and he asked me whether there are some similarities and differences between Li Hongzhang's view of enterprise management and the current reform perspectives of state-owned enterprises, and if there were areas worth exploring. Therefore, I owe the improvement of my dissertation to his patient instruction. Third, Prof. Shi Shiqi made clear his rigid requirements for me and provided me with earnest instruction. Prof. Shi was once the dean and secretary of the Party Committee of the Economics School of Peking University, and treats his students strictly. My tutor, Shi Shiqi carefully examined each draft of this dissertation, and made recommendations for its revision. He said I was the first doctoral candidate he had supervised; thus, if my dissertation did not meet the relevant requirements, he would not permit me to pass. I remember clearly that his evaluation of the first draft of my dissertation was that it was too rough, but he thought the second draft showed improvements. He also considered some parts of the work excellent as some materials were brand new, but thought that other parts could benefit from additional study and detail. He was essentially satisfied with the third draft of my dissertation, and believed that given extra time, it could be further improved. Therefore, without his earnest and rigid instruction, it would have been impossible for me to complete the dissertation. Fourth, my family gave me a great deal of support. My child was born while I was writing my dissertation. To ensure I could concentrate on writing it, my wife, parents, and parents-in-law undertook all the responsibilities of attending to my baby. I attribute the smooth completion of my dissertation to their support, and appreciate them very much.

Mr. Zhaojing, former president of the Association of the History of Chinese Economic Thought, a professor at Peking University, took the time to write the preface for this book despite his poor health. I was very moved by his gesture. His encouragement has driven me to progress further. In an age in which academic works are difficult to publish, this book was fortunately published with the great help of Zhang Quanxi, the general manager of Guanhuatong Trading Company (Beijing). This was a surprise for me, and to this end, I extend my thanks to Mr. Zhang. The publication of this book will give a sense of fulfilling my studies.

By Zhou Jianbo

December 10, 2000 at Peking University

References

Corpus

[1] Collected Works of Karl Marx and Friedrich Engels [C]. People's Publishing House, 1956–1985.

[2] Selected Works of Karl Marx and Frederick Engels [C]. People's Publishing House, 1972.

[3] Capital [C]. People's Publishing House, 1975.

[4] Selected Works of Mao Zedong, Volume1–4 [C]. People's Publishing House, 1991.

[5] Guan Zi [C]. Yuelu Press, 1993.

[6] Shi Ji: Biographies of Merchants [C]. Nanjing University Press, 1994.

[7] Gong Zizhen Complete Works [C]. Shanghai People's Publishing House, 1975.

[8] Lin Zexu Works [C]. Zhonghua Book Company, 1965.

[9] Wei Yuan Works [C]. Zhonghua Book Company, 1976.

[10] Zhang Jixin. The Sketch of Officialdom in the Reign of Dao-Xian [C]. Zhonghua Book Company, 1981.

[11] Feng Guifen. Reform Proposals written in Jiaoban Cabin [C]. Zhongzhou Classics Publishing House, 1998.

[12] Zheng Guanying Works, Vol. 1 [C]. Shanghai People's Publishing House, 1982.

[13] Ma Jianzhong: Political Proposals Written in Shike Study [C]. Zhonghua Book Company, 1960.

[14] Selected Works of Xue Fucheng [C]. Shanghai People's Publishing House, 1987.

[15] Chen Chi Works [C]. Zhonghua Book Company, 1997.

J. Zhou, *Westernization Movement and Early Thought of Modernization in China*, Palgrave Studies in Economic History, https://doi.org/10.1007/978-3-030-86985-4

[16] Wang Tao. "Tao Yuan" series, Zhongzhou Ancient Books Publishing House, 1998
[17] Kang Youwei Political Set [C]. Zhonghua Book Company, 1981.
[18] He Qi, Hu Liyuan. The real interpretation of the new policy [C]. Liaoning People's Publishing House, 1994.
[19] Guo Songtao Diary [C]. Hunan People's Publishing House, 1981.
[20] Guo Songtao Anthology [C]. Yuelu Press, 1984.
[21] Wuyong. On the Westward Hunting in Gengzi Year, Yuelu Press, 1984[22] Rong Hong. My Life in China and America [C]. Zhongzhou Classics Publishing House, 1998.
[23] Zhang Zhidong. Exhortation to Learning [C]. Zhongzhou Classics Publishing House, 1998.
[24] Works of Zeng Jize [C]. Yuelu Press, 1984.
[25] Works of Yan Fu [C]. Zhonghua Book Company, 1986.
[26] Tang Shouqian. *Tang's Righteous Words.*
[27] Shao Zuozhou. *Shao's Righteous Words.*
[28] Jing Yuanshan. *A Collection of Ju Yichu.*
[29] Zhong Tianwei. *Zhong's Righteous Words.*
[30] Huang Zunxian. *Annals of Japan.*
[31] Sheng Xuanhuai. *Memorials of Sheng Xuanhuai.*
[32] Yang Yuehan. *Biography of Yang Oufang.*
[33] Xu Run: *The Chronicle of Xu Yuzhai.*
[34] Liang Qichao. *Yinbing Mansion Compilations.*
[35] Guo Songtao. *Memorials of Guo Songtao.*
[36] Zhang Zhidong. *Collected Works of Zhang Wenxiang.*
[37] Liu Kunyi. *Works of Liu Kunyi, Memorials of Liu Zhuangsu.*
[38] Li Hongzhang. *Complete Works of Li Wenzhong, Letters of Li Wenzhong.*
[39] Zeng Guofan. *Complete Works of Zeng Wenzheng.*
[40] Zuo Zongtang. *Complete Works of Zuo Wenxiang.*
[41] Zhang Shusheng. *Memorials of Zhang Jingda.*
[42] Shen Baozhen: *Reform Proposals of Shen Wensu.*
[43] Zhang Jian. *Works of Zhang Jiuzi's Industrial Projects.*
[44] Wang Jingyu. Materials of Chinese Modern Industrial History (After 1895), Vol. 1 [C]. Science Press, 1957.
[45] Sun Yutang. Materials of Chinese Modern Industrial History (Before 1895), Vol. 2 [C]. Science Press, 1957.
[46] Chen Zhen. Materials of Chinese Modern Industrial History [C]. SDX Joint Publishing Company, 1961.
[47] Peng Zeyi. Materials for the Modern History of Handicrafts in China [C]. Zhonghua Book Company, 1962.
[48] Peng Zeyi. Historical Materials of Chinese Industry and Commerce Guild [C]. Zhonghua Book Company, 1995.

[49] Zhang Youyi. Materials of Chinese Modern Agricultural History [C]. SDX Joint Publishing Company, 1957.
[50] The Han-ye-ping Company: Archives Materials for Sheng Xuanhuai (Selected Four) [C]. Shanghai People's Publishing House, 1984.
[51] Westernization Movement [C]. Shanghai People's Publishing House, 1973.
[52] Wuxu Reform [C]. Shanghai People's Publishing House, 1972.
[53] History of Diplomatic Affairs in Late Qing Dynasty [C]. Zhonghua Book Company, 1979.
[54] The Chronicle of Zeng Guofan [C]. Yuelu Press, 1986.
[55] Draft History of Qing [C]. Zhonghua Book Company, 1977.
[56] The History of Modern China [C]. Sichuan People's Publishing House, 1985.

Newspapers

[1] Shun Pao.
[2] Domestic and Foreign News.
[3] Multinational Communique.
[4] China Gazette.

Monographs

[1] Zhang Kaiyuan. The Footprints of the Pioneer: The Biography of Zhang Jian [M]. Zhonghua Book Company, 1986.
[2] Feng Tianyu. The Critical Biography of Zhang Zhidong [M]. Henan Education Press, 1985.
[3] Zhao Jing, Shi Shiqi. The Course of the History of Chinese Economical Management Thoughts [M]. Peking University Press, 1993.
[4] Zhao Jing, Shi Shiqi. The General History of Chinese Economic Thoughts [M]. Peking University Press, 1991–1998.
[5] Zhao Jing, Yi Menghong. The Selections of the Modern Chinese Economic Thoughts [M]. Zhonghua Book Company, 1982.
[6] Hao Yanping. The Bridge between the Orient and the Occident—Chinese Comprador in the 19th Century [M]. Shanghai Academy of Social Sciences Press, 1988.
[7] Hao Yanping. The Commercial Revolution in Modern China [M]. Shanghai People's Publishing House, 1991.
[8] Hu Fuming. The Historical Process of Chinese Modernization [M]. Anhui People's Publishing House, 1994.
[9] Du Xuncheng. National Capitalism and the Old Chinese Government (1840–1937) [M]. Shanghai Social Science Press, 1991.

[10] Yuan Shuyi. The Biography of Li Hongzhang [M]. People's Publishing House, 1991.

[11] Yen Ching-hwang (Singapore).On the History of Overseas Chinese [M]. Singapore Society of Asian Studies, 1992.

[12] John K. Fairbank (U.S.). The Cambridge History of China, Vol. 10, Late Ch'ing [M]. China Social Sciences Press 1985.

[13] Hu Jichuang. The Outline of the History of Modern Chinese Economic Thoughts [M]. China Social Sciences Press, 1984.

[14] Li Renkai. The Ideological Trend of Modern China [M]. Henan People's Publishing House, 1996.

[15] Dong Caishi. The Critical Biography of Zuo Zongtang [M]. China Social Sciences Press, 1984.

[16] Yang Dongliang. The Critical Biography of Zuo Zongtang [M]. Hunan People's Publishing House, 1985.

[17] Wang Jingyu. The Western Capitalists' Economic Aggression against China in the 19th Century [M]. China Social Sciences Press, 1983.

[18] Wang Jingyu. The Study of Tang Tingshu [M]. China Social Sciences Press, 1983.

[19] Hu Weige. On the Ideological Trend of Modern China [M]. Northeast Normal University Press, 1996.

[20] Kwang-Ching Liu (U.S.). The Start of China's Modernization: The Biography of Li Hung-chang [M]. Shanghai Classics Publishing House, 1995.

[21] Chen Xulu. The Reform of Modern China [M]. Shanghai People's Publishing House, 1992.

[22] Chen Xulu. The Acadamic Works of Chen Xulu [M]. Shanghai People's Publishing House, 1990.

[23] Zhang Zhongli. The Chinese Gentry-On their Roles in the 19th China [M]. Shanghai Academy of Social Sciences Press, 1991.

[24] Wu Chengming. The Chinese Capitalism and Its Domestic Market [M]. China Social Sciences Press, 1985.

[25] Wu Chengming. Market, Modernization, Theory of Economic History [M]. Yunnan University Press, 1996.

[26] Lin Jinzhi. On the Modern History of the Investment of Overseas Chinese in Domestic Enterprises [M]. Fujian People's Publishing House, 1983.

[27] Luo Rongqu. The Explore of the Process of Chinese Modernization [M]. Peking University Press, 1992.

[28] Zhao Fengtian. Fifty Years History of Economic Thought in Late Qing Dynasty [M]. Harvard–Yenching Institute, 1939.

[29] Albert Feuerwerker (U.S.). The Early Modernization of China-Sheng Xuanhuai and Government-supervised and Merchant-managed Enterprises [M]. China Social Sciences Press, 1990.

[30] Xia Dongyuan. The History of Westernization Movement [M]. East China Normal University Press, 1992.
[31] Xia Dongyuan. The Biography of Sheng Xuanhuai [M]. Nankai University Press, 1998.
[32] Xia Dongyuan. On Westernization Movement in Late Qing [M]. Sichuan People's Publishing House, 1985.
[33] Xia Dongyuan. The Biography of Zheng Guanying [M]. Guangdong People's Publishing House, 1995.
[34] Wang Lixin. The American Missionaries and the Chinese Modernization in Late Qing Dynasty [M]. Tianjin People's Publishing House, 1997.
[35] Jiang Jianping. The History of China's Commerce Economic thoughts [M]. China Financial and Economic Publishing House, 1990.
[36] Tatsuo Yamada, Nakai Yoshihiro (Japan). The Sino-Japanese Comparative Modernization Theory [M]. Koyo Shobo Publisher, 1996.
[37] Gilbert Rozman (U.S.). The Modernization of China [M]. Jiangsu People's Publishing House, 1998.
[38] Xu Jilin. The History of China's Modernization [M]. Shanghai Joint Publishing Company, 1995.
[39] Xu Yi. Historical Essay of Foreign Debt in the Qing Dynasty [M]. China Financial Publishing House, 1996.
[40] Xin Ping. The Biography of Wang Tao [M]. East China Normal University Press, 1990.
[41] Mi Rucheng. A Comprehensive History of the Qing Dynasty, Vol. 8 [M]. Liaoning People's publishing House, 1993.

Index

A

Anglo-French forces, 4, 6, 20
Anhui Army, 10, 11, 13
The Art of War, 174
Asian Tigers, 52
Assistant Grand Secretary, 84

B

Beijing-QingJiangpu railway, 270
Book of Songs, 74
Buddhism, 351

C

Chen Chi, 32, 49, 50, 63, 66, 67, 72, 88, 143, 145, 161, 163, 182, 184, 185, 189, 223–225, 227–232, 235, 237, 238, 241, 244, 245, 247, 248, 250, 251, 259, 262, 266, 267, 273, 274, 277, 279, 280, 285, 287, 289, 290, 295, 302, 304, 356
Chen Chi Works, 50, 63, 66, 67, 72, 88, 144, 145, 161, 163, 185, 189, 224, 225, 228, 230–232, 235, 237, 238, 241, 245, 248–251, 263, 266, 267, 273, 278–281, 285, 286, 290, 295, 296, 302, 304
China Gazette, 133, 147–150, 153, 154
China Merchants Steamship Navigation Company, 51, 67, 105, 119–124, 138, 139, 144, 164, 167, 169, 173, 204–206, 212, 216, 217, 357
Collected Works of Karl Marx and Friedrich Engels, 103, 346
Collected Works of Liang Qichao, 310
Collected Works of Zhang Wenxiang, 61, 79, 87, 94–96, 100, 112, 113, 116, 148, 152, 192, 193, 225, 228, 234, 257, 258, 263, 271–273, 342
Commercial Bank of China, 289–291
Comprador, 22, 117–122, 124–126, 138, 173, 199, 202, 355, 357

J. Zhou, *Westernization Movement and Early Thought of Modernization in China*, Palgrave Studies in Economic History,
https://doi.org/10.1007/978-3-030-86985-4

Confucianism, 18, 25, 29–31, 34–37, 312, 313, 315, 316, 318, 319, 325, 351, 367
Convention of Peking, 4, 5, 8
Coup of 1861, 4, 6, 7
Crisis Awareness in Millenium, 68

D
Daoguang Reign, 310, 315
The Department of Water Transport, 300
Donation system/subscription system, 58, 355–357
Draft History of Qing, 5

E
Eagle dollar, 282, 283
Eight Banners, 302–305, 314
Europe, 33, 42, 61, 68, 80, 115, 132, 179, 248, 279, 294, 295, 331, 340, 342, 349–352, 368
Exchange shop, 287–289
Exhortation to Learning, 35, 36, 55, 60, 101, 111, 112, 115, 140, 224, 225, 228, 229, 243, 249, 257, 258, 266, 268

F
Feng Guifen, 13, 16, 20, 21, 29, 36, 82, 84, 88, 113, 222, 226, 245, 317, 328
Fuzhou Arsenal, 95, 108, 109, 111, 154, 156, 186, 198, 200

G
General administration, 107, 279
Government-run enterprise, 99, 118, 119, 149, 186–191, 194–197, 199, 321, 325, 333, 344, 361
Government-supervised and merchant-managed enterprises, 45, 94, 134, 173, 188, 189, 200–203, 205–217, 323, 344, 345
Governor, 6, 8, 12, 13, 15, 58, 61, 82, 84, 99, 110, 112, 120, 131, 149, 155, 176, 189, 191, 192, 194, 196, 200, 203, 217, 232, 234, 273, 279, 284, 301, 311, 314, 315, 320–322, 324, 357, 362, 364
Governor-general, 10, 82, 110, 123, 146, 149, 187, 191, 196, 202, 301, 315
the Governor-general of Guangdong and Guangxi provinces, 59, 95, 283
Governor-general of Jiangnan and Jiangxi, 14, 82
Grand academician, 4, 5
Great Learning, 71
Green Standards, 302, 314
Guangxu Reign, 10, 44, 47, 80, 125, 146, 147, 196, 202, 258, 360, 365
Guangzhou-Wuhan Railway, 192, 193
Guo Songtao, 10, 13, 20, 21, 26, 31, 33, 46–48, 61, 89, 186, 187, 254, 310, 328, 330, 344

H
Hanyeping Company, 200
Huai Army, 123, 239, 364
Huang Zunxian, 68, 80, 81, 96, 130, 131, 286, 356
Huizhou merchants, 351
Hunan and Anhui Military Groups, 8
Hunan Army, 9, 10

I

Illustrated Annals of Overseas Countries, 175
Imperial examination system, 56, 64, 113–116, 312, 316
Inspector General of Customs, 7
Investigating censor, 48

J

Jardine Matheson, 121, 361
Jiangnan Manufacturing Bureau, 41, 42, 104, 144, 147, 150, 153
Jiaqing Reign, 84, 310
Jin-Tong railway, 270
Junk, 47, 119, 121, 122

K

Kaiping Coal Mine, 120, 123, 147, 149, 153, 165
Kang Youwei, 12, 29, 341, 347, 364

L

late Qing Dynasty, 10, 69, 80, 85, 91, 100, 123, 131, 185, 194, 238, 283, 301, 309, 311, 316, 339, 357, 360, 364
Li Hongzhang, 10, 11, 13, 17, 19–23, 25–28, 30, 36, 39, 42, 46–48, 50, 56–60, 73, 74, 87, 89, 90, 104–106, 109–111, 114, 120–126, 150, 165, 169, 176, 189, 196, 200, 202–206, 208, 211, 218, 233, 242, 254, 261, 266, 270, 272, 275, 277, 283, 317–319, 341, 342, 356, 360, 361, 363–365, 368
Likin tax, 69, 89, 90, 162
Luhan Railway, 94, 124, 271, 272

M

Ma Jianzhong, 20, 21, 32, 33, 48, 61, 63, 89, 95, 97, 98, 203, 205, 214, 215, 234, 236, 240, 255, 260–262, 266, 269, 328, 344
Memorials, 6, 22, 35, 47, 48, 56, 59, 87, 96, 109, 111, 112, 181, 187, 190, 196, 197, 200, 203, 234
Memorials of Guo Songtao, 33
Memorials of Sheng Xuanhuai, 61, 124, 141, 180, 182, 284, 290, 291
Merchant-managed enterprise, 186, 188–192, 194, 199, 200, 208, 209, 317
Ming dynasty, 17, 51, 57, 70, 282, 303, 350
Minister, 5, 7, 58, 63, 81, 107, 108, 113, 118–120, 131, 187, 275, 279, 291, 300, 301, 361, 364
Ministry of Commerce, 62–64, 95, 177, 258, 283, 292
Ministry of Foreign Affairs, 6–8, 16, 19, 360, 361
Ministry of Justice, 7, 8
Ministry of Personnel, 62
Ministry of Revenue, 91, 92, 204, 282, 284, 290, 361
Ministry of Rites, 8
Ministry of War, 8
Ministry of Works, 8, 200
Mohe Gold Mine/Ore, 122, 234, 243
Money shop, 288, 289

N

Neo-Confucianism of the Song and Ming Dynasties, 18

O

Official Council of State, 301

Opium War, 26, 74, 82, 84, 85, 89, 91, 108, 114, 130, 132, 222, 253, 274, 303, 314, 315, 317, 318, 365
Overseas Chinese, 117, 125, 126, 130–133, 197, 205, 210, 355

P
Paper money, 285, 288, 290, 291, 299, 350
Political Proposals Written in Shike Study, 21, 95, 97, 99, 234, 237, 240, 256, 260–262, 267, 270, 282
Private capital, 45, 87, 92, 104, 127, 132, 134, 149, 185, 186, 188, 190–193, 201, 211–214, 333, 344, 345
Private Secretariats, 12–15, 21, 24, 118, 119, 122, 128

Q
Qianlong Reign, 309, 350
Qing government, 4, 8, 14, 16, 27, 28, 33, 42, 44–46, 59, 63, 68, 69, 82, 89, 99, 113–116, 122, 123, 128, 130–132, 140, 176, 178, 180, 186, 190, 191, 194, 198, 202, 204, 211, 215, 259, 261, 263, 264, 268, 305, 312, 326–328, 330–332, 344, 345, 359–368

R
Reform Proposals Written in Jiaoban Cabin, 13, 16, 21, 30, 226
Reforms and Opening-up, 352–354

S
Salt tax, 63, 80, 85–87
the Scholar-bureaucrats, 311–315, 317–319
School of Combined Learning (Tongwen Guan), 7, 115
Selected Works of Karl Marx and Frederick Engels, 41–43, 340, 360
Selected Works of Mao Zedong, 126
Selected Works of Xue Fucheng, 26, 32, 66, 69–71, 81, 97, 98, 131, 179, 227, 236, 240, 246, 254, 255, 267, 269, 271, 275, 294, 295, 297–299, 319, 341
Self-Strengthening movement, 23, 30, 32, 36, 82, 204, 206, 207, 209, 210, 212–218, 283, 285, 288, 289, 293
Shanghai Mechanical Textile Bureau, 44, 120, 122, 125, 154, 164, 171, 204, 205, 211, 212
Shanxi merchants, 287, 351
Shen Bao, 148, 171, 172, 212
Shen Baozhen, 10, 109, 124, 156, 200, 317
Sheng Xuanhuai, 105, 106, 108, 110, 118, 119, 122–124, 128, 134, 140, 141, 180–182, 199, 203–205, 209, 211, 274–277, 279, 280, 283, 290, 291, 355, 356, 361, 362
Shi, 84, 305
Silk Road, 349
Silver dollar, 45, 47, 278, 282, 283, 333, 335, 365
Sino-Japanese War in 1894–1895, 59, 60, 98, 99, 132, 186, 190, 191, 194, 197, 198, 199, 223, 256, 287, 332
Six Regulations of the Comprehensive Arrangement of the Westernization, 6
Song Dynasty, 36, 57, 285, 349, 350

Special economic zone, 263, 334
Swire Group, 361

T
Taiping Rebellion, 8–10, 12, 21, 30, 42, 58, 119, 123, 129, 363
Taoism, 351
Ten Great Merchant Guilds, 351
Ten Items on Business Expansion, 177, 179, 183, 185
Tongzhi Reign, 8, 47, 112, 146, 176, 319, 364
Trade war, 223, 256, 258
Translation Department/Head Department, 7
Treaty of Shimonoseki, 60, 96
Treaty of Tientsin, 4
the Turmoil of 1860, 16

V
Vice Minister, 4, 5, 10

W
Wang Tao, 20, 21, 26, 30, 36, 61, 62, 114, 127, 236, 245, 253, 255, 259, 330
Wanguo Gong Bao, 133
Wei Yuan, 108, 109, 175, 186, 309, 310, 313, 314, 316, 356
Westernization group, 19, 20, 23, 44, 49–52, 55, 58, 91–94, 97, 99, 105, 106, 108, 111, 124, 126, 130, 133–136, 139, 140, 143, 155, 156, 159, 160, 163, 165, 168, 175, 177, 178, 181, 183, 185, 190, 194, 196, 197, 222, 226, 229, 231, 236–238, 241, 277, 280, 282, 317–319, 322, 324
Westernizationists, 6, 9, 12, 27–29, 47, 106–108, 110–112, 114, 117, 118, 241, 243, 245–247, 249–251, 254–256, 258, 259, 261, 262, 265, 273–275, 285, 305, 339, 340, 343, 345–347
Westernization Movement, 4, 6, 7, 9, 11–15, 19–26, 29, 31–35, 37, 40–43, 45, 47, 48, 51, 55–63, 65, 69, 71, 74, 79, 80, 88, 104–106, 110, 111, 115, 120, 122–124, 127, 130, 137–139, 196, 202, 217, 218, 236, 254, 255, 260, 272, 279, 283, 288, 293, 296, 299, 300, 317–319, 322, 325, 326, 328, 329, 337, 339, 345–347, 349, 351–357, 360–363, 365, 368
Westernization thought, 9, 16, 34, 35, 51, 328, 345
Wuxu Reform, 35, 36, 347

X
Xianfeng Reign, 8, 15, 226, 315, 319
Xue Fucheng, 13, 20, 21, 26, 32, 61, 69–71, 81, 97, 131, 179–182, 226, 233, 235, 239, 240, 246, 253, 255, 267–269, 271, 275, 294, 297–299, 319, 340, 344, 356

Y
Yanguan System, 58
Yi Xin, 4–7, 18–20, 26, 27, 59
Yi Xin Group, 4, 6–8
Yuan Dynasty, 349

Z
Zeng Guofan, 6, 9, 11, 15, 18, 20, 21, 26, 27, 30, 34, 36, 56, 111, 120, 129, 165, 310, 347

Zhang Shusheng, 10, 59, 146

Zhang Zhidong, 20, 23, 35–37, 55, 60, 61, 79, 82, 88, 94–96, 100, 101, 104, 105, 110, 111, 115, 124, 140, 141, 148, 149, 152, 156, 161, 191, 192, 197–199, 204, 224, 228, 233, 243, 249, 256–258, 263, 266, 268, 271–273, 283, 341–343, 353, 354, 368

Zheng Guanying, 20, 22, 30, 32, 36, 46, 49, 61, 63–66, 68, 82, 83, 85, 86, 88, 90, 91, 96, 98, 107, 113, 114, 118–120, 133, 134, 140, 144, 161–164, 166–170, 174, 178, 180, 181, 187, 202, 204, 208–210, 212, 215, 223, 227, 229, 231–233, 236–238, 241, 243, 247–250, 256, 260, 261, 268, 270, 272, 273, 275, 277, 279, 280, 284, 289–291, 296, 301–305, 337, 341–344, 356

Zheng Guanying Works, 30, 46, 49, 63–66, 68, 69, 83, 85, 87, 90, 92, 93, 96, 98, 108, 113, 134, 135, 140, 145, 161, 163, 164, 166–170, 174, 176, 178, 181, 182, 187, 202, 208, 216, 223, 227, 229, 231, 236, 242, 244, 247–251, 259, 260, 262, 268, 270, 273–275, 277–280, 284, 289, 291, 292, 297, 300–305, 341, 343

Zhong's Righteous Words, 49, 92, 107, 150, 168, 173, 177, 179, 183–185, 195, 196, 207, 223, 225, 256, 260, 287, 295

Zhong Tianwei, 49, 92, 93, 97, 107, 150, 168, 173, 174, 177, 178, 183–185, 194, 196, 208, 209, 222, 225, 226, 228, 256, 260, 286, 295

Zuo Zongtang, 9, 10, 15, 20, 21, 44, 73–75, 105, 109, 111, 112, 146, 160, 176, 187, 189, 190, 200, 204, 333, 364, 368

CPSIA information can be obtained
at www.ICGtesting.com
Printed in the USA
LVHW040256020323
740706LV00017B/1719

9 783030 869878